Collective Intelligence in Action

Get the ebook FREE!

To get a free PDF copy of this book
(sold separately for $27.50) purchase the print
book and register it at the Manning website
following the instructions inside this insert.

That's it!

Thanks from Manning!

To register this book and download your free ebook:
1. Go to http://www.manning.com/ebookoffer
2. Enter the codes from this table when prompted
3. Download ebook using link emailed to you

	A	B	C	D	E	F	G	H	I
1	PT 502 6150	WF 779 6817	AK 567 2959	BY 872 4410	IM 227 8752	GR 418 9437	NM 141 6478	EV 359 1873	OH 373 0947
2	EY 971 1263	WF 345 2127	GW 310 1434	EI 828 9239	HV 638 5663	KG 777 2487	IG 713 5130	CX 489 1385	IK 760 7530
3	SL 113 1004	QR 161 1540	NO 114 1074	VQ 825 9561	SL 537 1916	SK 404 1958	EL 872 1327	QI 750 9646	LJ 306 5048
4	LY 494 4094	GP 747 9395	NU 330 7984	BM 142 7039	AZ 248 2402	UN 149 5117	AK 877 3629	QA 870 3409	LR 405 3433
5	AB 633 2980	PL 161 5438	BQ 106 7356	BI 240 7388	ZZ 255 8900	ZS 417 3034	KL 465 3815	MF 219 1344	TP 767 1214
6	LC 308 1300	AK 257 7760	WV 306 6653	HY 405 9274	MU 628 0596	SP 288 3390	EV 820 5702	JP 831 7928	HK 179 4839

	A	B	C	D	E	F	G	H	I
7	HI 912 9344	ZL 322 2419	MK 751 4959	KC 563 1448	CW 420 9482	EA 885 5934	IZ 582 8696	PO 772 5660	LH 958 9609
8	OH 733 5315	IQ 101 1088	NS 901 7590	HB 413 6081	WX 906 8113	HA 366 7742	LN 642 1021	FV 711 4187	XW 777 1512
9	NR 546 6736	GB 126 5496	RS 626 2199	OQ 523 2776	AK 876 2249	NW 289 1466	BS 896 5388	GA 929 9466	SZ 921 4743
10	EQ 555 3171	XR 752 1246	EH 727 4403	JH 650 1731	LO 248 9598	BU 753 9063	CW 105 7086	UU 939 8103	RT 833 4122
11	WH 712 2812	II 849 0382	HB 112 9346	NR 937 7260	WI 835 2769	LS 838 0088	NB 859 1920	XN 400 5241	JH 365 7587
12	HK 618 7458	RU 807 0724	QI 754 3734	QX 695 9637	PK 273 2560	GM 249 9890	XZ 221 3697	FA 874 6412	WI 115 7535
13	DH 813 4016	GB 919 6164	AK 674 7458	SV 955 2150	AS 409 8625	FC 239 6475	WP 940 2682	DK 439 1437	IW 892 8159
14	AK 383 0939	JJ 825 9054	RC 807 3765	VL 804 9583	NY 511 4264	ES 296 4742	RN 853 1099	ED 275 1483	GV 504 9222
15	WN 777 2640	JB 224 2771	ZF 108 3197	NF 767 1772	HQ 272 2735	XS 870 5275	KL 341 3307	QG 761 0934	JR 621 7901
16	AB 551 0658	YK 960 9482	YZ 995 9075	KE 781 4218	MO 394 1040	LL 293 8359	PD 238 3289	GV 444 3166	UA 793 5995
17	NV 601 1042	KT 255 0624	XO 837 9523	PJ 836 4722	KJ 196 9889	LG 841 9293	VJ 193 9757	VO 988 5574	PG 940 8434
18	CB 290 5545	JN 839 9639	SV 610 5906	KG 397 5401	GK 207 1050	KR 834 9137	IO 664 1901	FY 714 6637	XI 350 2766
19	TU 468 0887	JY 296 8314	MT 985 8604	WH 523 1489	IU 765 2365	LW 982 4509	RT 448 6010	MB 483 1475	WO 120 5858
20	BC 203 3659	AK 557 2373	IC 447 4945	QT 309 6323	CF 493 4820	XD 683 3342	PB 983 9328	IF 841 5752	YN 198 0298

Collective Intelligence in Action

SATNAM ALAG

MANNING

Greenwich
(74° w. long.)

To my dear sons, Ayush and Shray,
and my beautiful, loving, and intelligent wife, Alpana

	Development Editor:	Jeff Bleiel
Manning Publications Co.	Copyeditor:	Benjamin Berg
Sound View Court 3B	Typesetter:	Gordan Salinovic
Greenwich, CT 06830	Cover designer:	Leslie Haimes

ISBN 1933988312
Printed in the United States of America
1 2 3 4 5 6 7 8 9 10 – MAL – 13 12 11 10 09 08

brief contents

v

contents

foreword

When I founded ReadWriteWeb[1] back in April 2003, a tech news and analysis blog that is now one of the world's top 10 blogs,[2] my goal was to explore the current era of the web. The year 2003 was a time when the effects of the dot-com meltdown were still being felt, yet there was something new stirring on the web, too. I christened my new blog Read/Write Web (the slash and space have since been dropped) because this new era of the web seemed to embody the notion that Tim Berners-Lee had when he invented the web—that it ought to be editable by anyone and that *everyone* contributes in some way to the web's data.

As Satnam Alag writes in this book, *collective intelligence* as a research field actually predates the web. But it was after the dot-com era had ended that we began to see evidence of collective intelligence applied to the web. In 2003 we regularly saw it in sites like Amazon, with its user reviews and recommendations, eBay with its user-driven auctions, Wikipedia with its editable encyclopedia, and Google with its mysterious PageRank algorithm for ranking the popularity of web pages.

Sometime in 2004, O'Reilly & Associates coined the term *Web 2.0,* which eventually gained mainstream acceptance as the term for this era of the web (just as dot-com described the previous one). A central part of the new definition was the notion of *harnessing* collective intelligence, in which user contributions could be valuable in aggregate if mined and utilized in some way in your web site or application.

---

[1] http://www.readwriteweb.com/
[2] According to Technorati http://www.technorati.com/pop/blogs/

For all the popularity of Web 2.0, it remains difficult to implement many of its principles. This is where this book comes in, because it applies mathematical formulas and examples to the notion of collective intelligence (from now on simply known as *CI*). After explaining how to gather data and extract intelligence on the web, in part 2 of the book Satnam instructs you on specific CI techniques such as data mining, text analysis, clustering, and predictive technology.

And, *pssst,* do you want to know how to build a *recommendation engine?* This is an area of web technology that we at ReadWriteWeb have been covering with great interest in 2008. Recommendation engines, as Satnam notes, aim to show items of interest to a user. But in our reviews of the current wave of recommendation engines, we have seen that it's hard—very hard—to get recommendations right. Satnam shows how the leading practitioners, such as Amazon, Google News, and Netflix, build their recommendation engines. He also explains the different approaches you can take, with examples that developers can use and deploy in their own applications.

The Read/Write Web, or Web 2.0, or the Social Web, whatever you want to call it, relies on and builds value from user participation. If you're a web developer, you'll want to know how to use CI techniques to ensure that your web application can extract valuable data from its usage—and most importantly deliver that value right back to the users, where it belongs. This book goes a long way towards explaining how to do this.

RICHARD MACMANUS
FOUNDER/EDITOR, READWRITEWEB

preface

"What is the *virality coefficient* for your application?"

This is an increasingly common question being asked of young companies as they try to raise money from venture capitalists. New products are being designed that inherently take advantage of *virality* within the product. Companies such as YouTube, Facebook, Ning, LinkedIn, Skype, and more have grown from zero to millions of users by leveraging the power of virality. With little or no marketing, these types of companies rely on the wisdom of crowds to spread exponentially from one user to two users, then four, then eight, and so on. A simple link in an email, which worked for Hotmail to grow its user base, may no longer be adequate for your application. Facebook and LinkedIn enable users to build their networks by sending an invitation to others to connect as friends or connections; other applications such as Skype and Jaxtr provide free services as long as you're connecting to someone who's already a member, thus encouraging users to register.

It wasn't long ago when things were different. I still remember a few years back when I would ignore requests from others to connect on sites such as LinkedIn. Over a period of time, after repeatedly getting requests to connect from friends and acquaintances, I finally reached a *tipping point* and joined the network. The critical mass of users on the application, in addition to word-of-mouth recommendations, was good enough for me to see enough value to joining the network. Others had collectively convinced me to change my ways and join the application—this is one aspect of how collective intelligence is born and can manifest itself in your application.

Over the last few years, there's been a quiet revolution in the way users interact. *Time* magazine even declared "you," as in the collective set of users on the web, as the person of the year for 2006. Users are no longer shy about expressing themselves. This expression may be as simple as forwarding an interesting article to a friend, rating an item, or generating new content—commonly known as *user-generated content (UGC)*. To harness this user revolution, a new breed of applications, commonly known as *user-centric applications*, are being developed. Putting the user at the center of the application, leveraging social networks, and UGC are the new paradigms, and a high degree of personalization is now becoming the norm.

It's been almost two years since I first contacted Manning with the idea of writing a book on collective intelligence. Ever since my graduate school days, I've been fascinated by how you can discover interesting information by analyzing data. Over the years, I was able to ground a lot of theory in the practical world, especially in the context of large-scale web applications. One thing I knew was that there wasn't a practical book that could guide a developer through the various aspects of applying intelligence in an application. I could see a typical developer's eyes roll when delving into the inner workings of an algorithm or applying some of the collective intelligence features. There's immense value that an application can create by leveraging user-interaction data. As more and more companies joined the Web 2.0 parade, I wanted to write a book that would guide developers to understanding and implementing collective intelligence–related features in their applications.

It took longer to write this book than I had hoped. Most of the book was written while I was working full-time in demanding jobs. But the experience obtained by implementing these concepts in the real world provided good insight into what would be useful to others.

Remember, applications that make use of every user interaction to improve the value of the application for the user and other potential future users, and harness the power of virality, will dominate their markets. This book provides a set of tools that you'll need to leverage the information provided by the users on your site. Whatever forms of information may be available to you, this book will guide you in harnessing the potential of your information to personalize the site for your users. Focus on the user, and you shall succeed. For collective intelligence begins with a crowd of one.

acknowledgments

In the late seventeenth century, Sir Isaac Newton said, "If I have seen further, it is by standing on the shoulders of giants." Similarly, if I've been able to finish this book, it's with the help of a great number of people.

First, this book wouldn't have been possible without Associate Publisher Michael Stephens. Mike's passion and belief in the topic kept the book going. He's an excellent mentor and guides you through good times and bad. Just like Mike, my brain now converts all text into lists of lists. It was a real privilege to work with my development editor, Jeff Bleiel. Jeff spent countless hours providing feedback, digging deeper into why things were written in a certain way, and improving the flow of the text. Thanks to Marjan Bace, Manning's publisher, for helping fine-tune the table of contents, and for his guiding principle of keeping the book focused on new content. Special thanks to Karen Tegtmeyer for setting up and coordinating the peer reviews. And to the production team of Benjamin Berg, Katie Tennant, and Gordan Salinovic for turning my manuscript into the book that you are now holding. They spent countless hours checking and rechecking the manuscript. If you're thinking of writing a book, you won't find a better team than the one at Manning!

I'd like to thank all of the reviewers of my manuscript, many of whom spent large amounts of their free time on this task, for sending their excellent comments, suggestions, and criticisms. Some of the reviewers wished to remain anonymous...but here are a few I would like to acknowledge by name: Jérôme Bernard, Ryan Cox, Dave Crane, Roozbeh Daneshvar, Steve Gutz, Clint Howarth, Frank Jania, Gordon Jones,

Murali Krishnan, Darren Neimke, Sumit Pal, Muhammad Saleem, Robi Sen, Sopan Shewale, Srikanth Sundararajana, and John Tyler.

Special thanks to Shiva Paranandi, for his help in reviewing the text and the code, and for his technical proofread; Brendan Murray, for his technical proofread of the first half of the book; Sean Handel, for his detailed review of and suggestions on the first four chapters; Gautam Aggarwal, for his insightful comments; Krishna Mayuram, for his review of the third chapter; Mark Hornick, specification lead of JDM, for his suggestions on JDM-related chapters; Mayur Datar of Google, for reviewing the text for the Google News Personalization section in chapter 12; Mark Hall, Lead for Pentaho's data mining solutions (WEKA), for his comments on WEKA-related content; Shi Hui Liu, Murtaza Sonaseth, Kevin Xiao, Hector Villarreal, and the rest of the NextBio team, for their suggestions; Shahram Seyedin-Noor of NextBio, for his comments on the early chapters, encouragement, and his passionate philosophy on virality; and Ken DeLong and Mike McEvoy of BabyCenter, for their review and suggestions to improve the manuscript.

Special thanks to the awesome team at NextBio, especially the management team: Saeid Akhtari, Shahram Seyedin-Noor, Ilya Kupershmidt, and Mostafa Ronaghi, who introduced me to the field of data search and life sciences. We have a fantastic opportunity in intelligent search and user-centric applications; let's make it happen!

This book wouldn't have been possible without the support of a number of people whom I have worked for, including Patrick Grady, the charismatic CEO of Rearden Commerce; Michael McEvoy, CEO of QuickTrac Software; K.J., CEO 123signup.com, whom I thank for his mentorship; and Gordon Jones, SVP at TechWorks.

And finally, thanks to Richard MacManus, founder and editor of ReadWriteWeb, for taking the time to read the manuscript and write the foreword to the book.

This book took longer to finish than I had hoped, while I was working full-time. Consequently, it amounted to working all the time, even when we were on vacation. This book wouldn't have been possible without the active support of my wife, Alpana, and sons, and also the active encouragement and support provided by our extended families. On Alpana's side, dad diligently proofread and cheered raw early drafts; mom tried to free up my time; Rohini and Amit Verma provided constant encouragement. On my side, my mom helped in every way she could and kept me going, while my two adoring sisters, Nina and Amrita, made me feel as if I were the best writer in the world. Special thanks to Rajeev, Ankit, and Anish Suri for their encouragement.

Needless to say, this book was a nonstarter without the inspiration and support provided by Alpana, Ayush, and Shray. "Dad, how many chapters did you finish last night?" kept me going, as I didn't want to see the disappointment in my sons' eyes. Thank you, Alpana, for supporting me through this venture—it wouldn't have been possible without your sacrifices. I look forward to some quality time with the family, soon.

about this book

Collective Intelligence in Action is a practical book for applying collective intelligence to real-world web applications. I cover a broad spectrum of topics, from simple illustrative examples that explain the concepts and the math behind them, to the ideal architecture for developing a feature, to the database schema, to code implementation and use of open source toolkits. Regardless of your background and nature of development, I'm sure you'll find the examples and code samples useful. You should be able to directly use the code developed in this book. This is a practical book and I present a holistic view on what's required to apply these techniques in the real world. Consequently, the book discusses the architectures for implementing intelligence—you'll find lots of diagrams, especially UML diagrams, and a number of screenshots from well-known sites, in addition to code listings and even database schema designs.

There are a plethora of examples. Typically, concepts and the underlying math for algorithms are explained via examples with detailed step-by-step analysis. Accompanying the examples is Java code that demonstrates the concepts by implementing them, or by using open source frameworks.

A lot of work has been done by the open source community in Java in the areas of text processing and search (Lucene), data mining (WEKA), web crawling (Nutch), and data mining standards (JDM). This book leverages these frameworks, presenting examples and developing code that you can directly use in your Java application.

The first few chapters don't assume knowledge of Java. You should be able to follow the concepts and the underlying math using the illustrative examples. For the later chapters, a basic understanding of Java will be helpful. The book uses a number of diagrams and screenshots to illustrate the concepts. The Resources section of each chapter contains links to other useful content.

Roadmap

Chapter 1 provides a basic introduction to the field of collective intelligence (CI). CI is an active area of research, and I've kept the focus on applying CI to web applications. Section 1.2.1 is a personal favorite of mine; it provides a roadmap through a hypothetical example of how you can apply CI to your application. This is a must-read, since it helps to translate CI into features in your application and puts the flow of the book in perspective. Chapter 1 should also provide you with a good overview of the three forms of intelligence: direct, indirect, and derived.

The book is divided into three parts. Part 1 deals with collecting data, both within and outside the application, to be translated into intelligence later. Chapters 2 through 4 deal with gathering information from within one's application, while chapters 5 and 6 focus on gathering information from outside of one's application.

Chapter 2 provides an overview of the architecture required to embed CI in your application, along with a quick overview of some of the basic concepts that are needed to apply CI. Please take some time to go through section 2.2 in detail, as a firm understanding of the concepts presented in this section will be useful throughout the book. This chapter also shows how intelligence can be derived by analyzing the actions of the user. It's worthwhile to go through the example in section 2.4 in detail, as understanding the concepts presented there will also be useful throughout the book.

Chapter 3 continues with the theme of collecting data, this time from the user action of tagging. It provides an overview of the three forms of tags and how tagging can be leveraged. In section 3.3, we work through an example to show how tagging data can be converted into intelligence. This chapter also provides an overview of the ideal persistence architecture required to leverage tagging, and illustrates how to develop tag clouds.

Chapter 4 is focused on the different kinds of content that may be available in your application and how they can be used to derive intelligence. The chapter begins with providing an overview of the different architectures to embed content in your application. I also briefly discuss content that's typically associated with CI: blogs, wikis, and message boards. Next, we work through a step-by-step example of how intelligence can be extracted from unstructured text. This is a must-read section for those who want to understand text analytics.

The next two chapters are focused on collecting data from outside of one's application—first by searching the blogosphere and then by crawling the web.

Chapter 5 deals with building a framework to harvest information from the blogosphere. It begins with developing a generalized framework to retrieve blog entries. Next, it extends the framework to query blog-tracking providers such as Technorati, Blogdigger, Bloglines, and MSN.

Chapter 6 is focused on retrieving information from the web using web crawling. It introduces intelligent web crawling or focused crawling, along with a short discussion on dealing with hidden content. In this chapter, we first develop a simple web crawler. This exercise is useful to understand all the pieces that need to come together to build a web crawler and to understand the issues related to crawling the complete web. Next, for scalable crawling, we look at Nutch, an open source scalable web crawler.

Part 2 of the book is focused on deriving intelligence from the information collected. It consists of four chapters—an introduction to the data mining process, standards, and toolkits, and chapters on developing a text-analysis toolkit, finding patterns through clustering, and making predictions.

Chapter 7 provides an introduction to the process of data mining—the process and the various kinds of algorithms. It introduces WEKA, the open source data mining toolkit that's being extensively used, along with Java Data Mining (JDM) standard.

Chapter 8 develops a text analysis toolkit; this toolkit is used in the remainder of the book to convert unstructured text into a format that's usable for the mining algorithms. Here we leverage Lucene for text processing. In this section, we develop a custom analyzer to inject synonyms and detect phrases.

In chapter 9, we develop clustering algorithms. In this chapter, we develop the implementation for the k-means and hierarchical clustering algorithms. We also look at how we can leverage WEKA and JDM for clustering. Building on the blog harvesting framework developed in chapter 5, we also illustrate how we can cluster blog entries.

In chapter 10, we deal with algorithms related to making predictions. We first begin with classification algorithms, such as decision trees, Naïve Bayes' classifier, and belief networks. This chapter covers three algorithms for making predictions: linear regression, multi-layer perceptron, and radial basis function. It builds on the example of harvesting blog entries to illustrate how WEKA and JDM APIs can be leveraged for both classification and regression.

Part 3 consists of two chapters, which deal with applying intelligence within one's application.

Chapter 11 deals with intelligent search. It shows how you can leverage Lucene, along with other useful toolkits and frameworks that leverage Lucene. It also covers six different approaches being taken in the area of intelligent search.

The last chapter, chapter 12, illustrates how to build a recommendation engine using both content-based and collaborative-based approaches. It also covers real-world case studies on how recommendation engines have been build at Amazon, Google News, and Netflix.

Code conventions and downloads

All source code in listings or in text is in a `fixed-width font like this` to separate it from ordinary text. Method and function names, object properties, XML elements, and attributes in text are presented using this same font. Code annotations accompany many of the listings, highlighting important concepts. In some cases, numbered bullets link to explanations that follow the listing.

Source code for all of the working examples in this book is available for download from www.manning.com/CollectiveIntelligenceinAction. Basic setup documentation is provided with the download.

Author Online

The purchase of *Collective Intelligence in Action* includes free access to a private web forum run by Manning Publications, where you can make comments about the book, ask technical questions, and receive help from the authors and from other users. To access the forum and subscribe to it, point your web browser to www.manning.com/CollectiveIntelligenceinAction. This page provides information about how to get on the forum once you're registered, what kind of help is available, and the rules of conduct on the forum.

Manning's commitment to our readers is to provide a venue where a meaningful dialogue between individual readers and between readers and the author can take place. It isn't a commitment to any specific amount of participation on the part of the author, whose contribution to the forum remains voluntary (and unpaid). We suggest you try asking the author some challenging questions lest his interest stray! The Author Online forum and the archives of previous discussions will be accessible from the publisher's web site as long as the book is in print.

About the author

SATNAM ALAG, PH.D, is currently the vice president of engineering at NextBio (www.nextbio.com), a vertical search engine and a Web 2.0 user-centric application for the life sciences community. He's a seasoned software professional with more than 15 years of experience in machine learning and over a decade of experience in commercial software development and management. Dr. Alag worked as a consultant with Johnson & Johnson's BabyCenter, where he helped develop their personalization engine. Prior to that, he was the chief software architect at Rearden Commerce and began his career at

GE R&D. He's a Sun Certified Enterprise Architect (SCEA) for the Java Platform. Dr. Alag earned his Ph.D in engineering from UC Berkeley, and his dissertation was on the area of probabilistic reasoning and machine learning. He's published a number of peer-reviewed articles.

About the title

By combining introductions, overviews, and how-to examples, the *In Action* books are designed to help learning and remembering. According to research in cognitive science, the things people remember are things they discover during self-motivated exploration.

Although no one at Manning is a cognitive scientist, we're convinced that for learning to become permanent it must pass through stages of exploration, play, and, interestingly, retelling of what is being learned. People understand and remember new things, which is to say they master them, only after actively exploring them. Humans learn *in action*. An essential part of an *In Action* book is that it's example-driven. It encourages the reader to try things out, to play with new code, and explore new ideas.

There is another, more mundane, reason for the title of this book: our readers are busy. They use books to do a job or solve a problem. They need books that allow them to jump in and jump out easily and learn just what they want just when they want it. They need books that aid them *in action*. The books in this series are designed for such readers.

About the cover illustration

The figure on the cover of *Collective Intelligence in Action* is captioned "Le Champenois," a resident of the Champagne region in northeast France, best known for its sparkling white wine. The illustration is taken from a 19th century edition of Sylvain Maréchal's four-volume compendium of regional dress customs published in France. Each illustration is finely drawn and colored by hand. The rich variety of Maréchal's collection reminds us vividly of how culturally apart the world's towns and regions were just 200 years ago. Isolated from each other, people spoke different dialects and languages. In the streets or in the countryside, it was easy to identify where they lived and what their station in life was just by their dress.

Dress codes have changed since then and the diversity by region, so rich at the time, has faded away. It is now hard to tell apart the inhabitants of different continents, let alone different towns or regions. Perhaps we have traded cultural diversity for a more varied personal life—certainly for a more varied and fast-paced technological life.

At a time when it is hard to tell one computer book from another, Manning celebrates the inventiveness and initiative of the computer business with book covers based on the rich diversity of regional life of two centuries ago, brought back to life by Maréchal's pictures.

Part 1

Gathering data for intelligence

Chapter 1 begins the book with a brief overview of what collective intelligence is and how it manifests itself in your application. Then we move on to focus on how we can gather data from which we can derive intelligence. For this, we look at information both inside the application (chapters 2 through 4) and outside the application (chapters 5 and 6).

Chapter 2 deals with learning from the interactions of users. To get the ball rolling, we look at the architecture for embedding intelligence, and present some of the basic concepts related to collective intelligence (CI). We also cover how we can gather data from various forms of user interaction. We continue with this theme in chapter 3, which deals with tagging. This chapter contains all the information you need to build tagging-related features in your application. In chapter 4, we look at the various forms of content that are typically available in a web application and how to derive collective intelligence from it.

Next, we change our focus to collecting data from outside our application. We first deal with searching the blogosphere in chapter 5. This is followed by chapter 6, which deals with intelligently crawling the web in search of relevant content.

Understanding
collective intelligence

Web applications are undergoing a revolution.

In this post-dot-com era, the web is transforming. Newer web applications trust their users, invite them to interact, connect them with others, gain early feedback from them, and then use the collected information to constantly improve the application. Web applications that take this approach develop deeper relationships with their users, provide more value to users who return more often, and ultimately offer more targeted experiences for each user according to her personal need.

3

Web users are undergoing a transformation.

Users are expressing themselves. This expression may be in the form of sharing their opinions on a product or a service through reviews or comments; through sharing and tagging content; through participation in an online community; or by contributing new content.

This increased user interaction and participation gives rise to data that can be converted into intelligence in your application. The use of collective intelligence to personalize a site for a user, to aid him in searching and making decisions, and to make the application more sticky are cherished goals that web applications try to fulfill.

In his book, *Wisdom of the Crowds*, James Surowiecki, business columnist for *The New Yorker*, asserts that "under the right circumstances, groups are remarkably intelligent, and are often smarter than the smartest people in them." Surowiecki says that if the process is sound, the more people you involve in solving a problem, the better the result will be. A crowd's *collective intelligence* will produce better results than those of a small group of experts if four basic conditions are met. These four basic conditions are that "wise crowds" are effective when they're composed of individuals who have diverse opinions; when the individuals aren't afraid to express their opinions; when there's diversity in the crowd; and when there's a way to aggregate all the information and use it in the decision-making process.

Collective intelligence is about making your application more valuable by tapping into *wise crowds*. More formally, collective intelligence (CI) as used in this book simply and concisely means

> *To effectively use the information provided by others to improve one's application.*

This is a fairly broad definition of collective intelligence—one which uses all types of information, both inside and outside the application, to improve the application for a user. This book introduces you to concepts from the areas of machine learning, information retrieval, and data mining, and demonstrates how you can add intelligence to your application. You'll be exposed to how your application can learn about individual users by correlating their interactions with those of others to offer a highly personalized experience.

This chapter provides an overview of collective intelligence and how it can manifest itself in your application. It begins with a brief introduction to the field of collective intelligence, then goes on to describe the many ways it can be applied to your application, and finally shows how intelligence can be classified.

1.1 What is collective intelligence?

Collective intelligence is an active field of research that predates the web. Scientists from the fields of sociology, mass behavior, and computer science have made important contributions to this field. When a group of individuals collaborate or compete with each other, intelligence or behavior that otherwise didn't exist suddenly emerges; this is commonly known as *collective intelligence*. The actions or influence of a few individuals slowly spread across the community until the actions become the norm for the community. To better understand how this circle of influence spreads, let's look at a couple of examples.

In his book *The Hundredth Monkey*,[1] Ken Keyes recounts an interesting story about how change is propagated in groups. In 1952, on the isolated Japanese island of Koshima, scientists observed a group of monkeys. They offered them sweet potatoes; the monkeys liked the sweet potatoes but found the taste of dirt and sand on the potatoes unpleasant. One day, an 18-month-old monkey named Imo found a solution to the problem by washing the potato in a nearby stream of water. She taught this trick to her mother. Her playmates also learned the trick and taught it to their mothers. Initially, only adults who imitated their children learned the new trick, while the others continued eating the old way. In the autumn of 1958, a number of monkeys were washing their potatoes before eating. The exact number is unknown, but let's say that out of 1,000, there were 99 monkeys who washed their potatoes before eating. Early one sunny morning, a 100th monkey decided to wash his potato. Then, incredibly, by evening *all* monkeys were washing their potatoes. The 100th monkey was that *tipping point* that caused others to change their habits for the better. Soon it was observed that monkeys on other islands were also washing their potatoes before eating them.

As users interact on the web and express their opinions, they influence others. Their initial circle of influence is the group of individuals that they most interact with. Because the web is a highly connected network of sites, this *circle of influence* grows and may shape the thoughts of everybody in the group. This circle of influence also grows rapidly throughout the community—another example helps illustrate this further.

In 1918, as the influenza flu pandemic spread, nearly 14 percent of Fiji's population died in just 16 days. Nearly one third of the native population in Alaska had a similar fate; it's estimated that worldwide, nearly twenty-five million people died of the flu. A pandemic is a global disease outbreak and spreads from person to person. First, one person is affected, who then transmits it to another and then another. The newly infected person transmits the flu to others; this causes the disease to spread exponentially.

In October 2006, Google bought YouTube for $1.65 billion. In its 20 months of existence, YouTube had grown to be one of the busiest sites on the Internet, dishing out 100 million video[2] views a day. It ramped from zero to more than 20 million unique user visits a day, with mainly *viral marketing*—spread from person to person, similar to the way the pandemic flu spreads. In YouTube's case, each time a user uploaded a new video, she was easily able to invite others to view this video. As those others viewed this video, other related videos popped up as recommendations, keeping the user further engaged. Ultimately, many of these viewers also became submitters and uploaded their own videos as well. As the number of videos increased, the site became more and more attractive for new users to visit.

---

[1] http://en.wikipedia.org/wiki/Hundredth_Monkey
[2] As of September 2006

Whether you're a budding startup, a recognized market leader, or looking to take an emerging application or web site to the next level, harnessing information from users improves the perceived value of the application to both current and prospective users. This improved value will not only encourage current users to interact more, but will also attract new users to the application. The value of the application further improves as new users interact with it and contribute more content. This forms a self-reinforcing feedback loop, commonly known as a *network effect*, which enables wider adoption of the service. Next, let's look at CI as it applies to web applications.

1.2   *CI in web applications*

In this section, we look at how CI manifests itself in web applications. We walk through an example to illustrate how it can be used in web applications, briefly review its benefits, see how it fits in with Web 2.0 and can be leveraged to build user-centric applications.

Let's expand on our earlier definition of collective intelligence. Collective intelligence of users in essence is

- *The intelligence that's extracted out from the collective set of interactions and contributions made by your users.*
- *The use of this intelligence to act as a filter for what's valuable in your application for a user*—This filter takes into account a user's preferences and interactions to provide relevant information to the user.

This filter could be the simple influence that collective user information has on a user—perhaps a rating or a review written about a product, as shown in figure 1.1—or it may be more involved—building models to recommend personalized content to a user. This book is focused toward building the more involved models to personalize your application.

As shown in figure 1.2, there are three things that need to happen to apply collective intelligence in your application. You need to

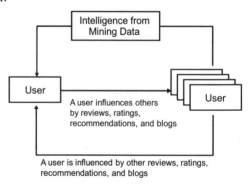

Figure 1.1   A user may be influenced by other users either directly or through intelligence derived from the application by mining the data.

1. Allow users to interact with your site and with each other, learning about each user through their interactions and contributions.
2. Aggregate what you learn about your users and their contributions using some useful models.
3. Leverage those models to recommend relevant content to a user.

Let's walk through an example to understand how collective intelligence can be a catalyst to building a successful web application.

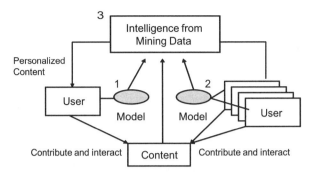

Figure 1.2 Three components to harnessing collective intelligence. 1: Allow users to interact. 2: Learn about your users in aggregate. 3: Personalize content using user interaction data and aggregate data.

1.2.1 Collective intelligence from the ground up: a sample application

In our example, John and Jane are two engineers who gave up their lucrative jobs to start a company. They're based in Silicon Valley and as is the trend nowadays, they're building their fledgling company without any venture capital on a shoestring budget leveraging open source software. They believe in fast-iterative agile-based development cycles and aren't afraid to release beta software to gain early feedback on their features.[3] They're looking to build a marketplace and plan to generate revenue both from selling ad space and from sharing revenue from sold items.

In their first iteration, they launched an application where users—mainly friends and family—could buy items and view relevant articles. There wasn't much in terms of personalization or user interaction or intelligence—a plain vanilla system.

Next, they added the feature of showing a list of top items purchased by users, along with a list of recently purchased items. This is perhaps the simplest form of applying collective intelligence—*providing information in aggregate to users.* To grow the application virally, they also enabled users to email these lists to others. Users used this to forward interesting lists of items to their friends, who in turn became users of the application.

In their next iteration, they wanted to learn more about their users. So they built a basic user profile mechanism that contained explicit and implicit profile information. The explicit information was provided directly by the users as part of their accounts—first name, age, and so on. The implicit information was collected from the user interaction data—this included information such as the articles and content users viewed and the products they purchased. They also wanted to show more relevant articles and content to each user, so they built a content-based *recommendation engine* that analyzed the content of articles—keywords, word frequency, location, and so forth to correlate articles with each other and recommend possibly interesting articles to each user.

Next, they allowed users to generate content. They gave users the ability to write about their experiences with the products, in essence writing reviews and creating their list of recommendations through both explicit ratings of individual products

---

[3] Note that beta doesn't mean poor quality; it just means that it's incomplete in functionality.

and a "my top 10 favorite products" list. They also gave users the capability to rate items and rate reviews. Ratings and reviews have been shown to influence other users, and numerical rating information is also useful as an input to a collaborative-based recommendation engine.

With the growing list of content and products available on the site, John and Jane now found it too cumbersome and expensive to manually maintain the classification of content on their site. The users also provided feedback that content navigation menus were too rigid. So they introduced dynamic navigation via a *tag cloud*—navigation built by an alphabetical listing of terms, where font size correlates with importance or number of occurrences of a tag. The terms were automatically extracted from the content by analyzing the content. The application analyzed each user's interaction and provided users with a personalized set of tags for navigating the site. The set of tags changed as the type of content visited by the users changed. Further, the content displayed when a user clicked on a tag varied from user to user and changed over time. Some tags pulled the data from a search engine, while others from the recommendation engine and external catalogs.

In the next release, they allowed the users to explicitly tag items by adding free text labels, along with saving or *bookmarking* items of interest. As users started tagging items, John and Jane found that there was a rich set of information that could be derived. First of all, users were providing new terms for the content that made sense to them— in essence they built *folksonomies*.[4] The tag cloud navigation now had both machine-generated and user-generated tags. The process of extracting tags using an automated algorithm could also be enhanced using the dictionary of tags built by the users. These user-added tags were also useful for finding keywords used by an ad-generation engine. They could also use the tags created by users to connect users with each other and with other items of interest. This is collective intelligence in action.

Next, they allowed their users to generate content. Users could now blog about their experiences, or ask and respond to questions on message boards, or participate in building the application itself by contributing to wikis. John and Jane quickly built an algorithm that could extract tags from the unstructured content. They then matched the interests of users—gained from analyzing their interaction in the applications—with those of other users to find relevant items. They were soon able to learn enough about their users to personalize the site for each user, and to provide relevant content—targeting niche items to niche users. They could also target relevant advertisements based on the user profile and context of interaction.

They also modified the search results to make them more relevant to each user, for which they used the user's profile and interaction history when appropriate. They customized advertising by using keywords that were relevant to both the user and the page content.

To make the application stickier, they started aggregating and indexing external content—they would crawl a select list of external web sites to index the content and present

---

[4] Folksonomies are classifications created through the process of users tagging items.

links to it when relevant. They also connected to sites that tracked the blogosphere, presenting the users with relevant content from what others were saying in blogs.

They also clustered users and items to find patterns in the data and built models to automatically classify content into one of many categories.

The users soon liked the application so much that they started recommending the application to their friends and relatives and the user base grew *virally*. In our example, after a couple of years, John and Jane retired to Hawaii, having sold the company for a gigantic amount, where they waited for the next web revolution… Web 3.0!

These in essence are the many ways by which collective intelligence will manifest itself in your application, and thus more or less the outline for this book. Table 1.1 summarizes the ways to harness collective intelligence in your application. Each of these is discussed throughout the book.

Table 1.1   Some of the ways to harness collective intelligence in your application

Techniques	Description
Aggregate information: lists	Create lists of items generated in the aggregate by your users. Perhaps, *Top List* of items bought, or *Top Search Items* or *List of Recent Items*.
Ratings, reviews, and recommendations	Collective information from your users influences others.
User-generated content: blogs, wikis, message boards	Intelligence can be extracted from contributions by users. These contributions also influence other users.
Tagging, bookmarking, voting, saving	Collective intelligence of users can be used to bubble up interesting content, learn about your users, and connect users.
Tag cloud navigation	Dynamic classification of content using terms generated via one or more of the following techniques: machine-generated, professionally-generated, or user-generated.
Analyze content to build user profiles	Analyze content associated with a user to extract keywords. This information is used to build user profiles.
Clustering and predictive models	Cluster users and items, build predictive models.
Recommendation engines	Recommend related content or users based on intelligence gathered from user interaction and analyzing content.
Search	Show more pertinent search results using a user's profile.
Harness external content	Provide relevant information from the blogosphere and external sites

John and Jane showed us a few nice things to apply to their site, but there are other benefits of applying collective intelligence to your application. Let's look at that next.

1.2.2   Benefits of collective intelligence

Applying collective intelligence to your application impacts it in the following manner:

- *Higher retention rates*—The more users interact with the application, the stickier it gets for them, and the higher the probability that they'll become repeat visitors.
- *Greater opportunities to market to the user*—The greater the number of interactions, the greater the number of pages visited by the user, which increases the opportunities to market to or communicate with the user.
- *Higher probability of a user completing a transaction and finding information of interest*—The more contextually relevant information that a user finds, the better the chances that he'll have the information he needs to complete the transaction or find content of interest. This leads to higher click-through and conversion rates for your advertisements.
- *Boosting search engine rankings*—The more users participate and contribute content, the more content is available in your application and indexed by search engines. This could boost your search engine ranking and make it easier for others to find your application.

Collective intelligence is a term that is increasingly being used in the context of Web 2.0 applications. Let's take a closer look at how it fits in with Web 2.0.

1.2.3 CI is the core component of Web 2.0

Web 2.0 is a term that has generated passionate emotions, ranging from being dismissed as marketing jargon to being anointed as the new or next generation of the Internet. There are seven principles that Web 2.0 companies demonstrate, as shown in table 1.2.[5]

Table 1.2 Seven principles of Web 2.0 applications

Principle	Description
The network is the platform	Companies or users who use traditional licensed software have to deal with running the software, upgrading it periodically to keep up with newer versions, and scaling it to meet appropriate levels of demand. Most successful Web 2.0 companies no longer sell licensed software, but instead deliver their software as a service. The end customer simply uses the service through a browser. All the headaches of running, maintaining, and scaling the software and hardware are taken care of by the service provider seamlessly to the end user. The software is upgraded fairly frequently by the service provider and is available 24 x 7.
Harnessing collective intelligence	The key to the success of Web 2.0 applications is how effectively they can harness the information provided by users. The more personalized your service, the better you can match a user to content of her choice.
Hard-to-replicate data as competitive advantage	Hard-to-replicate, unique, large datasets provide a competitive advantage to a company. Web 2.0 is *data* and *software* combined. One can't replicate Craigslist, eBay, Amazon, Flickr, or Google simply by replicating the software. The underlying data that the software generates from user activity is tremendously valuable. This dataset grows every day, improving the product daily.

---

[5] Refer to Tim O'Reilly's paper on Web 2.0.

Table 1.2 Seven principles of Web 2.0 applications *(continued)*

Principle	Description
The perpetual beta	Web 2.0 companies release their products early to involve their users and gain important feedback. They iterate often by having short release cycles. They involve the users early in the process. They instrument the application to capture important metrics on how a new feature is being used, how often it's being used, and by whom. If you aren't sure how a particular feature should look and have competing designs, expose a prototype of each to different sets of users and measure the success of each. Involve the customers and let them decide which one they like. By having short development cycles, it's possible to solicit user feedback, incorporate changes early in the product life cycle, and build what the users really want.
Simpler programming models	Simpler development models lead to wider adoption and reuse. Design your application for "hackability" and "remixability" following open standards, using simple programming models and a licensing structure that puts as few restrictions as necessary.
Software above the level of a single device	Applications that operate across multiple devices will be more valuable than those that operate in a single device.
Rich user experience	The success of AJAX has fueled the growing use of rich user interfaces in Web 2.0 applications. Adobe Flash/Flex and Microsoft Silverlight are other alternatives for creating rich UIs.

It is widely regarded that harnessing collective intelligence is the key or core component to Web 2.0 applications. In essence, Web 2.0 is all about inviting users to participate and interact. But what do you do with all the data collected from user participation and interaction? This information is wasted if it can't be converted into intelligence and channeled into improving one's application. That's where collective intelligence and this book come in.

Dion Hinchliffe, in his article, "Five Great Ways to Harness Collective Intelligence," makes an analogy to the apocryphal Einstein quote that compound interest was the most important force in the universe. Similarly, web applications that effectively harness collective intelligence can "benefit" in much the same way—harnessing collective intelligence is about those very same exponential effects.

NOTE *Collective intelligence is the heart of Web 2.0 applications.* It's generally acknowledged that one of the core components of Web 3.0 applications will be the use of artificial intelligence.[6] There's debate as to whether this intelligence will be attained by computers reasoning like humans or by sites leveraging the collective intelligence of humans using techniques such as collaborative filtering. Either way, having the dataset generated from real human interactions will be necessary and useful.

In order to effectively leverage collective intelligence, you need to put the user at the center of your application, in essence building a user-centric application.

---

[6] http://en.wikipedia.org/wiki/Web_3.0#An_evolutionary_path_to_artificial_intelligence

1.2.4   *Harnessing CI to transform from content-centric to user-centric applications*

Prior to the user-centric revolution, many applications put little emphasis on the user. These applications, known as *content-centric* applications, focused on the best way to present the content and were generally static from user to user and from day to day. User-centric applications leverage CI to fundamentally change how the user interacts with the web application. User-centric applications make the user the center of the web experience and dynamically reshuffle the content based on what's known about the user and what the user explicitly asks for.

As shown in figure 1.3, user-centric applications are composed of the following four components:

- *Core competency*—The main reason why a user comes to the application.
- *Community*—Connecting users with other users of interest, social networking, finding other users who may provide answers to a user's questions.
- *Leveraging user-generated content*—Incorporating generated content and interactions of users to provide additional content to users.
- *Building a marketplace*—Monetizing the application by product and/or service placements and showing relevant advertisements.

The user profile is at the center of the application. A part of the user profile may be generated by the user, while some parts of it may be learned by the application based on user interaction. Typically, sites that allow user-generated content have an abundance of information. User-centric sites leverage collective intelligence to present relevant content to the user.

Figure 1.4 shows a screenshot of one such user-centric application—LinkedIn,[7] a popular online network of more than 20 million professionals.[8] As shown in

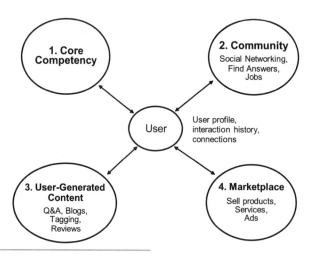

Figure 1.3   Four pillars for user-centric applications

---

[7] http://www.linkedin.com/static?key=company_info&trk=ftr_abt

[8] As of May 2008

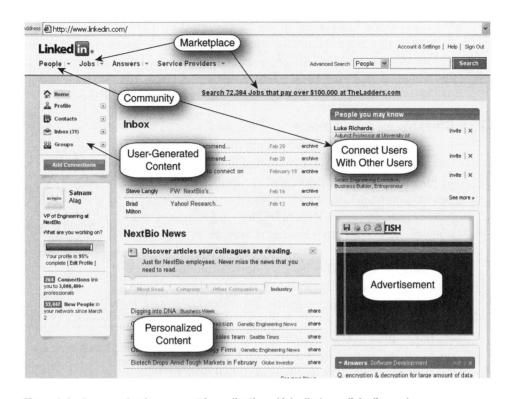

Figure 1.4   An example of a user-centric application—LinkedIn (www.linkedin.com)

the screenshot, the LinkedIn application leverages the four components of user-centric applications:

- *Core competency*—Users come to the site to connect with others and build their professional profiles.
- *Community*—Users create connections with other users; connections are used while looking up people, responding to jobs, and answering questions asked by other users. Other users are automatically recommended as possible connections by the application.
- *User-generated content*—Most of the content at the site is user-generated. This includes the actual professional profiles, the questions asked, the feed of actions—such as a user updating his profile, uploading his photograph, or connecting to someone new.
- *Marketplace*—The application is monetized by means of advertisements, job postings, and a monthly subscription for the power-users of the system, who often are recruiters. The monetization model used is also commonly known as *freemium*[9]—basic services are free and are used by most users, while there's a charge for premium services that a small minority of users pay for.

---

[9]   http://en.wikipedia.org/wiki/Freemium_business_model

For user-centric applications to be successful, they need to personalize the site for each user. CI can be beneficial to these applications. So far in this section, we've looked at what collective intelligence is, how it manifests itself in your application, the advantages of applying it, and how it fits in with Web 2.0. Next, we'll take a more detailed look at the many forms of information provided by the users.

1.3   *Classifying intelligence*

Figure 1.5 illustrates the three types of intelligence that we discuss in this book. First is explicit information that the user provides in the application. Second is implicit information that a user provides either inside or outside the application and is typically in an unstructured format. Lastly, there is intelligence that's derived by analyzing the aggregate data collected. This piece of derived intelligence is shown on the upper half of the triangle, as it is based on the information gathered by the other two parts.

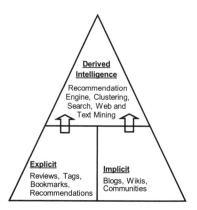

Figure 1.5   Classifying user-generated information

Data comes in two forms: structured data and unstructured data. Structured data has a well-defined form, something that makes it easily stored and queried on. User ratings, content articles viewed, and items purchased are all examples of structured data. Unstructured data is typically in the form of raw text. Reviews, discussion forum posts, blog entries, and chat sessions are all examples of unstructured data.

In this section, we look at the three forms of intelligence: explicit, implicit, and derived.

1.3.1   *Explicit intelligence*

This section deals with explicit information that a user provides. Here are a few examples of how a user provides explicit information that can be leveraged.

REVIEWS AND RECOMMENDATIONS

A recommendation made by a friend or a person of influence can have a big impact on other users within the same group. Moreover, a review or comments about a user's experience with a particular provider or service is contextually relevant for other users inquiring about that topic, especially if it's within the context of similar use.

TAGGING

Adding the ability for users to add tags—keywords or labels provided by a user—to classify items of interest such as articles, items being sold, pictures, videos, podcasts, and so on is a powerful technique to solicit information from the user. Tags can also be generated by professional editors or by an automated algorithm that analyzes content. These tags are used to classify data, bookmark sites, connect people with each other, aid users in their searches, and build dynamic navigation in your application, of which a tag cloud is one example.

Figure 1.6   This tag cloud from del.icio.us shows popular tags at the site.

Figure 1.6 shows a tag cloud showing popular tags at del.icio.us, a popular bookmarking site. In a tag cloud, tags are displayed alphabetically, with the size of the font representing the frequency of occurrence. The larger the font of the tag, the more frequently it occurs.

VOTING

Voting is another way to involve and obtain useful information from the user. Digg, a web site that allows users to contribute and vote on interesting articles, leverages this idea. Every article on Digg is submitted and voted on by the Digg community. Submissions that receive many votes in a short period tend to move up in rank. This is a good way to share, discover, bookmark, and promote important news. Figure 1.7 is a screenshot from Digg.com showing news items with the number of Diggs associated with each.

1.3.2   Implicit intelligence

This section deals with indirect information that a user provides. Here are a few examples of how a user provides this information.

Information relevant to your application may appear in an unstructured free-form text format through reviews, messages, blogs, and so forth. A user may express his opinion online, either within your application or outside the application, by writing in his blog or replying to a question in an online community. Thanks to the power of search engines and blog-tracking engines, this information becomes easily available to others and helps to shape their opinions.

You may want to augment your current application by aggregating and mining external data. For example, if your area is real estate applications, you may want to augment your application with additional data harvested from freely available external

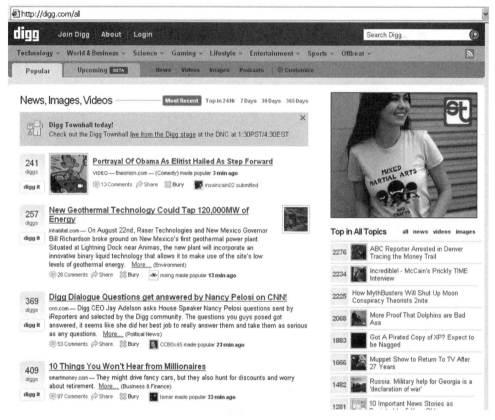

Figure 1.7   Screen shot from Digg.com showing news items with the number of diggs for each

sites, for example, public records on housing sales, reviews of schools and neighborhoods, and so on.

Blogs are online journals where information is displayed in reverse chronological order. The blogosphere—the collection of blogs on the net—is huge and growing fast. As of August 2008, Technorati, a private company that tracks blogs, was tracking 112.8 million blogs. With a new blog being created virtually every second, the blogosphere is an important source of information that can be leveraged in your application. People write blogs on virtually every topic.

Next, let's look at the third category of intelligence, which is derived from analyzing the data collected.

1.3.3   Derived intelligence

This section deals with information derived from the data you collect from users. Here are a few examples of techniques and features that deal with derived intelligence.

DATA AND TEXT MINING

The process of finding patterns and trends that would otherwise go undetected in large datasets using automated algorithms is known as *data mining*. When the data is in the form of text, the mining process is commonly known as *text data mining*. Another related field is *information retrieval*, which deals with finding relevant information by analyzing the content of the documents. Web and text mining deal with analyzing unstructured content to find patterns in them. Most applications are content-rich. This content is indexed by search engines and can be used by the recommendation engine to recommend relevant content to a user.

CLUSTERING AND PREDICTIVE ANALYSIS

Clustering and predictive analysis are two main components of data mining. Clustering techniques enable you to classify items—users or content—into natural groupings. Predictive analysis is a mathematical model that predicts a value based on the input data.

INTELLIGENT SEARCH

Search is one of the most commonly used techniques for retrieving content. In later chapters, we look at *Lucene*—an open source Java search engine developed through the Apache foundation. We look at how information about the user can be used to customize the search through intelligent filters that enhance search results when appropriate.

RECOMMENDATION ENGINE

A recommendation engine offers relevant content to a user. Again, recommendation engines can be built by analyzing the content, by analyzing user interactions (collaborative approach), or a combination of both. Figure 1.8 shows a screenshot from Yahoo! Music in which a user is recommended music by the application.

Figure 1.8 Screenshot from Yahoo! Music recommending songs of interest

Recommendation engines use inputs from the user to offer a list of recommended items. The inputs to the recommendation engine may be items in the user's shopping list, items she's purchased in the past or is considering purchasing, user-profile information such as age, tags and articles that the user has looked at or contributed, or any other useful information that the user may have provided. For large online stores such as Amazon, which has millions of items in its catalog, providing fast recommendations can be challenging. Recommendation engines need to be fast and scale independently of the number of items in the catalog and the number of users in the system; they need to offer good recommendations for new customers with limited interaction history; and they need to age out older or irrelevant interaction data (such as a gift bought for someone else) from the recommendation process.

1.4   Summary

Collective intelligence is powering a new breed of applications that invite users to interact, contribute content, connect with other users, and personalize the site experience.

Users influence other users. This influence spreads outward from their immediate circle of influence until it reaches a critical number, after which it becomes the norm. Useful user-generated content and opinions spread virally with minimal marketing.

Intelligence provided by users can be divided into three main categories. First is direct information/intelligence provided by the user. Reviews, recommendations, ratings, voting, tags, bookmarks, user interaction, and user-generated content are all examples of techniques to gather this intelligence. Next is indirect information provided by the user either on or off the application, which is typically in unstructured text. Blog entries, contributions to online communities, and wikis are all sources of intelligence for the application. Third is a higher level of intelligence that's derived using data mining techniques. Recommendation engines, use of predictive analysis for personalization, profile building, market segmentation, and web and text mining are all examples of discovering and applying this higher level of intelligence.

The rest of this book is divided into three parts. The first part deals with collecting data for analysis, the second part deals with developing algorithms for analyzing the data, and the last part deals with applying the algorithms to your application. Next, in chapter 2, we look at how intelligence can be gathered by analyzing user interactions.

1.5   Resources

"All things Web 2.0." http://www.allthingsweb2.com/component/option,com_mtree/
     Itemid,26/

Anderson, Chris. *The Long Tail: Why the Future of Business Is Selling Less of More*. 2006. Hyperion

Hinchliffe, Dion. "The Web 2.0 Is Here." http://web2.wsj2.com/web2ishere.htm

"Five Great Ways to Harness Collective Intelligence." January 17, 2006, http://web2.wsj2.com/
     five_great_ways_to_harness_collective_intelligence.htm

"Architectures of Participation: The Next Big Thing." August 1, 2006, http://web2.wsj2.com/
     architectures_of_participation_the_next_big_thing.htm

Jaokar, Ajit. "Tim O'Reilly's seven principles of web 2.0 make a lot more sense if you change the order." April 17, 2006, http://opengardensblog.futuretext.com/archives/2006/04/tim_o_reillys_s.html

Kroski, Ellyssa. "The Hype and the Hullabaloo of Web 2.0." http://infotangle.blogsome.com/2006/01/13/the-hype-and-the-hullabaloo-of-web-20/

McGovern, Gerry. "Collective intelligence: is your website tapping it?" April 2006, New Thinking, http://www.gerrymcgovern.com/nt/2006/nt-2006-04-17-collective-intelligence.htm

"One blog created 'every second'." BBC news, http://news.bbc.co.uk/1/hi/technology/4737671.stm

"Online Community Toolkit." http://www.fullcirc.com/community/communitymanual.htm

O'Reilly, Tim. "What Is Web 2.0: Design Patterns and Business Models for the Next Generation of Software." http://www.oreilly.com/pub/a/oreilly/tim/news/2005/09/30/what-is-web-20.html

"The Future of Technology and Proprietary Software." December 2003, http://tim.oreilly.com/articles/future_2003.html

"Web 2.0: Compact Definition?" October 2005, http://radar.oreilly.com/archives/2005/10/web_20_compact_definition.html

Por, George. "The meaning and accelerating the emergence of CI." April 2004, http://www.community-intelligence.com/blogs/public/archives/000251.html

Surowiecki, James. *The Wisdom of Crowds.* 2005. Anchor

Web 3.0. Wikipedia, http://en.wikipedia.org/wiki/Web_3.0#An_evolutionary_path_to_artificial_intelligence

Learning
from user interactions

2

This chapter covers

- Architecture for applying intelligence
- Basic technical concepts behind collective intelligence
- The many forms of user interaction
- A working example of how user interaction is
  converted into collective intelligence

Through their interactions with your web application, users provide a rich set of information that can be converted into intelligence. For example, a user rating an item provides crisp quantifiable information about the user's preferences. Aggregating the rating across all your users or a subset of relevant users is one of the simplest ways to apply collective intelligence in your application.

There are two main sources of information that can be harvested for intelligence. First is *content-based*—based on information about the item itself, usually keywords or phrases occurring in the item. Second is *collaborative-based*—based on the interactions of users. For example, if someone is looking for a hotel, the collaborative filtering engine will look for similar users based on matching profile attributes and find

20

hotels that these users have rated highly. Throughout the chapter, the theme of using content and collaborative approaches for harvesting intelligence will be reinforced.

First and foremost, we need to make sure that you have the right architecture in place for embedding intelligence in your application. Therefore, we begin by describing the ideal architecture for applying intelligence. This will be followed by an introduction to some of the fundamental concepts needed to understand the underlying technology. You'll be introduced to the fields of content and collaborative filtering and how intelligence is represented and extracted from text. Next, we review the many forms of user interaction and how that interaction translates into collective intelligence for your application. The main aim of this chapter is to introduce you to the fundamental concepts that we leverage to build the underlying technology in parts 2 and 3 of the book. A strong foundation leads to a stronger house, so make sure you understand the fundamental concepts introduced in this chapter before proceeding on to later chapters.

2.1 Architecture for applying intelligence

All web applications consist, at a minimum, of an application server or a web server—to serve HTTP or HTTPS requests sent from a user's browser—and a database that stores the persistent state of the application. Some applications also use a messaging server to allow asynchronous processing via an event-driven Service-Oriented Architecture (SOA). The best way to embed intelligence in your application is to build it as a set of *services*—software components that each have a well-defined interface.

In this section, we look at the two kinds of intelligence-related services and their advantages and disadvantages.

2.1.1 Synchronous and asynchronous services

For embedding intelligence in your application, you need to build two kinds of services: synchronous and asynchronous services.

Synchronous services service requests from a client in a synchronous manner: the client waits till the service returns the response back. These services need to be fast, since the longer they take to process the request, the longer the wait time for the client. Some examples of this kind of a service are the runtime of an item-recommendation engine (a service that provides a list of items related to an item of interest for a user), a service that provides a model of user's profile, and a service that provides results from a search query.

For scaling and high performance, synchronous services should be stateless—the service instance shouldn't maintain any state between service requests. All the information that the service needs to process a request should be retrieved from a persistent source, such as a database or a file, or passed to it as a part of the service request. These services also use caching to avoid round-trips to the external data store. These services can be in the same JVM as the client code or be distributed in their own set of machines. Due to their stateless nature, you can have multiple instances of the services running servicing requests. Typically, a load balancer is used in front of the multiple instances. These services scale nearly linearly, neglecting the overhead of load-balancing among the instances.

Asynchronous services typically run in the background and take longer to process. Examples of this kind of a service include a data aggregator service (a service that crawls the web to identify, gather, and classify relevant information) as well as a service that learns the profile of a user through a predictive model or clustering, or a search engine indexing content. Asynchronous learning services need to be designed to be stateless: they receive a message, process it, and then work on the next message. There can be multiple instances of these services all listening to the same queue on the messaging server. The messaging server takes care of load balancing between the multiple instances and will queue up the messages under load.

Figure 2.1 shows an example of the two kinds of services. First, we have the runtime API that services client requests synchronously, using typically precomputed information about the user and other derived information such as search indexes or predictive models. The intelligence-learning service is an asynchronous service that analyzes information from various types of content along with user-interaction information to create models that are used by the runtime API. Content could be either contained within your system or retrieved from external sources, such as by searching the blogosphere or by web crawling.

Table 2.1 lists some of the services that you'll be able to build in your application using concepts that we develop in this book.

As new information comes in about your users, their interactions, and the content in your system, the models used by the intelligence services need to be updated. There are two approaches to updating the models: event-driven and non-event-driven. We discuss these in the next two sections.

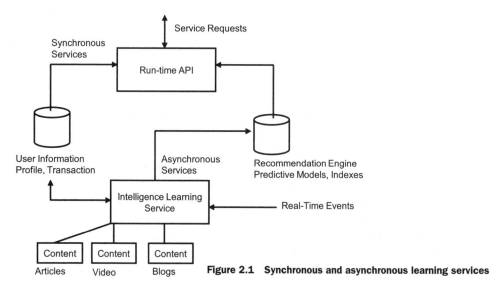

Figure 2.1 Synchronous and asynchronous learning services

Table 2.1 Summary of services that a typical application-embedding intelligence contains

Service	Processing type	Description
Intelligence Learning Service	Asynchronous	This service uses user-interaction information to build a profile of the user, update product relevance tables, transaction history, and so on.
Data Aggregator/ Classifier Service	Asynchronous	This service crawls external sites to gather information and derives intelligence from the text to classify it appropriately.
Search Service	Asynchronous Indexing Synchronous Results	Content—both user-generated and professionally developed—is indexed for search. This may be combined with user profile and transaction history to create personalized search results.
User Profile	Synchronous	Runtime model of user's profile that will be used for personalization.
Item Relevance Lookup Service	Synchronous	Runtime model for looking up related items for a given item.

2.1.2 Real-time learning in an event-driven system

As users interact on your site, perhaps by looking at an article or video, by rating a question, or by writing a blog entry, they're providing your application with information that can be converted into intelligence about them. As shown in figure 2.2, you can develop near–real-time intelligence in your application by using an event-driven Service-Oriented Architecture (SOA).

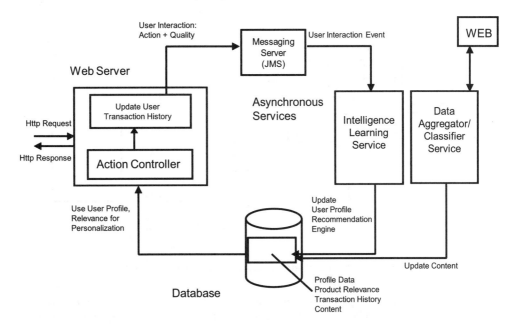

Figure 2.2   Architecture for embedding and deriving intelligence in an event-driven system

The web server receives a HTTP request from the user. Available locally in the same JVM is a service for updating the user transaction history. Depending on your architecture and your needs, the service may simply add the transaction history item to its memory and periodically flush the items out to either the database or to a messaging server.

Real-time processing can occur when a message is sent to the messaging server, which then passes this message out to any interested intelligence-learning services. These services will process and persist the information to update the user's profile, update the recommendation engine, and update any predictive models.[1] If this learning process is sufficiently fast, there's a good chance that the updated user's profile will be reflected in the personalized information shown to the user the next time she interacts.

NOTE   As an alternative to sending the complete user transaction data as a message, you can also first store the message and then send a lightweight object that's a pointer to the information in the database. The learning service will retrieve the information from the database when it receives the message. If there's a significant amount of processing and data transformation that's required before persistence, then it may be advantageous to do the processing in the asynchronous learning service.

2.1.3 *Polling services for non–event-driven systems*

If your application architecture doesn't use a messaging infrastructure—for example, if it consists solely of a web server and a database—you can write user transaction history to the database. In this case, the learning services use a poll-based mechanism to periodically process the data, as shown in figure 2.3.

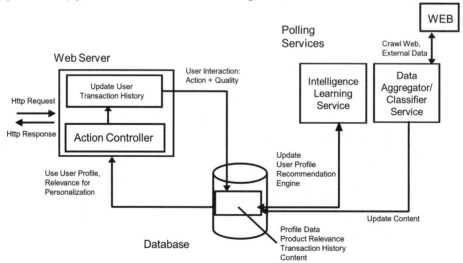

Figure 2.3 Architecture for embedding intelligence in a non-event-driven system

---

[1] The open source Drools complex-event-processing (CEP) framework could be useful for implementing a rule-based event-handling intelligent-learning service; see http://blog.athico.com/2007/11/pigeons-complex-event-processing-and.html.

So far we've looked at the two approaches for building intelligence learning services—event-driven and non–event-driven. Let's now look at the advantages and disadvantages of each of these approaches.

2.1.4 Advantages and disadvantages of event-based and non–event-based architectures

An event-driven SOA architecture is recommended for learning and embedding intelligence in your application because it provides the following advantages:

- *It provides more fine-grained real-time processing—every user transaction can be processed separately.* Conversely, the lag for processing data in a polling framework is dependent on the polling frequency. For some tasks such as updating a search index with changes, where the process of opening and closing a connection to the index is expensive, batching multiple updates in one event may be more efficient.
- *An event-driven architecture is a more scalable solution.* You can scale each of the services independently. Under peak conditions, the messaging server can queue up messages. Thus the maximum load generated on the system by these services will be bounded. A polling mechanism requires more continuous overhead and thus wastes resources.
- *An event-driven architecture is less complex to implement because there are standard messaging servers that are easy to integrate into your application.* Conversely, multiple instances of a polling service need to coordinate which rows of information are being processed among themselves. In this case, be careful to avoid using `select for update` to achieve this locking, because this often causes deadlocks. The polling infrastructure is often a source of bugs.

On the flip side, if you don't currently use a messaging infrastructure in your system, introducing a messaging infrastructure in your architecture can be a nontrivial task. In this case, it may be better to begin with building the learning infrastructure using a poll-based non–event-driven architecture and then upgrading to an event-driven architecture if the learning infrastructure doesn't meet your business requirements.

Now that we have an understanding of the architecture to apply intelligence in your application, let's next look at some of the fundamental concepts that we need to understand in order to apply CI.

2.2 Basics of algorithms for applying CI

In order to correlate users with content and with each other, we need a common language to compute relevance between items, between users, and between users and items. Content-based relevance is anchored in the content itself, as is done by information retrieval systems. Collaborative-based relevance leverages the user interaction data to discern meaningful relationships. Also, since a lot of content is in the form of unstructured text, it's helpful to understand how metadata can be developed from unstructured text. In this section, we cover these three fundamental concepts of learning algorithms.

We begin by abstracting the various types of content, so that the concepts and algorithms can be applied to all of them.

2.2.1 *Users and items*

As shown in figure 2.4, most applications generally consist of *users* and *items*. An *item* is any entity of interest in your application. Items may be articles, both user-generated and professionally developed; videos; photos; blog entries; questions and answers posted on message boards; or products and services sold in your application. If your application is a social-networking application, or you're looking to connect one user with another, then a user is also a type of item.

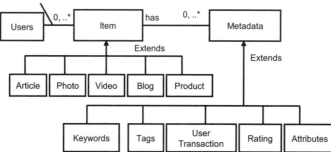

Figure 2.4 A user interacts with items, which have associated metadata.

Associated with each item is *metadata*, which may be in the form of professionally developed keywords, user-generated tags, keywords extracted by an algorithm after analyzing the text, ratings, popularity ranking, or just about anything that provides a higher level of information about the item and can be used to correlate items together. Think about metadata as a set of attributes that help qualify an item.

When an item is a user, in most applications there's no content associated with a user (unless your application has a text-based descriptive profile of the user). In this case, metadata for a user will consist of profile-based data and user-action based data. Figure 2.5 shows the three main sources of developing metadata for an item (remember a user is also an item). We look at these three sources next.

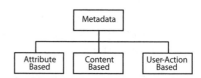

Figure 2.5 The three sources for generating metadata about an item

ATTRIBUTE-BASED

Metadata can be generated by looking at the attributes of the user or the item. The user attribute information is typically dependent on the nature of the domain of the application. It may contain information such as age, sex, geographical location, profession, annual income, or education level. Similarly, most nonuser items have attributes associated with them. For example, a product may have a price, the name of the author or manufacturer, the geographical location where it's available, the creation or manufacturing date, and so on.

CONTENT-BASED

Metadata can be generated by analyzing the content of a document. As we see in the following sections, there's been a lot of work done in the area of information retrieval and text mining to extract metadata associated with unstructured text. The title, subtitles, keywords, frequency counts of words in a document and across all documents of interest, and other data provide useful information that can then be converted into metadata for that item.

USER-ACTION-BASED

Metadata can be generated by analyzing the interactions of users with items. User interactions provide valuable insight into preferences and interests. Some of the interactions are fairly explicit in terms of their intentions, such as purchasing an item, contributing content, rating an item, or voting. Other interactions are a lot more difficult to discern, such as a user clicking on an article and the system determining whether the user liked that item or not. This interaction can be used to build metadata about the user and the item. This metadata provides important information as to what kind of items the user would be interested in; which set of users would be interested in a new item, and so on.

Think about users and items having an associated vector of metadata attributes. The similarity or relevance between two users or two items or a user and item can be measured by looking at the similarity between the two vectors. Since we're interested in learning about the likes and dislikes of a user, let's next look at representing information related to a user.

2.2.2 *Representing user information*

A user's profile consists of a number of *attributes*—independent variables that can be used to describe the item of interest. As shown in figure 2.6, attributes can be *numerical*—have a continuous set of values, for example, the age of a user—or *nominal*—have a nonnumerical value or a set of string values associated with them. Further, nominal attributes can be either *ordinal*—enumerated values that have ordering in them, such as low, medium, and high—or *categorical*—enumerated values with no ordering, such as the color of one's eyes.

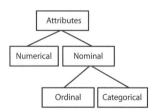

Figure 2.6 Attribute hierarchy of a user profile

All attributes are not equal in their predicting capabilities. Depending on the kind of learning algorithms used, the attributes can be *normalized*—converted to a scale of [0-1]. Different algorithms use either numerical or nominal attributes as inputs. Further, numerical and nominal attributes can be converted from one format to another depending on the kind of algorithms used. For example, the age of a user can be converted to a nominal attribute by creating *buckets*, say: "Teenager" for users under the

Table 2.2   Examples of user-profile attributes

Attribute	Type	Example	Comments
Age	Numeric	26 years old	User typically provides birth date.
Sex	Categorical	Male, Female	
Annual Income	Ordinal or Numeric	Between 50-100K or 126K	
Geographical Location	Categorical can be converted to numerical	Address, city, state, zip	The geo-codes associated with the location can be used as a distance measure to a reference point.

age of 18, "Young Person" for those between 18 and 25, and so on. Table 2.2 has a list of user attributes that may be available in your application.

In addition to user attributes, the user's interactions with your application give you important data that can be used to learn about your user, find similar users (clustering), or make a prediction. The number of times a user has logged in to your application within a period of time, his average session time, and the number of items purchased are all examples of derived attributes that can be used for clustering and building predictive models.

Through their interactions, users provide a rich set of information that can be harvested for intelligence. Table 2.3 summarizes some of the ways users provide valuable information that can be used to add intelligence to your application.

Table 2.3   The many ways users provide valuable information through their interactions

Technique	Description
Transaction history	The list of items that a user has bought in the past Items that are currently in the user's shopping cart or favorites list
Content visited	The type of content searched and read by the user The advertisements clicked
Path followed	How the user got to a particular piece of content—whether directly from an external search engine result or after searching in the application The intent of the user—proceeding to the e-commerce pages after researching a topic on the site
Profile selections	The choices that users make in selecting the defaults for their profiles and profile entries; for example, the default airport used by the user for a travel application
Feedback to polls and questions	If the user has responded to any online polls and questions
Rating	Rating of content
Tagging	Associating tags with items
Voting, bookmarking, saving	Expressing interest in an item

We've looked at how various kinds of attributes can be used to represent a user's profile and the use of user-interaction data to learn about the user. Next, let's look at how intelligence can be generated by analyzing content and by analyzing the interactions of the users. This is just a quick look at this fairly large topic and we build on it throughout the book.

2.2.3 *Content-based analysis and collaborative filtering*

User-centric applications aim to make the application more valuable for users by applying CI to personalize the site. There are two basic approaches to personalization: content-based and collaborative-based.

Content-based approaches analyze the content to build a representation for the content. Terms or phrases (multiple terms in a row) appearing in the document are typically used to build this representation. Terms are converted into their basic form by a process known as *stemming*. Terms with their associated weights, commonly known as *term vectors*, then represent the metadata associated with the text. Similarity between two content items is measured by measuring the similarity associated with their term vectors.

A user's profile can also be developed by analyzing the set of content the user interacted with. In this case, the user's profile will have the same set of terms as the items, enabling you to compute the similarities between a user and an item. Content-based recommendation systems do a good job of finding related items, but they can't predict the quality of the item—how popular the item is or how a user will like the item. This is where collaborative-based methods come in.

A collaborative-based approach aims to use the information provided by the interactions of users to predict items of interest for a user. For example, in a system where users rate items, a collaborative-based approach will find patterns in the way items have been rated by the user and other users to find additional items of interest for a user. This approach aims to match a user's metadata to that of other similar users and recommend items liked by them. Items that are liked by or popular with a certain segment of your user population will appear often in their interaction history—viewed often, purchased often, and so forth. The frequency of occurrence or ratings provided by users are indicative of the quality of the item to the appropriate segment of your user population. Sites that use collaborative filtering include Amazon, Google, and Netflix. Collaborative-based methods are language independent, and you don't have to worry about language issues when applying the algorithm to content in a different language.

There are two main approaches in collaborative filtering: memory-based and model-based. In memory-based systems, a similarity measure is used to find similar users and then make a prediction using a weighted average of the ratings of the similar users. This approach can have scalability issues and is sensitive to data sparseness. A model-based approach aims to build a model for prediction using a variety of approaches: linear algebra, probabilistic methods, neural networks, clustering, latent classes, and so on. They normally have fast runtime predicting capabilities. Chapter 12 covers building recommendation systems in detail; in this chapter we introduce the concepts via examples.

Since a lot of information that we deal with is in the form of unstructured text, it's helpful to review some basic concepts about how intelligence is extracted from unstructured text.

2.2.4   *Representing intelligence from unstructured text*

This section deals with developing a representation for unstructured text by using the content of the text. Fortunately, we can leverage a lot of work that's been done in the area of information retrieval. This section introduces you to terms and term vectors, used to represent metadata associated with text. Section 4.3 presents a detailed working example on this topic, while chapter 8 develops a toolkit that you can use in your application for representing unstructured text. Chapter 3 presents a collaborative-based approach for representing a document using user-tagging.

Now let's consider an example where the text being analyzed is the phrase "Collective Intelligence in Action."

In its most basic form, a text document consists of *terms*—words that appear in the text. In our example, there are four terms: *Collective, Intelligence, in,* and *Action.* When terms are joined together, they form *phrases. Collective Intelligence* and *Collective Intelligence in Action* are two useful phrases in our document.

The *Vector Space Model* representation is one of the most commonly used methods for representing a document. As shown in figure 2.7, a document is represented by a term vector, which consists of terms appearing in the document and a relative weight for each of the terms. The term vector is one representation of metadata associated with an item. The weight associated with each term is a product of two computations: *term frequency* and *inverse document frequency.*

Term frequency (TF) is a count of how often a term appears. Words that appear often may be more relevant to the topic of interest. Given a particular domain, some words appear more often than others. For example, in a set of books about Java, the word *Java* will appear often. We have to be more discriminating to find items that have these less-common terms: *Spring, Hibernate,* and *Intelligence.* This is the motivation behind *inverse document frequency (IDF).* IDF aims to boost terms that are less frequent. Let the total number of documents of interest be *n,* and let n_i be the number of times a given term appears across the documents. Then IDF for a term is computed as follows:

$$idf_i = \log\left(\frac{n}{n_i}\right)$$

Note that if a term appears in all documents, then its IDF is log(1) which is 0.

Commonly occurring terms such as *a, the,* and *in* don't add much value in representing the document. These are commonly known as *stop words* and are removed from the term vector. Terms are also

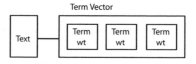

Figure 2.7   Term vector representation of text

converted to lowercase. Further, words are stemmed—brought to their root form—to handle plurals. For example, *toy* and *toys* will be stemmed to *toi*. The position of words, for example whether they appear in the title, keywords, abstract, or the body, can also influence the relative weights of the terms used to represent the document. Further, synonyms may be used to inject terms into the representation.

Figure 2.8 shows the steps involved in analyzing text. These steps are

1 *Tokenization*—Parse the text to generate terms. Sophisticated analyzers can also extract phrases from the text.

2 *Normalize*—Convert them into a normalized form such as converting text into lower case.

3 *Eliminate stop words*—Eliminate terms that appear very often.

4 *Stemming*—Convert the terms into their stemmed form to handle plurals.

Figure 2.8 Typical steps involved in analyzing text

A large document will have more occurrences of a term than a similar document of shorter length. Therefore, within the term vector, the weights of the terms are normalized, such that the sum of the squared weights for all the terms in the term vector is equal to one. This normalization allows us to compare documents for similarities using their term vectors, which is discussed next.

The previous approach for generating metadata is content based. You can also generate metadata by analyzing user interaction with the content—we look at this in more detail in sections 2.3 and 2.4; chapter 3 deals with developing metadata from user tagging.

So far we've looked at what a term vector is and have some basic knowledge of how they're computed. Let's next look at how to compute similarities between them. An item that's very similar to another item will have a high value for the computed similarity metric. An item whose term vector has a high computed similarity to that of a user's will be very *relevant* to a user—chances are that if we can build a term vector to capture the likes of a user, then the user will like items that have a similar term vector.

2.2.5 Computing similarities

A term vector is a vector where the direction is the magnitude of the weights for each of the terms. The term vector has multiple dimensions—thousands to possibly millions, depending on your application. Multidimensional vectors are difficult to visualize, but the principles used can be illustrated by using a two-dimensional vector, as shown in figure 2.9.

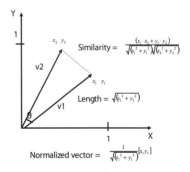

Figure 2.9 Two dimensional vectors, v1 and v2

Given a vector representation, we normalize the vector such that its length is of size 1 and compare vectors by computing the similarity between them. Chapter 8 develops the Java classes for doing this computation. For now, just think of vectors as a means to represent information with a well-developed math to compute similarities between them.

So far we've looked at the use of term vectors to represent metadata associated with content. We've also looked at how to compute similarities between term vectors. Now let's take this one step forward and introduce the concept of a dataset. Algorithms use data as input for analysis. This data consists of multiple instances represented in a tabular form. Based on how data is populated in the table, we can classify the dataset into two forms: densely populated, or high-dimensional sparsely populated datasets—similar in characteristics to a term vector.

2.2.6 *Types of datasets*

To illustrate the two forms of datasets used as input for learning by algorithms, let's consider the following example.

Let there be three users—John, Joe, and Jane. Each has three attributes: age, sex, and average number of minutes spent on the site. Table 2.4 shows the values for the various attributes for these users. This data can be used for clustering[2] and/or to build a predictive model.[3] For example, similar users according to age and/or sex might be a good predictor of the number of minutes a user will spend on the site.

In this example dataset, the age attribute is a good predictor for number of minutes spent—the number of minutes spent is inversely proportional to the age. The sex attribute has no effect in the prediction. In this made-up example, a simple linear model is adequate to predict the number of minutes spent (minutes spent = 50 – age of user).

	Age	Sex	Number of minutes per day spent on the site
John	25	M	25
Joe	30	M	20
Jane	20	F	30

Table 2.4   Dataset with small number of attributes

This is a densely populated dataset. Note that the number of rows in the dataset will increase as we add more users. It has the following properties:

- *It has more rows than columns*—The number of rows is typically a few orders of magnitude more than the number of columns. (Note that to keep things simple, the number of rows and columns is the same in our example.)
- *The dataset is richly populated*—There is a value for each cell.

---

[2] Chapter 9 covers clustering algorithms.

[3] Chapter 10 deals with building predictive models.

The other kind of dataset (high-dimensional, sparsely populated) is a generalization of the term vector representation. To understand this dataset, consider a window of time such as the past week. We consider the set of users who've viewed any of the videos on our site within this timeframe. Let n be the total number of videos in our application, represented as columns, while the users are represented as rows. Table 2.5 shows the dataset created by adding a 1 in the cell if a user has viewed a video. This representation is useful to find similar users and is known as the *User-Item matrix*.

	Video 1	Video 2	...	...	Video n
John	1				
Joe	1	1			
Jane					1

Table 2.5 Dataset with large number of attributes

Alternatively, when the users are represented as columns and the videos as rows, we can determine videos that are similar based on the user interaction: "Users who have viewed this video have also viewed these other videos." Such an analysis would be helpful in finding related videos on a site such as YouTube. Figure 2.10 shows a screenshot of such a feature at YouTube. It shows related videos for a video.

Figure 2.10 Screenshot from YouTube showing related videos for a video

This dataset has the following properties:

- *The number of columns is large*—For example, the number of products in a site like Amazon.com is in millions, as is the number of videos at YouTube.
- *The dataset is sparsely populated with nonzero entries in a few columns.*
- *You can visualize this dataset as a multidimensional vector*—Columns correspond to the dimensions and the cell entry corresponds to the weight associated for that dimension.

We develop a toolkit to analyze this kind of dataset in chapter 8. The dot product or cosine between two vectors is used as a similarity metric to compare two vectors.

Note the similarity of this dataset with the term vector we introduced in section 2.2.3. Let there be m terms that occur in all our documents. Then the term vectors corresponding to all our documents have the same characteristics as the previous dataset, as shown in table 2.6.

	Term 1	Term 2	..	..	Term m
Document 1	0.8				0.6
Document 2		0.7	0.7		
Document 3					1

Table 2.6 Sparsely populated dataset corresponding to term vectors

Now that we have a basic understanding of how metadata is generated and represented, let's look at the many forms of user interaction in your application and how they are converted to collective intelligence.

2.3 *Forms of user interaction*

To extract intelligence from a user's interaction in your application, it isn't enough to know what content the user looked at or visited. You also need to quantify the quality of the interaction. A user may like the article or may dislike it, these being two extremes. What one needs is a quantification of how the user liked the item relative to other items.

Remember, we're trying to ascertain what kind of information is of interest to the user. The user may provide this directly by rating or voting for an article, or it may need to be derived, for example, by looking at the content that the user has consumed. We can also learn about the item that the user is interacting with in the process.

In this section, we look at how users provide quantifiable information through their interactions; in section 2.4 we look at how these interactions fit in with collective intelligence. Some of the interactions such as ratings and voting are explicit in the user's intent, while other interactions such as using clicks are noisy—the intent of the user isn't known perfectly and is implicit. If you're thinking of making your application more interactive or intelligent, you may want to consider adding some of the functionality mentioned in this section. We also look at the underlying persistence architecture that's required to support the functionality. Let's begin with ratings and voting.

2.3.1   *Rating and voting*

Asking the user to rate an item of interest is an explicit way of getting feedback on how well the user liked the item. The advantage with a user rating content is that the information provided is quantifiable and can be used directly.

It's interesting to note that most ratings in a system tend to be positive, especially since people rate items that they've bought/interacted with and they typically buy/ interact with items that they like.

Next, let's look at how you can build this functionality in your application.

PERSISTENCE MODEL[4]

Figure 2.11 shows the persistence model for storing ratings. Let's introduce two entities: user and item. user_item_rating is a mapping table that has a composite key, consisting of the user ID and content ID. A brief look at the cardinality between the entities show that

- Each user may rate 0 or more items.
- Each rating is associated with only one user.
- An item may contain 0 or more ratings.
- Each rating is associated with only one item.

Based on your application, you may alternatively want to also classify the items in your application. It's also helpful to have a generic table to store the ratings associated with the items. Computing a user's average rating for an item or item type is then a simple database query.

In this design, answers to the following questions amount to a simple database query:

- What is the average rating for a given item?
- What is the average rating for a given item from users who are between the ages of 25 and 35?
- What are the top 10 rated items?

The last query can be slow, but faster performance can be obtained by having a user_item_rating_statistic table, as shown in figure 2.10. This table gets updated by a trigger every time a new row is inserted in the user_item_rating table. The average

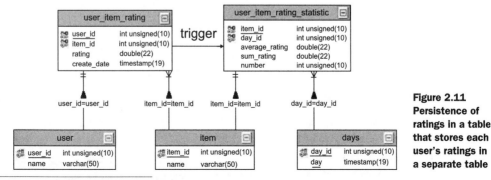

**Figure 2.11
Persistence of
ratings in a table
that stores each
user's ratings in
a separate table**

---

[4] The code to create the tables, populate the database with test data, and run the queries is available from the code download site for this book.

is precomputed and is calculated by dividing the cumulative sum by the number of ratings. If you want to trend the ratings of an item on a daily basis, you can augment the user_item_rating_statistic to have the day as another key.

VOTING—"DIGG IT"

Most applications that allow users to rate use a scale from zero to five. Allowing a user to vote is another way to involve and obtain useful information from the user. Digg, a website that allows users to contribute and vote on interesting articles, uses this idea. As shown in figure 2.12, a user can either *digg* an article, casting a positive vote, or *bury* it, casting a negative vote. There are a number of heuristics applied to selecting which articles make it to the top, some being the number of positive votes received by the article along with the date the article was submitted in Digg.

Figure 2.12   At Digg.com, users are allowed to vote on how they like an article—"digg it" is a positive vote, while "Bury" is a negative vote.

Voting is similar to rating. However, a vote can have only two values—1 for a positive vote and -1 for a negative vote.

2.3.2   *Emailing or forwarding a link*

As a part of viral marketing efforts, it's common for websites to allow users to email or forward the contents of a page to others. Similar to voting, forwarding the content to others can be considered a positive vote for the item by the user. Figure 2.13 is a screenshot from *The Wall Street Journal* showing how a user can forward an article to another user.

2.3.3   *Bookmarking and saving*

Online bookmarking services such as del. icio.us and spurl.net allow users to store and retrieve URLs, also known as bookmarks. Users can discover other interesting links that other users have bookmarked through

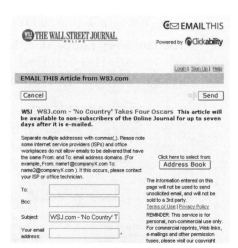

Figure 2.13   Screenshot from *The Wall Street Journal* (wsj.com) that shows how a user can forward/email an article to another user

recommendations, hot lists, and other such features. By bookmarking URLs, a user is explicitly expressing interest in the material associated with the bookmark. URLs that are commonly bookmarked bubble up higher in the site.

The process of saving an item or adding it to a list is similar to bookmarking and provides similar information. Figure 2.14 is an example from *The New York Times*, where a user can save an item of interest. As shown, this can then be used to build a recommendation engine where a user is shown related items that other users who saved that item have also saved.

Figure 2.14   Saving an item to a list (NY Times.com)

If a user has a large number of bookmarks, it can become cumbersome for the user to find and manage bookmarked or saved items. For this reason, applications allow their users to create *folders*—a collection of items bookmarked or saved together. As shown in figure 2.15, folders follow the composite design pattern,[5] where they're composed of bookmarked items. A folder is just another kind of item in your application that can be shared, bookmarked, and rated in your application. Based on their composition, folders have metadata associated with them.

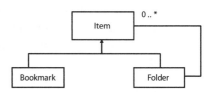

Figure 2.15   Composite pattern for organizing bookmarks together

Next, let's look at how a user purchasing an item also provides useful information.

2.3.4   Purchasing items

In an e-commerce site, when users purchase items, they're casting an explicit vote of confidence in the item—unless the item is returned after purchase, in which case it's a negative vote. Recommendation engines, for example the one used by Amazon (Item-to-Item recommendation engine; see section 12.4.1) can be built from analyzing the procurement history of users. Users that buy similar items can be correlated and items that have been bought by other users can be recommended to a user.

2.3.5   Click-stream

So far we've looked at fairly explicit ways of determining whether a user liked or disliked a particular item, through ratings, voting, forwarding, and purchasing items.

---

[5]   Refer to the Composite Pattern in the Gang of Four design patterns.

When a list of items is presented to a user, there's a good chance that the user will click on one of them based on the title and description. But after quickly scanning the item, the user may find the item to be not relevant and may browse back or search for other items.

A simple way to quantify an article's relevance is to record a positive vote for any item clicked. This approach is used by Google News to personalize the site (see section 12.4.2). To further filter out noise, such as items the user didn't really like, you could look at the amount of time the user spent on the article. Of course, this isn't fail proof. For example, the user could have left the room to get some coffee or been interrupted while looking at the article. But on average, simply looking at whether an item was visited and the time spent on it provides useful information that can be mined later. You can also gather useful statistics from this data:

- What is the average time a user spends on a particular item?
- For a user, what is the average time spent on any given article?

One of the ways to validate the data and clear out outliers is to use a *validation window*. To build a validation window, treat the amount of time spent by a user as a normal distribution (see figure 2.16) and compute the mean and standard deviation from the samples.

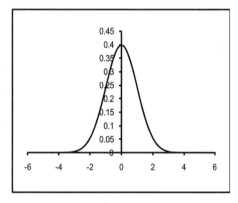

Let's demonstrate this with a simple example—it's fictitious, but illustrates the point well. Let the amount of time spent by nine readers on an article be [5, 47, 50, 55, 47, 54, 100, 45, 50] seconds. Computing the mean is simple (add them all up and divide it by nine, the number of samples); it's 50.33 seconds. Next, let's compute the standard

Figure 2.16   A normal distribution with a mean of 0 and standard deviation of 1

deviation. For this, take the difference of each of the samples from its mean and square it. This leads to [2055.11, 11.11, 0.11, 21.78, 11.11, 13.44, 2466.78, 28.44, 0.11]. Add them up and divide it by eight, the number of samples minus one. This gives us 576, and the square root of this is the standard deviation, which comes out to be 24. Now you can create a validation window two or three times the standard deviation from the mean. For our example, we take two times the standard deviation, which gives us a confidence level of 95 percent. For our example, this is [2.33 98]. Anything outside this range is an outlier.

So we flag the seventh sample of 100 seconds as an outlier—perhaps the user had stepped out or was interrupted while reading the article. Next, continue the same process with the remaining eight samples [5, 47, 50, 55, 47, 54, 45, 50]. The new mean and standard deviation is 44.125 and 16.18. The new confidence window is [11.76 76.49]. The first sample is an outlier; perhaps the user didn't find the article relevant.

Now let's remove this outlier and recompute the validation window for the sample set of [47, 50, 55, 47, 54, 45, 50]. The new mean and standard deviation is 49.71 and 3.73

respectively. The new confidence window is [42.26 57.17]. Most users will spend time within this window. Users that spent less time were probably not interested in the content of the article.

Of course, if you wanted to get more sophisticated (and a lot more complex), you could try to model the average time that a user spends on an item and correlate it with average time spent by a typical user to shrink or expand the validation window. But for most applications, the preceding process of validation window should work well. Or if you want to keep things even simpler, simply consider whether the article has been visited, irrespective of the time spent[6] reading it.

2.3.6 *Reviews*

Web 2.0 is all about connecting people with similar people. This similarity may be based on similar tastes, positions, opinions, or geographic location. Tastes and opinions are often expressed through reviews and recommendations. These have the greatest impact on other users when

- They're unbiased
- The reviews are from similar users
- They're from a person of influence

Depending on the application, the information provided by a user may be available to the entire population of users, or may be privately available only to a select group of users. This is especially the case for software-as-a-service (SaaS) applications, where a company or enterprise subscribing to the service forms a natural grouping of users. In such applications, information isn't usually shared across domains. The information is more contextually relevant to users within the company, anyway.

Perhaps the biggest reasons why people review items and share their experiences are to be discovered by others and for boasting rights. Reviewers enjoy the recognition, and typically like the site and want to contribute to it. Most of them enjoy doing it. A number of applications highlight the contributions made by users, by having a Top Reviewers list. Reviews from top reviewers are also typically placed toward the top and featured more prominently. Sites may also feature one of their top reviewers on the site as an incentive to contribute.

Some sites may also provide an incentive, perhaps monetary, for users to contribute content and reviews. Epinions.com pays a small amount to its reviewers. Similarly, Revver, a video sharing site, pays its users for contributed videos. It's interesting to note that even though sites like Epinions.com pay money to their reviewers, while Amazon doesn't, Amazon still has on order of magnitude more reviews from its users.

Users tend to contribute more to sites that have the biggest audience.

In a site where anyone can contribute content, is there anything that stops your competitors from giving you an unjustified low rating? Good reviewers, especially those that are featured toward the top, try to build a good reputation. Typically, an

---

[6] Google News, which we look at in chapter 12, simply uses a click as a positive vote for the item.

application has links to the reviewer's profile along with other reviews that he's written. Other users can also write comments about a review. Further, just like voting for articles at Digg, other users can endorse a reviewer or vote on his reviews. As shown in figure 2.17, taken from epinions.com, users can "Trust" or "Block" reviewers to vote on whether a reviewer can be trusted.

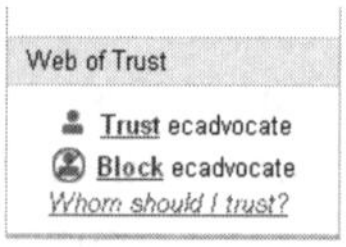

Figure 2.17   Epinions.com allows users to place a positive or negative vote of confidence in a reviewer.

The feedback from other users about how helpful the review was helps to weed out biased and unhelpful reviews. Sites also allow users to report reviewers who don't follow their guidelines, in essence allowing the community to police itself.

MODELING THE REVIEWER AND ITEM RELATIONSHIP

We need to introduce another entity—the reviewer, who may or may not be a user of your application. The association between a reviewer, an item, and an ItemReview is shown in figure 2.18. This is similar to the relationship between a user and ratings.

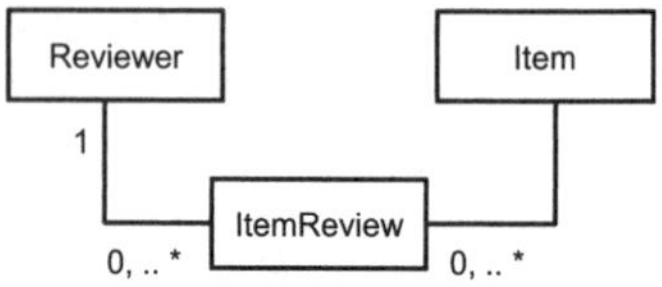

Figure 2.18   The association between a reviewer, an item, and the review of an item

- Each reviewer may write zero or more reviews.
- Each review is written by a reviewer.
- Each item may have zero or more reviews.
- Each review is associated with one item.

The persistence design for storing reviews is shown in figure 2.19, and is similar to the one we developed for ratings. Item reviews are in the form of unstructured text and thus need to be indexed by search engines.

So far, we've looked at the many forms of user interaction and the persistence architecture to build it in your application. Next, let's look at how this user-interaction information gets converted into collective intelligence.

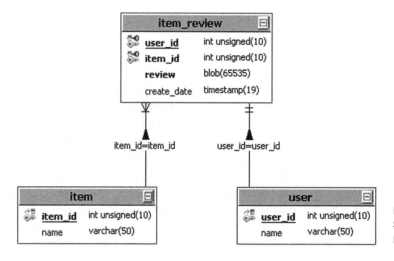

Figure 2.19 Schema design for persisting reviews

2.4   Converting user interaction into collective intelligence

In section 2.2.6, we looked at the two forms of data representation that are used by learning algorithms. User interaction manifests itself in the form of the sparsely populated dataset. In this section, we look at how user interaction gets converted into a dataset for learning.

To illustrate the concepts, we use a simple example dealing with three users who've rated photographs. In addition to the cosine-based similarity computation we introduced in section 2.2.5, we introduce two new similarity computations: correlation-based similarity computation and adjusted-cosine similarity computation. In this section, we spend more time on this example which deals with ratings to illustrate the concepts. We then briefly cover how these concepts can be generalized to analyze other user interactions in section 2.4.2. That section forms the basis for building a recommendation engine, which we cover in chapter 12.

2.4.1   Intelligence from ratings via an example

There are a number of ways to transform raw ratings from users into intelligence. First, you can simply aggregate all the ratings about the item and provide the average as the item's rating. This can be used to create a Top 10 Rated Items list. Averages work well, but then you're constantly promoting the popular content. How do you reach the potential of The Long Tail? A user is really interested in the average rating for content by users who have similar tastes.

Clustering is a technique that can help find a group of users similar to the user. The average rating of an item by a group of users similar to a user is more relevant to the user than a general average rating. Ratings provide a good quantitative feedback of how good the content is.

Let's consider a simple example to understand the basic concepts associated with using ratings for learning about the users and items of interest. This section introduces you to some of the basic concepts.

Let there be three users: John, Jane, and Doe, who each rate three items. As per our discussion in section 2.2.1, items could be anything—blog entries, message board questions, video, photos, reviews, and so on. For our example, let them rate three photos: Photo1, Photo2, and Photo3, as shown in table 2.7. The table also shows the average rating for each photo and the average rating given by each user. We revisit this example in section 12.3.1 when we discuss recommendation engines.

	Photo1	Photo2	Photo3	Average
John	3	4	2	3
Jane	2	2	4	8/3
Doe	1	3	5	3
Average	2	3	11/3	26/3

Table 2.7   Ratings data used in the example

Given this set of data, we answer two questions in our example:

- What are the set of related items for a given item?
- For a user, who are the other users that are similar to the user?

We answer these questions using three approaches: cosine-based similarity, correlation-based similarity, and adjusted-cosine-based similarity.

COSINE-BASED SIMILARITY COMPUTATION

Cosine-based similarity takes the dot product of two vectors as described in section 2.2.4. First, to learn about the photos, we transpose the matrix, so that a row corresponds to a photo while the columns (users) correspond to dimensions that describe the photo, as shown in table 2.8.

	John	Jane	Doe	Average
Photo1	3	2	1	2
Photo 2	4	2	3	3
Photo 3	2	4	5	11/3
Average	3	8/3	3	26/3

Table 2.8   Dataset to describe photos

Next, we normalize the values for each of the rows. This is done by dividing each of the cell entries by the square root of the sum of the squares of entries in a particular row. For example, each of the terms in the first row is divided by $\sqrt{3^2+2^2+1^2} = \sqrt{14} = 3.74$ to get the normalized dataset shown in table 2.9[7].

	John	Jane	Doe
Photo1	0.8018	0.5345	0.2673
Photo2	0.7428	0.3714	0.557
Photo3	0.2981	0.5963	0.7454

Table 2.9   Normalized dataset for the photos using raw ratings

We can find the similarities between the items by taking the dot product of their vectors. For example, the similarity between Photo 1 and Photo 2 is computed as $(0.8018 * 0.7428) + (0.5345 * 0.3714) + (0.2673 * 0.557) = 0.943$.

Using this, we can develop the item-to-item similarity table, shown in table 2.10. This table also answers our first question: what are the set of related items for a given item? According to this, Photo1 and Photo2 are very similar. The closer to 1 a value in the similarity table is, the more similar the items are to each other.

	Photo1	Photo2	Photo3
Photo1	1	0.943	0.757
Photo2	0.943	1	0.858
Photo3	0.757	0.858	1

Table 2.10   Item-to-item using raw ratings

---

[7] There is a unit test in the downloadable code that implements this example.

To determine similar users, we need to consider the original data in table 2.7. Here, associated with each user is a vector, where the rating associated with each item corresponds to a dimension in the vector. The analysis process is similar to our approach for calculating the item-to-item similarity table. We first need to normalize the vectors and then take a dot product between two normalized vectors to compute their similarities.

Table 2.11 contains the normalized vectors associated with each user. The process is similar to the approach taken to compute table 2.9 from table 2.8. For example, $\sqrt{3^2+4^2+2^2} = \sqrt{29} = 5.385$ is the normalizing factor for John's vector in table 2.7.

	Photo1	Photo2	Photo3
John	0.5571	0.7428	0.3714
Jane	0.4082	0.4082	0.8165
Doe	0.1690	0.5071	0.8452

Table 2.11   Normalized rating vectors for each user

Next, a user-to-user similarity table can be computed as shown in table 2.12 by taking the dot product of the normalized vectors for two users.

	John	Jane	Doe
John	1	0.83	0.78
Jane	0.83	1	0.97
Doe	0.78	0.97	1.00

Table 2.12   User-to-user similarity table

As shown in table 2.12, Jane and Doe are very similar. The preceding approach uses the raw ratings assigned by a user to an item. Another alternative is to focus on the deviations in the rating from the average values that a user provides. We look at this next.

CORRELATION-BASED SIMILARITY COMPUTATION

Similar to the dot product or cosine of two vectors, one can compute the correlation between two items as a measure of their similarity—the *Pearson-r correlation*. This correlation between two items is a number between –1 and 1, and it tells us the direction and magnitude of association between two items or users. The higher the magnitude—closer to either –1 or 1—the higher the association between the two items. The direction of the correlation tells us how the variables vary. A negative number means one variable increases as the other decreases, or in this example, the rating of one item decreases as the rating of another increases.

To compute the correlation, we need to isolate those cases where the users corated items—in our case, it's the complete set, as all the users have rated all the content. Let U be the set of users that have rated both item i and j.

Now the scary-looking formula to compute the correlation:

$$corr(i, j) = \frac{\sum_{u \in U}(R_{ui} - \overline{R_i})(R_{uj} - \overline{R_j})}{\sqrt{\sum_{u \in U}(R_{ui} - \overline{R_i})^2}\sqrt{\sum_{u \in U}(R_{uj} - \overline{R_j})^2}}$$

where $R_{u,i}$ is the rating of user u for item i and $\bar{R}_i$ is the average rating of item i. The correlation computation looks for variances from the mean value for the items.

Let's look at the correlation of Photo 1 and Photo 2.

Numerator $= (3-2)(4-3)+(2-2)(2-3)+(1-2)(3-3) = 1$

Denominator $= \sqrt{(3-2)^2+(2-2)^2+(1-2)^2}\sqrt{(4-3)^2+(2-3)^2+(3-3)^2} = 2$

Corr(1,2)=0.5

Alternatively, for the computation, it's useful to subtract the average value for a row as shown in table 2.13. Note that the sum of the numbers for each row is equal to zero.

	John	Jane	Doe
Photo1	1	0	-1
Photo 2	1	-1	0
Photo 3	-5/3	1/3	4/3

Table 2.13   Normalized matrix for the correlation computation

Table 2.14 shows the correlation matrix between the items and provides answers to our first question: what are the set of related items for a given item? According to this, Photo 1 and Photo 3 are strongly negatively correlated.

	Photo1	Photo2	Photo3
Photo1	1	0.5	-0.982
Photo2	0.5	1	-0.655
Photo3	-0.982	-0.655	1

Table 2.14   Correlation matrix for the items

Similarly, the correlation matrix between the users is computed along the rows of the data shown in table 2.7. Table 2.15 contains the normalized rating vectors for each user that will be used for computing the correlation. Note that the sum of the values for each row is 0.

	Photo1	Photo2	Photo3
John	0	0.7071	-0.7071
Jane	-0.4083	-0.4083	0.8166
Doe	-0.7071	0	0.7071

Table 2.15   Normalized rating vectors for each user

The resulting correlation matrix is shown in table 2.16 and provides answers to our second question: given a user, who are the other users that are similar to that user? Note that users Jane and Doe are highly correlated—if one likes an item, chances are the other likes it, too. John is negatively correlated—he dislikes what Jane and Doe like.

Since users Jane and Doe are highly correlated, you can recommend items that are rated highly by Jane to Doe and vice versa.

	John	Jane	Doe
John	1	-0.866	-0.5
Jane	-0.866	1	0.87
Doe	-0.5	0.87	1

Table 2.16 Correlation matrix for the users

ADJUSTED COSINE-BASED SIMILARITY COMPUTATION

One drawback of computing the correlation between items is that it doesn't take into account the difference in rating scale between users. For example, in the example data, user Doe is correlated highly with Jane but tends to give ratings toward the extremes.

An alternative formula, known as *adjusted cosine* is used, which is

$$similarity(i, j) = \frac{\sum_{u \in U}(R_{u,i} - \overline{R_u})(R_{u,j} - \overline{R_u})}{\sqrt{\sum_{u \in U}(R_{u,i} - \overline{R_u})^2}\sqrt{\sum_{u \in U}(R_{u,ij} - \overline{R_u})^2}}$$

where R_u is the average rating for user u. Here, instead of subtracting the average value for a row, the average value provided by a user is used.

To compute this, it's again useful to normalize the dataset by removing the average rating value from the column values. This leads to the data shown in table 2.17. Note that the sum of the entries for a column is equal to zero.

	John	Jane	Doe
Photo1	0	-2/3	-2
Photo2	1	-2/3	0
Photo3	-1	4/3	2

Table 2.17 Normalized matrix for the adjusted cosine-based computation

Table 2.18 shows the item-to-item similarity for the three items. Again, Photo1 and Photo3 are strongly negatively correlated, while Photo2 and Photo3 are similar.

	Photo1	Photo2	Photo3
Photo1	1	0.1754	-0.891
Photo2	0.1754	1	.604
Photo3	-0.891	.604	1

Table 2.18 Similarity between items using correlation similarity

Along the same lines, to compute the similarity between users, we subtract the average rating associated with each item in table 2.7. Table 2.19 shows the resulting table. Note that the sum of the values for a column is equal to 0.

	Photo1	Photo2	Photo3
John	1	1	-5/3
Jane	0	-1	1/3
Doe	-1	0	4/3

Table 2.19 Normalized rating vectors for each user

Again, normalizing each of the vectors to unit length leads to table 2.20.

	Photo1	Photo2	Photo3
John	0.4575	0.4575	-0.7625
Jane	0	-0.9486	0.3162
Doe	-0.6	0	0.8

Table 2.20   Normalizing the vectors to unit lengthr

Finally, table 2.21 contains the similarity matrix between the users by taking the dot product of their vectors.

	John	Jane	Doe
John	1	-0.675	-0.884
Jane	-0.675	1	-0.253
Doe	-0.884	-0.253	1.00

Table 2.21   Adjusted cosine similarity matrix for the users

So far in this section, we've looked at how to transform user rating data into a dataset for analysis, and we used three different similarity metrics to compute the similarities between various items and users. The method used for computing the similarity does have an effect on the result. Next, let's look at how this approach can be generalized for other interactions such as voting.

The analysis for using voting information is similar to that for rating. The only difference is that the cell values will be either 1 or –1 depending on whether the user voted for or against the item. The persistence model for representing voting is similar to that developed in the previous section for persisting ratings.

2.4.2   Intelligence from bookmarking, saving, purchasing Items, forwarding, click-stream, and reviews

In this section, we quickly look at how other forms of user-interaction get transformed into metadata. There are two main approaches to using information from users' interaction: content-based and collaboration-based.

CONTENT-BASED APPROACH

As shown in figure 2.20, metadata is associated with each item. This term vector could be created by analyzing the content of the item or using tagging information by users, as we discuss in the next chapter. The term vector consists of keywords or tags with a relative weight associated with each term. As the user saves content, visits content, or writes recommendations, she inherits the metadata associated with each.

This implies that both users and items are represented by the same set of dimensions—tags. Using this representation, one

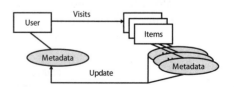

Figure 2.20   A user's metadata vector is created using the metadata vector associated with all the items visited.

can compare users with other users, users with items, and items with other items using cosine-based similarity. We see an example of this in the next chapter.

COLLABORATION-BASED APPROACH

The analysis of data collected by bookmarking, saving an item, recommending an item to another user, purchasing an item, or click-stream analysis is similar. To understand this, let's use the following example.

Consider data collected in a window of time. Again, let our three users John, Jane, and Doe bookmark three articles Article 1, Article 2, and Article 3, as shown in table 2.22. We've placed a 1 for articles that the user has bookmarked. This is a sparsely populated dataset as described in section 2.2.6. Using this data, you maybe interested in finding the

	Article 1	Article 2	Article 3
John	1		
Jane		1	1
Doe	1		1

Table 2.22 Bookmarking data for analysis

following answers:

- *What are other items that have been bookmarked by other users who bookmarked the same articles as a specific user?*—When the user is John, the answer is Article 3—Doe has bookmarked Article 1 and also Article 3.
- *What are the related items based on the bookmarking patterns of the users?*

To determine the answer to the last question, it's again useful to invert the dataset to the one shown in table 2.23. Again, the users correspond to the dimensions of the vector for an article. Similarities between two items are measured by computing the dot product between them.

	John	Jane	Doe
Article 1	1		1
Article 2		1	
Article 3		1	1

Table 2.23 Adjusted cosine similarity matrix for the users

The normalized matrix is shown in table 2.24.

	John	Jane	Doe
Article 1	0.7071		0.7071
Article 2		1	
Article 3		0.7071	0.7071

Table 2.24 Normalized dataset for finding related articles

The item-to-item similarity matrix based on this data is shown in table 2.25. According to this, if someone bookmarks Article 1, you should recommend Article 3 to the user, and if the user bookmarks Article 2, you should also recommend Article 3.

	Article 1	Article 2	Article 3
Article 1	1	0	0.5
Article 2	0	1	0.7071
Article 3	0.5	0.7071	1

Table 2.25   Related articles based on bookmarking

A similar analysis can be performed by using information from the items the user saves, purchases, and recommends. You can further refine your analysis by associating data only from users that are similar to a user based on user-profile information. In section 12.3, we further discuss this approach when we discuss building recommendation engines.

In this section, we looked at how we can convert user interactions into intelligence using a simple example of rating photos. We looked at finding items and users of interest for a user. We computed this by using three similarity computations.

2.5   Summary

Services for embedding intelligence in your applications can be divided into two types. First, synchronous services get invoked when the web server processes a request for a user. Second, asynchronous services typically run in the background and take longer to process. An event-driven SOA architecture is recommended for embedding intelligence.

There's a rich amount of information that can be used from user interaction. Metadata attributes can be used to describe items and users. Some interactions such as ratings, voting, buying, recommendations, and so forth are fairly explicit as to whether the user likes the item or not. There are two main approaches to finding items of interest for a user: content-based and collaborative-based. Content-based techniques build a term vector—a multidimensional representation for the item based on the frequency of occurrence and the relative frequency of the terms—and then associate similar items based on the similarities between term vectors. Collaborative-based techniques tend to automate "word of mouth recommendations" to find related items and users.

Metadata associated with users and items can be used to derive intelligence in the form of building recommendation engines and predictive models for personalization, and for enhancing search.

Tagging is another way that users interact with items and provide a rich set of information. We look at tagging next in chapter 3.

2.6   Resources

"All of Web2.0." Chrisekblog. http://chrisek.com/wordpress/2006/10/03/all-of-web-20/

Arthur, Charles. "What is the 1% rule?" July 2006. *The Guardian*. http://technology.guardian.co.uk/weekly/story/0,,1823959,00.html

Baeza-Yates, Ricardo, and Berthier Ribeiro-Neto. *Modern Information Retrieval*. Paperback, May 15, 1999.

Goldberg, David, David Nichols, Brian M. Oki, and Douglas Terry. *Using collaborative filtering to weave an information tapestry.* Communications of the ACM, 35(12):61-70, 1992.

Grossman, David A., and Ophir Frieder. *Information Retrieval: Algorithms and Heuristics (The Information Retrieval Series) (2nd Edition).* Paperback, Jan 23, 2006.

"Joshua Schachter." Joho the Blog. http://www.hyperorg.com/blogger/mtarchive/berkman_joshua_schachter.html

Kelly, Kevin. "A review of review sites." http://www.kk.org/cooltools/archives/000549.php

Kopelman, Josh. "53,651." Blog. May 2006 . http://redeye.firstround.com/2006/05/53651.html

Pulier, Eric, and Hugh Taylor. 2005. *Understanding Enterprise SOA.* Manning.

Sarwar, Badru, George Karypis, Joseph Konstan, and John Riedl. *Item-based Collaborative Filtering Recommendation Algorithms.* ACM, 2001. http://www10.org/cdrom/papers/519/node1.html

"Should top users be paid?" Stewtopia, Blog. September 11, 2006. http://blog.stewtopia.com/2006/09/11/should-top-users-be-paid/

Thornton, James. *Collaborative Filtering Research Papers.* http://jamesthornton.com/cf/

Wang, Jun, Arjen P. de Vries, and Marcel J.T. Reinders. *Unifying User-based and Item-based Collaborative Filtering Approaches by Similarity Fusion.* 2006. http://ict.ewi.tudelft.nl/pub/jun/sigir06_similarityfuson.pdf.

Extracting intelligence
from tags

This chapter covers

- Three forms of tagging and the use of tags
- A working example of how intelligence is extracted from tags
- Database architecture for tagging
- Developing tag clouds

In content-centric applications, users typically navigate content through categories or menus authored by the site editors. Each category can have a number of nested subcategories, allowing the user to drill down the subcategory tree and find content of interest. From a user-experience point of view, such navigation can be tedious. A user might need to navigate across multiple subtopics before finding the right item. This approach of manually categorizing items can be expensive and difficult to maintain over the long run due to the manpower involved, especially as the amount of content increases. As users generate content on your site, it'll be expensive and sometimes financially infeasible to manually categorize the content being created. Imagine a site like Flickr with millions of photographs and the effort that would be required if you tried to manually categorize each photo.

An alternative to manual categorization and rigid menus is to build a system that can learn about each user—what kind of content she's interested in—and dynamically build *navigation links*, hyperlinks to other relevant items, whose text or phrases are also familiar to the user. Further, such a system can be built in a cost-effective manner without having to rely on professional editors to categorize items.

Users tagging items—adding keywords or phrases to items—is now ubiquitous on the web. This simple process of a user adding labels or tags to items, bookmarking items, sharing items, or simply viewing items provides a rich dataset that can translate into intelligence, for both the user and the items. This intelligence can be in the form of finding items related to the one tagged; connecting with other users who have similarly tagged items; or drawing the user to discover alternate tags that have been associated with an item of interest and through that finding other related items.

In this chapter, we look at three forms of generating tags in your application: professionally generated tags, user-generated tags, and machine-generated tags. We review the advantages and disadvantages of each approach and develop guidelines for creating tags. We briefly review how you can use dynamic navigation in your application. We use a working example to illustrate the process of developing the term vector or metadata for the item and user. Next, we discuss how you can build this infrastructure in a scalable manner. For this, we first review the various designs used to persist tagging-related data and develop the recommended persistence architecture. Next, we develop code to build a tag cloud, one of the ways to add dynamic navigation to your application, and end with some practical issues.

3.1 Introduction to tagging

Tagging is the process of adding freeform text, either words or small phrases, to items. These keywords or tags can be attached to anything in your application—users, photos, articles, bookmarks, products, blog entries, podcasts, videos, and more.

In section 2.2.3, we looked at using term vectors to associate metadata with text. Each term or tag in the term vector represents a dimension. The collective set of terms or tags in your application defines the *vocabulary* for your application. When this same vocabulary is used to describe both the user and the items, we can compute the similarity of items with other items and the similarity of the item to the user's metadata to find content that's relevant to the user. In this case, tags can be used to represent metadata. Using the context in which they appear and to whom they appear, they can serve as *dynamic navigation links*. The tag cloud introduced later in the chapter is one example of such navigation.

In essence, tags enable us to

1 Build a metadata model (term vector) for our users and items. The common terminology between users and items enables us to compute the similarity of an item to another item or to a user.
2 Build dynamic navigation links in our application, for example, a tag cloud or hyperlinked phrases in the text displayed to the user.
3 Use metadata to personalize and connect users with other users.

4   Build a vocabulary for our application.

5   Bookmark items, which can be shared with other users.

In this section, we look at some basic information about tagging.

3.1.1 *Tag-related metadata for users and items*

Tags provide a common vocabulary to represent metadata associated with users and items. The metadata developed can be again divided into content-based metadata and collaborative-based metadata.

In the content-based approach, metadata associated with the item is developed by analyzing the item's content as explained in section 2.2.3. This is represented by a term vector, a set of tags with their relative weights. Similarly, metadata can be associated with the user by aggregating the metadata of all the items visited by the user within a window of time, as explained in section 2.4.2.

In the collaborative approach, user actions are used for deriving metadata. User tagging is an example of such an approach, and we illustrated with the example in section 2.2. Basically, the metadata associated with the item can be computed by computing the term vector from the tags—taking the relative frequency of the tags associated with the item and normalizing the counts.

When you think about metadata for a user and item using tags, think about a term vector with tags and their related weights.

We can categorize tags based on who generated them. As shown in figure 3.1, there are three main types of tags: professionally generated, user-generated, and machine-generated.

Next, we look at each of these three types of tags.

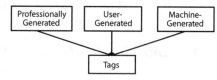

Figure 3.1   Three ways to generate tags

3.1.2 *Professionally generated tags*

There are a number of applications that are content rich and provide different kinds of content—articles, videos, photos, blogs—to their users. Vertical-centric medical sites, news sites, topic-focused group sites, or any site that has a professional editor generating content are examples of such sites. In these kinds of sites, the professional editors are typically domain experts, familiar with content domain, and are usually paid for their services. The first type of tags we cover is tags generated by such domain experts, which we call professionally generated tags.

Tags that are generated by domain experts have the following characteristics:

- They bring out the concepts related to the text.
- They capture the associated semantic value, using words that may not be found in the text.
- They can be authored to be displayed on the user interface.

- They can provide a view that isn't centered around just the content of interest, but provides a more global overview.
- They can leverage synonyms—similar words.
- They can be multi-term phrases.
- The set of words used can be controlled, with a controlled vocabulary.

Professionally generated tags require a lot of manpower and can be expensive, especially if a large amount of new content is being generated, perhaps by the users. These characteristics can be challenging for an automated algorithm.

3.1.3   User-generated tags

It's now common to allow users to tag items. Tags generated by the users fall into the category of user-generated tags, and the process of adding tags to items is commonly known as *tagging*.

Tagging enables a user to associate freeform text to an item, in a way that makes sense to him, rather than using a fixed terminology that may have been developed by the content owner or created professionally.

Figure 3.2 shows the process of tagging at del.icio.us. Here, a user can associate any tag or keyword with a URL. The system displays a list of recommended and popular tags to guide the user.

The use of users to create tags in your application is a great example of leveraging the collective power of your users. Items that are popular will tend to be frequently tagged. From an intelligence point of view, for a user, what matters most is which items people similar to the user are tagging.

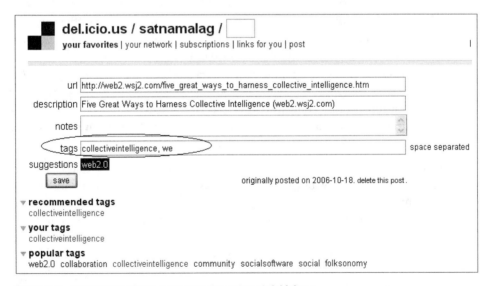

Figure 3.2   Screenshot of how a user creates a tag at del.icio.us

User-generated tags have the following characteristics:

- They use terms that are familiar to the user.
- They bring out the concepts related to the text.
- They capture the associated semantic value, using words that may not be found in the text.
- They can be multi-term phrases.
- They provide valuable collaborative information about the user and the item.
- They may include a wide variety of terms that are close in meaning.

User-generated tags will need to be *stemmed* to take care of plurals and filtered for obscenity. Since tags are freeform, variants of the same tag may appear. For example, *collective intelligence* and *collectiveintelligence* may appear as two tags. As shown in figure 3.2, you may want to offer recommended tags to the user based on the dictionary of tags created in your application and the first few characters typed by the user.[1] We discuss user-generated tags and tagging in more detail later in the next section.

3.1.4   *Machine-generated tags*

Tags or terms generated through an automated algorithm are known as machine-generated tags. In section 2.2.3, we briefly reviewed the steps involved in generating tags using an automated algorithm. Section 4.3 has a working example of how tags can be generated by analyzing the text. We develop the toolkit to extract tags in chapter 8. An algorithm generates tags by parsing through text and detecting terms and phrases.

Machine-generated tags have the following characteristics:

- *They use terms that are contained in the text, with the exception of injected synonyms.*
- *They're usually single terms*—Multi-term phrases are more difficult to extract and are usually done using a set of predefined phrases. These predefined phrases can be built using either professional or user-generated tags.
- *They can generate a lot of noisy tags—tags that can have multiple meanings based on the context, including polysemy[2] and homonyms.[3]*—For example, the word *gain* can have a number of meanings—height gain, weight gain, stock price gain, capital gain, amplifier gain, and so on. Again, detecting multiple-term phrases, which are a lot more specific than single terms, can help solve this problem.

In the absence of user-generated and professionally generated tags, machine-generated tags are the only alternative. This is especially true for analyzing user-generated content.

Chances are that you'll be using tags for both dynamic navigation in your application and for representing metadata. The next section covers some tips on how to tag items that I've learned from my experience.

---

[1]   This is commonly done using AJAX.

[2]   A word that has multiple related meanings depending on the context.

[3]   A word that has multiple unrelated meanings depending on the context.

3.1.5   *Tips on tagging*

Here are a few guidelines for how to create tags:

- *If possible, build a tag dictionary for your product*—Further tags can be organized in a "is-a" hierarchy. While tagging, build a synonym dictionary—a set of tags that have the same meaning. Leverage this dictionary to extract phrases while analyzing content and inject synonyms automatically while parsing text (see chapter 8).

- *Avoid tags that can have multiple meanings based on their context*—For example, *gain* can have multiple meanings as discussed in the previous section. Use a more qualified phrase, such as *weight gain* or *stock price gain.*

- *Don't use multiple tags to capture both singular and plurals, since the tags will be stemmed*—Similarly, don't worry about capitalization—all tags will be converted to lowercase.

- *Multi-term phrases are rarer in occurrence and therefore can give highly relevant matches*—To detect multi-term phrases using an automated algorithm, you may need to use a phrase dictionary. This is discussed more in chapter 8.

- *For a system that uses only professionally generated tags, the weight associated with each tag is related to the number of other tags used to describe the item and the inverse-document-frequency (idf) for the tag*—Every additional tag can dilute the weight of the other tags for an item. Use adequate but only relevant tags for an item.

- *You can use a combination of the three sources of tag generation.*

- *While tagging, build a synonym dictionary—a set of tags that have the same meaning.*

So far we've looked at the three forms of tagging and some pointers on how to tag. You may wonder what motivates a user to tag information; we look at this next.

3.1.6   *Why do users tag?*

In its most basic form, people may tag things so as to organize items of interest and remember them. For example, if you have a large number of files on your computer, you normally create folders to organize your files. Tagging is similar—you create categories or buckets and associate them with the item of interest. An item can be tagged with multiple labels, as shown in figure 3.3, a screenshot from Amazon.com, where users are allowed to add multiple tags to an item. By tagging items, users can use tags that make sense to them and don't have to use the classification of the content owner or site.

Users also tag items so that they can share the information with others, find related items that others have tagged in the same category, and also when they want to be found by others (mainly in social-networking sites).

As shown in figure 3.3, let's assume that a user is interested in management and has placed a *management* tag for his items of interest. Over a period of time, if the user would like to see all items related to management, he can look at all items that have been tagged with management. Tags help users organize and find items of interest.

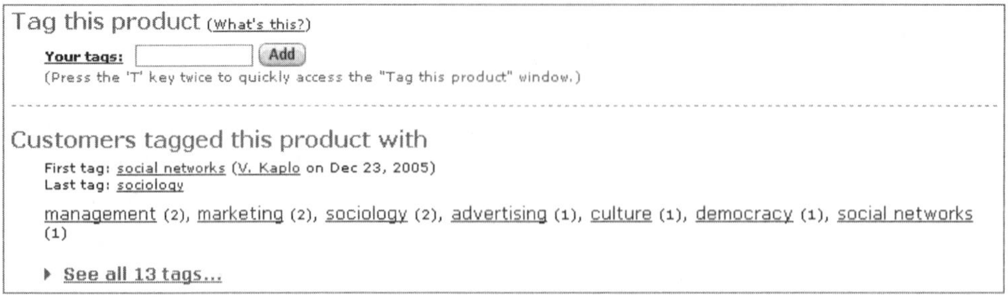

Figure 3.3   **Amazon allows users to tag a product and see how others have tagged the same product.**

Another feature that's actively used, especially for social networking applications, is allowing users to explore tags. In our example, any user would be able to click on the management link and see other items that have been tagged by other users with the same tag. This helps them discover new items of interest. User can also look at which users have used the same tag, thus helping them find other users with similar interests.

You can also find similar tags. The same item may have been tagged by others with different keywords. By following the links, you can associate similar tags. For example, in figure 3.3, the same item has been tagged as *social networks, sociology, management, marketing,* and so on. These four tags may be similar, especially if they're repeated consistently across multiple items.

So far, we've looked at what tags are and how they're generated. At the beginning of the section, we listed how tags can be used in your application. Next, we go through each use case in more detail.

3.2   How to leverage tags

It's useful to build metadata by analyzing the tags associated with an item and placed by a user. This metadata can then be used to find items and users of interest for the user. In addition to this, tagging can be useful to build dynamic navigation in your application, to target search, and to build folksonomies. In this section, we briefly review these three use cases.

3.2.1   Building dynamic navigation

In early applications, content would be categorized by professional authors. A user would navigate to the content by first selecting a category and then drilling down the category tree until the content was found. Tags provide an alternative to this rigid categorization, with a tag cloud as one manifestation of this dynamic navigation. Hyperlinks within content are another manifestation of this dynamic navigation. It's now fairly common for applications to hyperlink cities, phone numbers, and certain keywords as they display content on their sites. You must have seen this kind of hyperlinking, perhaps in your Yahoo! or Gmail email account.

As shown in figure 3.4, a tag cloud shows a list of tags, typically arranged alphabetically, with the font size representing the tag's frequency of use. The bigger the font in

Figure 3.4 Tag cloud from squidoo.com

a tag cloud, the more frequently it's used. Some tag clouds also use different font colors in their tag clouds.

Figure 3.5 shows the tag cloud of all-time most popular tags at Flickr. There are a number of interesting things that we can learn from this tag cloud. First, tags are not stemmed—plurals are treated as separate tags. For example, *animal* and *animals* are treated as separate tags, as are *flower* and *flowers*.

Note that the tag cloud here has only single-term tags—*new, york,* and *newyork* are three separate tags. The tag *San* could be a part of *San Diego, San Jose,* or *San Francisco.* Clearly, in this case, the content parsing isn't intelligent enough to extract the content in a way that makes sense.

All time most popular tags

Figure 3.5 Tag cloud of all-time most popular tags at Flickr

Toward the center of the tag cloud, you'll see the tag *nyc*. Clearly, *nyc* is a synonym for *new york city*, but these two phrases are treated as separate tags. To properly leverage tags, we need to do the following:

- Stem tags to take care of plurals.
- Detect multi-term phrases.
- Handle synonym tags.

The process of stemming, detecting phrases, and injecting synonyms is illustrated in section 4.3, and the infrastructure for such an analysis is developed in chapter 8.

A tag cloud needs terms and their relative weights, and that's what's contained in a term vector! Whereas a term vector is one way to represent metadata, a tag cloud is a visual representation of the metadata associated with an item or a user.

A tag cloud can be created for each user using her metadata—her term vectors—whether that metadata is learned from the content or from a collaborative-based approach or a combination of the two. In essence, a tag cloud associated with a user or an item is dynamic—it's dependent on the tags that users have assigned to it or that the user has visited.

When a user clicks on a tag in a tag cloud, you have the context for the tag—the associated metadata —and this can be converted into a call to the recommendation engine, where you search for content that's related to the user and the tag of interest. We look at building a tag cloud in detail in section 3.4.

3.2.2   *Innovative uses of tag clouds*

At the beginning of the chapter, we mentioned the use of tags to create dynamic navigation. Every day, more and more personalized tag clouds are appearing in applications. The tags in these clouds are being generated in one or more of three ways: professional, automated, or user-generated. Figure 3.6 shows the basic strategy used. Use the set of contents associated with the user—visited, subscribed to, and so on as shown on the right side of the figure—to get a combined term vector and then display it to the user. Remember that a tag cloud in essence is a visualization of a term vector.

Here are a couple of other interesting examples of using tag clouds. John Herren provides a good example of how different APIs can be combined to build powerful applications. He built a prototype application, Yahoo! News Tag Soup (http://yahoo.theherrens.com/index.php), that combines Yahoo!'s content analysis web service with Yahoo! News feeds. The service extracts keywords from the news article,

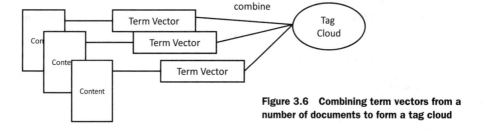

Figure 3.6   Combining term vectors from a number of documents to form a tag cloud

using Yahoo!'s content analysis web service. He then uses that information to build a dynamic tag cloud. This idea was further developed to provide users with their own personal tag cloud at TagCloud.com (http://www.tagcloud.com/). At this site, users can register themselves, and based on the news feeds that they register for, a personal tag cloud is generated for each user.

ZoomCloud (http://zoomclouds.egrupos.net/) provides the capability to add a tag cloud to your application. You can create a tag cloud on the ZoomCloud site by feeding in an RSS feed. ZoomCloud provides a template to customize the look-and-feel of the cloud and code that you can embed in your site. The tag cloud is hosted on their site, and can be customized for your blog or application.

In the future, look for more personalized tag clouds that combine multiple sources of information.

3.2.3 Targeted search

In June 2005, in its quest to challenge Google's search engine, Yahoo! launched its new search technology called MyRank. Google's search engine, which holds 50–60 percent[4] of the search market share, is based on the PageRank algorithm—the number of connections to a page, indicating the importance of the page. MyRank instead taps into the collective intelligence generated by a community of users. MyRank powers Yahoo!'s community, MyWeb 2.0. Users can save copies of web pages of interest in their personal cache and tag them. Search results for each user are dependent on the items saved and tagged by that user and his community of friends; results depend on the "quality" of a user's community and the pages they save and tag. Now let's look at the use of tags beyond MyRank.

Just like Google's page rank system looks at the number of links to a page as a metric to quantify the page's importance in its search engine, tags provide a similar metric. If an article is being tagged by many users using the same tag, it's probably very relevant to that topic and of interest to other users.

As shown in figure 3.7, you can combine the tag's context with the user's metadata as a query to the search engine to get relevant results for the user.

An example illustrates this approach well. Let's say that a tag *Spring* appears in a tag cloud that's used for navigating books in the application. Further, the user's profile identifies her as a developer. Here, the context of the query is books, while the metadata associated with the user is from her profile—developer. Relevant results can be shown to the user when she clicks on the tag *Spring* by making the following query to the search engine: *Books Spring Developer.*

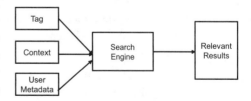

Figure 3.7 Using a tag, the context that it appears in, and user metadata to get relevant results from a search engine

---

[4] Nelsen/Netratings gave the number as 59% for the month of May 2008: http://www.nielsen-netratings.com/pr/pr_080619V.pdf.

3.2.4   *Folksonomies and building a dictionary*

User-generated tags provide an ad hoc way of classifying items, in a terminology that's relevant to the user. This process of classification, commonly known as *folksonomies*, enables users to retrieve information using terms that they're familiar with. There are no controlled vocabularies or professionally developed taxonomies.

The word *folksonomy* combines the words *folk* and *taxonomy.* Blogger Thomas Vander Wal is credited with coining the term.

Folksonomies allow users to find other users with similar interests. A user can reach new content by visiting other "similar" users and seeing what other content is available. Developing controlled taxonomies, as compared to folksonomies, can be expensive both in terms of time spent by the user using the rigid taxonomy, and in terms of the development costs to maintain it. Through the process of user tagging, users create their own classifications. This gives useful information about the user and the items being tagged.

The tags associated with your application define the set of terms that can be used to describe the user and the items. This in essence is the vocabulary for your application. Folksonomies are built from user-generated tags. Automated algorithms have a difficult time creating multi-term tags. When a dictionary of tags is available for your application, automated algorithms can use this dictionary to extract multi-term tags. Well-developed ontologies, such as in the life sciences, along with folksonomies are two of the ways to generate a dictionary of tags in an application.

Now that we've looked at how tags can be used in your application, let's take a more detailed look at user tagging.

3.3   *Extracting intelligence from user tagging: an example*

In this section, we illustrate the process of extracting intelligence from the process of user tagging. Based on how users have tagged items, we provide answers to the following three questions:

- Which items are related to another item?
- Which items might a user be interested in?
- Given a new item, which users will be interested in it?

To illustrate the concepts let us look at the following example. Let's assume we have two users: John and Jane, who've tagged three articles: Article1, Article2, and Article3, as follows:

- John has tagged Article1 with the tags apple, fruit, banana
- John has tagged Article2 with the tags orange, mango, fruit
- Jane has tagged Article3 with the tags cherry, orange, fruit

Our vocabulary for this example consists of six tags: *apple, fruit, banana, orange, mango,* and *cherry.* Next, we walk through the various steps involved in converting this information into intelligence. Lastly, we briefly review why users tag items.

Let the number of users who've tagged each of the items in the example be given by the data in table 3.1. Let each tag correspond to a dimension. In this example, each item is associated with a six-dimensional vector. For your application, you'll probably have thousands of unique tags. Note the last column, *normalizer*, shows the magnitude of the vector. The normalizer for Article1 is computed as $\sqrt{4^2+8^2+6^2+3^2} = 11.18$.

Table 3.1 Raw data used in the example

	apple	fruit	banana	orange	mango	cherry	normalizer
Article1	4	8	6	3			11.18
Article2		5		8	5		10.68
Article3	1	4		3		10	11.22

Next, we can scale the vectors so that their magnitude is equal to 1. Table 3.2 shows the normalized vectors for the three items—each of the terms is obtained by dividing the raw count by the normalizer. Note that the sum of the squares of each term after normalization will be equal to 1.

Table 3.2 Normalized vector for the items

	apple	fruit	banana	orange	mango	cherry
Article1	.3578	.7156	.5367	.2683		
Article2		.4682		.7491	0.4682	
Article3	.0891	.3563		.2673		.891

3.3.1 Items related to other items

Now we answer the first of our questions: which items are related to other items?

To find out how "similar" or relevant each of the items are, we take the dot product for each of the item's vector to obtain table 3.3. This in essence is an item-to-item recommendation engine.

To get the relevance between Article1 and Article2 we took the dot product:

(.7156 * .4682 + .2683 * .7491) = .536

According to this, Article2 is more relevant to Article1 than Article3.

	Article1	Article2	Article3
Article1	1	.5360	.3586
Article2	.5360	1	.3671
Article3	.3586	.3671	1

Table 3.3 Similarity matrix between the items

3.3.2 Items of interest for a user

This item-to-item list is the same for all users. What if you wanted to take into account the metadata associated with a user to tailor the list to his profile? Let's look at this next.

Based on how users tagged items, we can build a similar matrix for users, quantifying what items they're interested in as shown in table 3.4. Again, note the last column, which is the normalizer to convert the vector into a vector of magnitude 1.

Table 3.4   Raw data for users

	apple	fruit	banana	orange	mango	cherry	normalizer
John	1	2	1	1	1		2.83
Jane		1		1		1	1.73

The normalized metadata vectors for John and Jane are shown in table 3.5.

Table 3.5   The normalized metadata vector for the two users

	apple	fruit	banana	orange	mango	cherry
John	.3536	.7071	.3536	.3536	.3536	
Jane		.5773		.5773		.5773

Now we answer our second question: which items might a user be interested in?

To find out how relevant each of the items are to John and Jane, we take the dot product of their vectors. This is shown in table 3.6.

	Article1	Article2	Article3
John	.917	.7616	.378
Jane	.568	.703	.8744

Table 3.6   Similarity matrix between users and items

As expected in our fictitious example, John is interested in Article1 and Article2, while Jane is most interested in Article3. Based on how the items have been tagged, she is also likely to be interested in Article2.

3.3.3   *Relevant users for an item*

Next, we answer the last question: given a new item, which users will be interested in it?

When a new item appears, the group of users who could be interested in that item can be obtained by computing the similarities in the metadata for the new item and the metadata for the set of candidate users. This relevance can be used to identify users who may be interested in the item.

In most practical applications, you'll have a large number of tags, items, and users. Next, let's look at how to build the infrastructure required to leverage tags in your application. We begin by developing the persistence architecture to represent tags and related information.

3.4   *Scalable persistence architecture for tagging*

Web 2.0 applications invite users to interact. This interaction leads to more data being available for analysis. It's important that you build your application for scale. You need a strong foundation to build features for representing metadata with tags, representing information in the form of tag clouds, and building metadata about users and items. In this section, we concentrate on developing the persistence model for tagging in your application. Again, the code for the database schemas is downloadable from the download site.

This section draws from previous work done in the area of building the persistence architecture for tagging, but generalizes it to the three forms of tags and illustrates the concepts via examples.

In chapter 2, we had two main entities: user and item. Now we introduce two new entities: *tags* and *tagging source.* As shown in figure 3.8, all the tags are represented in the `tags` table, while the three sources of producing tags—professional, user, and automated—are represented in the `tagging_source` table.

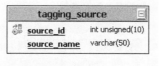

Figure 3.8 The `tags` and `tagging_source` database tables

The `tags` table has a unique index on the `tag_text` column: there can be only one row for a tag. Further, there may be additional columns to describe the tag, such as `stemmed_text`, which will help identify duplicate tags, and so forth.

Now let's look at developing the tables for a user tagging an item. There are a number of approaches to this. To illustrate the benefits of the proposed design, I'm going to show you three approaches, with each approach getting progressively better. The schema also gets progressively more normalized. If you're familiar with the principles of database design, you can go directly to section 3.4.2.

3.4.1 *Reviewing other approaches*

To understand some of the persistence schemas used for storing data related to user tagging, we use an example. Let's consider the problem of associating tags with URLs; here the URL is the item. In general, the URL can be any item of interest, perhaps a product, an article, a blog entry, or a photo of interest. MySQLicious, Scuttle, and Toxi are the three main approaches that we're using.

I've always found it helpful to have some sample data and represent it in the persistence design to better understand the design. For our example, let a user bookmark three URLs and assign them names and place tags, as shown in table 3.7.[5]

Table 3.6 **Data used for the bookmarking example**

Url	Name	Tags
http://nanovivid.com/projects/mysqlicious/	MySQLicious	Tagging schema denormalized
http://sourceforge.net/projects/scuttle/	Scuttle	Database binary schema
http://toxi.co.uk/	Toxi	Normalized database schema

MYSQLICIOUS

The first approach is the MySQLicious approach, which consists of a single denormalized table, `mysqlicious`, as shown in figure 3.9. The table consists of an autogenerated

---

[5] The URLs are also reference to sites where you can find more information to the persistence architectures: MySQLicious, Scuttle, and Toxi.

primary key, with tags stored in a space-delimited manner. Figure 3.8 also shows the sample data for our example persisted in this schema. Note the duplication of *database* and *schema* tags in the rows. This approach also assumes that tags are single terms.

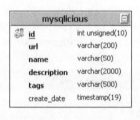

url	name	tags
http://nanovivid.com/projects/mysqlicious/	MySQLicious	tagging schema denormalized
http://sourceforge.net/projects/scuttle/	Scuttle	database binary schema
http://toxi.co.uk/	Toxi	normalized database schema

Figure 3.9 The MySQLicious schema with sample data

Now, let's look at the SQL you'd have to write to get all the URLs that have been tagged with the tag *database*.

```
Select url from mysqlicious where tags like "%database%"
```

The query is simple to write, but "like" searches don't scale well. In addition, there's duplication of tag information. Try writing the query to get all the tags. This denormalized schema won't scale well.

TIP   Avoid using space-delimited strings to persist multiple tags; you'll have to parse the string every time you need the individual tags and the schema won't scale. This doesn't lend well to stemming words, either.

Next, let's improve on this solution by looking at the second approach: the Scuttle approach.

SCUTTLE SOLUTION

The Scuttle solution uses two tables, one for the bookmark and the other for the tags, as shown in figure 3.10. As shown, each tag is stored in its own row.

The SQL to get the list of URLs that have been tagged with *database* is much more scalable than for the previous design and involves joining the two tables:

```
Select b.url from scuttle_bookmark b, scuttle_tags t where
    b.bookmark_id = t.bookmark_id and
    t.tag = 'database' group by b.url
```

The Scuttle solution is more normalized than MySQLicious, but note that tag data is still being duplicated.

Next, let's look at how we can further improve our design. Each bookmark can have multiple tags, and each tag can have multiple bookmarks. This many-to-many relationship is modeled by the next solution, known as Toxi.

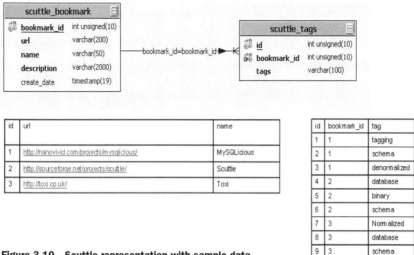

id	url	name
1	http://nanovivid.com/projects/mysqlicious/	MySQLicious
2	http://sourceforge.net/projects/scuttle/	Scuttle
3	http://toxi.co.uk/	Toxi

id	bookmark_id	tag
1	1	tagging
2	1	schema
3	1	denormalized
4	2	database
5	2	binary
6	2	schema
7	3	Normalized
8	3	database
9	3	schema

Figure 3.10   Scuttle representation with sample data

TOXI

The third approach that's been popularized on the internet is the Toxi solution. This solution uses three tables to represent the many-to-many relationship, as shown in figure 3.11. There's no longer duplication of data. Note that the `toxi_bookmark` table is the same as the `scuttle_bookmark` table.

So far in this section, we've shown three approaches to persisting tagging information. Each gets progressively more normalized and scalable, with Toxi being the closest to the recommended design. Next, we look at the recommended design, and also generalize the design for the three forms of tags: professionally generated, user-generated, and machine-generated.

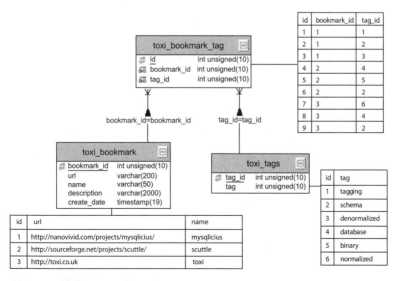

Figure 3.11   The normalized Toxi solution with sample data

3.4.2 *Recommended persistence architecture*

The scalable architecture presented here is similar to the one presented at MySQL-Forge called *TagSchema*, and the one presented by Jay Pipes in his presentation "Tagging and Folksonomy Schema Design for Scalability and Performance." We generalize the design to handle the three kinds of tags and illustrate the design via an example.

Let's begin by looking at how to handle user-generated tags. We use an example to explain the schema and illustrate how commonly used queries can be formed for the schema.

SCHEMA FOR USER-GENERATED TAGS

Let's continue with the same example that we began with at the beginning of section 3.3.2. Let's add the user dimension to the example—there are users who are tagging items. We also generalize from bookmarks to items.

In our example, John and Jane are two users:

- *John has tagged item1 with the tags* tagging, schema, denormalized
- *John has tagged item2 with the tags* database, binary, schema
- *Jane has tagged item3 with the tags* normalized, database, schema

As shown in figure 3.12, there are three entities—user, item, and tags. Each is represented as a database table, and there is a fourth table, a mapping table, user_item_tag.

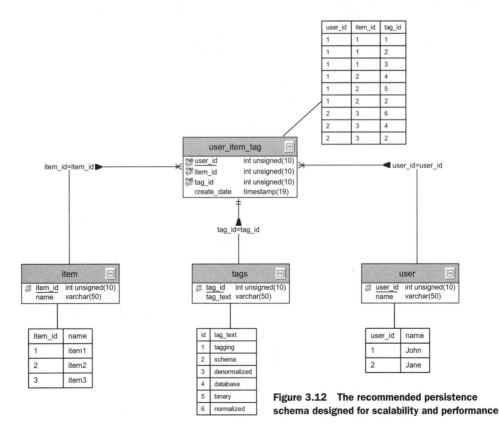

Figure 3.12 The recommended persistence schema designed for scalability and performance

Let's look at how the design holds up to two of the common use cases that you may apply to your application:

- What other tags have been used by users who have at least one matching tag?
- What other items are tagged similarly to a given item?

As shown in figure 3.13 we need to break this into three queries:

1 First, find the set of tags used by a user, say John.
2 Find the set of users that have used one of these tags.
3 Find the set of tags that these users have used.

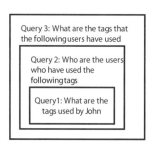

Figure 3.13   Nesting queries to get the set of tags used

Let's write this query for John, whose user_id is 1. The query consists of three main parts.

First, let's write the query to get all of John's tags. For this, we have to inner-join tables `user_item_tag` and `tags`, and use the distinct qualifier to get unique tag IDs.

```
Select distinct t.tag_id, t.tag_text from tags t, user_item_tag uit where
    t.tag_id = uit.tag_id and uit.user_id = 1;
```

If you run this query, you'll get the set (*tagging, schema, denormalized, database, binary*).

Second, let's use this query to find the users who've used one of these tags, as shown in listing 3.1.

Listing 3.1   Query for users who have used one of John's tags

```
Select distinct uit2.user_id from user_item_tag uit2, tags t2 where
    uit2.tag_id = t2.tag_id and
    uit2.tag_id in (Select distinct t.tag_id from tags t, user_item_tag uit
wheret.tag_id = uit.tag_id and uit.user_id = 1)          subquery
```

Note that the first query:

```
Select distinct t.tag_id, t.tag from tags t, user_item_tag uit where
    t.tag_id = uit.tag_id and uit.user_id = 1
```

is a subquery in this query. The query selects the set of users and will return user_ids 1 and 2.

Third, the query to retrieve the tags that these users have used is shown in listing 3.2

Listing 3.2   The final query for getting all tags that other users have used

```
Select uit3.tag_id, t3.tag_id, count(*)  from user_item_tag uit3, tags t3
whereuit3.tag_id = t3.tag_id and uit3.user_id
    in (Select distinct uit2.user_id from user_item_tag uit2, tags t2
where uit2.tag_id = t2.tag_id and
    uit2.tag_id in (Select distinct t.tag_id from tags t, user_item_tag uit
        where t.tag_id = uit.tag_id and uit.user_id = 1) )
    group by uit3.tag_id
```

Note that this query was built by using the query developed in listing 3.1. The query will result in six tags, which are shown in table 3.8, along with their frequencies.

tag_id	tag_text	count(*)
1	tagging	1
2	schema	3
3	denormalized	1
4	database	2
5	binary	1
6	normalized	1

Table 3.8   The result for the query to find other tags used by user 1

Now let's move on to the second question: what other items are tagged similarly to a given item? Let's find the other items that are similarly tagged to item1.

First, let's get the set of tags related to item1, which has an item_id of 1—this set is (*tagging, schema, normalized*):

```
Select uit.tag_id from user_item_tag uit, tags t where
    uit.tag_id = t.tag_id and
    uit.item_id = 1
```

Next, let's get the list of items that have been tagged with any of these tags, along with the count of these tags:

```
Select uit2.item_id, count(*) from user_item_tag uit2 where
  uit2.tag_id in (Select uit.tag_id from user_item_tag uit, tags t where
    uit.tag_id = t.tag_id and uit.item_id = 1)
      group by uit2.item_id
```

This will result in table 3.9, which shows the three items with the number of tags.

item_id	count(*)	Tags
1	3	tagging, schema, normalized
2	1	schema
3	1	schema

Table 3.9   Result of other items that share a tag with another item

So far, we've looked at the normalized schema to represent a user, item, tags, and users tagging an item. We've shown how this schema holds for two commonly used queries. In chapter 12, we look at more advanced techniques—*recommendation engines*—to find related items using the way items have been tagged.

Next, let's generalize the design from user tagging to also include the other two ways of generating tags: professionally and machine-generated tags.

SCHEMA FOR PROFESSIONALLY AND MACHINE-GENERATED TAGS

We add a new table, item_tag, to capture the tags associated with an item by professional editors or by an automated algorithm, as shown in figure 3.14. Note that there's also a weight column—this table is in essence storing the metadata related with the item.

Finding tags and their associated weights for an item is simply with this query:

```
Select tag_id, weight from item_tag
  where item_id = ? and
  tagging_source_id = ?
```

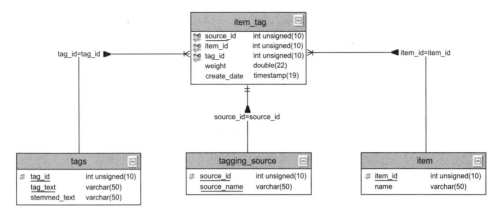

Figure 3.14 Table to store the metadata associated with an item via tags

In this section, we've developed the schema for persisting tags in your application. Now, let's look at how we can apply tags to your application. We develop tag clouds as an instance of dynamic navigation, which we introduced in section 3.1.4.

3.5   Building tag clouds

In this section, we look at how you can build tag clouds in your application. We first extend the persistence design to support tag clouds. Next, we review the algorithm to display tag clouds and write some code to implement a tag cloud.

3.5.1   Persistence design for tag clouds

For building tag clouds, we need to get a list of tags and their relative weights. The relative weights of the terms are already captured in the `item_tag` table for professionally generated and machine-generated tags. For user tagging, we can get the relative weights and the list of tags for the tag cloud with this query:

```
Select t.tag, count(*) from user_item_tag uit, tags t where
    Uit.tag_id = t.tag_id group by t.tag
```

This results in table 3.10, which shows the six tags and their relative frequencies for the example in section 3.3.3.

The use of `count(*)` can have a negative effect on scalability. This can be eliminated by using a summary table. Further, you may want to get the count of tags based on different time windows. To do this, we add two more tables, `tag_summary` and `days`, as shown in figure 3.15. The `tag_summary` table is updated on every insert in the `user_item_tag` table.

The tag cloud data for any given day is given by the following:

Table 3.10   Data for the tag cloud in our example

tag_text	count(*)
tagging	1
schema	3
denormalized	1
database	2
binary	1
normalized	1

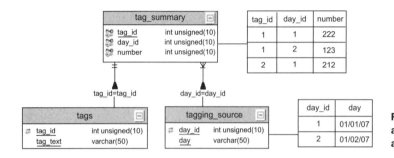

Figure 3.15   **The addition of summary and days tables**

```
select t.tag, ts.number from tags t, tag_summary ts where
    t.tag_id = ts.tag_id and
    ts.day = 'x'
```

To get the frequency over a range of days, you have to use the sum function in this design:

```
select t.tag, sum(ts.number) from tag tags t, tag_summary ts where
    t.tag_id = ts.tag_id and
    ts.day > 't1' and ts.day <'t2' group by t.tag
```

When a user clicks on a particular tag, we need to find out the list of items that have been tagged with the tag of interest. There are a number of approaches to showing results when a user clicks on a tag. The tag value could be used as an input to a search engine or recommendation engine, or we can query the userItemTag or the itemTag tables. The following query retrieves items from the userItemTag table:

```
select uit.item_id, count(*) from user_item_tag uit where
    uit.tag_id = 'x' group by uit.item_id
```

Similarly, for professional and automated algorithm generated tags we can write the query

```
select item_id from item_tag where tag_id = ? order by weight desc
```

Since we've developed the database query for building the tag cloud, let's next look at how we can build a tag cloud after we have access to a list of tags and their frequency.

3.5.2   *Algorithm for building a tag cloud*

There are five steps involved in building a tag cloud:

1   The first step in displaying a tag cloud is to get a list of tags and their frequencies—a list of <Tag name, frequency>.

2   Next, compute the minimum and maximum occurrence of each tag. Let's call these numberMin and numberMax.

3   Decide on the number of font sizes that you want to use; generally this number is between 3 and 20. Let's call this number numberDivisions.

4 Create the ranges for each font size. The formula for this is

$$
\begin{aligned}
&\text{...visions} \\
&\text{...n} + (i - 1) * (\text{numberMax} - \text{numberMin}) / \text{numberDivisions} \\
&i * (\text{numberMax} - \text{numberMin}) / \text{numberDivisions}
\end{aligned}
$$

...berMin, numberMax, and numberDivisions are (20, 80, 3),
...0, 40–60, 60–80).

...ts and iterate over all the items to display the tag

...e, it can be quite powerful in displaying the infor-
...r "In Search of … The Perfect Tag Cloud," pro-
...e the log of the frequency and create the buckets for
...—to distribute the font size in a tag cloud.
...ts for the tags have been normalized (when the
..., the linear scaling works fairly well, unless the
...from the other values.
...htforward. It's now time to roll up our sleeves
...e in your application to implement a tag cloud

...implementing a tag cloud. We also use this code
...ry[6] design pattern to factor out the scaling algo-
...also helpful to define interfaces TagCloud and
...re can be different implementations for them.
...of this section gets into the details of implementing the code
related to developing a tag cloud. Figure 3.16 shows the classes that we develop in this
section.

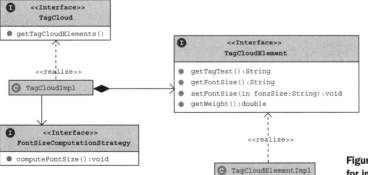

Figure 3.16 Class design for implementing a tag cloud

---

6 Gang of Four—Strategy pattern

TAGCLOUD

First, let's begin with the `TagCloud` interface, which is shown in listing 3.3.

Listing 3.3   The `TagCloud` interface

```
package com.alag.ci.tagcloud;

import java.util.List;

public interface TagCloud {
    public List<TagCloudElement> getTagCloudElements();
}
```

This is simple enough, and has one method to get the `List` of `TagCloudElements`.

TAGCLOUDELEMENT

The `TagCloudElement` interface corresponds to a tag and contains methods to get the tag text, the tag weight, and the computed font size. This is shown in listing 3.4 .

Listing 3.4   The `TagCloudElement` interface

```
package com.alag.ci.tagcloud;                    Extends Comparable to sort entries

public interface TagCloudElement extends Comparable<TagCloudElement> {
    public String getTagText();
    public double getWeight();            Double to represent
    public String getFontSize();          relative weight
    public void setFontSize(String fontSize);
}
```

The `TagCloudElement` interface extends the `Comparable` interface, which allows Tag-Cloud to return these elements in a sorted manner. I've used a `String` for the font size, as the computed value may correspond to a style sheet entry in your JSP. Also a `double` is used for the `getWeight()` method.

FONTSIZECOMPUTATIONSTRATEGY

The `FontSizeComputationStrategy` interface has only one method, as shown in listing 3.5.

Listing 3.5   The `FontSizeComputationStrategy` interface

```
package com.alag.ci.tagcloud;

import java.util.List;

public interface FontSizeComputationStrategy {
    public void computeFontSize(List<TagCloudElement> elements);
}
```

The method

```
void computeFontSize(List<TagCloudElement> elements);
```

computes the font size for a given `List` of `TagCloudElements`.

TAGCLOUDIMPL

`TagCloudImpl` implements the `TagCloud` and is fairly simple, as shown in listing 3.6.

Listing 3.6 Implementation of `TagCloudImpl`

```
package com.alag.ci.tagcloud.impl;

import java.util.*;

import com.alag.ci.tagcloud.*;

public class TagCloudImpl implements TagCloud {

    private List<TagCloudElement> elements = null;

    public TagCloudImpl(List<TagCloudElement> elements,
                  FontSizeComputationStrategy strategy) {
      this.elements = elements;
      strategy.computeFontSize(this.elements);
      Collections.sort(this.elements);
    }

    public List<TagCloudElement> getTagCloudElements() {
      return this.elements;
    }

  //to String
  }
```

> **FontSizeComputationStrategy computes font size**

> **Sorts entries alphabetically**

It has a list of `TagCloudElements` and delegates the task of computing the font size to `FontSizeComputationStrategy`, which is passed in its constructor. It also sorts the `List<TagCloudElement>` elements alphabetically.

TAGCLOUDELEMENTIMPL

`TagCloudElementImpl` is shown in listing 3.7.

Listing 3.7 The implementation of `TagCloudElementImpl`

```
package com.alag.ci.tagcloud.impl;

import com.alag.ci.tagcloud.TagCloudElement;

public class TagCloudElementImpl implements TagCloudElement {
    private String fontSize = null;
    private Double weight = null;
    private String tagText = null;

    public TagCloudElementImpl(String tagText, double tagCount) {
       this.tagText = tagText;
       this.weight = tagCount;
    }

    public int compareTo(TagCloudElement o) {
       return this.tagText.compareTo(o.getTagText());
    }
  //get and set methods
  }
```

> **Implements Comparable for alphabetical sorting**

`TagCloudElementImpl` is a pure bean object that implements the `Comparable` interface for alphabetical sorting of tag texts as shown in listing 3.7.

FONTSIZECOMPUTATIONSTRATEGYIMPL

The implementation for the base class `FontSizeComputationStrategyImpl` is more interesting and is shown in listing 3.8.

Listing 3.8   Implementation of `FontSizeComputationStrategyImpl`

```java
package com.alag.ci.tagcloud.impl;

import java.util.List;

import com.alag.ci.tagcloud.*;

public abstract class FontSizeComputationStrategyImpl implements
        FontSizeComputationStrategy {
    private static final double PRECISION = 0.00001;
    private Integer numSizes = null;
    private String prefix = null;

    public FontSizeComputationStrategyImpl(int numSizes, String prefix) {
        this.numSizes = numSizes;
        this.prefix = prefix;
    }

    public int getNumSizes() {
        return this.numSizes;
    }

    public String getPrefix() {
        return this.prefix;
    }

    public void computeFontSize(List<TagCloudElement> elements) {
        if (elements.size() > 0) {
            Double minCount = null;
            Double maxCount = null;
            for (TagCloudElement tce: elements) {
                double n = tce.getWeight();
                if ( (minCount == null) || (minCount > n)) {
                    minCount = n;
                }
                if ( (maxCount == null) || (maxCount < n)) {
                    maxCount = n;
                }
            }
            double maxScaled = scaleCount(maxCount);
            double minscaled = scaleCount(minCount);
            double diff = (maxScaled - minscaled)/(double)this.numSizes;
            for (TagCloudElement tce: elements) {
                int index = (int)
                    Math.floor((scaleCount(tce.getWeight()) - minscaled)/diff);
                if (Math.abs(tce.getWeight() - maxCount) < PRECISION) {
                    index = this.numSizes - 1;
                }
                tce.setFontSize(this.prefix + index);
            }
        }
    }
    protected abstract double scaleCount(double count) ;
}
```

Annotations:
- `Used to check equality of doubles` (points to `PRECISION = 0.00001`)
- `Compute min and max count`
- `Scale the counts`
- (unlabeled arrow pointing to the second `for` loop)
- `Compute appropriate font bucket`
- `Abstract forces inheriting classes to implement` (points to `protected abstract double scaleCount`)

This takes in the number of font sizes to be used and the prefix to be set for the font. In your application, there might be an enumeration of fonts and you may want to use `Enum` for the different fonts. I've made the class `abstract` to force the inheriting classes to overwrite the `scaleCount` method, as shown in figure 3.16.

The method `computeFontSize` first gets the minimum and the maximum and then computes the bucket for the font size using the following:

```
for (TagCloudElement tce: elements) {
    int index = (int) Math.floor((scaleCount(tce.getWeight()) -
        minscaled)/diff);
    if (Math.abs(tce.getWeight() - maxCount) < PRECISION){
        index = this.numSizes - 1;
    }
    tce.setFontSize(this.prefix + index);
    }
}
```

To understand the formula used to calculate the font index, let, x be the scaled value of the number of times a tag appears then that tag falls in bin n, where

$$n = \frac{(x - \min scaled)}{(\max scaled - \min scaled)} numSizes$$

Note that when x is the same as *maxscaled*, n is *numSizes*. This is why there's a check for *maxCount*:

```
if (tce.getWeight() == maxCount) {
```

This implementation is more efficient than creating an array with the ranges for each of the bins and looping through the elements.

EXTENDING FONTSIZECOMPUTATIONSTRATEGYIMPL

Lastly, the two classes extending `FontSizeComputationStrategyImpl` simply need to implement the `scaleCount` method and have a constructor that calls super, as shown in figure 3.17.

First, let's look at the implementation of `LinearFontSizeComputationStrategy`, which simply overrides the `scaleCount` method:

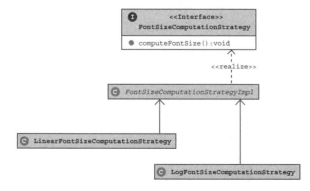

Figure 3.17 The class diagram for `FontSizeComputationStrategy`

```
protected double scaleCount(double count) {
    return count;
}
```

Similarly, `LogFontSizeComputationStrategy` implements the same method as the following:

```
protected double scaleCount(double count) {
    return Math.log10(count);
}
```

You can implement your own variant of the `FontSizeComputationStrategy` by simply overwriting the `scaleCount` method. Some other strategies that you may want to consider are using clustering (see chapter 9) or assigning the same number of items (or nearly the same) for each of the font sizes. For this, sort the items by weight and assign the items to the appropriate bins.

Now that we've implemented a tag cloud, we need a way to visualize it. Next, we develop a simple class to generate HTML to display the tag cloud.

3.5.4 *Visualizing a tag cloud*

We use the Decorator design pattern, as shown in figure 3.18, to define an interface `VisualizeTagCloudDecorator`. It takes in a `TagCloud` and generates a `String` representation.

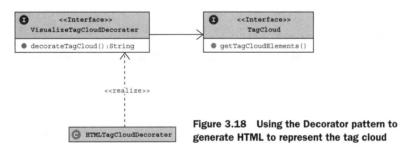

Figure 3.18   Using the Decorator pattern to generate HTML to represent the tag cloud

The code for `VisualizeTagCloudDecorator` is shown in listing 3.9.

Listing 3.9 `VisualizeTagCloudDecorator` interface

```
package com.alag.ci.tagcloud;

public interface VisualizeTagCloudDecorator {
    public String decorateTagCloud(TagCloud tagCloud);
}
```

There's only one method to create a `String` representation of the `TagCloud`:

```
public String decorateTagCloud(TagCloud tagCloud);
```

Let's write a concrete implementation of `HTMLTagCloudDecorator`, which is shown in listing 3.10.

Listing 3.10 Implementation of `HTMLTagCloudDecorator`

```java
package com.alag.ci.tagcloud.impl;

import java.io.StringWriter;
import java.util.*;

import com.alag.ci.tagcloud.*;

public class HTMLTagCloudDecorator implements VisualizeTagCloudDecorator {
    private static final String HEADER_HTML =
        "<html><br><head><br><title>TagCloud <br></title><br></head>";
    private static final int NUM_TAGS_IN_LINE = 10;
    private Map<String, String> fontMap = null;

    public HTMLTagCloudDecorator() {
        getFontMap();                                          // Get mapping
    }                                                          // from font-bin
                                                               // or XML file
    private void getFontMap() {
        this.fontMap = new HashMap<String,String>();
        fontMap.put("font-size: 0", "font-size: 13px");
        fontMap.put("font-size: 1", "font-size: 20px");
        fontMap.put("font-size: 2", "font-size: 24px");
    }
                                                               // Generates
    public String decorateTagCloud(TagCloud tagCloud) {        // HTML file
        StringWriter sw = new StringWriter();
        List<TagCloudElement> elements = tagCloud.getTagCloudElements();
        sw.append(HEADER_HTML);
        sw.append("<br><body><h3>TagCloud (" + elements.size() +")</h3>");
        int count = 0;
        for (TagCloudElement tce :  elements) {
            sw.append(" <a style=\""+
             fontMap.get(tce.getFontSize())+";\">" );
            sw.append(tce.getTagText() +"</a> ");
            if (count++ == NUM_TAGS_IN_LINE) {
                count = 0;
                sw.append("<br>" );
            }
        }
        sw.append("<br></body><br></html>");
        return sw.toString();
    }
}
```

Here, the title of the generated page is hard-coded to `TagCloud`:

```java
private static final String HEADER_HTML =
    "<html><br><head><br><title>TagCloud <br></title><br></head>";
```

The method `getFontMap()` simply creates a `Map` of font strings that will be used:

```java
private void getFontMap() {
    this.fontMap = new HashMap<String,String>();
    fontMap.put("font-size: 0", "font-size: 13px");
    //... other font mapping
}
```

For your application, you'll probably read this mapping from an XML file or from the database.

The rest of the code generates the HTML for displaying the tag cloud:

```
for (TagCloudElement tce : elements) {
    sw.append(" <a style=\""+
        fontMap.get(tce.getFontSize())+";\">" );
    sw.append(tce.getTagText() +"</a> ");
    if (count++ == NUM_TAGS_IN_LINE) {
        count = 0;
        sw.append("<br>" );
    }
}
```

A simple test program is shown in listing 3.11. The asserts have been removed to make it easier to read. This code creates a `TagCloud` and creates an HTML file to display it.

Listing 3.11 Sample code for generating tag clouds

```
package com.alag.ci.tagcloud.test;

import java.io.*;
import java.util.*;

import com.alag.ci.tagcloud.*;
import com.alag.ci.tagcloud.impl.*;

import junit.framework.TestCase;

public class TagCloudTest extends TestCase {

    public void testTagCloud() throws Exception {
        String firstString = "binary";
        int numSizes = 3;
        String fontPrefix = "font-size: ";

        List<TagCloudElement> l = new ArrayList<TagCloudElement>();
        l.add(new TagCloudElementImpl("tagging",1));
        l.add(new TagCloudElementImpl("schema",3));
        l.add(new TagCloudElementImpl("denormalized",1));
        l.add(new TagCloudElementImpl("database",2));
        l.add(new TagCloudElementImpl(firstString,1));
        l.add(new TagCloudElementImpl("normalized",1));

        FontSizeComputationStrategy strategy =
            new LinearFontSizeComputationStrategy(numSizes,fontPrefix);
        TagCloud cloudLinear = new TagCloudImpl(l,strategy);
        System.out.println(cloudLinear);

        strategy = new LogFontSizeComputationStrategy(numSizes,fontPrefix);
        TagCloud cloudLog = new TagCloudImpl(l,strategy);
        System.out.println(cloudLog);

        //write to file
        String fileName = "testTagCloudChap3.html";
        writeToFile(fileName,cloudLinear);
    }

    private static void writeToFile(String fileName, TagCloud cloud)
```

```
        throws IOException {
        BufferedWriter out = new BufferedWriter(
            new FileWriter(fileName));
        VisualizeTagCloudDecorator decorator = new HTMLTagCloudDecorator();
        out.write(decorator.decorateTagCloud(cloud));
        out.close();
    }
}
```

A TagCloud is created by the following code:

```
List<TagCloudElement> l = new ArrayList<TagCloudElement>();
l.add(new TagCloudElementImpl("tagging",1));
....

FontSizeComputationStrategy strategy =
    new LinearFontSizeComputationStrategy(numSizes,fontPrefix);
TagCloud cloudLinear = new TagCloudImpl(l,strategy);
```

The method `writeToFile` simply writes the generated HTML to a specified file:

```
BufferedWriter out = new BufferedWriter(
    new FileWriter(fileName));
VisualizeTagCloudDecorator decorator = new HTMLTagCloudDecorator();
out.write(decorator.decorateTagCloud(cloud));
out.close();
```

Figure 3.19 shows the tag cloud developed for our example.[7] Note that *schema* has the biggest font, followed by *database*.

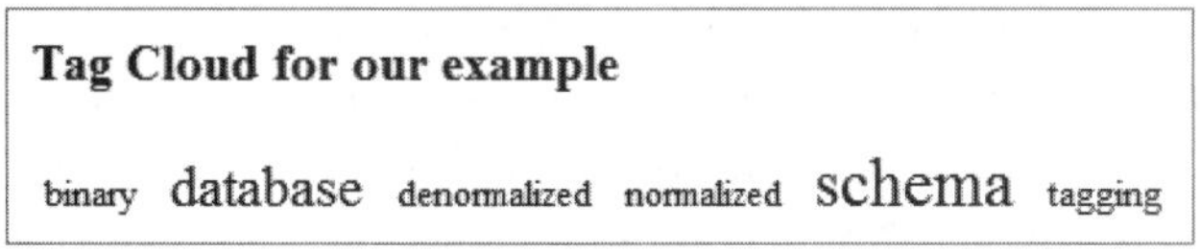

Tag Cloud for our example

binary database denormalized normalized schema tagging

Figure 3.19 The tag cloud for our example

In this section, we developed code to implement and visualize a tag cloud. Next, let's look at a few interesting topics related to tags that you may run into in your application.

3.6   *Finding similar tags*

As of February 2007, 35 percent[8] of all posts tracked by Technorati used tags. As of October 2006, Technorati was tracking 10.4 million tags. There were about half a million unique tags in del.icio.us, as of October 2005, with each item averaging about two tags. Given the large number of tags, a good question is how to find tags that are related to each other—tags that are synonymous or that show a parent-child relationship. Building this manually is too expensive and nonscalable for most applications.

A simple approach to finding similar tags is to stem—convert the word into its root form—to take care of differences in tags due to plurals after removing *stop*

---

[7] Both the linear and logarithmic functions gave the same font sizes for this simple example when three font sizes were used, but they were different when five were used.

[8] http://technorati.com/weblog/2007/04/328.html

words—commonly occurring words. Having a synonym dictionary also helps keep track of tags that are similar. When dealing with multi-term phrases, two tags could be similar but may have their terms in different positions. For example, *weight gain* and *gain weight* are similar tags.

Another approach is to analyze the co-occurrences of tags. Table 3.11 shows data that can be used for this analysis. Here, the rows correspond to tags and the columns are the items in your system. There's a 1 if an item has been tagged with that tag. Note the similarity to the table we looked at in section 2.4. You can use the correlation similarity computation to find correlated tags. Matrix dimensionality reduction using *Latent Semantic Indexing (LSI)* is also used (see section 12.3.3). LSI has been used to solve the problems of synonymy and polysemy.

	Item 1	Item 2	Item 3
Tag1	1		
Tag2		1	1
Tag3	1		1

Table 3.11 Bookmarking data for analysis

When finding items relevant to a tag, don't forget to first find a similar set of tags to the tag of interest and then find items related to the tag by querying the `item_tag` table.

3.7 Summary

Tagging is the process of adding freeform text, either words or small phrases, to items. These keywords or labels can be attached to anything—another user, photos, articles, bookmarks, products, blog entries, podcasts, videos, and more. Tagging enables users to associate freeform text with an item, in a way that makes sense to them, rather than using a fixed terminology that may have been developed by the content owner.

There are three ways to generate tags: have professional editors create tags, allow users to tag items, or have an automated algorithm generate tags. Tags serve as a common vocabulary to associate metadata with users and items. This metadata can be used for personalization and for targeting search to a user.

User-centric applications no longer rigidly categorize items. They offer dynamic navigation, which is built from tags to their users. A tag cloud is one example of dynamic navigation. It visually represents the term vector—tags and their relative weights. We looked at how tags can be persisted in your application and how you can build a tag cloud.

In the next chapter, we look at the different kinds of content that are used in application and how they can be abstracted from an analysis point of view. We also demonstrate the process of generating a term vector from text using a simple example.

3.8 Resources

"All of Web2.0." Chrisekblog, http://chrisek.com/wordpress/2006/10/03/all-of-web-20/

"Building a tag cloud in Java." http://randomcoder.com/articles/building-a-tag-cloud-in-java

"Everything Web2.0." Matt's blog. http://yahoolog.com/blog/?p=94

Freitag,Pete. "How to make a tag cloud." http://www.petefreitag.com/item/396.cfm

Gamma, Eric, et. al. *Design Patterns - Elements of Reusable Object-Oriented Software.* 1995, Addison-Wesley Professional.

Green,Heather. "A Tag Team's Novel Net Navigation." *BusinessWeek.* February 28, 1995. http://www.businessweek.com/technology/content/feb2005/tc20050228_6395_tc024.htm?chan=search

Grossman, Frieder. *Information Retrieval: Algorithms and Heuristics.* 2006. Springer.

Hoffman, Kevin. "In Search of a Perfect Tag Cloud." http://files.blog-city.com/files/J05/88284/b/insearchofperfecttagcloud.pdf

"Homonyms." wikipedia.org, http://en.wikipedia.org/wiki/Homonyms

Keller, Philipp. "Tags Database Schema." http://www.pui.ch/phred/archives/2005/04/tags-database-schemas.html

Konchady, Manu. "Text Mining Application Programming." 2006. Thomson Delmar Learning.

Kopelman, Josh. "53,651." May 2006. http://redeye.firstround.com/2006/05/53651.html

MySQLicious. http://nanovivid.com/projects/mysqlicious/

"Nielsen Net Ratings Announces February U.S Search Share Rankings." January, 2008. http://www.nielsen-netratings.com/pr/pr_080118.pdf

Pipes, Jay. "Tagging and Folksonomy Schema Design for Scalability and Performance." MySQL Inc.

"Polysemy." wikipedia.org, http://en.wikipedia.org/wiki/Polysemy

Scuttle. http://sourceforge.net/projects/scuttle/

Sinha,Rashmi. "A social analysis of tagging (or how tagging transforms the solitary browsing experience into a social one)." January 18, 2006. http://www.rashmisinha.com/archives/06_01/social-tagging.html

"Tag Schema." MySQL Inc. http://forge.mysql.com/wiki/TagSchema#Tagging_and_Folksonomy_Schema_Concepts

"Tagcloud examples." http://microformats.org/wiki/tagcloud-examples

Toxi. http://toxi.co.uk/

"Zoom Clouds." http://zoomclouds.egrupos.net/

Extracting intelligence from content

This chapter covers
- Architecture for integrating various types of content
- A more detailed look at blogs, wikis, and message boards
- A working example of extracting intelligence from unstructured text
- Extracting intelligence from different types of content

Content as used in this chapter is any item that has text associated with it. This text can be in the form of a title and a body as in the case of articles, keywords associated with a classification term, questions and answers on message boards, or a simple title associated with a photo or video. Content can be developed either professionally by the site provider or by users (commonly known as *user-generated content*), or be harvested from external sites via web crawling.[1]

Content is the fundamental building block for developing applications. This chapter provides background on integrating and analyzing content in your application.

---

[1] Web crawling is covered in chapter 6.

It'll be helpful to go through the example developed in section 4.3, which illustrates how intelligence can be extracted from analyzing content.

In this chapter, we take a deeper look into the many types of content, and how they can be integrated into your application for extracting intelligence. A book on collective intelligence wouldn't be complete without a detailed discussion of content types that get associated with collective intelligence and involve user interaction: blogs, wikis, groups, and message boards. Next, we use an example to demonstrate step by step how intelligence can be extracted from content. Having learned the similarities among these content types, we create an abstraction model for analyzing the content types for extracting intelligence.

4.1 Content types and integration

Classifying content into different content types and mapping each content type into an abstraction (see section 4.4) allows us to build a common infrastructure for handling various kinds of content.

In this section, we look at the many forms of content in an application and the various forms of integration that you may come across to integrate these content types.

4.1.1 Classifying content

Table 4.1 shows some of the content types that are used in applications along with the way they're typically created. Chances are that you're already familiar with most of the content types.

Table 4.1 The different content types

Content type	Description	Source
Articles	Text on a particular topic. Has a title, body, and, optionally, subtitles.	Professionally created, user-generated, news feeds, aggregated from other sites
Products	An item being sold on your site. Typically has title, description, keywords, reviews, ratings, other attributes such as price, manufacturer, and availability in particular geographic location.	Created by the site, user-generated in a marketplace like eBay, linking to partner sources
Classification terms	Ad hoc terms, such as *collective intelligence* with keywords or tags associated with them. Created for user navigation.	Professionally created, machine-generated; user tagging is also an instance of this
Blogs	Online personal journals where you write about things you want to share with others; others can comment on your entries and link to your site.	Site management, company employees, user-generated
Wikis	Online collaboration tool where users can very easily edit, add, or delete web pages.	Mainly user-generated
Groups and message boards	Places where you can place questions and others can respond to them, as well as rate them for usefulness. Mainly in the form of questions and answers.	Mainly user-generated, expert answers may be provided by experts working for the site

Table 4.1   The different content types *(continued)*

Content type	Description	Source
Photos and video	Rich media in the form of photos and videos.	Professionally created, user-generated
Polls	Questions asked of a user, with the response being one of a handful of options.	Professionally or user-generated
Search terms	Search queries by user. Similar to dynamic classification.	User-generated
Profile pages	Profile page for a user. Typically, created by the user listing preferences and information about the user.	User-generated
Tools and worksheets	Tools and worksheets that may be available at the site.	Professionally created
Chat logs	Transcripts of online chats.	Expert talking to users, users talking to users
Reviews	Reviews about an item, which could be any of the other content types.	Professionally or user-generated
Classifieds	Advertisements with a title and a body. Optionally, may have keywords associated with it.	Professionally or user-generated
Lists	List of items—any of the other content types—combined together.	Professionally or user-generated

You're probably familiar with articles and products. We talked about classification terms in section 3.2.1 and their use for dynamic navigation links. Classification terms are any ad hoc terms that may be created; they're similar to topic headers. An example best illustrates them.

Let's say that one of the features in your application is focused on providing relevant news items. You know that global warming is an important area of interest to your users. So you create the classification term *global warming* and assign it appropriate tags or keywords. Then the process of finding relevant content for this term for a user can be treated as a classification problem—using the user's profile and the keywords assigned to the term, find other items that the user will be interested in. The other content types could be news articles, blog entries, information from message boards and chat logs, videos, and so on.

Another manifestation of classification terms is when information is extracted from a collection of content items to create relevant keywords. In the previous example, rather than assigning tags or keywords to the term *global warming*, you'd take a set of items that you think best represents the topic and let an automated algorithm extract tags from the set of articles. In essence, you'll get items that are similar to the set of learning items.

In section 4.2, we take a more detailed look at three content types that are normally associated with collective intelligence: blogs, wikis, and groups and message boards. All three of these involve user-generated content. The remaining content types are fairly straightforward.

So far we've looked at some of the different kinds of content that you may use in your application. We need to integrate these content types into our intelligence learning services that we talked about in section 2.1.

4.1.2 Architecture for integrating content

At the beginning of chapter 2, we looked at the architecture for integrating intelligence into your application. Let's extend it for integrating content into your application. Based on your business requirements and existing infrastructure, you'll face one of the following three ways to integrate content into your application:

1 Use standalone, freely available open source or commercial software within your firewall, hosted as a separate instance.
2 Rebuild the basic functionality within your application.
3 Integrate data from an externally hosted site.

This section covers how each of these cases can be integrated into your application to extract data. There are two forms of information that we're interested in:

- The user interaction with the content. This could be in the form of authoring the content, rating it, reading it, bookmarking it, sharing it with others, and so on.
- The actual content itself. We need it to index it in our search engine and extract metadata from it.

Let's look at the first case, in which the functionality is available in a server hosted within your firewall but as a separate instance.

INTERNALLY HOSTED SEPARATE INSTANCE

Figure 4.1 shows the architecture for integrating content from separate servers hosted within your firewall. Here, the application server could either make REST calls to the other server or redirect the HTTP request to the external server. Since all calls go through the application server, both user interaction information and the content when edited can be persisted to the database for use by the intelligence learning services.

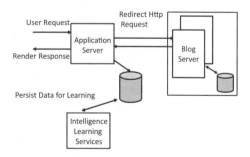

Figure 4.1 Architecture for integrating internally hosted separate instances server

INTEGRATED INTO THE APPLICATION

The second case is when the basic functionality for the feature—for example, blogs—is built within the web app of your application server. You may choose this approach to integrate this functionality into your application when you need a lot more control over the look-and-feel than hosting it as a separate instance. In this case, the architecture for learning is the same as we covered in section 2.1.

EXTERNALLY HOSTED

Many times you may have a relationship with an external vendor to outsource certain features of your application, or need to integrate content from another partner. The simplest way to integrate is to provide a link to the externally hosted server. In essence, as users click on the link, they're transferred to the other site—your application loses the user. There's no information available to your application, unless the external site posts you that information, as to what the user did on the site. If you want to learn from what users did at the external site, you'll need their user-interaction information and the text for the content.

Another challenge is coordinating sessions. The user's session shouldn't time out in your application as she interacts on the other site. Managing single-signons and receiving data are some of the technical challenges that you'll face in this approach. Though this is probably the easiest approach to add new functionality, it's the least user friendly and least desirable approach from an intelligence point of view.

So far, we've classified content into different content types and looked at three ways of integrating them in your application. Next, let's take a more detailed look at a few of the content types that are associated with collective intelligence.

4.2   *The main CI-related content types*

In this section, we look at three content types that are typically associated with collective intelligence: blogs, wikis, and groups and message boards. All these content types are user generated, and users through their opinions and contributions with these content types shape the thoughts of others.

User-generated content plays an important part in influencing others—here's an example of how they affected me last year. Last summer, my printer stopped working after I'd changed the cartridge. After reinstalling the cartridge a few times and trying to print, I gave up. On searching the web, I found an online community where others had written in detail about similar problems with the same brand of printer. Evidently, there was a problem with the way the printing head was designed that caused it to fail occasionally while changing cartridges. Going through the postings, I found that initially a number of users had expressed their frustration at the failure of the printer, promising never to buy again from the vendor. After a few initial postings, I found that someone had left information about how to contact the customer support department for the vendor. The manufacturer was shipping an upgraded version of the printer to anyone who had experienced the problem. The recent postings tended to have a positive tone, as the users got a brand-new printer from the manufacturer. The next morning, I called the manufacturer's customer support number and had a new printer in a few days.

For each of these three content types, we describe what they are and how they are used, and model the various elements and develop the persistence schema. We use blogs as an example to illustrate the process of extracting intelligence from content in the second and third part of the book. It's therefore helpful to understand the structure of a blog in detail.

4.2.1 Blogs

Blogs, short for *weblogs*, are online personal journals where you write about things you want to share with others; others can comment on your entries and link to your site. Blogs typically are written in a diary style and contain links to other websites. There are blogs on virtually every topic; a blog may cover a range of topics from the personal to the political, or focus on one narrow subject.

USE OF BLOGS

As a part of writing this book, I went through numerous blogs. There were blogs on almost every topic covered in this book, as you can see from the references in the various chapters. The popularity of blogs can be measured by both the number of blogs in the blogosphere and the references to blogs that people cite in publications.

Blogs appear in three different contexts:

1 *In a corporate website*—Corporations use blogs to connect with their shareholders, customers, staff, and others. Blogs can be used to solicit feedback on important decisions and policies. Blogs also serve as a good forum for conveying the rationale for certain decisions or policies and for getting feedback on product features that you're developing. An internal blog within the company may be a good medium for groups to collaborate together, especially if they're geographically dispersed. Similarly, consultants often develop their brands and reputations with their blogs.

2 *Within your application*—Applications can leverage blogs both internally and externally by providing contextually relevant information. Allowing users to blog within your application generates additional content that can be viewed by others. User-generated content and blogging in particular can help improve the visibility of your application and boost your search index ranking. If your blog is widely followed, with a number of people linking to it, it'll show up higher in search engine results. Furthermore, if your application or corporate website is linked to your blog, its ranking will be boosted further, since it's connected to a highly linked page.

3 *All other blogs in the blogosphere*—Other blogs in the blogosphere can have an impact on your brand. A favorable blog entry by an influential person can create a buzz around your product, while a negative reference could spell doom for the product.

So far we've looked at what blogs are and how they're used. If you're thinking of building blogs in your application, it's useful to look at the various elements of a blog. Reviewing the class diagram to model blogs and a typical persistence schema for blogs should help you understand the basic elements. This information will also be useful in the next chapter, where we look at searching the blogosphere. We review these next.

MODELING THE ELEMENTS OF BLOG

As shown in figure 4.2, a `Blog` consists of a number of blog entries such as `BlogEntry`—a `BlogEntry` is fully contained in a `Blog`. Associated with a `BlogEntry` are comments made by others, represented as a `List` of `BlogEntryComments`. The `BlogEntry` may

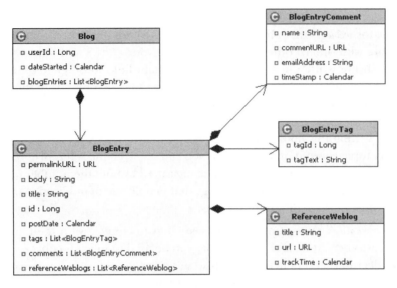

Figure 4.2   Class model for representing a blog for a user

have been tagged by the author; this is contained in `BlogEntryTag`. References by other blogs are contained in a `List` of `ReferenceWeblogs`.

Using the class diagram, we can build a corresponding persistence schema for blogs using five tables, as described in table 4.2.

Table 4.2   Description of the tables used for persistence

Table	Description
blog	Represents the blogs for the various users.
blog entry	Each blog entry is represented as a row. If you allow users to modify their blogs and want to keep a history of changes then you need to keep a version ID. The `version id` is incremented after every modification to the blog-entry.
blog entry history	This is a history table that's updated via a trigger whenever there's a modification to the `BlogEntry` table. The primary key for this table is `blog entry id`, `version id`.
reference-weblog	Stores the list of blogs referencing the blog entry.
blog Entry comment	This stores the list of comments associated with the blog entry.

Figure 4.3 shows the persistence schema for a blog. There are a few things to note about the schema design. If you want to keep a history of modifications made by users in their blog entries, you need to have a `version_id` associated with every blog entry. This gets updated after every modification. There's a corresponding history table `blog_entry_history` that can be populated via a database trigger.

Using the class diagram and the persistence schema, you should have a good understanding of elements of a blog, blog entries, blog comments, and reference

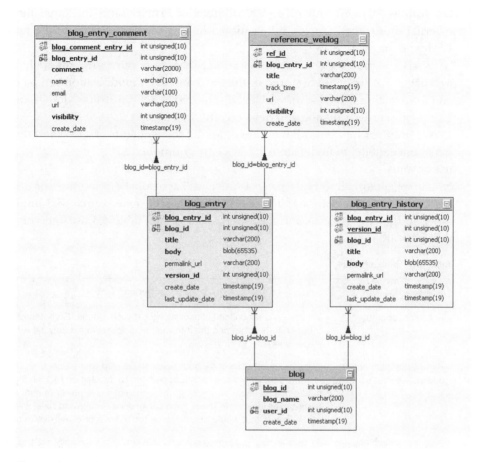

Figure 4.3   Persistence schema for blogs

weblogs. This information is also useful in the next chapter, which deals with searching the blogosphere. Next, we briefly look at the second content type that is associated with collective intelligence: wikis.

4.2.2   *Wikis*

In May 2006, Meebo (www.meebo.com) was getting requests for Spanish-language translations of its application. Meebo is a startup company that uses AJAX to build a browser-based application that can connect to multiple instant messengers in one location. Meebo set up a wiki and allowed their users to submit translations in different languages. Last I checked, there were more than 90 different languages that users were contributing to.

Wikipedia, with more than five million articles in 229 languages, is probably the poster child of how wikis can be used to develop new applications. Wikipedia is cited by Alexa as one of the top 20 visited sites and is widely cited. If you're interested in a topic and search for it, chances are that a Wikipedia article will show up in the first few listings—the breadth of topics, number of articles, and the large number of external sites (blogs, articles, publications) linking to its articles boost the ranking of Wikipedia pages.

Wikis are good for online collaboration, since users can easily edit, add, or delete web pages. All changes are stored in the database. Each modification can be reviewed and information can be reverted back if required. The wiki style of development promotes consensus or democratic views on a topic.

We briefly review how wikis are used. Model the elements of a wiki and develop its persistence model to understand a wiki's core components.

USE OF WIKIS

Nowadays, almost all software projects use a wiki as a collaboration tool for documenting and developing software. There are a number of open source wiki implementations, so the cost associated with having a wiki is low. Table 4.3 list some of the ways that wikis are used.

Table 4.3   Uses of wikis

Use	Description
Online collaboration	They're good for online collaborations between groups. Each person can contribute her thoughts and the information is accessible to anyone with access to the wiki.
Harnessing user contributions—crowd sourcing	Wikis are good at involving your users to develop your product. You may want to start a wiki in your application, perhaps to develop an FAQ, an installation guide, help section, or anything where the collective power of user contributions can be leveraged. Users get a sense of ownership and cover a wide range of use cases that would otherwise be too difficult or expensive to build.
Boosting search engine ranking	As with all user-generated content, wiki content, especially if it's extensively linked, can help improve the search rank visibility of your application.
Knowledge repository	How many times have you been working on a project and someone starts an email chain discussing an issue? As the email chain gets longer and longer, it's more and more difficult and time consuming to keep up with it. This information is also available to only those who participate in the email chain. The barrage of emails can also slow productivity for those who don't want to actively participate in the discussion. Wikis offer an excellent alternative. Unlike email, Wiki content is available for anyone and can be searched and retrieved easily.

There are literally hundreds of Wiki software programs available in dozens of languages (see http://c2.com/cgi/wiki?WikiEngines). Wikipedia has a good comparison between the features of the top WikiEngines at http://en.wikipedia.org/wiki/Comparison_of_wiki_software. There is good information on how to choose a Wiki at http://c2.com/cgi/wiki?ChoosingaWiki.

MODELING THE USERS, PAGES, AND CATEGORIES

Every wiki consists of a number of categories. Within each category are zero or more pages, as shown in figure 4.4. A page can belong to one or more categories.

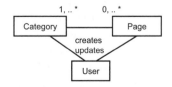

Figure 4.4   Relationship between a page, a category, and a user in a wiki

Users create and edit pages, categories, and the relationship between the pages and the categories.

The category page is an example of the `CompositeContentType` that we introduce in section 4.4 for extracting intelligence.

Figure 4.5 shows a persistence model for a wiki. Also, a *blob* is used for the text of a page, allowing the users to create a large document.

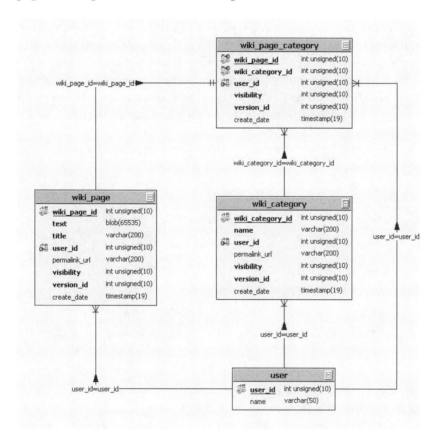

Figure 4.5   Persistence model for a wiki

We've briefly reviewed wikis: what they are, how they're used, the elements of a wiki, and how they can be persisted. Lastly, let's look at the third content type associated with collective intelligence: groups and message boards.

4.2.3   *Groups and message boards*

Message boards are places where you can ask questions and others can respond to them, as well as rate them for usefulness. Message boards are usually associated with groups. A group is a collection of users that share a common interest, where users can participate in threaded conversations. Groups usually have a mailing list associated with them where members can get updates over email. Yahoo! has more than a million groups on virtually every subject, from data mining, to groups on companies, dogs, and marathons. There are hundreds of message boards, and you can find a list of them at http://www.topology.org/net/mb.html and http://dmoz.org/Computers/Internet/On_the_Web/Message_Boards/.

USE OF MESSAGE BOARDS

Groups can be useful in your application for bringing together people with similar interests and tastes. In a blog, people respond to writing by a single user or a group of bloggers, who collectively share the responsibility of writing blog entries; this is especially true in the case of corporate blogs. However, in a group or a message board, any user can pose a question to which others can respond. Message boards along with wikis are more collaborative. Since multiple people can post and comment on questions, message boards need to be moderated and managed to weed out spam and flames. Each entry in a message board should be indexed separately by a search engine.

MODELING GROUPS AND MESSAGE BOARDS

As shown in table 4.4, groups, topics, questions, messages, and users are the main entities for groups and message boards.

Table 4.4   Entities for message boards and groups

Entity	Description
Groups	Collections of users that have a common cause or interest
Topics	Groups consist of a number of topics or categories
Questions	Users pose questions within a topic
Messages	Posted in response to a question or an answer provided
User	Can create, become a member of, view, or rate any of the above entities

As shown in figure 4.6, each group consists of a number of topics; each topic has a number of questions; each question has a number of messages or answers. A user can belong to multiple groups; can create a group, topic, question, or answer; and can rate any of these entities. Again, groups, topics, and question are all examples of CompositeContentTypes, which we discuss in section 4.3. Figure 4.7 shows the schema for the elements of a message board.

In this section, we've looked at three content types that are typically associated with collective intelligence: blogs, wikis, and groups and message boards. We've looked at the elements of these content types, how they're used, and the relationship between

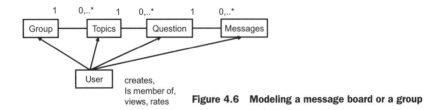

Figure 4.6   Modeling a message board or a group

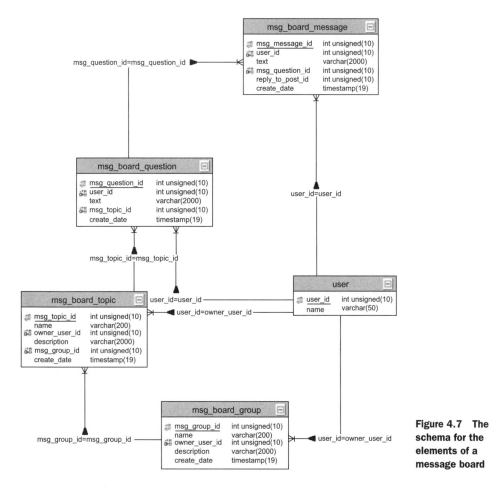

Figure 4.7 The schema for the elements of a message board

their various elements. Now we're ready to take a more detailed look at how intelligence is extracted from analyzing content.

4.3　*Extracting intelligence step by step*

In section 2.2.3, we introduced the use of term vectors to represent metadata associated with text. We also introduced the use of term frequency and inverse document frequency to compute the weight associated with each term. This approach is an example of using the content to generate the metadata. In section 3.3, we demonstrated a collaborative approach using user tagging to generate similar metadata with text.

At this stage, it's helpful to go through an example of how the term vector can be computed by analyzing text. The intent of this section is to demonstrate concepts and keep things simple; therefore we develop simple classes for this example. Later, in chapter 8, we use open source libraries for analyzing text, but going through the code developed in this chapter should give you good insight into the fundamentals involved.

If you haven't done so already, it's worthwhile to review section 2.2.3, which gives an overview of generating metadata (term vectors) from text, and section 3.2.1 on tag clouds, which we use to visualize the data.

Remember, the typical steps involved in text analysis are shown in figure 4.8:

1 *Tokenization*—Parse the text to generate terms. Sophisticated analyzers can also extract phrases from the text.

2 *Normalize*—Convert them to lowercase.

3 *Eliminate stop words—Eliminate terms that appear very often.*

4 *Stemming*—Convert the terms into their stemmed form—remove plurals.

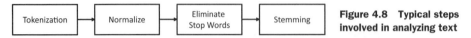

Figure 4.8 Typical steps involved in analyzing text

In this section, we set up the example that we'll use. We first use a simple but naïve way to analyze the text—simply tokenizing the text, analyzing the body and title, and taking term frequency into account. Next, we show the results of the analysis by eliminating the stop words, followed by the effect of stemming. Lastly, we show the effect of detecting phrases on the analysis.

4.3.1 Setting up the example

Let's assume that a reader has posted the following blog entry:

Title: *Collective Intelligence and Web2.0*
Body: *Web2.0 is all about connecting users to users, inviting users to participate, and applying their collective intelligence to improve the application. Collective intelligence enhances the user experience.*

There are a few interesting things to note about the blog entry:

- It discusses collective intelligence, Web 2.0, and how they affect users.
- There are a number of occurrences of *user* and *users*.
- The title provides valuable information about the content.

We've talked about metadata and term vectors; code for this is fully developed in chapter 8. So as not to confuse things for this example, simply think of metadata being represented by an implementation of the interface `MetaDataVector`, as shown in listing 4.1.

Listing 4.1 The `MetaDataVector` interface

```
package com.alag.ci;

import java.util.List;

public interface MetaDataVector {
    public List<TagMagnitude> getTagMetaDataMagnitude() ;
    public MetaDataVector add(MetaDataVector other);
}
```

Gets sorted list of terms and weights

Gives result from adding another MetaDataVector

We have two methods: one for getting the terms and their weights and the second to add another `MetaDataVector`. Further, assume that we have a way to visualize this `MetaDataVector`; after all, it consists of tags or terms and their relative weights.[2]

---

[2] If you really want to see the code for the implementation of the `MetaDataVector`, jump ahead to chapter 8 or download the available code.

Let's define an interface `MetaDataExtractor` for the algorithm that will extract metadata, in the form of keywords or tags, by analyzing the text. This is shown in listing 4.2.

Listing 4.2 The `MetaDataExtractor` interface

```
package com.alag.ci.textanalysis;

import com.alag.ci.MetaDataVector;

public interface MetaDataExtractor {
    public MetaDataVector extractMetaData(String title, String body);
}
```

The interface has only one method, `extractMetaData`, which analyzes the title and body to generate a `MetaDataVector`. The `MetaDataVector` in essence is the term vector for the text being analyzed.

Figure 4.9 shows the hierarchy of increasingly complex text analyzers that we use in the next few sections. First, we use a simple analyzer to create tokens from the text. Next, we remove the common words. This is followed by taking care of plurals. Lastly, we detect multi-term phrases. With this background, we're now ready to have some fun and work through some code to analyze our blog entry!

4.3.2 Naïve analysis

Let's begin by tokenizing the text, normalizing it, and getting the frequency count associated with each term. We also analyze the body and text separately and then combine the information from each. For this we use `SimpleMetaDataExtractor`, which is a naïve implementation for our analyzer, shown in listing 4.3.

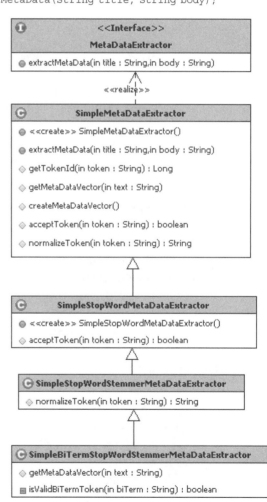

Figure 4.9 The hierarchy of analyzers used to create metadata from text

Listing 4.3 Implementation of the `SimpleMetaDataExtractor`

```
package com.alag.ci.textanalysis.impl;

import java.util.*;
import com.alag.ci.*;
```

```
import com.alag.ci.impl.*;
import com.alag.ci.textanalysis.MetaDataExtractor;

public class SimpleMetaDataExtractor implements MetaDataExtractor {
    private Map<String, Long> idMap = null;                          Keeps
    private Long currentId = null;                  Used to          map of
                                                    generate         all tags
    public SimpleMetaDataExtractor() {              unique           found
        this.idMap = new HashMap<String,Long>();    IDs
        this.currentId = new Long(0);
    }

    public MetaDataVector extractMetaData(String title, String body) {
        MetaDataVector titleMDV = getMetaDataVector(title);         Places equal
        MetaDataVector bodyMDV = getMetaDataVector(body);           weight on title
        return titleMDV.add(bodyMDV);                               and body
    }

    private Long getTokenId(String token) {          Generates
        Long id = this.idMap.get(token);             unique IDs for
        if (id == null) {                            tags found
            id = this.currentId ++;
            this.idMap.put(token, id);
        }
        return id;
    }
}
```

Since the title provides valuable information as a heuristic, let's say that the resulting
`MetaDataVector` is a combination of the `MetaDataVectors` for the title and the body.
Note that as tokens or tags are extracted from the text, we need to provide them with
a unique ID; the method `getTokenId` takes care of it for this example. In your application, you'll probably get it from the `tags` table.

The following code extracts metadata for the article:

```
MetaDataVector titleMDV = getMetaDataVector(title);
MetaDataVector bodyMDV = getMetaDataVector(body);
return titleMDV.add(bodyMDV);
```

Here, we create `MetaDataVectors` for the title and the body and then simply combine
them together.

As new tokens are extracted, a unique ID is assigned to them by the code:

```
private Long getTokenId(String token) {
    Long id = this.idMap.get(token);
    if (id == null) {
        id = this.currentId ++;
        this.idMap.put(token, id);
    }
    return id;
}
```

The remaining piece of code, shown in listing 4.4, is a lot more interesting.

Listing 4.4   Continuing with the implementation of `SimpleMetaDataExtractor`

```
private MetaDataVector getMetaDataVector(String text) {
    Map<String,Integer> keywordMap = new HashMap<String,Integer>();
```

```
StringTokenizer st = new StringTokenizer(text);        ◁─┐ Uses space
while (st.hasMoreTokens()) {                              │ delimited
   String token = normalizeToken(st.nextToken());        │ StringTokenizer
   if (acceptToken(token)) {                    ◁─┐
      Integer count = keywordMap.get(token);       │ Should we accept
      if (count == null) {                         │ token as valid?
         count = new Integer(0);
      }                                        Keeps
      count ++;                                frequency count
      keywordMap.put(token, count);     ◁─┘
   }                                                        Creates
}                                                          MetaDataVector
   MetaDataVector mdv = createMetaDataVector(keywordMap);  ◁─┘
return mdv;
}

protected boolean acceptToken(String token) {   ◁─┐ Method to decide if
   return true;                                   │ token is accepted
}

protected String normalizeToken(String token) {   ◁─┐ Convert to
   String normalizedToken = token.toLowerCase().trim();  │ lowercase/
   if ( (normalizedToken.endsWith(".")) ||               │ remove
      (normalizedToken.endsWith(",")) ) {                │ punctuation
      int size = normalizedToken.length();
      normalizedToken = normalizedToken.substring(0, size -1);
   }
   return normalizedToken;
}
}
```

Here, we use a simple `StringTokenizer` to break the words into their individual form:

```
StringTokenizer st = new StringTokenizer(text);
while (st.hasMoreTokens()) {
```

We want to normalize the tokens so that they're case insensitive—that is, so user and User are the same word—and also remove the punctuation (comma and period).

```
String token = normalizeToken(st.nextToken());
```

The `normalizeToken` simply lowercases the tokens and removes the punctuation:

```
protected String normalizeToken(String token) {
   String normalizedToken = token.toLowerCase().trim();
      if ( (normalizedToken.endsWith(".")) ||
         (normalizedToken.endsWith(",")) ) {
         int size = normalizedToken.length();
         normalizedToken = normalizedToken.substring(0, size -1);
      }
      return normalizedToken;
}
```

We may not want to accept all the tokens, so we have a method `acceptToken` to decide whether a token is to be expected:

```
if (acceptToken(token)) {
```

All tokens are accepted in this implementation.

The logic behind the method is simple: find the tokens, normalize them, see if they're to be accepted, and then keep a count of how many times they occur. Both title and body are equally weighted to create a resulting `MetaDataVector`. With this, we've met our goal of creating a set of terms and their relative weights to represent the metadata associated with the content.

A tag cloud is a useful way to visualize the output from the algorithm. First, let's look at the title, as shown in figure 4.10. The algorithm tokenizes the title and extracts four equally weighted terms: *and, collective, intelligence,* and *web2.0.* Note that *and* appears as one of the four terms and *collective* and *intelligence* are two separate terms.

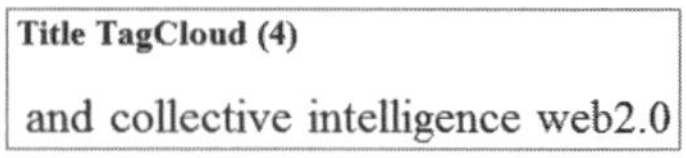

Title TagCloud (4)

and collective intelligence web2.0

Figure 4.10   The tag cloud for the title consists of four terms.

Similarly, the tag cloud for the body of the text is shown in figure 4.11. Note that words such as *the* and *to* occur frequently, and *user* and *users* are treated as separate terms. There are a total of 20 terms in the body.

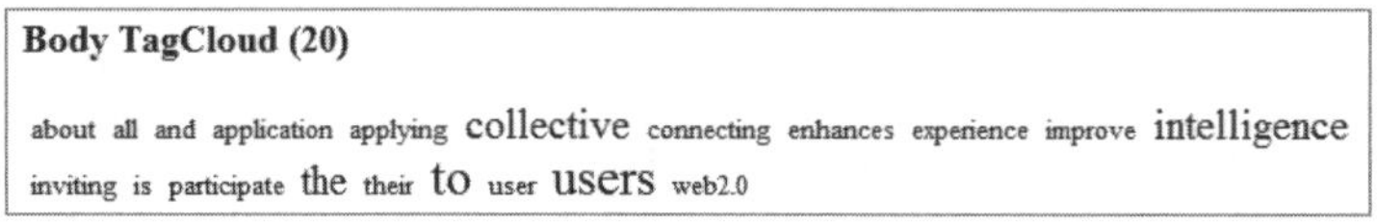

Body TagCloud (20)

about all and application applying collective connecting enhances experience improve intelligence inviting is participate the their to user users web2.0

Figure 4.11   The tag cloud for the body of the text

Combining the vectors for both the title and the body, we get the resulting `MetaData-Vector`, whose tag cloud is shown in figure 4.12.

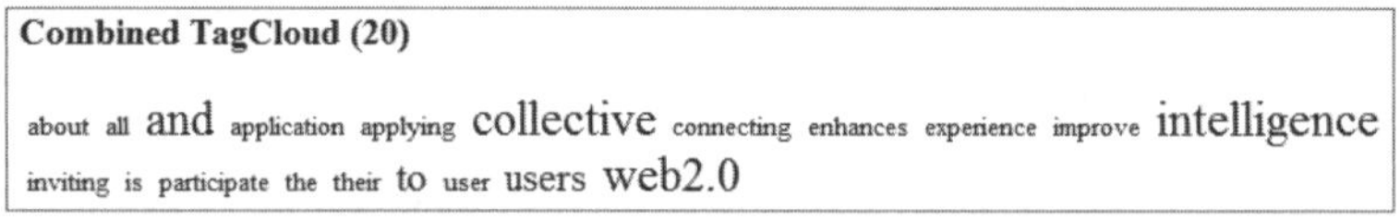

Combined TagCloud (20)

about all and application applying collective connecting enhances experience improve intelligence inviting is participate the their to user users web2.0

**Figure 4.12
The resulting tag cloud obtained by combining the title and the body**

The three terms *collective, intelligence,* and *web2.0* stand out. But there are quite a few noise words such as *all, and, is, the,* and *to* that occur so frequently in the English language that they don't add much value. Let's next enhance our implementation by eliminating these terms.

4.3.3   *Removing common words*

Commonly occurring terms are also called *stop terms* (see section 2.2) and can be specific to the language and domain. We implement `SimpleStopWordMetaDataExtractor` to remove these stop words. The code for this is shown in listing 4.5.

Listing 4.5   Implementation of `SimpleStopWordMetaDataExtractor`

```
package com.alag.ci.textanalysis.impl;

import java.util.*;

public class SimpleStopWordMetaDataExtractor
    extends SimpleMetaDataExtractor {
    private static final String[] stopWords =
```

```
        {"and","of","the","to","is","their","can","all", ""};    ◄─  Dictionary
    private Map<String,String> stopWordsMap = null;                   of stop
                                                                      words
    public SimpleStopWordMetaDataExtractor() {
        this.stopWordsMap = new HashMap<String,String>();
        for (String s: stopWords) {
            this.stopWordsMap.put(s, s);
        }
    }
                                                    Don't accept
                                                    token if stop word
    protected boolean acceptToken(String token) {  ◄──┘
        return !this.stopWordsMap.containsKey(token);
    }
}
```

This class has a dictionary of terms that are to be ignored. In our case, this is a simple list; for your application this list will be a lot longer.

```
    private static final String[] stopWords =
        {"and","of","the","to","is","their","can","all", ""};
```

The `acceptToken` method is overwritten to not accept any tokens that are in the stop word list:

```
    protected boolean acceptToken(String token) {
        return !this.stopWordsMap.containsKey(token);
    }
```

Figure 4.13 shows the tag cloud after removing the stop words. We now have 14 terms from the original 20. The terms *collective, intelligence,* and *web2.0* stand out. But *user* and *users* are still fragmented and are treated as separate terms.

After Removing Stop Words: Combined TagCloud (14)
about application applying collective connecting enhances experience improve intelligence inviting participate user users web2.0

Figure 4.13
The tag cloud after removing the stop words

To combine *user* and *users* as one term, we need to stem the words.

4.3.4   Stemming

Stemming is the process of converting words to their stemmed form. There are fairly complex algorithms for doing this, *Porter stemming* being the most commonly used.

There's only one plural in our example: *users.* For now, we enhance our implementation with `SimpleStopWordStemmerMetaDataExtractor`, whose code is in listing 4.6.

Listing 4.6   Implementation of `SimpleStopWordStemmerMetaDataExtractor`

```
package com.alag.ci.textanalysis.impl;

public class SimpleStopWordStemmerMetaDataExtractor extends
    SimpleStopWordMetaDataExtractor {

    protected String normalizeToken(String token) {      If rejected,
        if (acceptToken(token)) {                   ◄──┘ don't normalize
            token = super.normalizeToken(token);
```

```
        if (token.endsWith("s")) {                      ◁─┐ Normalize
            int index = token.lastIndexOf("s");            │ strings
            if (index > 0) {
                token = token.substring(0, index);
            }
        }
    }
    return token;
}
}
```

Here, we overwrite the `normalizeToken` method. First, it checks to make sure that the token isn't a stop word:

```
protected String normalizeToken(String token) {
    if (acceptToken(token)){
        token = super.normalizeToken(token);
```

Then it simply removes "s" from the end of terms.

Figure 4.14 shows the tag cloud obtained by stemming the terms. The algorithm transforms *user* and *users* into one term: *user.*

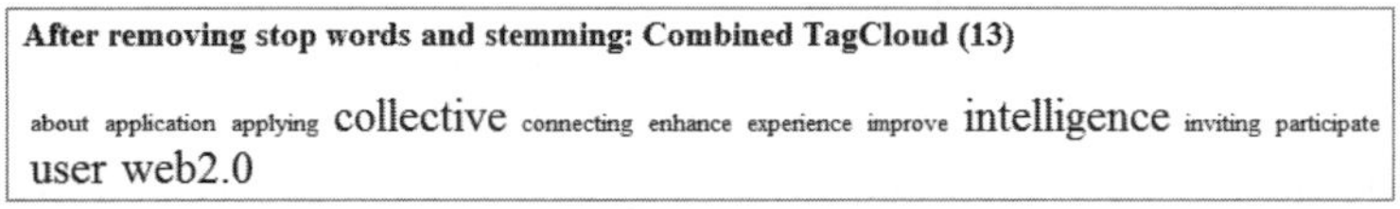

After removing stop words and stemming: Combined TagCloud (13)
about application applying **collective** connecting enhance experience improve intelligence inviting participate user web2.0

**Figure 4.14
The tag cloud
after normalizing
the terms**

We now have four terms to describe the blog entry: *collective, intelligence, user,* and *web2.0.* But *collective intelligence* is really one phrase, so let's enhance our implementation to detect this term.

4.3.5   Detecting phrases

Collective intelligence is the only two-term phrase that we're interested in. For this, we will implement `SimpleBiTermStopWordStemmerMetaDataExtractor`, the code for which is shown in listing 4.7.

Listing 4.7   Implement `SimpleBiTermStopWordStemmerMetaDataExtractor`

```
package com.alag.ci.textanalysis.impl;

import java.util.*;

import com.alag.ci.MetaDataVector;

public class SimpleBiTermStopWordStemmerMetaDataExtractor extends
        SimpleStopWordStemmerMetaDataExtractor {

    protected MetaDataVector getMetaDataVector(String text) {
        Map<String,Integer> keywordMap = new HashMap<String,Integer>();
        List<String> allTokens = new ArrayList<String>();
        StringTokenizer st = new StringTokenizer(text);
        while (st.hasMoreTokens()) {
            String token = normalizeToken(st.nextToken());
            if (acceptToken(token)) {
                Integer count = keywordMap.get(token);
```

```
            if (count == null) {
                count = new Integer(0);
            }
            count ++;
            keywordMap.put(token, count);        ┌─ Store normalized
            allTokens.add(token);        ◄───────┘  tokens in order
        }
    }
    String firstToken = allTokens.get(0);
    for (String token: allTokens.subList(1, allTokens.size())) {
        String biTerm = firstToken + " " + token;
        if (isValidBiTermToken(biTerm)) {     ◄──────┐  Take two tokens
            Integer count = keywordMap.get(biTerm);  │  and check validity
            if (count == null) {
                count = new Integer(0);
            }
            count ++;
            keywordMap.put(biTerm, count);
        }
        firstToken = token;
    }
    MetaDataVector mdv = createMetaDataVector(keywordMap);
    return mdv;                                        ┌─ Phrases tested
}                                                      │  against phrase
                                               ◄──────┘  dictionary
private boolean isValidBiTermToken(String biTerm) {
    if ("collective intelligence".compareTo(biTerm) == 0) {
        return true;
    }
    return false;
}
}
```

Here, we overwrite the `getMetaDataVector` method. We create a list of valid tokens and store them in a list, `allTokens`.

Next, the following code combines two tokens to check whether they're valid:

```
String firstToken = allTokens.get(0);
for (String token: allTokens.subList(1, allTokens.size())) {
    String biTerm = firstToken + " " + token;
    if (isValidBiTermToken(biTerm)) {
```

In our case, there's only one valid phrase, *collective intelligence*, and the check is done in the method.

```
private boolean isValidBiTermToken(String biTerm) {
    if ("collective intelligence".compareTo(biTerm) == 0) {
        return true;
    }
    return false;
}
```

Figure 4.15 shows the tag cloud for the title of the blog after using our new analyzer. As desired, there are four terms: *collective, collective intelligence, intelligence,* and *web2.0.*

Title TagCloud (4)

collective collective intelligence intelligence web2.0

Figure 4.15 Tag cloud for the title after using the bi-term analyzer

The combined tag cloud for the blog now contains 14 terms, as shown in figure 4.16. There are five tags that stand out: *collective, collective intelligence, intelligence, user,* and *web2.0.*

After stop words, stemming, and bi-terms: Combined TagCloud (14)

about application applying collective collective intelligence connecting enhance experience improve intelligence inviting participate user web2.0

Figure 4.16   Tag cloud for the blog after using a bi-term analyzer

Using phrases in the term vector can improve finding other similar content. For example, if we had another article, "Intelligence in a Child," with tokens *intelligence* and *child*, there'd be a match on the term *intelligence*. But if our analyzer was intelligent enough to simply extract *collective intelligence* without the terms *collective* and *intelligence*, there would be no match between the two pieces of content.

Hopefully, this gives you a good overview of how text can be analyzed automatically to extract relevant keywords or tags and build a `MetaDataVector`.

Now, every item in your application has an associated `MetaDataVector`. As users interact on your site, you can use the `MetaDataVector` associated with the items to develop a profile for the user. Finding similar items deals with finding items that have similar `MetaDataVectors`.

Intelligence in your application will manifest itself in three main forms—predictive models, search, and recommendation engines—each of which is covered in the latter half of this book.

In this section, we've worked with a simple example to understand how intelligence can be extracted from text. Text processing involves a number of steps, including creating tokens from the text, normalizing the text, removing common words that aren't helpful, stemming the words to their roots, injecting synonyms, and detecting phrases. With this basic understanding of text processing, we can now tie this back to section 4.1, where we discussed the different content types. For text processing, we can classify content into two types: simple and composite.

4.4   *Simple and composite content types*

In your application, you may want to show related videos for an article, or related blog entries for a product. Classifying the content into content types as done in section 4.4.1 enables you to do this analysis. Basically, you should consider only desired content types as candidate items. The content types we've developed are mutually exclusive; an item can only belong to one content type. Therefore, we enhance the `Item` table introduced in section 2.3.1 to also contain the content type. There's also another table, `content_type`, that contains a list of content types, as shown in figure 4.17.

Figure 4.17 Adding `item_type` to the item table

Based on how the term vectors for the content types are extracted, we can define content types—`SimpleContentType` and `CompositeContentType`—shown in figure 4.18.

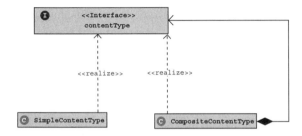

Figure 4.18 Classifying content types

Both the simple and the composite content types are described in table 4.5.

Table 4.5 Content type categorization

Content Type	Description	Examples
Simple content type	Items of this content type aren't dependent on other items .	Articles, photos, video, blogs, polls, products
Composite content type	Items of this content type are dependent on other items.	Questions with their associated set of answers Categorized terms with an associated set of items to describe the term Boards with associated group of messages Categories of items

Note that for certain content types such as questions and answers, answers are fully contained within the context of the question. You typically won't show the answer without the context of the question. The same is true for a list of items that a user may have saved together. The term vectors for `CompositeContentType` are obtained by combining the term vectors for each of their children items. The `MetaDataVector` for a `CompositeContentType` is obtained by combining the `MetaDataVector` for each of its children items.

4.5 *Summary*

Content is the foundation for building applications. It's one of the main reasons why users come to your application. There are a number of different types of content, such as articles, photos, video, blogs, wikis, classification terms, polls, lists, and so forth. These can be created professionally, created by users, or aggregated from external sites. Depending on your business requirements, there are three main ways of integrating content into your application: on a separate server hosted within your firewall, embedded in your application, and linked to an external site.

Intelligence or metadata can be extracted by analyzing text. The process consists of creating tokens, normalizing the tokens, validating them, stemming them, and detecting phrases. This metadata is in addition to the collaborative approach for generating metadata for content that we looked at in chapter 3.

Blogs, wikis, and groups are some ways by which users interact, both within and outside your application. Each tool is potentially useful within your application. User-generated content in your application can boost your search engine ranking, influence users, make your application stickier, and increase the content available in your application.

Content can be classified into simple and composite content types based on how metadata is extracted.

In the last three chapters, we looked at gathering intelligence from information within your application. The next two chapters deal with collecting information from outside your application. Chapter 5 deals with searching the blogosphere for relevant content, while chapter 6 introduces how to crawl the web in search of relevant content. Both techniques can be helpful in aggregating external relevant information for your application.

4.6 *Resources*

"All Things Web 2.0: Message Boards." http://www.allthingsweb2.com/component/ option,com_mtree/task,search/Itemid,26/searchword,message%20boards/cat_id,0/

"Axamol Message Board." http://www.slamb.org/projects/axamol/message-board/

"Blog Software Breakdown." http://asymptomatic.net/blogbreakdown.htm

"Blog software comparison chart." *Online Journalism Review.* http://www.ojr.org/ojr/images/ blog_software_comparison.cfm

"Blogging Strategy 101: A Primer." http://www.scoutblogging.com/blogs101.html

"Blogs Will Change Your Business." May 2, 2005. *BusinessWeek.* http://www.businessweek.com/ magazine/content/05_18/b3931001_mz001.htm

"Blogware choice." http://asymptomatic.net/2004/05/28/2040/blogware-choice

"Building Online Communities, Chromatic." O'Reilly. October 2002. http://www.oreilly-net.com/pub/a/network/2002/10/21/community.html

"Choosing a Wiki", http://c2.com/cgi/wiki?ChoosingaWiki

"Comparison of Wiki Software." http://en.wikipedia.org/wiki/Comparison_of_wiki_software

"Corporate Blogging: Is it worth the hype?" Backbone Media, 2005. http:// www.backbonemedia.com/blogsurvey/blogsurvey2005.pdf

Edelman, Richard. "A Commitment." October 16, 2006. http://www.edelman.com/speak_up/ blog/archives/2006/10/a_commitment.html#trackbacks

Fish, Shlomi. "July 2006 Update to Which Wiki." http://www.shlomifish.org/philosophy/ computers/web/which-wiki/update-2006-07/

———"Which Open Source Wiki Works For You?" November, 2004. http://www.onlamp.com/pub/a/onlamp/2004/11/04/which_wiki.html

———"Fortune 500 Business Blogging Wiki." http://www.socialtext.net/bizblogs/index.cgi

Friedman, Tom. *The World is Flat*. 2005. Penguin Books.

Gardner, Susannah. "Time to check: Are you using the right blogging tool?" *Online Journalism Review*. July 14, 2005. http://www.ojr.org/ojr/stories/050714gardner/

Goodnoe, Ezra. "How To Use Wikis For Business." *InformationWeek*, August 8, 2005. http://informationweek.com/shared/printableArticle.jhtml?articleID=167600331

Green, Heather. "Meebo and its Language Wiki." *BusinessWeek*. July 11, 2006. http://www.businessweek.com/the_thread/blogspotting/archives/2006/07/meebo_and_its_m.html?chan=search

Hof, Rob. "JotSpot Intros Wiki 2.0." *BusinessWeek*. July 24, 2006. http://www.businessweek.com/the_thread/techbeat/archives/2006/07/jotspot_intros.html?chan=search

Holohan, Catherine. "Six Apart's Booming Blogosphere." September 25, 2006. *BusinessWeek*. http://www.businessweek.com/technology/content/sep2006/tc20060925_607937.htm?chan=search

Horrigan, John, and Lee Rainie. "The Internet's Growing Role in Life's Major Moments." http://www.pewinternet.org/pdfs/PIP_Major%20Moments_2006.pdf

"Internet Message Boards." http://www.topology.org/net/mb.html

Kirkby, Jennifer. "Welcome to the Blogosphere." The Customer Management Community. http://www.insightexec.com/newswire_archive/20060322_monthly.html

Lee, Felicia. "Survey of the Blogosphere Finds 12 Million Voices." *New York Times*. July 20, 2006. http://select.nytimes.com/search/restricted/article?res=FA0613F63D5B0C738EDDAE0894DE404482

Li, Charlene. "Blogging policy examples." November 8, 2004. http://forrester.typepad.com/charleneli/2004/11/blogging_policy.html

Lenhrt, Amanda, and Susannah Fox. "Bloggers: A portrait of the internet's new storytellers." July 19, 2006. Pew Internet & American Life Project. http://www.pewinternet.org/PPF/r/186/report_display.asp

Leuf, Bo, and Ward Cunningham. "The Wiki Way: Collaboration and Sharing on the Internet." 2001. Addison Wessley.

"Message Boards." http://dmoz.org/Computers/Internet/On_the_Web/Message_Boards/

"Online Community Toolkit." http://www.fullcirc.com/community/communitymanual.htm

Open Directory, Message Boards. http://dmoz.org/Computers/Internet/On_the_Web/Message_Boards/

"Open Source Bloggers in Java." http://java-source.net/open-source/bloggers

Pilgrim, Mark. "What is RSS?" XML.com. 2002. http://www.xml.com/pub/a/2002/12/18/dive-into-xml.html

Quick, William. "Blogosphere." http://www.iw3p.com/DailyPundit/2001_12_30_dailypundit_archive.php#8315120

"Reports Family, Friends, and Community." http://www.pewinternet.org/report_display.asp?r=47

"Roller open source blog server." http://rollerweblogger.org/

Scoble, Robert, and Shell Israel. "Naked Conversations: How Blogs Are Changing the Way Businesses Talk with Customers." Wiley. 2006.

Sifry, Dave. "State of the Blogosphere, August 2005, Part 1: Blog Growth." August 2, 2005. http://www.technorati.com/weblog/2005/08/34.html

Singer, Suzette Cavanaugh. "NeoMarketing." June, 2006. Class notes, UC SC Extension.

"State of the Blogosphere, April 2006, Part 1: Blog Growth." August 2, 2006. http://technorati.com/weblog/2006/04/96.html

"State of the Blogosphere, August 2005, Part 2: Posting Volume." August 2, 2005. http://technorati.com/weblog/2005/08/35.html

"The Best of Web2.0 Wiki." http://www.allthingsweb2.com/component/option,com_mtree/task,listcats/cat_id,120/Itemid,26/

"Top ten Wiki Engines." http://c2.com/cgi-bin/wiki?TopTenWikiEngines

"Twiki." http://www.twiki.org/

Udell, John. "Year of the enterprise Wiki." *InfoWorld*. December 2004. http://www.infoworld.com/article/04/12/30/01FEtoycollab_1.html

"Virtual Community, Wikipedia." http://en.wikipedia.org/wiki/Virtual_community

"What is Wiki?" Wiki.org. http://wiki.org/wiki.cgi?WhatIsWiki

"Wiki Engines." http://c2.com/cgi/wiki?WikiEngines

Wolley, David. "Forum Software for the Web: An independent guide to discussion forum & message board software." http://thinkofit.com/webconf/forumsoft.htm

"10 Tips for Becoming a Great Corporate Blogger." Backbone Media. http://www.scoutblogging.com/tips.html

Searching the blogosphere 5

This chapter covers

- A brief introduction to the blogosphere
- A framework for searching the blogosphere
- Integrating Technorati and Bloglines
- Integrating MSN and Blogdigger using RSS

In early 2007, Microsoft was slated to launch its much-awaited new operating system—Vista. Perhaps tacitly acknowledging the growing power of the blogosphere—the collection of blogs on the web—and the impact it has in shaping the thoughts of others, a Microsoft employee contacted about 90 influential bloggers in late December 2006, offering them each a laptop, probably worth about $2,000, preloaded with Vista, and encouraging them to blog about their experiences with the new operating system. Leaving aside issues related to ethics and conflict of interest, public relations firms are now reaching out to bloggers, podcasters, and people who post video clips on the Internet to promote their products.

What people say about your product or application has an impact on others and affects your brand—it's important to track what others are saying about your product or application. In this chapter, we look at how we can search the blogosphere to discover nuggets of relevant information. The infrastructure developed here to retrieve blog entries is leveraged in the remaining part of the book to build examples to illustrate various algorithms.

In the previous three chapters, we looked at how to gather information from within your application. Collective intelligence deals with using information both within and outside one's application. In this and the next chapter, we focus on gathering relevant information from outside your application.

In section 4.2.1, we briefly looked at the elements of a blog. Searching for relevant information within blogs in your application is straightforward—index all content with a search engine and derive metadata from it. But harvesting information from the millions of blog entries not within your application is more involved. There are a large number of companies,[1] blog-tracking providers, that are in the business of tracking blogs. These companies provide APIs to query for relevant blog entries, usually using RSS (introduced in section 5.1.2) and/or proprietary APIs.

This chapter shows how to search blog-tracking providers. We leverage this infrastructure again in chapter 9 to illustrate the clustering process, in chapter 10 to illustrate predictive models, in chapter 11 to illustrate a search engine, and in chapter 12 to illustrate building a recommendation engine.

In this chapter, we build a generalized framework so you can start using blog-tracking providers to search blogs. We begin with a brief introduction to the blogosphere, RSS, and blog-tracking providers. Next, we build a generalized framework for searching blogs. This is followed by building the base implementation, which takes care of most of the heavy lifting.

There are a number of blog-tracking providers. Fortunately, most of them provide an RSS API in addition to any proprietary APIs to search for blogs they're tracking. We show how to integrate blog-tracking providers into the framework by integrating Technorati and Bloglines using their proprietary APIs, followed by integrating other providers, MSN and Blogdigger, using RSS 2.0. Other formats and providers can be integrated in a similar manner.

5.1   *Introducing the blogosphere*

People blog on virtually every topic, and there are literally millions of blogs in the blogosphere.[2] Further, people may blog within your application. All these blog entries contain a rich set of information, which when relevant could be valuable to users. The universe of blogs in essence is a good example of collective intelligence in action; here, the collective contributions of millions of people shape the thoughts of others.

In this section, we look at some of the benefits associated with searching the blogosphere; briefly look at RSS, a standard publishing format; and provide an overview of the different blog tracking providers.

5.1.1   *Leveraging the blogosphere*

In the previous chapter, I mentioned that content is the building block for applications. Many times, you have to go outside your application to get relevant content. It's

---

[1] As of September 2008, there were more than 150 companies that tracked various kinds of RSS feeds.
[2] As of September 2008, Technorati was tracking more than 112 million blogs.

common for applications to get news feeds and then show relevant news based on the context and the user. Similarly, the growing blogosphere provides a rich set of content—the collective set of blogs that can shape the minds of others—that can be aggregated and shown when relevant. Continuing with our example, if your application were in the business of selling the latest version of an operating system, perhaps it would be useful to show users blog entries from people who've expressed their experiences in using the new operating system.

Finding relevant content consists of two parts: first you need to aggregate or find content, and second you need to determine whether the context is relevant. This chapter focuses on the first part. You should be able to determine the relevance of the retrieved document to an item of interest using the similarities in the term vectors for the two items. The infrastructure for this similarity computation is developed in chapter 8.

Using the framework developed in this chapter, you should be able to build a feature that periodically queries the blogosphere for relevant blog entries. This could be helpful in protecting your brand; you can automate the retrieval of relevant blog entries and extract keywords to determine either positive or negative comments about your brand. The retrieved items could also be classified for review by a human.

Next, let's briefly look at RSS, one of the key enabling technologies for searching the blogosphere. If you're already familiar with RSS, you can skip this section.

5.1.2 *RSS: the publishing format*

Chances are that there are hundreds of articles or other content that you'd like to keep track of on the Internet. This could be tracking blog entries of your favorite bloggers or following news as it unfolds. It's virtually impossible to manually go and check for updates for each of these. Fortunately, software is pretty good at automating this repetitive task. Most sites publish their content in a standard format, RSS, that's understood by programs such as RSS readers or aggregators, which automatically check for updates and retrieve new content when available.

RSS allows you to publish content to the Web in an XML format that's commonly understood and also track other sites for updates using a similar format. Formats for publishing content on the Web have existed from the early days of the Internet. RSS has a rich history, and the acronym *RSS* stands for different things, as we'll soon see. Given the various formats, it's helpful to spend a few minutes understanding its history.

In March 1999, the first version of RSS[3]—RDF Site Summary—was created by Netscape. This version became known as RSS 0.9. There were two camps in the RSS community. The first camp wanted to make better use of RDF in RSS, while the other camp wanted to simplify the format and remove RDF. A few months later, in June 1999, Dan Libby produced a prototype called RSS 0.91 that simplified the format, removed all reference to RDF, and incorporated parts of an earlier syndication format created by Dave Winer, an influential blogger from Userland Software. In this version, RSS stood for *Rich Site Summary*. In late December 2000, Dave Winer released RSS 0.92, and then released a final version in September 2002, known as RSS 2.0. Here, RSS stands for *Really*

---

[3] Resource Description Framework—a language for describing resources on the web

Simple Syndication; RSS 2.0 is the most widely used newsfeed format. But there's more to this story.

In 2003, a group of influential bloggers and XML experts got together to develop a new newsfeed format known as Atom. Almost every part of RSS 2.0 is optional, and developers can extend the specification by using namespace-qualified vocabularies. This vagueness caused issues with interoperability among different vendor implementations. The influential bloggers joined forces with the Internet Engineering Task Force (IETF) and aimed to develop a new format that was

> *100 percent vendor-neutral, implemented by everybody, freely extensible by anybody, and cleanly and thoroughly specified.*
>
> —The Atom Wiki, June 2003.
> http://www.intertwingly.net/wiki/pie/RoadMap

IETF developed the Atom Publishing Format and Atom Publishing Protocol, and released Atom as an internet standard in 2005. Most blog search providers, with the exception of Blogger.com, provide results in RSS 2.0 format (see http://blogs.law. harvard.edu/tech/rss). Blogger.com provides results in the Atom format.

Listing 5.1 shows a sample of an RSS 2.0 output from Blogdigger.com. We later use this listing in section 5.6 to integrate Blogdigger. Each channel has a number of different `<item>`s associated with it. This XML snippet gives you a sense of the elements used in RSS 2.0, perhaps the most commonly used RSS version.

Listing 5.1   Example of RSS 2.0 from Blogdigger.com

```
<rss version="2.0">
  <channel>
    <title>Blogdigger search for collective intelligence</title>
    <link>://www.blogdigger.com/search/collective+intelligence</link>
    <description>Blogdigger search for collective intelligence
    </description>
    <ttl>60</ttl>
    <image>
       <url>http://www.blogdigger.com/images/blogd_logo01a.gif</url>
       <title>Blogdigger search for collective intelligence</title>
       <link>http://www.blogdigger.com/search?q=collective+intelligence
       </link>
       <width>144</width>
       <height>55</height>
    </image>
  <item>
     <title>Water - the basic system flow and missing learning …</title>
     <link>http://waterangels.blogspot.com/2006/12/water-basic-system-
flow-and-missing.html</link>
     <description>When info from our various network … ….</description>
     <pubDate>Mon, 1 Jan 2007 00:38:00 EST</pubDate>

     <source url="http://waterangels.blogspot.com/atom.xml">what the …
     </source>
     <author>macrae.nets</author>
  </item>
</channel>
<?xml version="1.0" encoding="UTF-8"?></rss>
```

If you want to find out more about RSS, Manning has an excellent book on RSS and Atom, *RSS and Atom in Action: Web 2.0 Building Blocks*, by Dave Johnson. Chapter 12 of the book, *Searching and Monitoring the Web*, also presents a good overview of blog search engines.

Next, let's look at companies that are in the business of tracking blogs and other RSS newsfeeds.

5.1.3   *Blog-tracking companies*

Fueled by the growth of the self-publishing phenomenon, a large number of companies track what's being published on the Web. As of early 2008, there were more than 40 blog-search engines; some of the best are Technorati, Google, Yahoo!, MSN, Sphere, IceRocket, Bloglines, Blogdigger, DayPop, Zopto, Postami, and Read A Blog.

If you publish content, you want others to find it. This is most easily done by notifying blog-tracking providers of the change. A number of companies allow you to notify multiple blogs and feed-tracking providers. By pinging these providers, you're notifying these services that content on your site has changed, and they then crawl your site to get the new content and publish it. By pinging these services, you decrease how long it takes before your content is published by these content-tracking providers. Pingoat (http://www.pingoat.com/), Pingomatic (http://pingomatic.com/), Blogflux (http://pinger.blogflux.com/), Feedshark (http://feedshark.brainbliss.com/), and King Ping (http://kping.com/) are examples of services that ping multiple providers.

APIs provided by these providers typically include the ability to search for relevant blogs using search terms or tags, as well as information on who's connecting to various blogs using either HTTP Get or HTTP Post. We discuss these kinds of APIs in sections 5.4 and 5.5.

With this background, we're now ready to build a framework to search the blogosphere. We follow a step-by-step approach, beginning with a generalized framework, building the base classes, and then integrating various providers.

5.2   *Building a framework to search the blogosphere*

Given the large number of blog-tracking providers, chances are that you may want to integrate more than one of them in your application. The framework we develop in this chapter abstracts out the differences between the APIs for these different providers; thus it's easy for your application to add new providers and not be coupled to a specific API or a single provider.

As shown in figure 5.1, there are four steps involved in searching the blogosphere:

1   Create a query that's submitted to a blog searcher.
2   The blog searcher translates this query into a format that can be understood by the blog-tracking provider and sends this information to the provider using either HTTP Get or HTTP Post.
3   The blog-tracking provider processes the request and sends back an XML response.
4   The response is parsed by the blog searcher and a response in a standard format is sent back to the client.

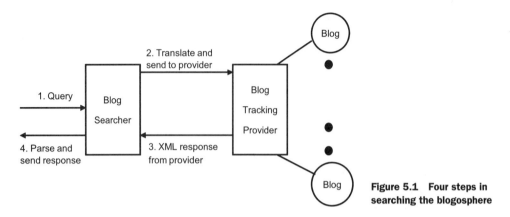

Figure 5.1   Four steps in searching the blogosphere

Therefore, to develop a generic framework, we need the four main interfaces that are shown in figure 5.2:

- `BlogQueryParameter`: captures the query made by the client
- `BlogSearcher`: translates and submits the query to the provider
- `BlogSearchResponseHandler`: used by the BlogSearcher to process the response XML
- `BlogQueryResult`: the canonical response to query

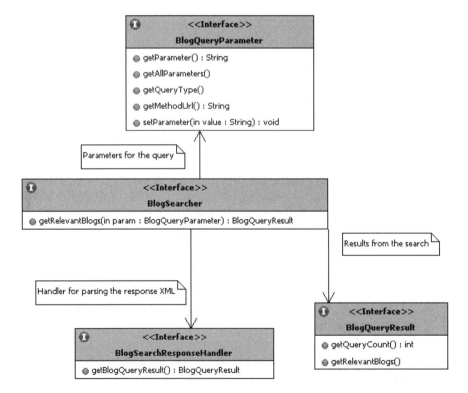

Figure 5.2   The generic architecture for the blog searcher

Next, let's look at each of these main interfaces. The API is fairly generic, using generic objects as input to the methods and for the results from the query. The API should be resilient to changes as you integrate more blog-tracking providers.

5.2.1 *The searcher*

The `BlogSearcher` is the main class that coordinates the process of searching. Listing 5.2 shows the `BlogSearcher` interface.

Listing 5.2 `BlogSearcher` interface

```
package com.alag.ci.blog.search;

public interface BlogSearcher {
    public BlogQueryResult getRelevantBlogs(BlogQueryParameter param)
        throws BlogSearcherException;          ◁─┐ Return relevant blogs
}                                                 │ using query parameters
```

BlogSearcher contains only one method:

```
public BlogQueryResult getRelevantBlogs(BlogQueryParameter param)
        throws BlogSearcherException;
```

which takes a `BlogQueryParameter`, returns a `BlogQueryResult`, and throws a `BlogSearcherException`.

Next, let's look at the input to the search: `BlogQueryParameter`.

5.2.2 *The search parameters*

Parameters for the search are encapsulated in the `BlogQueryParameter` interface, whose code is shown in listing 5.3.

Listing 5.3 The `BlogQueryParameter` interface

```
package com.alag.ci.blog.search;

import java.util.Collection;
                                               ┌ Type of
public interface BlogQueryParameter {          │ search
    public enum QueryType {SEARCH,TAG};    ◁───┘
    public enum QueryParameter {KEY, APIUSER, START_INDEX, LIMIT,
      QUERY, TAG,SORTBY, LANGUAGE};                       ◁─┐ Type of query
                                                            │ parameters
    public String getParameter(QueryParameter param);
    public void setParameter(QueryParameter param, String value);
    public Collection<QueryParameter> getAllParameters();
    public QueryType getQueryType();
    public String getMethodUrl();
}
```

There are two enums: `QueryType` and `QueryParameter`. There are two types of queries that can be made—search by a query string or search by a specified tag:

```
enum QueryType {SEARCH,TAG};
```

You may want to generalize to additional search commands in your application. Similarly, the following

```
public enum QueryParameter {KEY, APIUSER, START_INDEX, LIMIT,
  QUERY, TAG, SORTBY, LANGUAGE};
```

specifies the different parameters that can be set for the query. It's nearly impossible to list all parameters (a lot of them optional) across the various blog-tracking providers. The enumerated list is the subset of features that we support in our API. Table 5.1 contains a description of the QueryParameters.

Table 5.1 Description of the QueryParameters

QueryParameter	Description
KEY, APIUSER	A unique-token KEY and APIUSER name that may need to be passed to the provider. This key and name identify the caller to the provider. The provider may authenticate if the caller has privileges to make the call. This also gives the provider the capability to charge for calls made if required.
START_INDEX, LIMIT	There may be a large number of results available from the query. Typically, LIMIT specifies the maximum number of results returned from the START INDEX. For example, if there are 100 results, specifying START INDEX of 20 and LIMIT of 10 will return results 20–29.
QUERY, TAG	The query string is populated either as a QUERY or a TAG based on whether we're interested in search queries or tag related blog entries.
SORTBY	Specifies how the results should be sorted, for example, by date or title.
LANGUAGE	Language of blog entries.

There are two methods to retrieve the QueryParameter:

```
String getParameter(QueryParameter param);
Collection<QueryParameter> getAllParameters();
```

The URL for connecting to a provider is dependent on the type of search and the provider. This can be retrieved using String getMethodUrl();. This doesn't need to be specified by the calling client code. We'll build implementations of QueryParameter that automatically set the URL for each provider.

Next, let's look at how results are returned by the BlogSearcher.

5.2.3 *The query results*

BlogQueryResult is a container object that contains the result of the blog search query, as shown in figure 5.3. For building a generic API that will be resilient to changes over time, it's almost always better to return a rich object such as the container Blog-QueryResult rather than just a List. You can add more details to the BlogQuery-Result, perhaps by how long the query took or whether multiple blog-tracking providers were queried. Listing 5.4 shows the code for the BlogQueryResult, which consists of two methods.

Listing 5.4 The BlogQueryResult interface

```
package com.alag.ci.blog.search;
import java.util.List;
```

```
public interface BlogQueryResult {
    public Integer getQueryCount();          ←——— Returns total
    public List<RetrievedBlogEntry> getRelevantBlogs();  number of results
}                                                                    Returns list of
                                                                     blog entries
```

The number of results returned by the query is accessed through the following method:

```
int getQueryCount();
```

Note that this count is the total number of results, not necessarily the same as the number of blog entries retrieved in this query. The list of blog entries retrieved is

```
List<RetrievedBlogEntry> getRelevantBlogs();
```

`RetrievedBlogEntry` represents one retrieved blog entry, and its specification is shown in figure 5.3. The attributes of `RetrievedBlogEntry` are a subset of all the attributes of a blog entry (see `BlogEntry` in section 4.3.1) and represent common attributes that are available across different blog-tracking providers. Note that some providers may expose only a subset of these attributes in their APIs. `RetrievedBlogEntry` contains the name of the blog, `getName()`, which is different from the title of the blog entry, `String getTitle();`.

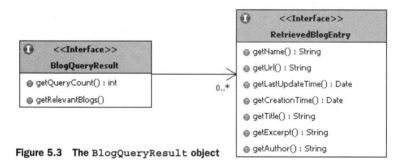

Figure 5.3   The `BlogQueryResult` object

The `BlogSearcher` normally receives an XML response from the provider. This XML is handled by a `BlogSearchResponseHandler`, which parses the response and converts it into `BlogQueryResult`.

5.2.4   *Handling the XML response*

The response XML received from a provider is handled by `BlogSearchResponse-Handler`. The `BlogSearchResponseHandler` interface, as shown in figure 5.4, consists of a single method, `getBlogQueryResult()`. For parsing the XML results, it uses `Xml-Token` objects, corresponding to the XML tags.

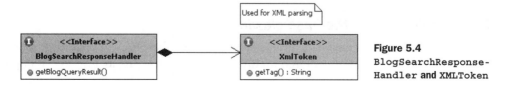

Figure 5.4
`BlogSearchResponse-`
`Handler` **and** `XMLToken`

Listing 5.5 contains the code for the interface `BlogSearchResponseHandler`.

Listing 5.5 The `BlogSearchResponseHandler` interface

```
package com.alag.ci.blog.search;

public interface BlogSearchResponseHandler {                    Retrieves result
    public BlogQueryResult getBlogQueryResult();    ◁──┘       from blog query
}
```

The code `BlogQueryResult getBlogQueryResult();` returns the resulting result object from the parsed XML.

The SAX parsing deals with tokens, which are represented by the interface shown in figure 5.4. The `XmlToken` interface has only one method, `String getTag();`, which returns the associated XML tag.

A number of exceptions can be thrown while talking to external providers. Next, let's look at how exceptions are handled in the framework.

5.2.5 Exception handling

All exceptions are wrapped in a common exception, `BlogSearcherException`, which is used for throwing exceptions throughout the package. Listing 5.6 contains the code for the `BlogSearcherException`, which is a *checked exception*, so the caller code needs to handle it.

Listing 5.6 Implementation of `BlogSearcherException`

```
package com.alag.ci.blog.search;

public class BlogSearcherException extends Exception {
    public BlogSearcherException(String message, Throwable cause) {   ◁──┐
        super(message, cause);
    }                                                        Constructor to
    public BlogSearcherException(String message) {           chain exceptions
        super(message);
    }
}
```

The constructor `BlogSearcherException` nests the underlying `Throwable`, and the new exception is created with the original cause attached, as is typically done with chained exceptions.

So far we've looked at the process of searching the blogosphere and introduced interfaces for the main entities that will be used in our framework. Next, let's implement the base classes for these interfaces. Provider-specific implementations will extend these base classes.

5.3 Implementing the base classes

We'd like most of the heavy lifting to be done by the base implementations, so as to minimize the amount of code required to integrate a new provider. Next, we implement each of the interfaces introduced in the previous section; we begin with an easy one: `BlogQueryParameterImpl`.

5.3.1 Implementing the search parameters

Each provider has a unique URL, and we'll have multiple implementations of the `BlogQueryParameter` that will extend from the base class `BlogQueryParameterImpl`.

   `BlogQueryParameterImpl` is an abstract class, whose implementation is shown in listing 5.7.

Listing 5.7   Implementation of `BlogQueryParameterImpl`

```
package com.alag.ci.blog.search.impl;

import java.util.*;

import com.alag.ci.blog.search.BlogQueryParameter;

public abstract class BlogQueryParameterImpl
implements BlogQueryParameter {                               Uses Map to store
    private Map<QueryParameter,String> params = null;    ⊲─┘  QueryParameters
    private QueryType queryType = null;
    private String methodUrl = null;

    public BlogQueryParameterImpl(QueryType queryType, String methodUrl)  ⊲┐
        this.queryType = queryType;
        this.methodUrl = methodUrl;                            Constructor to
        this.params = new HashMap<QueryParameter,String>();    set queryType
    }                                                          and methodUrl

//get methods

    public void setParameter(QueryParameter param, String value) {
      this.params.put(param, value);
    }
}
```

`BlogQueryParameterImpl` uses the following to store the `QueryParameters`:

```
private Map<QueryParameter,String> params = null;
```

It also has a variable `QueryType` to store the type of query being made and `methodUrl` to store the provider URL. The rest of the code consists of get methods for the three attributes. The constructor `BlogQueryParameterImpl` sets the `queryType` and the `methodUrl`. There are no set methods for these two attributes—the derived classes will pass these two attributes to the constructor.

   Next, let's look at implementing the result objects.

5.3.2 Implementing the result objects

As shown in figure 5.5, `BlogQueryResultImpl` implements `BlogQueryResult`. `Null-BlogQueryResultImpl` extends `BlogQueryResultImpl` and represents the case when there are no results found for a blog query.

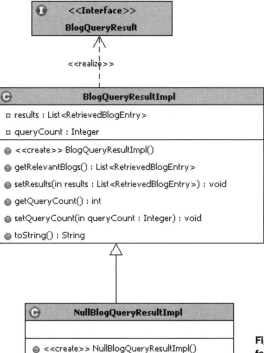

**Figure 5.5   Two implementations
for** `BlogQueryResult`

The implementation of `BlogQueryResultImpl` is straightforward. It consists of two
attributes. The first stores the `List` of retrieved blog entries:

```
private List<RetrievedBlogEntry> results = null;
```

The other stores the query count:

```
private Integer queryCount = null;
```

`NullBlogQueryResultImpl` extends `BlogQueryResultImpl` and has a constructor that
sets the results `List` to an empty `Collections.EMPTY_LIST`:

```
public NullBlogQueryResultImpl() {
   super();
   this.setResults(Collections.EMPTY_LIST);
}
```

The method `getRelevantBlogs` returns a `List` of `RetrievedBlogEntry` objects,
which is implemented by `RetrievedBlogEntryImpl`. `RetrievedBlogEntryImpl` is a
JavaBean object with seven attributes to implement the interface `RetrievedBlog-
Entry`. There are standard get and set methods and a `toString` method to print out
the attributes.

So far we've implemented the classes for representing the query and the results.
Next, let's look at the implementation of the `BlogSearcher`, which is responsible for
coordinating the search.

5.3.3 *Implementing the searcher*

Implementations of `BlogSearcher` are responsible for converting the input query from the client into a format that the blog-tracking provider can understand and then processing the XML response back from the provider. Figure 5.6 shows the base implementation for the `BlogSearcher`. Note that there is only one public method that needs to be implemented:

```
public BlogQueryResult getRelevantBlogs(BlogQueryParameter param)
        throws BlogSearcherException {
```

We use SAX[4] parsing to process the XML returned by the provider. We use JAXP[5]—a small layer on top of SAX—to plug in parsers from different vendors without changing

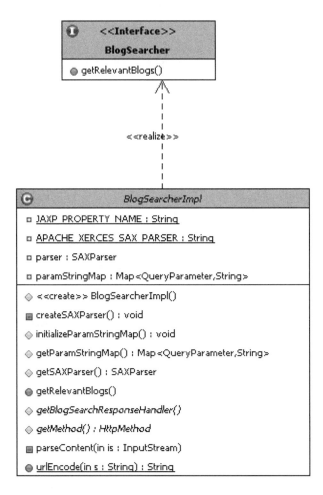

Figure 5.6   Base implementation for `BlogSearcher`

---

[4] http://www.saxproject.org/apidoc/overview-summary.html
[5] http://java.sun.com/webservices/jaxp/index.jsp

the basic code. We use the Apache Xerces-J[6] parser. SAX parsing consists of creating a content handler and invoking the parser with the content handler.

Communication with blog-tracking providers occurs using the Hypertext Transfer Protocol (HTTP). The `java.net` class provides basic functionality for accessing resources via HTTP. However, the Apache Jakarta Commons `HttpClient`[7] package provides an easy way to use the HTTP protocol. This open source project follows the Apache Source License and provides flexibility for source and binary reuse.

NOTE You can download the `HttpClient` library from http://jakarta.apache.org/commons/httpclient/downloads.html. Don't forget to also download the dependent jar files: commons-codec.jar and commons-logging.jar.

Listing 5.8 contains the first half of the code for `BlogSearcherImpl`. This half deals with creating the SAX parser.

Listing 5.8 First half of `BlogSearcherImpl`—SAX parser

```
package com.alag.ci.blog.search.impl;

import java.io.*;                    ◁─────┐  See downloaded
import java.net.URLEncoder;                │  code for full list
import java.util.*;

import javax.xml.parsers.*;

import org.apache.commons.httpclient.*
import org.apache.commons.httpclient.params.HttpMethodParams;
import org.xml.sax.SAXException;
import org.xml.sax.helpers.DefaultHandler;

import com.alag.ci.blog.search.*;
import com.alag.ci.blog.search.BlogQueryParameter.QueryParameter;

public abstract class BlogSearcherImpl implements BlogSearcher {
   private static final String JAXP_PROPERTY_NAME =     ◁──────┐ Sets name
      "javax.xml.parsers.SAXParserFactory";                    │ of SAX
   private static final String APACHE_XERCES_SAX_PARSER =      │ parser
      "org.apache.xerces.jaxp.SAXParserFactoryImpl";           │ factory

   private SAXParser parser = null;
   private Map<QueryParameter, String> paramStringMap = null;

   protected BlogSearcherImpl() throws BlogSearcherException {
      createSAXParser();          ◁─────┐                          Creates instance
      initializeParamStringMap();        │  Creates instance       of parser factory
   }                                     │  of SAX parser

   private void createSAXParser() throws BlogSearcherException {
      if (System.getProperty(JAXP_PROPERTY_NAME) == null) {
        System.setProperty(JAXP_PROPERTY_NAME,APACHE_XERCES_SAX_PARSER);─┐
      }                                                                  │
      SAXParserFactory factory = SAXParserFactory.newInstance();  ◁──────┘
      try {
```

---

[6] http://xerces.apache.org/xerces2-j/
[7] http://jakarta.apache.org/commons/httpclient/

```
      this.parser = factory.newSAXParser();
    } catch(ParserConfigurationException e) {
      throw new BlogSearcherException("SAX parser not found",e);
    } catch(SAXException se) {
      throw new BlogSearcherException("SAX exception",se);
    }
  }
}
```
Uses factory to create instance of parser

```
  protected void initializeParamStringMap() {
    paramStringMap = new HashMap<QueryParameter, String>();
  }

  protected Map<QueryParameter, String> getParamStringMap() {
    return paramStringMap;
  }

  protected SAXParser getSAXParser() {
    return this.parser;
  }
```

The system property javax.xml.parsers.SAXParserFactory needs to be set to specify which instance of the SAX parser is to be used. This is set to org.apache.xerces.jaxp.SAXParserFactoryImpl in our case. The constructor creates an instance of the SAX parser:

```
  protected BlogSearcherImpl() throws BlogSearcherException {
    createSAXParser();
```

For this, it first creates a SAXParserFactory:

```
SAXParserFactory factory = SAXParserFactory.newInstance();
```

And through the factory, it creates an instance of the parser:

```
this.parser = factory.newSAXParser();
```

The attribute paramStringMap stores a Map of QueryParameters and their values.

Next, let's look at listing 5.9, which deals with submitting an HTTP request and handling the XML response.

Listing 5.9 Second half of BlogSearcherImpl—HTTP and parsing response

```
public BlogQueryResult getRelevantBlogs(BlogQueryParameter param)
    throws BlogSearcherException {
  BlogQueryResult result = new NullBlogQueryResultImpl();
  HttpClient client = new HttpClient();
  HttpMethod method = getMethod(param);
    method.getParams().setParameter(HttpMethodParams.RETRY_HANDLER,
      new DefaultHttpMethodRetryHandler(3, false));

  try {
    int statusCode = client.executeMethod(method);
    if (statusCode == HttpStatus.SC_OK) {
      InputStream is = method.getResponseBodyAsStream();
      result = parseContent(is);
      is.close();
    }
```
Initialized with null response

Could be POST or GET

Custom retry

Execute method

Parse content

```
      } catch (HttpException he) {
         throw new BlogSearcherException("HTTP exception ", he);
      } catch (IOException ioe) {
         throw new BlogSearcherException(
               "IOException while getting response body", ioe);
      } finally {
         method.releaseConnection();
      }
      return result;
   }

   protected abstract HttpMethod getMethod(BlogQueryParameter param);

   protected abstract BlogSearchResponseHandler
      getBlogSearchResponseHandler();

   private BlogQueryResult parseContent(InputStream is)
      throws BlogSearcherException {
      try {
         BlogSearchResponseHandler h = getBlogSearchResponseHandler();
         this.getSAXParser().parse(is, (DefaultHandler) h);
         return h.getBlogQueryResult();
      } catch (SAXException se) {
         throw new BlogSearcherException("Error parsing Response XML",
               se);
      } catch (IOException ioe) {
         throw new BlogSearcherException("IOException while parsing
               XML", ioe);
      }
   }
   public static String urlEncode(String s) {
      String result = s;
      try {
         result = URLEncoder.encode(s, "UTF-8");
      } catch (UnsupportedEncodingException e) {
         System.out.println("Unsupported encoding exception thrown");
      }
      return result;
   }
}
```

> Parse content using custom handler

> GET methods must be URL-encoded

> UTF-8 is supported

Initially, the result `BlogQueryResult` is initialized to a null implementation, in case of no response back from the provider:

```
BlogQueryResult result = new NullBlogQueryResultImpl();
```

The code first creates an instance of the `HttpClient`:

```
HttpClient client = new HttpClient();
```

Next, it creates an instance of `HttpMethod`, either Get or Post:

```
HttpMethod method = getMethod(param);
```

The `getMethod()` method is abstract and will be implemented by the inheriting classes. The method is executed on the client and a status code is returned, which can be used to determine if the request was successful.

There are two kinds of exceptions that can be thrown:

- *HttpException*—Represents a logical error.
- *IOException*—Represents a transport error. This is likely to be an I/O error.

The following code sets the default recovery procedure to recover when a plain `IOException` is thrown:

```
method.getParams().setParameter(HttpMethodParams.RETRY_HANDLER,
            new DefaultHttpMethodRetryHandler(3, false));
```

`HttpClient` will retry the request three times, provided the request was never fully submitted to the blog-tracking provider.

Next, the response back from the provider is read in as a stream:

```
InputStream is = method.getResponseBodyAsStream();
result = parseContent(is);
```

The `parseContent()` method gets the appropriate response handler to parse the response.

Parameters for get methods need to be URL-encoded—for example, *collective intelligence* gets converted to *collective+intelligence*. The following code

```
public static String urlEncode(String s)
```

is available for inheriting classes to encode the parameters using UTF-8 encoding, which is the recommended encoding scheme.

In this section, we developed the base class for coordinating the search. The last class to be implemented is the base class for handling the XML response.

5.3.4 *Parsing XML response*

An implementation of the `BlogSearchResponseHandler` is responsible for parsing the XML response from the provider and creating a `BlogQueryResult`. `BlogSearch-ResponseHandlerImpl` is the base class that other instances extend. This base class does most of the heavy lifting for writing a specific implementation of `BlogSearchResponse-Handler`. Figure 5.7 shows the methods in `BlogSearchResponseHandlerImpl`. `Default-Handler`[8] is the base class for SAX event handlers and contains default implementations for the callbacks.

For consistency across the different parsers, we use Java 1.5's `Enum`[9] capabilities. Each XML file has different tokens for the returning values. Each of the XML tokens that we're interested in is enumerated in an `Enum` that implements the `XMLToken` interface. This abstraction helps factor a lot of the XML processing out to the base class.

Typically, the retrieved response from the providers contains date strings; for example, the last updated time for the blog entry or the date the blog entry was created. Unfortunately, different providers use different formats for the date string.

---

[8] http://java.sun.com/j2se/1.4.2/docs/api/org/xml/sax/helpers/DefaultHandler.html
[9] http://java.sun.com/j2se/1.5.0/docs/guide/language/enums.html

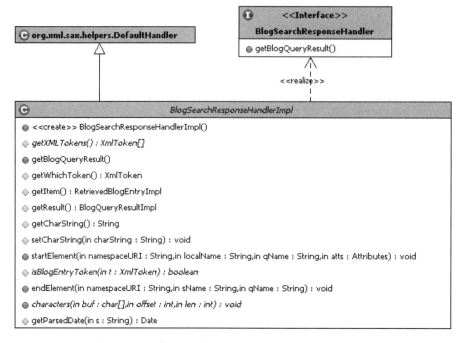

Figure 5.7   The base class for SAX parsing handlers

"Mon, 01 Jan 2007 04:20:38 GMT" and "24 Dec 06 01:44:00 UTC" are examples of date formats that are returned from providers—refer to table 5.2 for a more complete list. A `DateFormat` object is used to parse the `String` into a `Date` object.

Table 5.2   The different date formats returned by the different providers

Date format	Example	Blog-tracking providers
yyyy-MM-dd HH:mm:ss	2008-01-10 11:25:56	Technorati—tag search
EEE, dd MMM yy HH:mm:ss zzz	Mon, 01 Jan 2007 04:20:38 GMT	Bloglines
yyyy-MM-dd HH:mm:ss zzz	2007-01-10 19:21:49 GMT	Technorati—query search
dd MMM yy HH:mm:ss zzz	24 Dec 06 01:44:00 UTC	RSS feed, MSN, Blogdigger

With that overview, let's look at listing 5.10, which has the first part of the code for `BlogSearchResponseHandlerImpl`. This listing shows the constructor along with the attributes for the class.

Listing 5.10   Constructor and attributes for `BlogSearchResponseHandlerImpl`

```
package com.alag.ci.blog.search.impl;

import java.text.*;
import java.util.*;
```

```
import org.xml.sax.*;
import org.xml.sax.helpers.DefaultHandler;

import com.alag.ci.blog.search.*;

public abstract class BlogSearchResponseHandlerImpl extends
  DefaultHandler implements BlogSearchResponseHandler {
    private BlogQueryResultImpl result = null;              ⟵─┐ Stores result
    private List<RetrievedBlogEntry> entries = null;
    private RetrievedBlogEntryImpl item = null;
    private XmlToken whichToken = null;              ⟵──┐ Tracks which token
    private Map<String, XmlToken> tagMap = null;        │ is being parsed
    private String charString = null;
    private DateFormat dateFormat = null;
    private DateFormat timeZoneDateFormat = null;        ⟵─┐ Formats for handling
    private DateFormat timeZoneDayDateFormat = null;        │ date parsing
    private DateFormat timeZoneYearDateFormat = null;

    public BlogSearchResponseHandlerImpl() {
        this.result = new BlogQueryResultImpl();
        this.entries = new ArrayList<RetrievedBlogEntry>();
        this.result.setResults(this.entries);
        this.tagMap = new HashMap<String, XmlToken>();
        for (XmlToken t : getXMLTokens()) {              ⟵─┐ XML tokens we're
            this.tagMap.put(t.getTag(), t);                 │ interested in
        }
        this.dateFormat = new SimpleDateFormat("yyyy-MM-dd HH:mm:ss");
        this.timeZoneDayDateFormat =
    new SimpleDateFormat("EEE, dd MMM yy HH:mm:ss zzz");
      this.timeZoneYearDateFormat =
    new SimpleDateFormat("yyyy-MM-dd HH:mm:ss zzz");
        this.timeZoneDateFormat =
    new SimpleDateFormat("dd MMM yy HH:mm:ss zzz");
    }
                                                     Determines if
                                                     token create
    protected abstract XmlToken [] getXMLTokens();    new item

protected abstract boolean isBlogEntryToken(XmlToken t) ;    ⟵─┘

//get methods
    }
```

The attributes

```
    private BlogQueryResultImpl result = null;
    private List<RetrievedBlogEntry> entries = null;
    private RetrievedBlogEntryImpl item = null;
```

store the resulting BlogQueryResult, the List of RetrievedBlogEntry objects, and the current RetrievedBlogEntry being processed. tagMap contains the list of tokens we're interested in. Each subclass implements the abstract getXMLTokens() method to return an array of tokens we're interested in. The subclasses also implement another abstract method, isBlogEntryToken(), which specifies which XML token creates a new entry in the result object.

Next, let's look at listing 5.11, which contains the parsing-related methods.

Listing 5.11   Parsing-related code for `BlogSearchResponseHandlerImpl`

```
    public void startElement(String namespaceURI, String localName,
        String qName, Attributes atts) throws SAXException {
  XmlToken t = this.tagMap.get(qName);
      if (t != null) {                        Create new instance
        this.whichToken = t;                  for new item
        if (isBlogEntryToken(t)) {     ◁
          this.item = new RetrievedBlogEntryImpl();
          this.entries.add(this.item);
        }
      }                             Reinitialize it for
      charString = "";      ◁───    new XML token
    }

    public void endElement(String namespaceURI, String sName, String qName)
     throws SAXException {
       this.whichToken = null;
    }

    public abstract void characters(char buf[], int offset, int len)
     throws SAXException ;

  //get/set charString
  //protected Date getParsedDate(String s) {      ◁── Parse date string
  }
```

In SAX parsing, `startElement` and `endElement` are the methods that get called at the start and end of an element. The `startElement` method takes four parameters. The first is the `namespaceURI`, which is left empty if there is no namespace. The second is `localName` (without prefix), or an empty `String` if namespace processing isn't being performed—both the namespaceURI and `localName` are empty strings for our sample XML. The third is the fully qualified element name; for example, `weblog` or `name`. The fourth parameter lists any attributes attached to the element. The `endElement` takes only the first three parameters, since end tags aren't permitted any attributes.

The following code

```
    public void startElement(String namespaceURI, String localName,
        String qName, Attributes atts) throws SAXException {
```

checks to see if a new instance of an item is available and resets the `charString`. The method `characters()` gets called by the SAX parser to report each chunk of character data. This method may be called multiple times for an element; the `charString` takes care of concatenating the String of characters together.

The utility method `getParsedDate()` contains logic to select the right date parser and convert the `String` to a `Date` object.

That takes care of all the base implementations in our framework. Now, let's look at how this framework will be extended to integrate the different blog-tracking providers.

5.3.5 Extending the framework

Figure 5.8 gives an overview of the classes that we build. Basically, for each integration, we extend the three classes: `BlogSearcherImpl` for blog searching, `BlogSearch-ResponseHandlerImpl` for handling the XML response, and `BlogQueryParameterImpl` for configuring the search parameters.

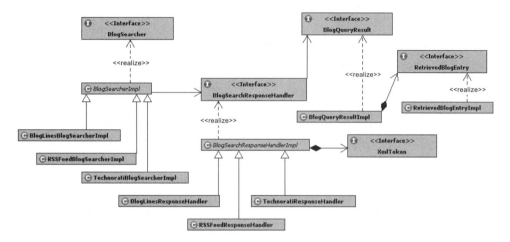

Figure 5.8   The interfaces and their implementing classes

Figure 5.9 shows the classes that will extend `BlogQueryParameterImpl` to configure the URL that the instance of `BlogSearcher` will access.

So far we've implemented the base classes for our framework. Now let's integrate various blog-tracking providers. We begin with integrating Technorati, who tracks the largest number of blogs—more than 112.8 million blogs as of September 2008. I selected Technorati and Bloglines for their popularity, as well as to illustrate how to integrate a custom API.

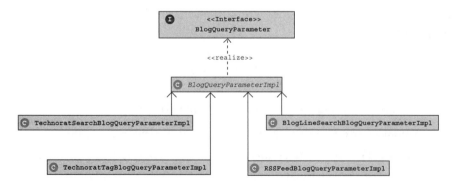

Figure 5.9   The classes extending `BlogQueryParameterImpl`

5.4   *Integrating Technorati*

In early December 2006, Jeremy Caplan of Time magazine profiled Technorati, calling it the "Searchlight for the Blogosphere." In his words:

> *If Google is the Web's reference library, Technorati is becoming its coffeehouse, where people go to find out what's being said and by whom. Rather than send you to Madonna's web site if you punch her name into its search box, Technorati tells you the latest buzz about her career—and her adoption saga.*

Technorati provides an API[10] that allows developers to

- Search for blog postings that use specified keywords or are tagged with those keywords. Furthermore, you can find out which blogs link to a particular URL.
- Get the list of top tags that have been indexed by Technorati.
- Get detailed information about a blog, such as its available feeds and how many other blogs link to it.
- Get information about a Technorati member.

In this section, we look at how to use our framework to search for relevant blogs using the two APIs provided, search and tag. Using this approach, you should be able to extend the framework to query Technorati for other functionality.

To access Technorati's API, you first need to sign up for the Technorati developer program and agree to the terms of service. Technorati's API returns results in its own proprietary XML as well as common feed formats such as RSS. In this section, we extend our framework to use Technorati's custom API, which provides a richer set of information than the RSS feed. Once you sign up for the service, you'll get a unique API key from Technorati, which you can see at the Technorati API information page.

5.4.1   *Technorati search API overview*

Using the Technorati API, you can search for blog entries using either the search query or the tag query. The query parameters and response XML are similar in both cases. Technorati uses a RESTful interface for their API, where you can send either a Post or a Get. Let's look at the details for both these queries.

TECHNORATI SEARCH QUERY

The search API allows you to search for blog entries that contain the given search string. This gives the same result as entering a search string into Technorati's search box. We need to send either a Get or a Post to

http://api.technorati.com/**search**?key=*[apikey]*&query=*[words]*

with mandatory parameters key and query, and the following optional parameters:

- format: Output format, either XML or RSS, with XML being the default.
- language: Two-character language code to retrieve results specific in that language. For example, en for English. This feature is in beta and may not work for all languages.

---

[10] http://www.technorati.com/developers/api/

- start: This parameter, along with the next one (limit), is useful for retrieving paginated results. If the limit is set to 20, its default value, and start is set to 0, the API will return entries from 0 to 20. Similarly, if you set start to 40+1, you'll get the third set of results from 41 to 60.

- limit: The number of values returned, which should be between 0 and 100. There are two more optional parameters: authority, to filter results to those from blogs with at least the Technorati Authority specified, and claim, to include user information with each link. We ignore these parameters, as they aren't supported by other providers. If you'd like to add them to the API, you need to extend the enums in QueryParameters and modify the Technorati-BlogSearcherImpl to take these into account.

Listing 5.12 shows the response XML for the search request, with elements that we're interested in shown in **bold**.

Listing 5.12   Technorati response XML for search query

```xml
<?xml version="1.0" encoding="utf-8"?>
<!-- generator="Technorati API version 1.0 /search" -->
<!DOCTYPE tapi PUBLIC "-//Technorati, Inc.//DTD TAPI 0.02//EN"
    "http://api.technorati.com/dtd/tapi-002.xml">
<tapi version="1.0">
<document>
<result>
 <query>[query string]</query>
 <querycount>[number of matches]</querycount>
 <querytime>[duration of query]</querytime>
 <rankingstart>[value of start parameter]</rankingstart>
</result>
<item>
 <weblog>
  <author>
    <firstname></firstname>
    <lastname></lastname>
    <username>[username]</username>
    <description></description>
    <bio></bio>
   <thumbnailpicture></thumbnailpicture>
  </author>
  <name>[name of blog containing match]</name>
  <url>[blog URL]</url>
  <rssurl>[blog RSS URL]</rssurl>
  <atomurl>[blog Atom URL]</atomurl>
  <inboundblogs>[inbound blogs]</inboundblogs>
  <inboundlinks>[inbound links]</inboundlinks>
  <lastupdate>[date blog last updated]</lastupdate>
 </weblog>
 <title>[title of entry]</title>
 <excerpt>[blurb from entry with search term highlighted]</excerpt>
 <created>[date entry was created]</created>
 <permalink>[URL of blog entry]</permalink>
</item>
```

```
...
</document>
</tapi>
```

The element `querycount` gives the total number of responses. `firstname` and `last-name` correspond to the first and last name of the author—these are combined together. `name`, `url`, `title`, `excerpt`, and `created` correspond to elements in the `RetrievedBlogEntry`.

TECHNORATI TAG QUERY

The tag query returns a list of blog entries that have the given tag associated with them. The API consists of sending either a Get or a Post to http://api.technorati.com/tag?key=[apikey]&tag=[tag] with the mandatory parameters `key` and `tag`, along with additional optional parameters. `format`, `limit`, and `start` are the same parameters as described for the search query. There are two other optional parameters:

- `excerptsize`: The number of word characters to include in the post excerpt. We use the default 100 word characters.
- `topexcerptsize`: The number of word characters to include in the first post excerpt. We use the default 150 word characters.

The XML response is similar to that for the search query.

5.4.2 *Implementing classes for integrating Technorati*

There are four classes that we need to implement:

- `TechnoratiSearchBlogQueryParameterImpl`: a search-related query parameter
- `TechnoratiTagBlogQueryParameterImpl`: a tag-related query parameter
- `TechnoratiBlogSearcherImpl`: an instance of `BlogSearcher` that coordinates the search
- `TechnoratiResponseHandler`: to handle the XML response

Let's begin by looking at the two implementations for the `QueryParameters`.

TECHNORATI QUERY PARAMETERS

`TechnoratiSearchBlogQueryParameterImpl` implements the `QueryParameter` for the search query as shown in listing 5.13.

Listing 5.13 `TechnoratiSearchBlogQueryParameterImpl`

```
package com.alag.ci.blog.search.impl.technorati;

import com.alag.ci.blog.search.impl.BlogQueryParameterImpl;

public class TechnoratiSearchBlogQueryParameterImpl extends
    BlogQueryParameterImpl {                                    ◁─── URL for
    private static final String TECHNORATI_SEARCH_API_URL =          search query
        "http://api.technorati.com/search";          ◁─┘

    public TechnoratiSearchBlogQueryParameterImpl() {       Sets
        super(QueryType.SEARCH,TECHNORATI_SEARCH_API_URL);  ◁─┘ query type
    }
}
```

The constructor simply sets the query type to search and the URL for the query. Note that the client code simply needs to create an instance, such as

```
BlogQueryParameter tbqp = new TechnoratiSearchBlogQueryParameterImpl();
```

without having to worry about the URL or kind of search.

Similarly, `TechnoratiTagBlogQueryParameterImpl` sets the query type to tag-related search and sets the URL for the tag search:

```
private static final String  TECHNORATI_TAG_API_URL =
     "http://api.technorati.com/tag";
```

TECHNORATIBLOGSEARCHERIMPL

Listing 5.14 contains the code for `TechnoratiBlogSearcherImpl`, the Technorati-related blog searcher. Remember there are two abstract method that this extending class needs to implement. Further, since both Get and Post can be used, we develop methods for both.

Listing 5.14 `TechnoratiBlogSearcherImpl`

```
package com.alag.ci.blog.search.impl.technorati;
import java.util.*;

import org.apache.commons.httpclient.HttpMethod;
import org.apache.commons.httpclient.methods.GetMethod;
import org.apache.commons.httpclient.methods.PostMethod;

import com.alag.ci.blog.search.BlogQueryParameter;
import com.alag.ci.blog.search.BlogSearchResponseHandler;
import com.alag.ci.blog.search.BlogSearcherException;
import com.alag.ci.blog.search.BlogQueryParameter.QueryParameter;
import com.alag.ci.blog.search.impl.BlogSearcherImpl
public class TechnoratiBlogSearcherImpl extends BlogSearcherImpl {
    public TechnoratiBlogSearcherImpl() throws BlogSearcherException {
    }
    protected void initializeParamStringMap() {           ◁── Maps parameters to
        super.initializeParamStringMap();                      Technorati-specific strings
        Map<QueryParameter, String> paramStringMap = getParamStringMap();
        paramStringMap.put(QueryParameter.KEY, "key");
        paramStringMap.put(QueryParameter.START_INDEX, "start");
        paramStringMap.put(QueryParameter.LIMIT, "limit");
        paramStringMap.put(QueryParameter.QUERY, "query");
        paramStringMap.put(QueryParameter.TAG, "tag");
        paramStringMap.put(QueryParameter.LANGUAGE, "language");
    }

    protected HttpMethod getMethod(BlogQueryParameter param) {    ◁─┐
        // return getPostMethod(param);                             │
        return getGetMethod(param);                        Use either │
    }                                                      Get or Post│

    private HttpMethod getPostMethod(BlogQueryParameter param) {
        PostMethod method = new PostMethod(param.getMethodUrl());
        Collection<QueryParameter> paramColl = param.getAllParameters();
        for (QueryParameter qp : paramColl) {
```

```
        String key = getParamStringMap().get(qp);
        if (key != null) {
            method.addParameter(key, param.getParameter(qp));
        }
    }
    return method;
}

    private HttpMethod getGetMethod(BlogQueryParameter param) {
        String url = param.getMethodUrl() + "?";
        Collection<QueryParameter> paramColl = param.getAllParameters();
        for (QueryParameter qp : paramColl) {
            String key = getParamStringMap().get(qp);
            if (key != null) {
                url += "&" + key + "=" + urlEncode(param.getParameter(qp));
            }
        }
        return new GetMethod(url);
    }

    protected BlogSearchResponseHandler getBlogSearchResponseHandler() {
        return new TechnoratiResponseHandler();
    }
}
```

The method `initializeParamStringMap()` sets the strings for the various query parameters to those expected by Technorati. These parameters are set in the Post method and the Get method to compose the URL.

NOTE   You can use either Get or Post within our framework, and most of the work is done by the base class that `TechnoratiBlogSearcherImpl` extends. However, some providers support only HTTP GET.

Lastly, we need to look at `TechnoratiResponseHandler`, which handles the response and is shown in listing 5.15. Note that most of the implementation deals with implementing the three abstract methods that were specified in the base class `BlogSearch-ResponseHandlerImpl`: `getXMLTokens()`, `isBlogEntryToken()`, and `characters()`.

Listing 5.15   `TechnoratiResponseHandler`

```
package com.alag.ci.blog.search.impl.technorati;

import org.xml.sax.SAXException;

import com.alag.ci.blog.search.XmlToken;
import com.alag.ci.blog.search.impl.*;

public class TechnoratiResponseHandler                          Tokens we're
        extends BlogSearchResponseHandlerImpl {                 interested in
    public enum TechnoratiXmlToken implements XmlToken {   ◁──┘
      COUNT("querycount"), POSTSMATCHED("postsmatched"), WEBLOG("weblog"),
      NAME("name"), LASTUPDATE("lastupdate"), URL("url"), TITLE("title"),
      EXCERPT("excerpt"), ITEM("item"), CREATED("created"),
      FIRSTNAME("firstname"),LASTNAME("lastname");
```

```
        private String tag = null;

        TechnoratiXmlToken(String tag) {
            this.tag = tag;
        }

        public String getTag() {
            return this.tag;
        }
    }

    private String firstName = null;

    protected XmlToken [] getXMLTokens() {
        return TechnoratiXmlToken.values();
    }

    protected boolean isBlogEntryToken(XmlToken t) {
        return (TechnoratiXmlToken.ITEM.compareTo(
            (TechnoratiXmlToken)t) == 0);
    }

    public void characters(char buf[], int offset, int len)
        throws SAXException {
        String s = this.getCharString() + new String(buf, offset, len);
        this.setCharString(s);
        TechnoratiXmlToken token = (TechnoratiXmlToken) getWhichToken();
        RetrievedBlogEntryImpl item = getItem();
        if (token != null) {
            switch (token) {
                case POSTSMATCHED: {
                    this.getResult().setQueryCount(new Integer(s));
                    break;
                }
//… Setting other fields when appropriate tokens are matched
            }
        }
    }
}
```

Which token
corresponds
to new item (annotation pointing to `isBlogEntryToken`)

Set attribute
based on token (annotation pointing to `if (token != null)`)

The `TechnoratiXmlToken` contains a list of XML tokens that we're interested in; this list is returned to the base class by the `getXMLToken()` method.

New blog entries are created whenever `TechnoratiXmlToken.ITEM` token is encountered, as shown by the implementation of the `isBlogEntryToken()` method:

```
    protected boolean isBlogEntryToken(XmlToken t) {
        return (TechnoratiXmlToken.ITEM.compareTo(
            (TechnoratiXmlToken)t) == 0);
    }
```

Lastly, in the `characters()` method, appropriate fields in `RetrievedBlogEntryImpl` and `BlogQueryResultImpl` are populated.

That's all that's required to integrate Technorati into our framework. Next, let's look at how to call this API. Listing 5.16 shows the output from a unit test that calls this API.

Listing 5.16   Output from Technorati search for "collective intelligence"

```
http://api.technorati.com/search?&language=en&
        key=xxx&query=collective+intelligence&limit=1        ◁        Replace xxx
Total=25618                                              ◁            with your
1 Name: Gab Communicates To All (GCTA) …       Total number          key code
Url: http://gabrielcomia.multiply.com/blog
Title: The Great Cross of Hendaye, France       ◁── Blog entry details
Excerpt: The Great Cross of Hendaye, ….
LastUpdateTime: Thu Jan 11 17:02:36 PST 2007
CreationTime: Fri Jan 19 06:04:08 PST 2007       | Author not available
Author:                                        ◁ |
```

This output was generated using the unit test in listing 5.17.

Listing 5.17   Unit test to call Technorati search

```java
public void testTechnoratiSearchQuery() throws Exception {      Create instance of
    BlogSearcher bs = new TechnoratiBlogSearcherImpl();   ◁──┘   Technorati blog searcher

    BlogQueryParameter searchQueryParam = new
        TechnoratiSearchBlogQueryParameterImpl();                        ◁─
    searchQueryParam.setParameter(QueryParameter.KEY,"[your key]");
    searchQueryParam.setParameter(QueryParameter.LIMIT, "1");     Create
    searchQueryParam.setParameter(QueryParameter.QUERY,     query parameters
     "collective intelligence");
    searchQueryParam.setParameter(QueryParameter.LANGUAGE, "en");

    BlogQueryResult searchResult =bs.getRelevantBlogs(searchQueryParam);  ◁┐

    System.out.println(searchResult);                    Do the search
    assertTrue("No results", searchResult.getRelevantBlogs().size() >0);
}
```

Searching Technorati using our framework consists of three steps. First, we create an instance of `TechnoratiBlogSearcherImpl`:

```java
BlogSearcher bs = new TechnoratiBlogSearcherImpl();
```

Second, we create an instance of `TechnoratiSearchBlogQueryParameterImpl` and set the query parameters. In this case, we're searching for English blog entries containing the keyword *collective intelligence*.

```java
BlogQueryParameter searchQueryParam = new
    TechnoratiSearchBlogQueryParameterImpl();
```

Third, we perform the search:

```java
BlogQueryResult searchResult =bs.getRelevantBlogs(searchQueryParam);
```

Doing a tag-based search is similar, except you'll create an instance of `Technorati-TagBlogQueryParameterImpl`:

```java
BlogQueryParameter tagQueryParam = new
    TechnoratiTagBlogQueryParameterImpl();
```

and set the parameter:

```java
tagQueryParam.setParameter(QueryParameter.TAG,
    "collective intelligence");
```

With this example, you should have a sense of how easy it is to integrate new blog providers and invoke them to get relevant blogs. In the next section, we integrate another blog-tracking provider, Bloglines, using their custom API. This demonstrates how to handle responses that return information in attributes.

5.5 *Integrating Bloglines*

Time featured Bloglines as one of its 50 coolest websites in 2004.[11] Bloglines is a free online service that allows people to search, subscribe, share, and create new feeds, blogs, and rich content. The site indexes "tens of millions of live Internet content feeds, including articles, blogs, images, and audio," and allows people to create personalized news pages. Based in San Francisco, Bloglines is a fully owned subsidiary of IAC/InterActiveCorp.

In this section, we look at how to integrate Bloglines into our framework to search for relevant blogs. Let's begin by briefly looking at their API.

5.5.1 *Bloglines search API overview*

In addition to the blog search API, Bloglines provides three other APIs. These are

- *Notifier*—For counting unread items in a Bloglines account
- *Sync*—For accessing subscription lists and unread blog items
- *Blogroll*—For incorporating subscription lists into other sites

We concentrate on the search API in this section, but you should be able to use the concepts developed in this chapter to access the other APIs.

BLOGLINES SEARCH API

The search API requires a username and key to be submitted in the request for user authentication. You need to register with Bloglines to retrieve your key. You can find your key once you're logged in under the Developers tab under My Account.

The search API supports Get calls with four required parameters:

- `format=publicapi`: specifies that the search page return a `publicapi` query result in XML
- `apiuser`: the username or email address from the user's Bloglines account
- `apikey`: the API key generated on the Developer Tools tab under Profile Options
- `q`: the URL-encoded search query terms

Here is an example URL call:

```
http://www.bloglines.com/search?format=publicapi&apiuser=myusername
    &apikey=275938797F98797FA9879AF&q=collective+intelligence
```

Listing 5.18 contains a sample response with the tokens that we're interested in shown in **bold.**

---

[11] http://www.time.com/time/techtime/200406/news.html

Listing 5.18   Example response from Bloglines search

```
<publicapi>
  <link type="rss" title="Bloglines Search: [search-term]" href=[GET URL]/>
  <resultset set="main" qtype="article"
      estimate="115" found="71">                          ◁────┐  Total number
    <result id="0" siteid="521144" itemid="455" inline="0"  │  of results
      date="Fri, 26 Jan 2007 20:46:00 GMT" citations="0">  ◁─┘  found
      <site nsubs="26">
        <name>[site name]</name>                    Specific to
        <url>[site url]</url>                        each entry
        <feedurl[feed url]</feedurl>
      </site>
      <title>[title of blog entry]</title>
      <author>[author]</author>
      <abstract>[abstract]</abstract>
      <url>[url for blog entry]</url>
    </result>
  <result>           ┌── Repeated for
  ....          ◁────┘   all entries
  </result>
  </resultset>
</publicapi>
```

Note that the total number of items retrieved is listed in the attributes for resultset with the name found, and the date of the blog entry is an attribute for the element result.

5.5.2   *Implementing classes for integrating Bloglines*

To integrate Bloglines, we need to create three classes: BlogLineSearchBlogQuery-ParameterImpl for the query parameters, BlogLinesBlogSearcherImpl for searching, and BlogLinesResponseHandler for handling the XML response.

BlogLineSearchBlogQueryParameterImpl is similar to the TechnoratiSearch-BlogQueryParameterImpl class shown in listing 5.13, except that the URL passed in is http://www.bloglines.com/search. The constructor BlogLineSearchBlogQuery-ParameterImpl() also sets the query type to search.

Next, let's look at the implementation of the BlogLinesBlogSearcherImpl, which carries out the search.

IMPLEMENTING BLOGLINESBLOGSEARCHERIMPL

BlogLinesBlogSearcherImpl is responsible for carrying out the search, and simply needs to implement the two abstract methods in the base class:

```
protected abstract BlogSearchResponseHandler
   getBlogSearchResponseHandler();
protected abstract HttpMethod getMethod(BlogQueryParameter param);
```

The implementation for BlogLinesBlogSearcherImpl is shown in listing 5.19.

Listing 5.19   Implementation of BlogLinesBlogSearcherImpl

```
package com.alag.ci.blog.search.impl.bloglines;

import org.apache.commons.httpclient.HttpMethod;
import org.apache.commons.httpclient.methods.GetMethod;
```

```
import com.alag.ci.blog.search.BlogQueryParameter;
import com.alag.ci.blog.search.BlogSearchResponseHandler;
import com.alag.ci.blog.search.BlogSearcherException;
import com.alag.ci.blog.search.BlogQueryParameter.QueryParameter;
import com.alag.ci.blog.search.impl.BlogSearcherImpl;
public class BlogLinesBlogSearcherImpl extends BlogSearcherImpl {
   public BlogLinesBlogSearcherImpl() throws BlogSearcherException {
   }

   protected BlogSearchResponseHandler getBlogSearchResponseHandler() {
      return new BlogLinesResponseHandler();
   }

   protected HttpMethod getMethod(BlogQueryParameter param) {
      String url = param.getMethodUrl() + "?" +
      "format=publicapi&apiuser=" +
      param.getParameter(QueryParameter.APIUSER)+
      "&apikey=" + param.getParameter(QueryParameter.KEY)+
      "&q=" + urlEncode(param.getParameter(QueryParameter.QUERY));

      GetMethod method = new GetMethod(url);
      return method;
   }
}
```

Specifies response handler

Creates HttpMethod

The method getMethod() takes three parameters: APIUSER, KEY, and a QUERY set in a BlogQueryParameter to compose the URL.

Lastly, we need to create a handler, BlogSearchResponseHandler, to handle the XML response.

IMPLEMENTING BLOGLINESRESPONSEHANDLER

BlogLinesResponseHandler is responsible for parsing the XML returned from Bloglines and converting it to a BlogQueryResult object. Listing 5.20 contains the code for BlogLinesResponseHandler.

Listing 5.20 `BlogSearchResponseHandler`

```
package com.alag.ci.blog.search.impl.bloglines;

import org.xml.sax.Attributes;
import org.xml.sax.SAXException;

import com.alag.ci.blog.search.XmlToken;
import com.alag.ci.blog.search.impl.BlogSearchResponseHandlerImpl;
import com.alag.ci.blog.search.impl.RetrievedBlogEntryImpl;
public class BlogLinesResponseHandler
    extends BlogSearchResponseHandlerImpl {
   public enum BlogLinesXmlToken implements XmlToken {
       NAME("name"), URL("url"), TITLE("title"), RESULT("result"),
//.. and other tokens specific to BlogLines
   }

   protected XmlToken [] getXMLTokens() {
      return BlogLinesXmlToken.values();
   }

   protected boolean isBlogEntryToken(XmlToken t) {
      return (BlogLinesXmlToken.RESULT.compareTo(
```

Enum for elements of interest

Tag for next item

```
                (BlogLinesXmlToken)t) == 0);
    }

    public void startElement(String namespaceURI, String localName,
            String qName, Attributes atts) throws SAXException {
        super.startElement(namespaceURI, localName, qName, atts);

        String dateValue = atts.getValue(
            BlogLinesXmlToken.CREATED.getTag());        ⟵── Get date
        if (dateValue != null) {
            RetrievedBlogEntryImpl item = getItem();
            item.setCreationTime(getParsedDate(dateValue));
        }
        String numFound = atts.getValue(              ┐ Get total number
            BlogLinesXmlToken.FOUND.getTag());      ⟵─┘ of responses
        if (numFound != null) {
            this.getResult().setQueryCount(new Integer(numFound));
        }
        this.setCharString("");
    }

    public void characters(char buf[], int offset, int len)
            throws SAXException {
        String s = this.getCharString() + new String(buf, offset, len);
        this.setCharString(s);
        BlogLinesXmlToken token = (BlogLinesXmlToken) this.getWhichToken();
        RetrievedBlogEntryImpl item = getItem();    ┐ Set other
        if (token != null) {                      ⟵─┘ attributes
            switch (token) {
            //set item elements base on token
            }
        }
    }
}
}
```

The enum `BlogLinesXmlToken` keeps a list of tokens that we're interested in. New
blog entries are created by the tag RESULT, which leads to the implementation of the
abstract `isBlogEntryToken()` method:

```
protected boolean isBlogEntryToken(XmlToken t) {
    return (BlogLinesXmlToken.RESULT.compareTo(
        (BlogLinesXmlToken)t) == 0);
}
```

The date of the blog entry and the number of items are extracted from the attributes
in the method `startElement()`, while the other attributes are set in the method
`characters()`.

   That takes care of all the classes we need to implement to integrate Bloglines. The
process of calling Bloglines is similar to that for Technorati. There are three steps
involved in executing the search.

   First, we need to create an instance of the `BlogSearcher`:

```
BlogSearcher bs = new BlogLinesBlogSearcherImpl();
```

Second, we need to set the parameters: login-name, key, and the search query:

```
BlogQueryParameter searchQueryParam =
    new BlogLineSearchBlogQueryParameterImpl();
searchQueryParam.setParameter(
    QueryParameter.APIUSER, "[login-name]");
searchQueryParam.setParameter(QueryParameter.KEY, "[key]");
searchQueryParam.setParameter(
    QueryParameter.QUERY, "collective intelligence");
```

Third, we need to execute the search:

```
BlogQueryResult searchResult = bs.getRelevantBlogs(searchQueryParam);
```

The output from this query is similar to the one for Technorati.

So far, we've demonstrated how two different blog-tracking providers, Technorati and Bloglines, can be integrated using their proprietary APIs. Most blog-tracking providers provide an RSS 2.0 XML response. Though this RSS response may not be as rich in content as a provider's proprietary API, it can still be useful for integrating providers.

5.6 *Integrating providers using RSS*

In section 5.1.2, we briefly reviewed RSS and its history. Most providers support the RSS 2.0 format for responding to a search query. A typical RSS 2.0 XML response was shown in listing 5.1. The total number of results isn't available in this XML response.

Adding a new provider consists of adding three new classes:

- An instance of the QueryParameter
- An instance of the BlogSearcher that implements getMethod()
- An instance of BlogSearchResponseHandler that handles the XML parsing

In this section, we develop each of these classes in a generic manner.

5.6.1 *Generalizing the query parameters*

Rather than creating a specific instance of these classes for each provider, let's generalize the approach. Table 5.3 shows the URL used to query MSN and Blogdigger.

Table 5.3   Query URLs for some blog-tracking providers

Provider	URL
MSN	http://search.msn.com/results.aspx?q=collective+intelligence&format=rss&first=1&count=2
Blogdigger	http://www.blogdigger.com/rss.jsp?sortby=date&q=collective+intelligence&si=1&pp=2

You can decompose the query URL into five elements, as shown in table 5.4. These elements are

- *URL*—The provider URL for the query
- *First element*—The term used to specify the index of the first element
- *Number items*—The term used to specify the number of items
- *Sort*—The term used to specify the sort element
- *Format type*—The term used to specify the format used

Table 5.4   Decomposing the query parameters across providers

Provider	URL	First element	Number items	Sort	Format type
MSN	http://search.msn.com/results.aspx	first	count		format
Blogdigger	http://www.blogdigger.com/rss.jsp	si	pp	sortby	

RSSFeedBlogQueryParameterImpl, whose code is shown in listing 5.21, encapsulates the parameters shown in table 5.4.

Listing 5.21   `RSSFeedBlogQueryParameterImpl`

```
package com.alag.ci.blog.search.impl.rss;
import com.alag.ci.blog.search.impl.BlogQueryParameterImpl;

public class RSSFeedBlogQueryParameterImpl extends BlogQueryParameterImpl {

      public enum RSSProviderURL {
BLOGDIGGER("http://www.blogdigger.com/rss.jsp","si","pp","sortby","",
      QueryType.SEARCH),
MSN ("http://search.msn.com/results.aspx","first","count","",
       "format",QueryType.SEARCH),                         ◁──┐ Parameters for
      private String url = null;           ◁──┐                the providers
      private String firstKey = null;          │  Attributes
      private String numKey = null;            │  for enum
      private String sortKey = null;
      private String formatKey = null;
      private QueryType queryType = null;

      RSSProviderURL(String url,String firstKey, String numKey,
            String sortKey, String formatKey, QueryType queryType) {
//set the instance variables
      }
//Get methods for the parameters
    }
                                               ┌── Each instance has
    private RSSProviderURL rssProviderUrl = null;  ◁─┘  RSSProviderURL
    public RSSFeedBlogQueryParameterImpl(RSSProviderURL rssProviderUrl) {
       super(rssProviderUrl.getQueryType(),rssProviderUrl.getUrl());
       this.rssProviderUrl = rssProviderUrl;
    }

    public RSSProviderURL getRSSProviderURL() {
       return this.rssProviderUrl;
    }
}
```

The enum RSSProviderURL has an enumerated type for each of the providers that specifies the values for the various parameters. Now we can use this to develop a generic instance of the blog searcher.

5.6.2   *Generalizing the blog searcher*

Most of the heavy lifting required to implement RSSFeedBlogQueryParameterImpl has already been done in the base class, as shown in listing 5.22.

Listing 5.22 `RSSFeedBlogQueryParameterImpl`

```
package com.alag.ci.blog.search.impl.rss;

import org.apache.commons.httpclient.HttpMethod;
import org.apache.commons.httpclient.methods.GetMethod;

import com.alag.ci.blog.search.*;
import com.alag.ci.blog.search.impl.rss.RSSFeedBlogQueryParameterImpl.
    ➥RSSProviderURL;

public class RSSFeedBlogSearcherImpl extends BlogSearcherImpl {
    public RSSFeedBlogSearcherImpl() throws BlogSearcherException {
    }

    protected HttpMethod getMethod(BlogQueryParameter param) {
        RSSFeedBlogQueryParameterImpl rssParam =
          (RSSFeedBlogQueryParameterImpl)param;
        RSSProviderURL rssProvider = rssParam.getRSSProviderURL();
        String url = param.getMethodUrl() + "?q=" +
          urlEncode(param.getParameter(QueryParameter.QUERY))+
          "&" + rssProvider.getFirstKey() + "=" +
          param.getParameter(QueryParameter.START_INDEX)+
          "&" + rssProvider.getNumKey() + "=" +
           param.getParameter(QueryParameter.LIMIT);
    if ("".compareTo(rssProvider.getSortKey())  != 0) {      ◄── Append sort term when appropriate
        String sortBy = "date";
        if (param.getParameter(QueryParameter.SORTBY) != null ) {
           sortBy = param.getParameter(QueryParameter.SORTBY);
        }
        url += "&" + rssProvider.getSortKey() + "=" + sortBy;
    }
    if ("".compareTo(rssProvider.getFormatKey())  != 0) {     ◄── Append format term when appropriate
        url += "&" + rssProvider.getFormatKey() + "=rss" ;
    }

    return new GetMethod(url);
    }
}
```

`RSSFeedBlogQueryParameterImpl` needs to implement the abstract method get-Method(). This method uses the parameters specified in `RSSFeedBlogQueryParameterImpl` to create the appropriate query URL.

The last thing we need to implement is the handler to parse the XML, which is in RSS 2.0 format.

5.6.3 *Building the RSS 2.0 XML parser*

Listing 5.23 shows the implementation for `RSSFeedResponseHandler`, which is the handle for parsing the RSS 2.0 XML response.

Listing 5.23 `RSSFeedResponseHandler`

```
package com.alag.ci.blog.search.impl.rss;

import org.xml.sax.SAXException;

import com.alag.ci.blog.search.XmlToken;
```

```
import com.alag.ci.blog.search.impl.*;

public class RSSFeedResponseHandler extends BlogSearchResponseHandlerImpl {

    public enum RSSFeedXmlToken implements XmlToken {
        ITEM("item"), TITLE("title"), AUTHOR("author"), LINK("link"),
            DESCRIPTION("description"), PUBDATE("pubDate");

        private String tag = null;

        RSSFeedXmlToken(String tag) {
            this.tag = tag;
        }

        public String getTag() {
            return this.tag;
        }
    }

    protected XmlToken[] getXMLTokens() {
        return RSSFeedXmlToken.values();
    }

    protected boolean isBlogEntryToken(XmlToken t) {
        return (RSSFeedXmlToken.ITEM.compareTo((RSSFeedXmlToken) t) == 0);
    }

    public void characters(char buf[], int offset, int len)
        throws SAXException {
        String s = this.getCharString() + new String(buf, offset, len);
        this.setCharString(s);
        RSSFeedXmlToken token = (RSSFeedXmlToken) this.getWhichToken();
        RetrievedBlogEntryImpl item = getItem();
        if (token != null) {
            switch (token) {
            case LINK: {
                if (item != null) {
                    item.setUrl(s);
                }
                break;
            }
          //similar handling of tokens
            }
        }
    }
}
```

◁─┐ Tokens that
  │ are handled

◁─┐ Handling of
  │ tokens to set
  │ attribute

There are six tokens that are handled:

```
ITEM("item"), TITLE("title"), AUTHOR("author"), LINK("link"),
    DESCRIPTION("description"), PUBDATE("pubDate");
```

Appropriate elements of the items are also set.

A typical result using the RSS feed is shown in listing 5.24. Note that the total number of blog entries isn't returned.

Listing 5.24 Output from Blogdigger query for "collective intelligence"

```
http://www.blogdigger.com/rss.jsp?q=collective+intelligence&si=1&
    pp=2&sortby=date
Total=null
1 Name: BLOG: Random Thoughts From Last Night
```

◁─┐ **URL for query**   **Total number of
                          results not returned**

```
Url: http://baseballcrank.com/archives2/2007/05/blog_random_tho.php
Title: BLOG: Random Thoughts From Last Night
Excerpt: I was switching back and forth last night between the ...
LastUpdateTime: Wed May 16 10:30:45 PDT 2007
Author: Baseball Crank
```

The code was generated using the test shown in listing 5.25, which is similar to listing 5.17.

Listing 5.25 Output from Blogdigger query for "collective intelligence"

```
public void runBlogdiggerTest() throws Exception{          Specify provider as
    BlogQueryParameter tagQueryParam = new                      Blogdigger
     RSSFeedBlogQueryParameterImpl(RSSProviderURL.BLOGDIGGER);  ◄──────
    BlogSearcher bs = new RSSFeedBlogSearcherImpl();

    tagQueryParam.setParameter(QueryParameter.START_INDEX, "1");
    tagQueryParam.setParameter(QueryParameter.LIMIT, "1");
    tagQueryParam.setParameter(QueryParameter.QUERY,
       "collective intelligence");
    BlogQueryResult tagResult = bs.getRelevantBlogs(tagQueryParam);
    System.out.println(tagResult);
}
```

You can add other providers by decomposing the query URL into the five parameters specified in table 5.4 and adding an enum value to RSSFeedBlogQueryParameterImpl. RSSProviderURL.

In this section, we've shown how blog-tracking providers can be added using RSS. The approach is generic and can be extended to add other blog-tracking providers. Once you have the URL to the blog, you can download the text of the blog entry, analyze it to generate its term vector, and compute its similarity to items of interest.

5.7 *Summary*

It's helpful to search the blogosphere to obtain relevant information and to monitor what's being said about your product and application. There are a number of blog-tracking providers, companies that track what's being said in the blogosphere. RSS is an XML specification that's widely used for content changes. Most blog-tracking providers provide an RSS-based API to query.

In this chapter, we've developed a generic framework for searching the blogosphere by integrating blog-tracking providers. Searching the blogosphere involves four steps: creating the search query, sending it to a blog-tracking provider in a format the provider can understand, parsing the response from the provider, and lastly, converting it to a standard result format. We've demonstrated this process by adding four providers, two using proprietary APIs and the rest using RSS.

In the next chapter, we continue with our theme of collecting relevant information from outside your application by looking at web crawling.

5.8 *Resources*

Apache commons.feedparser. http://jakarta.apache.org/commons/sandbox/feedparser/
"Argos." https://argos.dev.java.net/

"Argos: Simple Java Search Engine Wrapper API." techno.blog("Dion"). April, 2005. http://almaer.com/blog/argos-simple-java-search-engine-wrapper-api

Atom. http://atomenabled.org/

Atom Publishing Format and Protocol (atompub). http://www.ietf.org/html.charters/atompub-charter.html

Blog Search Engine. http://www.blogsearchengine.com/

Blogdigger. http://www.blogdigger.com/rss.jsp

Blogger Data API. http://code.google.com/apis/blogger/gdata.html

Bloglines API Documentation. http://www.bloglines.com/services/api/

BlogPulse API FAQ. http://www.blogpulse.com/about.html#showcase_3

Brown, Larry, and Marty Hall. *XML Processing with Java*. 2002. Prentice Hill. http://www.phptr.com/articles/article.asp?p=26351&seqNum=4&rl=1

Caplan, Jeremy. "Searchlight for the Blogosphere." *Time*. Dec. 3, 2006. http://www.time.com/time/globalbusiness/article/0,9171,1565540,00.html

DateFormat and SimpleDateFormat Examples. http://javatechniques.com/public/java/docs/basics/dateformat-examples.html

Dmoz open directory. http://dmoz.org/Computers/Internet/On_the_Web/Weblogs/Search_Engines/

Fagan Finder, Blogs and RSS Search Engines. http://www.faganfinder.com/blogs/

Full list of ping services to go. http://www.onlinemoneytip.com/blogging/rss-ping-list/

Google Blog Search. http://www.google.com/help/about_blogsearch.html

HttpClient Tutorial. http://jakarta.apache.org/commons/httpclient/tutorial.html

Icerocket.com. http://www.icerocket.com/

Jakarta Commons HttpClient. http://hc.apache.org/httpclient-3.x/

"Java API for XML Processing (JAXP) Sources." Sun Microsystems Inc. https://jaxp-sources.dev.java.net/

Johnson, Dave. *RSS and Atom in Action*. 2006. Manning Publications.

MSN Live Search. http://search.msn.com/results.aspx

RSS, Wikipedia. http://en.wikipedia.org/wiki/RSS_%28file_format%29

RSS 2.0 Specification. RSS Advisory Board. http://www.rssboard.org/rss-specification

RSS 2.0 Specification. http://blogs.law.harvard.edu/tech/rss

RSS Tutorial for Content Publishers and Webmasters. http://www.mnot.net/rss/tutorial/

Sayer, Robert. "Atom: The Standard in Syndication." *IEEE Internet Computing*, vol. 9, no. 2, 2005, pp. 71-75.

SAX API Javadoc. http://www.saxproject.org/apidoc/overview-summary.html

SimpleDateFormat. http://java.sun.com/j2se/1.4.2/docs/api/java/text/SimpleDateFormat.html

Tailrank. http://tailrank.com/code.php

Technorati API Documentation. http://www.technorati.com/developers/api/

"Time's 50 Best Websites."

Time. http://www.time.com/time/techtime/200406/news.html

UrlEncoder. http://java.sun.com/j2se/1.4.2/docs/api/java/net/URLEncoder.html

Winer, Dave. "RSS History." April, 2004. http://blogs.law.harvard.edu/tech/rssVersionHistory

"Xerces2 Java Parser Readme." Apache XML. http://xerces.apache.org/xerces2-j/

Intelligent web crawling 6

This chapter covers
- A brief overview of web crawling and intelligent crawling
- A step-by-step implementation of a web crawler
- Crawling with Nutch
- Scalable web crawling

No one knows the exact number of web pages on the Internet. But we do know that the World Wide Web is

- Huge, with billions of web pages
- Dynamic, with pages being constantly added, removed, or updated
- Growing rapidly

Given the huge amount of information available on the Internet, how does one find information of interest?

In this chapter, we continue our theme of gathering information from outside one's application. You'll be introduced to the field of intelligent web crawling to retrieve relevant information. Search engines crawl the web periodically to index available content. You may be interested in crawling the web to harvest information from external sites, which can then be used in your application. Search engines such as Google and Yahoo! constantly crawl the web to gather data for their search results.

HOW BIG IS THE WEB? In late July 2008, Google announced that they had detected more than a trillion unique URLs on the web; with the internet growing by several billion individual pages every day. Of course, not all the content has been indexed by Google, but a large portion has. To get a sense of the number of pages indexed by Google it is useful to look at the number of pages indexed by Google for a site—type site:*website*, for example, site:facebook.com, to search for the pages indexed by Google for Facebook (this number incidentally was more than 76 million pages as of July 2008). Other providers, such as Alexa, Compete.com, and Quantcast also provide useful data on the kinds of searches carried out on various sites.

This chapter is organized in three sections:

- First, we look at the field of web crawling, how it can be used in your application, the details of the crawling process, how the process can be made intelligent, how to access pages that aren't retrievable using traditional methods, and the available public domain crawlers that you can use.
- Second, to understand the basics of intelligent (focused) crawling, we implement a simple web crawler that highlights the key concepts related to web crawling.
- Third, we use Apache Nutch, an open source Java-based scalable crawler. We also discuss making Nutch distributed and scalable, using concepts known as Hadoop and MapReduce.

6.1   Introducing web crawling

Web crawling is the automated process of visiting web pages with the aim of retrieving content. The content being extracted could be in many forms: text, images, or videos. A *web crawler* is a program that systematically visits web pages, retrieves content, extracts URLs to other relevant links, and then in turn visits those links if allowed. Web crawlers are also commonly known as *web spiders*, *bots*, or *automated indexers*.

As we'll see later in this chapter, it's easy to write a simple web crawler. But building a crawler that's sophisticated enough to efficiently crawl the complete web (or parts of it that can be crawled) is a whole different ball game. We discuss these challenges throughout this chapter.

In this section, we look at how crawling the web may be useful to you, the basics of web crawling, how crawling can be made focused or intelligent, how invisible content can be made available, and some of the available open source web crawlers.

6.1.1   Why crawl the Web?

The primary goal of web crawling is to collect data from external sites. Following are some of the many ways web crawling is typically used:

- *Content aggregation and indexing external content*—Search engines build a catalog of content available on the web by periodically crawling the web. They then allow their users to search for relevant content using the data retrieved. You can also aggregate external data that may be relevant to your application and present hyperlinks to those pages from within your application.[1]

- *Searching for specific information*—Focused crawling deals with crawling the web specifically looking for relevant information. In essence, the crawler visits a fraction of the total pages available by visiting pages that show promise. We also refer to this as *intelligent crawling*.

- *Triggering events*—Based on your domain, it may be helpful to crawl a set of web sites in search of relevant information that can be used as triggers or events in your application. For example, if your application is in the real estate domain, where you provide a valuation for a house, it may be helpful to crawl public domain sites that post information about recent sales. A house sale could be an event in your financial model for the price of homes in a neighborhood.

- *Detecting broken links*—Since a web crawler is good at visiting a page, extracting hyperlinks, and then visiting those pages, you can use a web crawler to detect whether you have any broken links in your application.

- *Searching for copyright infringement*—If you have copyrighted content, you can use intelligent web crawling to detect sites that are inappropriately using your content.

Next, let's look at the process of crawling the web used by web crawlers.

6.1.2 *The crawling process*

The basic process of web crawling is fairly straightforward, as shown in figure 6.1. Later, in section 6.2, we implement a simple web crawler using the algorithm outlined in figure 6.1. The basic steps involved in web crawling are

1 *Seeding the web crawler*—The web crawler is seeded with a set of URLs to be visited. Place these URLs in a queue data structure. The crawler queries the queue to get the next URL that it needs to crawl.

2 *Checking for exit criteria*—As long as the criteria for the crawler to continue crawling are met, the crawler retrieves the next URL to be visited. The exit criteria for a crawler could be based on one of many conditions—when the number of pages retrieved or visited reaches a certain threshold, how long the crawler has run, when there are no more available URLs to visit, and so on.

3 *Get the next URL to be visited*—There are some sites that don't allow crawlers to visit certain pages. Sites typically give permissions to crawlers to visit a set of pages in a file called robots.txt. The next step is to get the next URL that the crawler is allowed to visit.

---

[1] It may not be appropriate to show the content within your application if it is copyrighted.

4 *Retrieve content*—The crawler visits the URL and retrieves the content. Since you want the crawling process to be efficient—to avoid duplication—the URL visited is added to the list of URLs visited.

5 *Is the retrieved content relevant?*—This step is optional and is used when implementing focused crawling. Here, the retrieved content is checked against a model to see if the content is relevant to what we're searching for. If it is, then the content is saved locally.

6 *Extract URLs*—When the content is of interest, the text in the content is parsed for hyperlinks. Hyperlinks that haven't been visited are then placed in the queue of URLs.

7 *Inject delay*—If the crawling process is too fast or if multiple threads are being used, it can sometimes overwhelm the site. Sites protect themselves by blocking the IP addresses of misbehaving crawlers. You may want to optionally inject a delay between subsequent hits to a site.

This algorithm carries out its search using *breadth-first search (BFS)*—the roots of extracted URLs are visited first before going deep and visiting the children. Given that there are costs associated with the time to crawl, the network bandwidth used, and the number of machines used in the crawl, sophisticated methods have been developed to determine which URL should be visited next. These methods to estimate the potential quality of a URL include using historic information from previous crawls to determine a URL's weight, using the number of pages connecting to the URL (also known as *authority*) and the number of outward links, and analyzing the graph of connections on the site. Of course, though understanding these basic analysis algorithms is conceptually simple, the practical details of implementing them are complex and usually proprietary.

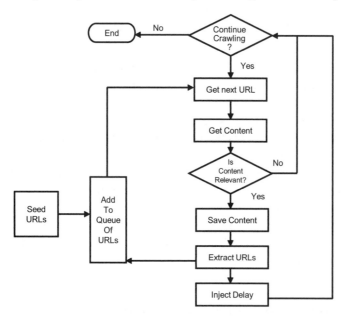

Figure 6.1 The basic process of web crawling

Web crawlers typically work in combination with a search library, which is used to index and search the content retrieved. For example, Nutch, which we use in section 6.3, uses Lucene, a Java-based open source search engine library, which we also use later in this book.

Given the dynamic nature of the Web, with pages being constantly added, modified, or deleted, crawling is performed periodically to keep the pages fresh. A site may have a number of *mirror* sites, and smart crawlers can detect these sites and avoid duplication by downloading from the fastest or freshest server.

A crawler can face a number of challenges during the crawl process, one of them being a *spider trap*. A spider trap could be created unintentionally or intentionally to guard a site against spam crawlers. Common techniques used to create spider traps include creating an infinitely deep directory structure and creating an infinite number of dynamically generated pages. Most crawlers stay with five levels of URL hierarchy.

Spammers use a variety of methods to mislead crawlers and boost their search engine rankings. These techniques include

- *Doorway pages*—Pages that are optimized for a single keyword, which then redirects to the real target page.
- *Keyword spamming*—Location and word frequency are two commonly used metrics used by text analysis algorithms. Spammers add misleading meta-keywords, repeat words excessively, or add hidden text.
- *Link spamming*—Some sites have numerous domains that point or redirect to a target page.
- *Cloaking*—Some sites detect when a request is from a web crawler and may serve fake spam content.

With this general overview of the crawling process, let's next focus on step 5 of the crawling process—focused crawling, where we want to focus the crawling process to get only items of interest.

6.1.3 *Intelligent crawling and focused crawling*

Given the sheer size of the web and the time and cost associated, crawling the complete Web can be daunting and potentially infeasible. Many times you may be interested in gathering information relevant to a particular domain or a topic; this is where focused crawling, also known as *topical crawling*, comes into play. Focused crawling is based on the simple principle that the more relevant a page to a topic of interest, the higher the probability that the linked pages contain relevant content. Therefore, it's advantageous to first explore these linked pages. A simple way to compute the relevancy of a page to a topic of interest is to match on keywords. The use of similarity computation between two term vectors using the term-frequency and inverse-document-frequency (TF-IDF) computation is a generalization of this idea.

Charkrabarti formally introduced focused crawling in 1999. In focused crawling, one first builds a model, also known as a *classifier*, that's trained to predict how relevant a piece of content is to the topic being searched. If you're searching for content that's similar to a set of documents, a simple approach is to create a composite term-vector representation, similar to `CompositeContentTypes`, which we looked at in section 4.4.1, and then compute the similarity between the retrieved content and this composite representation. Of course, there are a variety of approaches that can be used to build predictive models, which we discuss in part 2 of this book.

Assume that we've built a classifier that can emit a number between 0 and 1 to predict the *relevancy* of a piece of content, such that the higher the number, the higher the probability that the item is relevant to our topic. Content that has a value above a certain threshold is accepted, and hyperlinks from these pages are added to the pool of URLs to be visited with the weight of the relevancy of the parent. The URLs in the URL queue are sorted by relevancy, such that the URL with the highest predicted relevancy is selected.

A metric commonly used to measure the effectiveness of a crawler is its *harvest rate*: the proportion of pages retrieved that are relevant to the topic of interest for the crawler. Typically, a number of heuristics depending on the domain and the item being searched for are used to improve a crawler's harvest rate.

In the sixth step of the crawling process, we discussed how the crawler finds additional links by parsing through the content. However, not all content is accessible through this process. Next, let's look at how this content can be made available to the web crawler.

6.1.4   *Deep crawling*

Deep or invisible web pages are pages that can't be reached by following the links on a page. This is especially true when a site uses AJAX and crawlers can't navigate to the content. One way to solve this is to use the sitemaps protocol, a URL inclusion protocol. Sitemaps work together with the robots.txt specification, which is a URL exclusion protocol. The sitemap protocol has wide adoption, including support from AOL, Microsoft, and Yahoo!

Sitemaps are XML documents that tell web crawlers which URLs are available for crawling. They also contain additional information about the URLs, such as how often they change, when they were last updated, and the relative importance of a URL with respect to other URLs on the site. For more details on the sitemaps specification, refer to the official site at http://www.sitemaps.org/protocol.php and the Google sitemap site at https://www.google.com/webmasters/tools/docs/en/protocol.html. Since there is a limit of 50,000 URLs and up to 10MB for a sitemap file, you can also use a sitemap index specifying the locations of your sitemap files. You can have up to 1,000 sitemaps, and can specify the location of your sitemap in your robots.txt file, which we look at in section 6.2.2.

Leveraging search engine optimization and the use of sitemaps is one of the cheapest ways of marketing your content. When done correctly, your application web page will show up high in the search results of search engines such as Google and Yahoo!, and this could generate relevant traffic to your site. To show up high on results from search engines such as Google, you also need to increase the authority—sites linking to your site—of your domain. For more information on making your site Google crawler-friendly, check out the Google Webmaster site: https://www.google.com/webmasters/tools/docs/en/about.html. Using the Google Webmaster tools, you can see information about what content has been indexed by the Google crawler, Googlebot; when it was last indexed; pages that the crawler had problems with; and so forth. As shown in figure 6.2, you can also submit a link to your sitemap file through the Google Webmaster tools and check for any errors in the XML files.

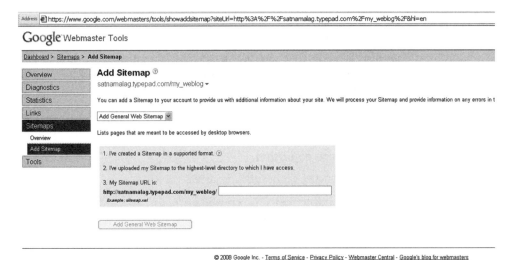

Figure 6.2   Submitting your site's sitemap using Google Webmaster tools

It's also helpful to list your site with the Open Directory Project (http://www.dmoz.org/), which is used by a number of search crawlers and will help you increase the page rank for your site.

6.1.5   *Available crawlers*

A number of open source web crawlers written in Java are available. Refer to http://www.manageability.org/blog/stuff/open-source-web-crawlers-java/view for a list of available open source crawlers, with Nutch[2] and Heritrix[3] perhaps being the two most popular.

Heritrix is the Internet Archive's open source, extensible, web-scale web crawler project. Nutch was built by Doug Cutting in an effort to provide a free and open web search engine. It's built on top of Lucene,[4] which we use in chapter 11 when we discuss intelligent search, and has shown good scalability. Nutch has been designed to scale to over 1 billion pages, and a demo index of more than 100 million documents was created in 2003. Both Nutch and Lucene are Apache projects and carry the Apache license.

---

[2]   http://lucene.apache.org/nutch/
[3]   http://crawler.archive.org/
[4]   Lucene is an open source software library for full-text search.

Later, in section 6.3, we use Nutch to crawl the web. Before we use an out-of-the-box crawler such as Nutch, it's useful to go through the process of building a web crawler ourselves—it'll help us better appreciate the complexities associated with crawling, especially as we try to make it scale.

Now that we know the basics of web crawling, let's systematically build a simple web crawler. This will give us useful insight into the inner workings of web crawlers and some of the issues related to web crawling.

6.2   Building an intelligent crawler step by step

In this section, we build a simple focused web crawler that follows hyperlinks to gather URLs of interest. To make the crawl focused, we use a regular expression matcher as the model for computing the relevance of content visited by the crawler. I've found this crawler to be useful in retrieving content of interest when I'm researching a particular topic. In our example, we retrieve content related to "collective intelligence" and seed the crawler by pointing it to the page on Wikipedia on collective intelligence.

6.2.1   Implementing the core algorithm

To implement our crawler, we build two classes:

1 `NaiveCrawler` implements the crawling process.
2 `CrawlerUrl` encapsulates the URL visited by the crawler.

Let's begin by looking at listing 6.1, which shows the `crawl()` method implemented by the crawler. This method follows the steps outlined in figure 6.1.

Listing 6.1   The `crawl()` method in the `NaiveCrawler` class

```
public void crawl() throws Exception {
    while (continueCrawling()) {              ❶
        CrawlerUrl url = getNextUrl();        ❷
        if (url != null) {
            printCrawlInfo();
            String content = getContent(url);   ❸
            if (isContentRelevant(content, regexpSearchPattern)) {   ❹
                saveContent(url, content);       ❺
                Collection<String> urlStrings =
                    extractUrls(content, url);    ❻
                addUrlsToUrlQueue(url, urlStrings);   ❼
            } else {
                System.out.println(url + " is not relevant ignoring ...");
            }
            Thread.sleep(this.delayBetweenUrls);   ❽
        }
    }
    closeOutputStream();
}
```

The crawler consists of eight steps:

❶ `continueCrawling()`: checks to make sure that the crawl exit criteria aren't met

❷ `getNextUrl()`: gets the next URL to be visited

③ getContent(url): retrieves the content associated with the URL

④ isContentRelevant(content, this.regexpSearchPattern): checks to see if the retrieved content is of interest

⑤ saveContent(url, content): saves the content if the URL is of interest

⑥ extractUrls(content, url): extracts URLs by parsing the content

⑦ addUrlsToUrlQueue(url, urlStrings): adds the extracted URLs to the URL queue

⑧ Thread.sleep(this.delayBetweenUrls): injects a delay before processing the next URL

We visit each of these steps in the next few sections. Before we go too far, let's look at the constructor for the NaiveCrawler, which is shown in listing 6.2.

Listing 6.2   The constructor for NaiveCrawler

```java
package com.alag.ci.webcrawler;

import java.io.*;
import java.net.URL;
import java.util.*;
import java.util.regex.*;

import org.apache.commons.httpclient.*;
import org.apache.commons.httpclient.methods.GetMethod;
import org.apache.commons.httpclient.params.HttpMethodParams;

public class NaiveCrawler {
    private static final String USER_AGENT = "User-agent:";
    private static final String DISALLOW = "Disallow:";
    public static final String REGEXP_HTTP = "<a href=\"http://(.)*\">";
    public static final String REGEXP_RELATIVE = "<a href=\"(.)*\">";
    private int maxNumberUrls;
    private long delayBetweenUrls;
    private int maxDepth;
    private Pattern regexpSearchPattern;
    private Pattern httpRegexp;
    private Pattern relativeRegexp;
    private Map<String, CrawlerUrl> visitedUrls = null;
    private Map<String, Collection<String>> sitePermissions = null;
    private Queue<CrawlerUrl> urlQueue = null;
    private BufferedWriter crawlOutput = null;
    private BufferedWriter crawlStatistics = null;
    private int numberItemsSaved = 0;

    public NaiveCrawler(Queue<CrawlerUrl> urlQueue, int maxNumberUrls,
      int maxDepth, long delayBetweenUrls, String regexpSearchPattern)
            throws Exception {
        this.urlQueue =
    urlQueue;
        this.maxNumberUrls = maxNumberUrls;
        this.delayBetweenUrls = delayBetweenUrls;
        this.maxDepth = maxDepth;
        this.regexpSearchPattern = Pattern.compile(regexpSearchPattern);
        this.visitedUrls = new HashMap<String, CrawlerUrl>();
```

Annotations:
- **Regular expression to extract out URLs** (pointing to REGEXP_HTTP / REGEXP_RELATIVE)
- **Regular expression pattern to focus crawling** (pointing to regexpSearchPattern)
- **Map keeps track of URLs visited** (pointing to visitedUrls)
- **Map keeps track of site permissions** (pointing to sitePermissions)
- **Extract next URL to visit** (pointing to urlQueue)
- **Output URLs stored in two files** (pointing to crawlOutput / crawlStatistics)

```
    this.sitePermissions = new HashMap<String, Collection<String>>();
    this.httpRegexp = Pattern.compile(REGEXP_HTTP);
    this.relativeRegexp = Pattern.compile(REGEXP_RELATIVE);
    crawlOutput = new BufferedWriter(new FileWriter("crawl.txt"));
    crawlStatistics = new BufferedWriter(new FileWriter(
        "crawlStatistics.txt"));
}
```

The crawler is seeded with an initial queue of `CrawlerUrls`, the maximum number of URLs to be visited, the maximum depth to be visited, the delay to be injected between visiting URLs, and a regular expression to guide the crawling process. This is shown in the constructor:

```
public NaiveCrawler(Queue<CrawlerUrl> urlQueue, int maxNumberUrls,
int maxDepth, long delayBetweenUrls, String regexpSearchPattern)
        throws Exception
```

At this point it's also helpful to look at the code for `CrawlerUrl`, as shown in listing 6.3.

Listing 6.3   The code for `CrawlerUrl`

```
package com.alag.ci.webcrawler;

import java.net.MalformedURLException;
import java.net.URL;

public class CrawlerUrl {
    private int depth = 0;                              ← Depth of URL
    private String urlString = null;                   ← String value for URL
    private URL url = null;
    private boolean isAllowedToVisit;                  ← Determines if crawler is allowed to visit this URL
    private boolean isCheckedForPermission = false;    ← Determines if crawler has visited this URL
    private boolean isVisited = false;

    public CrawlerUrl(String urlString, int depth) {
        this.depth = depth;
        this.urlString = urlString;
        computeURL();
    }

    private void computeURL() {
        try {
            url = new URL(urlString);
        } catch (MalformedURLException e) {
            // something is wrong
        }
    }

    public URL getURL() {
        return this.url;
    }

    public int getDepth() {
        return this.depth;
    }

    public boolean isAllowedToVisit() {
```

```java
        return isAllowedToVisit;
    }

    public void setAllowedToVisit(boolean isAllowedToVisit) {
        this.isAllowedToVisit = isAllowedToVisit;
        this.isCheckedForPermission = true;
    }

    public boolean isCheckedForPermission() {
        return isCheckedForPermission;
    }

    public boolean isVisited() {
        return isVisited;
    }

    public void setIsVisited() {
        this.isVisited = true;
    }

    public String getUrlString() {
        return this.urlString;
    }

    @Override
    public String toString() {
        return this.urlString + " [depth=" + depth + " visit="
                + this.isAllowedToVisit + " check="
                + this.isCheckedForPermission + "]";
    }

    @Override
    public int hashCode() {
        return this.urlString.hashCode();
    }

    @Override
    public boolean equals(Object obj) {
        return obj.hashCode() == this.hashCode();
    }

}
```

The CrawlerUrl class represents an instance of the URL that's visited by the crawler. It has utility methods to mark whether the URL has been visited and whether the site has given permission to crawl the URL.

Next, let's look in more detail at how the crawler gets the next URL for the crawl, which is shown in listing 6.4.

Listing 6.4 Getting the next url for the crawler

```java
    private boolean continueCrawling() {
        return ((!urlQueue.isEmpty()) && (getNumberOfUrlsVisited() <
            this.maxNumberUrls));
    }

    private CrawlerUrl getNextUrl() {
        CrawlerUrl nextUrl = null;
```

Next unvisited URL in queue

Run till out of URLs or exceed threshold

```
        while ((nextUrl == null) && (!urlQueue.isEmpty())) {
            CrawlerUrl crawlerUrl = this.urlQueue.remove();
            if (doWeHavePermissionToVisit(crawlerUrl)
                  && (!isUrlAlreadyVisited(crawlerUrl))
                  && isDepthAcceptable(crawlerUrl)) {
              nextUrl = crawlerUrl;
            }
        }
    }
    return nextUrl;
}
```

```
private void printCrawlInfo() throws Exception {      ◁——  Prints details
    StringBuilder sb = new StringBuilder();                  of crawler run
    sb.append("Queue length = ").append(this.urlQueue.size()).append(
            " visited urls=").append(getNumberOfUrlsVisited()).append(
            " site permissions=").append(this.sitePermissions.size());
    crawlStatistics.append("" + getNumberOfUrlsVisited()).append(
            "," + numberItemsSaved).append("," + this.urlQueue.size())
            .append("," + this.sitePermissions.size() + "\n");
    crawlStatistics.flush();
    System.out.println(sb.toString());
}
```

```
private int getNumberOfUrlsVisited() {      ◁——  Returns number
    return this.visitedUrls.size();                of URLs visited
}
```

```
private void closeOutputStream() throws Exception {      ◁——  Closes all
    crawlOutput.flush();                                       output streams
    crawlOutput.close();
    crawlStatistics.flush();
    crawlStatistics.close();
}
```

```
private boolean isDepthAcceptable(CrawlerUrl crawlerUrl) {      ◁——  Checks
    return crawlerUrl.getDepth() <= this.maxDepth;                    depth
}                                                                     of URL
```

```
private boolean isUrlAlreadyVisited(CrawlerUrl crawlerUrl) {   ◁——
    if ((crawlerUrl.isVisited())
          || (this.visitedUrls.containsKey(                    Checks if
              crawlerUrl.getUrlString())))) {                  URL has
      return true;                                             been visited
    }
    return false;
}
```

The method `continueCrawling` checks whether the crawler should stop crawling. Crawling stops when we run out of URLs to crawl or we've visited the maximum number of specified URLs. The method `getNextUrl` retrieves the next available URL that hasn't been visited, has acceptable depth, and that we're allowed to visit. To find out if we're allowed to visit a particular URL, we need to look at the robots.txt file.

6.2.2   *Being polite: following the robots.txt file*

A site can disallow web crawlers from accessing certain parts of the site by creating a robots.txt file and making it available via HTTP at the local URL /robots.txt. The robots.txt[5] specification was created in 1994. There's no agency that enforces the permissions provided by the site to the web crawlers, but it's considered good manners to respect the permissions provided by the site to the crawlers. Web crawlers that don't follow the guidelines risk having their IP blocked.

Let's look at a sample robots.txt file that I've taken from the Manning web site. It's shown in listing 6.5. This will help us understand the structure and the terms used to allow and disallow access to certain URLs.

Listing 6.5   Example robots.txt file at http://www.manning.com/robots.txt

```
User-agent: *
Disallow: /_mm/
Disallow: /_notes/
Disallow: /_baks/
Disallow: /MMWIP/

User-agent: googlebot
Disallow: *.csi
```

Note the following about the permissions set in this robots.txt file:

`User-agent: *` implies that this set of rules is valid for all web crawlers.

```
Disallow: /_mm/
Disallow: /_notes/
Disallow: /_baks/
Disallow: /MMWIP/
```

This specifies that no robots are allowed to visit content in any of the following directories: /_mm/, /_notes/, /_baks/, /MMWIP/.

The next specification, `User-agent: googlebot`, is applicable for the web crawler `googlebot`, which is forbidden to visit any pages that end with `.csi`. The specification requires only one directory per `Disallow:` line.

If for whatever reason you don't want any crawlers visiting your site, simply create the following robots.txt file:

```
User-agent: *
Disallow: /
```

Next, let's look at listing 6.6, which contains the methods to parse through the robots.txt file at a site to see if the crawler is allowed to visit the specified URL.

Listing 6.6   Parsing the robots.txt file to check for permissions

```
public boolean doWeHavePermissionToVisit(CrawlerUrl crawlerUrl) {
    if (crawlerUrl == null) {
        return false;
    }
    if (!crawlerUrl.isCheckedForPermission()) {
        crawlerUrl
        .setAllowedToVisit(computePermissionForVisiting(crawlerUrl));
    }
```

---

[5] www.robotstxt.org/wc/norobots.html

```
        return crawlerUrl.isAllowedToVisit();
    }

    private boolean computePermissionForVisiting(CrawlerUrl crawlerUrl) {
        URL url = crawlerUrl.getURL();
        boolean retValue = (url != null);                    Site permissions
        if (retValue) {                                      cached in local
            String host = url.getHost();          ◁───────┘  variable
            Collection<String> disallowedPaths =
                this.sitePermissions.get(host);
            if (disallowedPaths == null) {
                disallowedPaths = parseRobotsTxtFileToGetDisallowedPaths(
                    host);     ◁───┐  Parses content
            }                       of robots.txt
            String path = url.getPath();                ◁───┐  Checks for
            for (String disallowedPath : disallowedPaths) {    disallowed path
                if (path.contains(disallowedPath)) {
                    retValue = false;
                }
            }
        }
        return retValue;
    }

    private Collection<String> parseRobotsTxtFileToGetDisallowedPaths(
            String host) {
        String robotFilePath = getContent(            Gets robots.txt file
            "http://" + host + "/robots.txt");      ◁───┘
        Collection<String> disallowedPaths = new ArrayList<String>();
        if (robotFilePath != null) {
            Pattern p = Pattern.compile(USER_AGENT);    ◁──────┐  Pattern
            String[] permissionSets = p.split(robotFilePath);     matching
            String permissionString = "";                         to extract
            for (String permission : permissionSets) {            disallowed
                if (permission.trim().startsWith("*")) {          paths
                    permissionString = permission.substring(1);
                }
            }
            p = Pattern.compile(DISALLOW);
            String[] items = p.split(permissionString);
            for (String s : items) {
                disallowedPaths.add(s.trim());
            }
        }
        this.sitePermissions.put(host, disallowedPaths);
        return disallowedPaths;
    }
```

Once the robots.txt file has been parsed for a site, the permissions are cached in a local variable `disallowedPaths`. This ensures that we don't waste resources hitting the site unnecessarily.

The location of the sitemap can be specified in the robots.txt file by adding the following line (see section 6.1.4):

```
Sitemap: <sitemap location>
```

Next, let's look at how our crawler retrieves content.

6.2.3 *Retrieving the content*

As in the previous chapter, we retrieve content from a URL by using the org.apache.
commons.httpclient package, as shown in listing 6.7.

Listing 6.7   Retrieving content from URLs

```
private String getContent(String urlString) {
    return getContent(new CrawlerUrl(urlString, 0));
}

private String getContent(CrawlerUrl url) {
    HttpClient client = new HttpClient();
    GetMethod method = new GetMethod(url.getUrlString());         ⟵ Retrieves
    method.getParams().setParameter(HttpMethodParams.RETRY_HANDLER,   content
        new DefaultHttpMethodRetryHandler(3, false));              from URL
    String text = null;
    try {
        int statusCode = client.executeMethod(method);
        if (statusCode == HttpStatus.SC_OK) {
            text = readContentsFromStream(new InputStreamReader(method
                .getResponseBodyAsStream(),
                method.getResponseCharSet()));        ⟵ Used as
        }                                                recommended
    } catch (Throwable t) {                              by package
        System.out.println(t.toString());
        t.printStackTrace();
    } finally {
        method.releaseConnection();
    }
    markUrlAsVisited(url);                        Converts
    return text;                                  stream to String
}                                                 representation

private static String readContentsFromStream(Reader input)   ⟵
        throws IOException {
    BufferedReader bufferedReader = null;
    if (input instanceof BufferedReader) {
        bufferedReader = (BufferedReader) input;
    } else {
        bufferedReader = new BufferedReader(input);
    }
    StringBuilder sb = new StringBuilder();
    char[] buffer = new char[4 * 1024];
    int charsRead;
    while ((charsRead = bufferedReader.read(buffer)) != -1) {
        sb.append(buffer, 0, charsRead);
    }
    return sb.toString();                        Marked as visited
}                                                when content is
private void markUrlAsVisited(CrawlerUrl url) {   ⟵ retrieved
    this.visitedUrls.put(url.getUrlString(), url);
    url.setIsVisited();
}
```

The method getContent retrieves the content for the specified URL using the Http-
Client and GetMethod objects. The method extracts the content from the visited URL

by using the method `readContentsFromStream`. Once we have the content, we need to go through it to extract additional URLs that are within the content.

6.2.4   *Extracting URLs*

We extract two types of hyperlinked URLs.

First are hyperlinks with an absolute path, for example:

```
<a href=http://www.bath.ac.uk/carpp/davidskrbina/chap8.pdf
  class="external autonumber">[1]</a>
```

For this, we use the simple regular expression `<a href=\"http://(.)*\">`. This regular expression looks for strings starting with `<a href=\"http://"` and ending with the matching `\">`. Note the `\` after `href=`, which is used to escape the " character in Java.

Second are relative paths, an example of which is

```
<li><a href="/wiki/Systems_intelligence" title="Systems intelligence">
  Systems intelligence</a></li>
```

For this, we use the simple regular expression `<a  href=\"(.)*\">`. The code to extract these two kinds of URLs is shown in listing 6.8.

Listing 6.8   Extracting the URLs

```
public List<String> extractUrls(String text, CrawlerUrl crawlerUrl) {
   Map<String, String> urlMap = new HashMap<String, String>();
   extractHttpUrls(urlMap, text);                              Extracts
   extractRelativeUrls(urlMap, text, crawlerUrl);             HTTP-based
   return new ArrayList<String>(urlMap.keySet());            absolute URLs
}

private void extractHttpUrls(Map<String, String> urlMap, String text) {
   Matcher m = httpRegexp.matcher(text);
   while (m.find()) {
      String url = m.group();
      String[] terms = url.split("a href=\"");
      for (String term : terms) {
         if (term.startsWith("http")) {
            int index = term.indexOf("\"");
            if (index > 0) {
               term = term.substring(0, index);
            }
            urlMap.put(term, term);
         }
      }
   }
}

private void extractRelativeUrls(Map<String, String> urlMap,
   String text, CrawlerUrl crawlerUrl) {          Extracts
   Matcher m = relativeRegexp.matcher(text);      relative
   URL textURL = crawlerUrl.getURL();             URLs
   String host = textURL.getHost();
   while (m.find()) {
      String url = m.group();
      String[] terms = url.split("a href=\"");
```

```
        for (String term : terms) {
            if (term.startsWith("/")) {
                int index = term.indexOf("\"");
                if (index > 0) {
                    term = term.substring(0, index);
                }
                String s = "http://" + host + term;
                urlMap.put(s, s);
            }
        }
    }
}
```
Adds extracted
URLs to queue
if unvisited
```
private void addUrlsToUrlQueue(CrawlerUrl url,
    Collection<String> urlStrings) {        ◄──────┘
    int depth = url.getDepth() + 1;
    for (String urlString : urlStrings) {
        if (!this.visitedUrls.containsKey(urlString)) {
            this.urlQueue.add(new CrawlerUrl(urlString, depth));
        }
    }
}
```

The method `extractUrls` extracts two types of URLs. First, using the method `extractHttpUrls`, it extracts URLs that begin with `http` and follow a particular pattern. Second, using the method `extractRelativeUrls`, it extracts relative URLs using the a `href` prefix. All extracted URLs are added to the queue.

So far we've looked at the basic implementation of the crawler. Next, let's look at what's required to make the crawler intelligent or focused.

6.2.5 *Making the crawler intelligent*

To guide the crawling process, we use a simple regular expression pattern matcher as shown in listing 6.9.

Listing 6.9 Checking for relevant content

```
public static boolean isContentRelevant(String content,
        Pattern regexpPattern) {       ◄──┐  Content is relevant
    boolean retValue = false;             │  when it matches pattern
    if (content != null) {
        Matcher m = regexpPattern.matcher(content.toLowerCase());
        retValue = m.find();
    }
    return retValue;
}
```
Relevant
URLs written
to file
```
private void saveContent(CrawlerUrl url, String content)
    throws Exception {                         ◄──────┘
    this.crawlOutput.append(url.getUrlString()).append("\n");
    numberItemsSaved++;
}
```

The implementation of the `isContentRelevant` method simply tests to see if the content matches a regular expression. In our case, the `saveContent` method simply adds the URL to the list of interesting URLs.

We're now ready to make the crawler do some work for us.

6.2.6   *Running the crawler*

Now we're ready to launch our crawler to find relevant information for us in the web. Since this book is about collective intelligence, we use our crawler to find content related to collective intelligence. We seed our crawler with the page on Wikipedia relating to collective intelligence—http://en.wikipedia.org/wiki/Collective_intelligence—as shown in listing 6.10.

Listing 6.10   Main program for the crawler

```
public static void main(String[] args) {                    Seed crawler with
    try {                                                    Wikipedia page
        Queue<CrawlerUrl> urlQueue = new LinkedList<CrawlerUrl>();
        String url =
          "http://en.wikipedia.org/wiki/Collective_intelligence";
        String regexp = "collective.*intelligence";
        urlQueue.add(new CrawlerUrl(url, 0));
        NaiveCrawler crawler = new NaiveCrawler(urlQueue, 2000, 5,
          1000L, regexp);                Visit 2000 sites, depth
        crawler.crawl();                 of 5, wait I second      Crawl focused for
    } catch (Throwable t) {                                      terms *collective*
        System.out.println(t.toString());          }            and *intelligence*
    }
}
```

In our main program, we simply seed the crawler with a link to the Wikipedia site, set it to search for content having phrase *collective intelligence*, and allow the crawler to crawl.

Figure 6.3 shows the graph of the number of relevant URLs found by the crawler as a function of how many URLs it visits. Note the couple of steep gradients where the crawler finds a bunch of relevant content and then chugs along.

Listing 6.11 shows a sample of the relevant URLs that were discovered by the crawler. Imagine the usefulness of this tool when you're researching a particular topic of interest. This simple crawler can save you a considerable amount of time and effort by automating the process of following hyperlinks to discover relevant content.

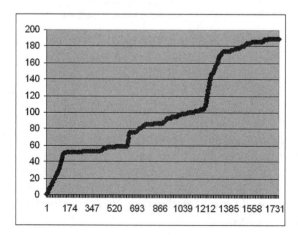

Figure 6.3   Number of relevant URLs retrieved as a function of number of URLs visited

Listing 6.11   Sample of the URLs retrieved by the crawler

```
http://en.wikipedia.org/wiki/Collective_intelligence
http://en.wikipedia.org/wiki/Douglas_Engelbart
http://en.wikipedia.org/wiki/Francis_Heylighen
http://ko.wikipedia.org/wiki/%EC%A7%91%EB%8B%A8%EC%A7%80%EC%84%B1
http://de.wikipedia.org/wiki/Kollektive_Intelligenz
http://en.wikipedia.org/wiki/Category:Collective_intelligence
http://en.wikipedia.org/wiki/Superorganism
http://en.wikipedia.org/wiki/Crowd_psychology
http://pt.wikipedia.org/wiki/Intelig%C3%AAncia_coletiva
http://en.wikipedia.org/wiki/Collaborative_filtering
http://en.wikipedia.org/wiki/Group_think
http://zh.wikipedia.org/wiki/%E7%BE%A4%E9%AB%94%E6%99%BA%E6%85%A7
http://www.TheTransitioner.org
http://it.wikipedia.org/wiki/Intelligenza_collettiva
http://en.wikipedia.org/wiki/Swarm_Intelligence
http://en.wikipedia.org/wiki/Special:Whatlinkshere/Collective_intelligence
http://www.axiopole.com/pdf/Managing_collective_intelligence.pdf
http://www.communicationagents.com/tom_atlee/
http://cci.mit.edu/index.html
http://www.pmcluster.com/
...
```

In section 11.5.4, we use this output to create a specialized search engine.

So far in this section, we've implemented a simple web crawler and made it intelligent. This gave you an overview of the various components that are required to make a crawler. Before we can use this in the real world, we need to make some enhancements, which we look at next.

6.2.7   *Extending the crawler*

If your goal is to crawl the entire Web or major parts of it, you'll need a crawler that's much more efficient than our simple single-threaded crawler. The bottleneck in a typical crawling process is the network delay in downloading content. Ideally, you want to download content from different hosts simultaneously. For this, you may want to enhance the crawler to have a pool of worker threads that work in parallel drawing URLs from the URL queue. Or even better, you may want to enhance the crawler to execute in parallel on distributed machines. You'll need to store the URLs visited and the queue of URLs to be visited in a database that's accessible to all the machines. You may also want to partition the URL space among the many machines, perhaps using namespaces for the URLs.

The model that we've used to focus the search is a simple pattern matcher. You'll want to use more sophisticated models, which we develop in the second part of this book. You may also want to enhance your crawler to visit URLs based on their relevance. Some crawling processes prefer to visit URLs that are referenced by many other sites; that is, sites with a high authority. Hubs—summary pages with many outgoing links—are also typically preferred by crawlers.

Given the dynamic nature of the web, you'll want to visit pages periodically to keep the content fresh. Commercial crawlers refresh content more often from sites that have shown to be historically more dynamic. For example, a news site or the home page of a site with user-generated content is far more dynamic than static web pages for a company web site. Efficient crawlers also have a way to detect mirror sites and duplicate pages that a site may contain. Our simple crawler injects time delay between successive URL requests; you may want to enhance it to inject a delay between successive URL requests to the same host.

By this time, you should have a good understanding of how a web crawler works and the issues related to building a truly scalable web crawler, which is a nontrivial task. For large-scale web crawling, you'll really want to use a scalable open source crawler, such as Nutch, which we look at next.

6.3   Scalable crawling with Nutch

Nutch is a Java-based open source web crawler that has been demonstrated to scale well. It was developed by Doug Cutting and is built on top of Lucene, an API for indexing and searching that we use throughout this book. Nutch uses a plug-in–based architecture, allowing it to be easily customized. Its processing is segmented, allowing it to be distributed. Nutch consists of two main components: the crawler and the searcher.

There are some excellent freely available tutorials to help set up Nutch and crawl the Web.[6] There are a couple of excellent articles on Java.net by Tim White that provide a great overview of how to crawl and search with Nutch version 0.7.

In this section, we briefly go through the process of setting up and running version 0.9 of Nutch on Windows. This section consolidates information from the many tutorials and articles available on the Net, and there are some differences between 0.9 and the earlier versions. This section may well save you hours going through the various tutorials on the Web. After this section, we talk about more advanced concepts of Hadoop and MapReduce, which are used by Nutch to scale and run in a distributed mode. If you're serious about large-scale crawling, you probably want to go through this section and its referenced material in detail.

6.3.1   Setting up Nutch

Let's set up Nutch to crawl Wikipedia, starting with the Wikipedia page on collective intelligence. For this, we seed the engine with the same base URL that we used in the previous section: http://en.wikipedia.org/wiki/Collective_intelligence. You need to perform the following eight steps to carry out this intranet crawl.

GETTING THE REQUIRED SOFTWARE

1 Download Nutch. You can download the latest version from http://apache. mirrors.hoobly.com/lucene/nutch/. This section works with version 0.9 (nutch-0.9. tar.gz; about 68Mb), which was released in April 2007. Unzip the contents of the zipped file to create a directory nutch/nutch -0.9.

2 Nutch requires a Unix-like environment to run its shell scripts to create indexes. If you're trying this out in the Windows environment, you'll need to download and install Cygwin (http://www.cygwin.com/).

---

[6]   See http://wiki.apache.org/nutch/Nutch_-_The_Java_Search_Engine, http://wiki.apache.org/ nutch/Nutch_0%2e9_Crawl_Script_Tutorial, and http://lucene.apache.org/nutch/tutorial.html.

3 We need a servlet container. If you don't already have one, download Apache Tomcat from http://tomcat.apache.org/download-55.cgi. I used Tomcat version 6.0.13 (apache-tomcat-6.0.13.zip; 6.2 Mb).

4 Set NUTCH_JAVA_HOME to the root of your JVM installation. You'll need Java 1.4.x or better. For example, I set this variable to C:\dev\Java\jdk1.5.0_06 on my local system.

5 Make sure that Java, Tomcat, and Nutch are in your classpath. For example, my classpath includes C:\nutch\nutch-0.9\bin;C:\apache-tomcat-6.0.13\apache-tomcat-6.0.13\bin; %JAVA_HOME%.

CREATING AN INDEX

6 Nutch uses a file to create an index of the content retrieved. Create a file nutch/nutch-0.9/urls on your local file system.

7 Create a file called seed-urls with the following as the only entry in the file: http://en.wikipedia.org/wiki/Collective_intelligence

CONFIGURING FOR INTRANET CRAWL

8 Edit the file conf/crawl-urlfilter.txt and replace MY.DOMAIN.NAME with the name of the domain you wish to crawl. For our example, we limit the crawl to the wikipedia.org domain, so the line should read

```
# accept hosts in MY.DOMAIN.NAME
+^http://([a-z0-9]*\.)*wikipedia.org/
```

This regex will include any URL in the domain wikipedia.org.

6.3.2 *Running the Nutch crawler*

You're now ready to launch the Wikipedia crawl. In your Cygwin window, go to the directory nutch/nutch-0.9 and run this command:

```
nutch crawl urls -dir crawl.wiki-ci -depth 2
```

This launches the crawl process with a maximum depth of 2. The -dir option specifies the directory in which content from the crawl should be stored. This creates a directory crawl.wiki-ci under the nutch directory (C:\nutch\nutch-0.9\crawl.wiki-ci on my system). Your Cygwin window should be similar to the one shown in figure 6.4.

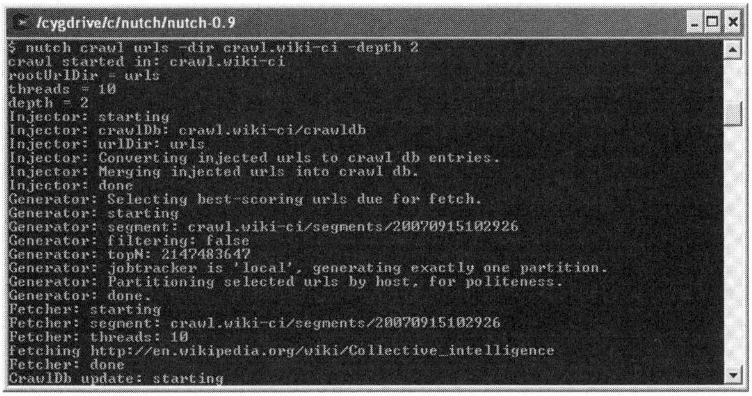

Figure 6.4 The Cygwin window after the crawl command

After a few minutes, the crawl should finish and there should be a new directory under nutch-0.9 called crawl.wiki-ci, as shown in figure 6.5.

Nutch has created four main directories to store the crawling information:

- *Crawldb*—Stores the state of the URLs along with how long it took to fetch, index, and parse the data.
- *Indexes*—A set of indexes created by Lucene.
- *Linkdb*—This directory contains the links associated with each URL, including the source URL and the anchor text of the link.
- *Segments*—There are a number of segments in this directory. Each segment is named based on the date and time that it was created and contains the pages that are fetched by the crawler during a particular run.

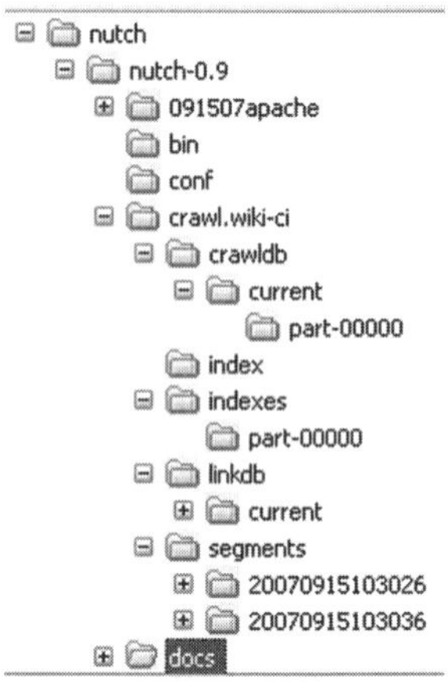

Figure 6.5 The directory structure after the crawl

Next, let's look at statistics associated with the crawldb. Execute the following command:

```
nutch readdb crawl.wiki-ci/crawldb -stats
```

You should see output similar to that shown in figure 6.6.

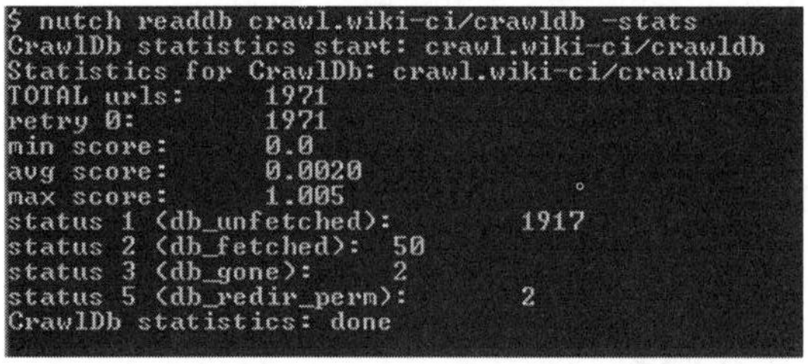

Figure 6.6 The stats associated with the crawldb

It's also helpful to dig deeper into the crawldb and get a dump of the contents in the database. Execute the following command:

```
nutch readdb crawl.wiki-ci/crawldb -dump crawl.wiki-ci/stats
```

This generates a file C:\nutch\nutch-0.9\crawl.wiki-ci\stats part-000, the contents of which will be similar to listing 6.12.

Listing 6.12 Dump of the URLs from the crawldb

```
http://ar.wikipedia.org/wiki/%D8%BA%D8%A8%D8%A7%D8%A1  Version: 5
Status: 1 (db_unfetched)
Fetch time: Sat Sep 15 10:32:03 PDT 2007
Modified time: Wed Dec 31 16:00:00 PST 1969
Retries since fetch: 0
Retry interval: 30.0 days
Score: 2.3218017E-4
```

```
Signature: null
Metadata: null

http://ca.wikipedia.org/wiki/M%C3%A8trica_%28matem%C3%A0tiques%29
     Version: 5
Status: 1 (db_unfetched)
Fetch time: Sat Sep 15 10:32:02 PDT 2007
Modified time: Wed Dec 31 16:00:00 PST 1969
Retries since fetch: 0
Retry interval: 30.0 days
Score: 3.1979533E-4
Signature: null
Metadata: null
```

You can look into the contents of the segments in a similar manner:

```
nutch readseg -dump crawl.wiki-ci/
  segments/20070915103026 crawl.wiki-ci/stats/segments
```

This create a file dump in C:\nutch\nutch-0.9\crawl.wiki-ci\stats\segments.

Next, in listing 6.13 let's see how we can search the newly created search index using the Nutch web application.

Listing 6.13 Dump of a Nutch segment

```
Recno:: 0
URL:: http://en.wikipedia.org/

CrawlDatum::
Version: 5
Status: 67 (linked)
Fetch time: Sat Sep 15 10:30:33 PDT 2007
Modified time: Wed Dec 31 16:00:00 PST 1969
Retries since fetch: 0
Retry interval: 30.0 days
Score: 0.016949153
Signature: null
Metadata: null

Recno:: 1
URL:: http://en.wikipedia.org/skins-1.5

CrawlDatum::
Version: 5
Status: 67 (linked)
Fetch time: Sat Sep 15 10:30:33 PDT 2007
Modified time: Wed Dec 31 16:00:00 PST 1969
Retries since fetch: 0
Retry interval: 30.0 days
Score: 0.016949153
Signature: null
Metadata: null
```

With this overview, let's next look at how we can set up Nutch to search for the contents that have been crawled.

6.3.3   *Searching with Nutch*

When you unzip your Nutch installation, you should find the nutch.war file. Place this war file in your Tomcat webapps directory. The Nutch web application finds its indexes in the /segments directory where you start Tomcat, so we need to point Nutch to where we have the crawled data. Therefore, go to

> C:\apache-tomcat-6.0.13\apache-tomcat-6.0.13\webapps\nutch\WEB-INF\classes\ nutch-site.xml

Change the contents of this file to those shown in listing 6.14.

Listing 6.14   Configuring nutch-site.xml

```
<?xml version="1.0"?>
<?xml-stylesheet type="text/xsl" href="configuration.xsl"?>

<!-- Put site-specific property overrides in this file. -->
<configuration>
<property>
<name>searcher.dir</name>                         Directory where
<value>C:\nutch\nutch-0.9\crawl.wiki-ci</value> ◁─── Nutch should get data
</property>
</configuration>
```

Now, start up Tomcat (startup.sh) and point your browser to the following URL (assuming that Tomcat is running on its default port of 8080):

```
http://localhost:8080/nutch
```

Your browser window should show the Nutch search screen, as shown in figure 6.7.

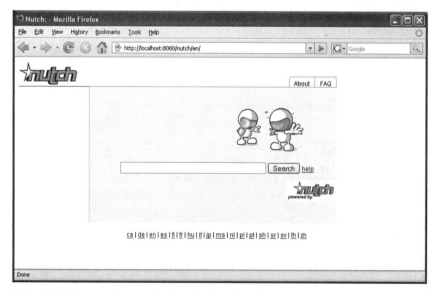

Figure 6.7   The search screen for the Nutch application

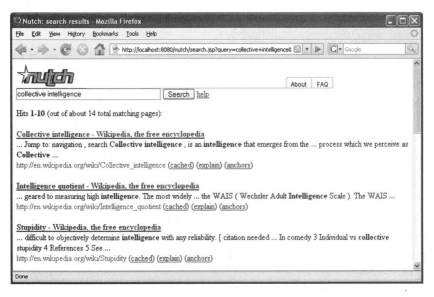

Figure 6.8 Searching for *collective intelligence* using the Nutch search application

Search for the term *collective intelligence* and your browser should look similar to the one in figure 6.8. Play around with the various links, especially the explain and anchors links that are associated with each result.

So far in this section, we've gone through a simple example to crawl Wikipedia, starting with its page on collective intelligence. We've gone through the various directories generated by Nutch and looked at how to use the search tool. This should have given you a good overview of how to use Nutch. I referred you to the various references to set up the system to do a full Internet crawl and maintain the crawled data. Before we end this section, it's useful to briefly go through two important concepts: Apache Hadoop and MapReduce. These are the principles on which Nutch has been built to scale to billions of pages using commodity hardware in a distributed platform.

6.3.4 *Apache Hadoop, MapReduce, and Dryad*

Apache Hadoop is a software platform that lets you write and run applications for processing large datasets using commodity hardware in a distributed platform. Hadoop uses the Hadoop Distributed File System[7] (HDFS) and implements MapReduce.[8]

HDFS is a part of Apache Hadoop project, which in turn is a subproject of Apache Lucene. HDFS is motivated by concepts used in the Google File System.[9] The MapReduce concept has been extensively used by Google and deals with dividing the application into small units of work that can be executed in a distributed environment.

---

[7] See http://lucene.apache.org/hadoop/hdfs_design.htm.
[8] See Dean, J., and Ghemawat, S., MapReduce: Simplified Data Processing on Large Clusters, http://labs.google.com/papers/mapreduce.html.
[9] http://labs.google.com/papers/gfs.html

Apache Hadoop aims to provide an open source implementation of MapReduce that anyone can use in their own distributed environment.

In the MapReduce paradigm, computation is split into two parts. First, apply a `map` function to each logical record to generate a set of intermediate key/value pairs. Then apply a `reduce` operation to compute a final answer that combines all the values for a given key.

A simple example best illustrates the paradigm, and is illustrated in figure 6.9. Assume that we need to compute the term frequencies associated with the various terms in a page. Using part of the example we looked at in section 4.3, let's assume that a page consists of the following text:

Collective Intelligence: Collective intelligence improves user experience

To process this, we would write a `map` method that is passed, say, an ID for the page as the key and the page text as the value. This method then generates seven intermediate key value pairs, one for each word, as shown in figure 6.9. These intermediate values are processed by the `reduce` function that counts the values for each of the keys. The output from the `reduce` function consists of five terms with their associated frequencies. Using this paradigm, a developer doesn't need to worry about distribution; the code is automatically parallelized.

Nutch uses Apache Hadoop and the MapReduce paradigm to scale to crawling and indexing billions of pages. For more details on Hadoop and MapReduce, see the references on this topic.

Microsoft's answer to MapReduce has been the development of Dryad.[10] Dryad is a distributed computing platform developed by Microsoft Research and designed to provide operating system–level abstraction for thousands of PCs in a data center. Like MapReduce, a programmer can leverage parallel processing capabilities of thousands of machines without knowing anything about concurrent programming. With Dryad, you write several sequential programs and then connect them using one-way channels.

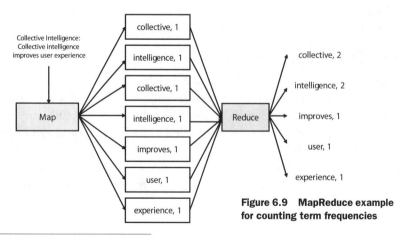

Figure 6.9   MapReduce example for counting term frequencies

---

[10] http://research.microsoft.com/research/sv/dryad/

The computation can be represented as a directed graph, with each vertex corresponding to a program and channels corresponding to the edges of the graph. A job in Dryad corresponds to traversing a directed acyclic graph, whose structure can change even during execution. Dryad infrastructure manages the creation, management, monitoring, and visualization of jobs. It provides fault-tolerance to machine failures and automatically re-executes failed jobs.

In this section, we looked at using the open source crawler, Nutch, for crawling the web. We also looked at how Nutch can be used for searching through the retrieved content and the various options for building a scalable web crawler.

6.4   Summary

Web crawlers are programs that retrieve content from sites by following hyperlinks in the document. Crawlers are useful for retrieving content from external sites. When the crawling process is guided by relevancy, it's called focused or intelligent crawling.

A typical focused crawling process consists of seeding the crawler with some seed URLs. The crawler visits the next available URL, retrieves the content, and measures the relevance of the content to the topic of interest. If the content is acceptable, then it parses the content to extract URLs and in turn visits these URLs.

There are significant costs associated with crawling the entire Web. These include costs for the software and hardware, high-speed network access, storage devices, and administrating the infrastructure. Using a focused crawler can help retrieve relevant information by crawling a subset of available crawling URLs.

With this chapter, we conclude the first part of the book that deals with gathering information from within and outside your application. In the next part, we look at how to analyze this information and build models to make your application more intelligent.

6.5   Resources

A Standard for Robots Exclusion. http://www.robotstxt.org/wc/norobots.html

Chakrabarti , Soumen. *Mining the Web. Discovering Knowledge from Hypertext Data*. 2005. Morgan Kaufmann Publishers.

Chakrabarti, Soumen, Martin H. Van den Berg, and Byron E. Dom. "Focused Crawling: A New Approach to Topic-Specific Web Resource Discovery." 1999. Proceedings of the 8th International WWW Conference, pp. 545-562.

Cutting, Doug. "MapReduce in Nutch." http://wiki.apache.org/nutch-data/attachments/Presentations/attachments/mapred.pdf

Dean, J., and S. Ghemawat. "MapReduce: Simplified Data Processing on Large Clusters." http://labs.google.com/papers/mapreduce.html

De Bra, Paul, Geert-Jan Houben, Yoram Kornatzky, and Renier Post. "Information Retrieval in Distributed Hypertexts." 1994. Proceedings of the 4th RIAO (Computer Assisted Information Retrieval) Conference, pp. 481-491.

Ghemawat, Sanjay, Howard Gobioff, and Shun-Tak Leung. "The Google File System." http://labs.google.com/papers/gfs.html

Gulli, A., and A. Signorini. "The Indexable Web is more than 11.5 billion pages." 2005. http://www.cs.uiowa.edu/~asignori/web-size/

Hadoop. http://lucene.apache.org/hadoop/

"How Google Works." http://www.baselinemag.com/article2/0,1540,1985048,00.asp

Isard, Michael, Mihai Budiu, Yuan Yu, Andrew Birrell, and Dennis Fetterly. "Dryad, Distributed Data-Parallel Programs from Sequential Building Blocks." Eurosys '07. http://research.microsoft.com/users/mbudiu/eurosys07.pdf

Lucene Hadoop Wiki. http://labs.google.com/papers/gfs.html

"Nutch 0.9 Crawl Script Tutorial." http://wiki.apache.org/nutch/Nutch_0%2e9_Crawl_Script_Tutorial

Nutch, the Java Search Engine. http://wiki.apache.org/nutch/Nutch_-_The_Java_Search_Engine

Nutch Wiki. http://wiki.apache.org/nutch/

NutchHadoop Tutorial. "How to Setup Nutch and Hadoop."

http://wiki.apache.org/nutch/NutchHadoopTutorial

Perez, Juan Carlos, IDG News Service. "Google Counts More Than 1 Trillion Unique Web URLs", http://www.pcworld.com/businesscenter/article/148964/google_counts_more_than_1_trillion_unique_web_urls.html

"Simple MapReduce Tutorial." http://wiki.apache.org/nutch/SimpleMapReduceTutorial

Sitemaps. http://en.wikipedia.org/wiki/Sitemaps

"The Hadoop Distributed File System: Architecture and Design." http://lucene.apache.org/hadoop/hdfs_design.htm

What are sitemaps? http://www.sitemaps.org/

White, Tom. Tom White's Blog. "MapReduce." http://weblogs.java.net/blog/tomwhite/archive/2005/09/mapreduce.html

"Introduction to Nutch, Part 1: Crawling." http://today.java.net/pub/a/today/2006/01/10/introduction-to-nutch-1.html

"Introduction to Nutch, Part 2: Searching." http://today.java.net/pub/a/today/2006/02/16/introduction-to-nutch-2.html

Zhuang, Ziming, Rohit Wage, and C. Lee Giles. "What's There and What's Not? Focused Crawling for Missing Documents in Digital Libraries." 2005. JCDL, pp. 301-310.

Part 2

Deriving intelligence

Now that we've collected data, in this part we focus on deriving intelligence from it. Part 2 consists of four chapters—an introduction chapter to the data mining process, standards, and toolkits, followed by chapters on developing a text-analysis toolkit, finding patterns through clustering, and making predictions.

Chapter 7 should give you a good overview of the data mining process, along with a basic understanding of WEKA, the open source data mining toolkit, and JDM, the standard data mining API. Next, in chapter 8 we develop a text-processing toolkit to analyze unstructured content. This toolkit is useful for converting text into a format that's usable by the learning algorithms. Chapter 9 deals with finding patterns of similar items using the process of clustering. Lastly, chapter 10 looks at how we can make predictions by using classification and regression algorithms.

At the end of this part, you should have a good understanding of the data mining process, the various APIs, and the key algorithms for deriving intelligence.

Data mining: process, toolkits, and standards

7

This chapter covers
- A brief overview of the data mining process
- Introduction to key mining algorithms
- WEKA, the open source data mining software
- JDM, the Java Data Mining standard

The data mining process enables us to find gems of information by analyzing data. In this chapter, you'll be introduced to the field of data mining. The various data mining algorithms, tools, and data mining jargon can be overwhelming. This chapter provides a brief overview and walks you through the process involved in building useful models. Implementing algorithms takes time and expertise. Fortunately, there are free open source data mining frameworks that we can leverage. We use WEKA—Waikato Environment for Knowledge Analysis—a Java-based open source toolkit that's widely used in the data mining community. We look at the core packages of WEKA and work through a simple example to show how WEKA can be used for learning. We really don't want our implementation to be specific to WEKA. Fortunately, two initiatives through the Java Community Process—JSR 73 and JSR 247—provide a standard API for data mining. This API is known as *Java Data Mining (JDM)*. We discuss JDM in the last section of this chapter and review its core components. We take an even deeper look at JDM in chapters 9 and 10, when we discuss clustering and predictive models.

7.1   *Core concepts of data mining*

Data mining is the automated process of analyzing data to discover patterns and build predictive models. Data mining has a strong theoretical foundation and draws from many fields, including mathematics, statistics, and machine learning. *Machine learning* is a branch of artificial intelligence that deals with developing algorithms that machines can use to learn the patterns in data in an automated manner. Data mining is different from data analysis, which typically deals with fitting data to already-known models. Querying for data and analyzing the data for summaries and trends—commonly known as *reporting* and *OLAP (online analytic processing)*—are common forms of data analysis. Data mining, on the other hand, deals with the discovery of previously unknown patterns or models by analyzing the data. They provide new insight into the data being analyzed. Reporting, OLAP, and data mining all fall in the general area of *business intelligence.*

In this section, we look at some of the core concepts associated with the process of data mining. We first discuss the three forms of attributes: numerical, ordinal, and nominal. Next, we look at supervised and unsupervised learning, some of the key learning algorithms, and the data mining process.

7.1.1   *Attributes*

A learning algorithm needs data in order to learn and find patterns; this data can be in the form of examples, where each example consists of a set of *attributes* or *dimensions.* Each attribute should be independent of other attributes; it shouldn't be possible to compute the value of an attribute based on another attribute's value. Depending on whether the attributes can be ordered and the kind of values they can take, we can categorize attributes into the following three forms:

- *Numerical* values have a real number associated with them. Two numerical values can be compared. Further, numerical values can be continuous (for example, a person's age) or can take only discrete values, such as the number of images uploaded by a user. Since every numerical value can be compared to another numerical value, there is ordering associated with numerical attributes. Furthermore, the difference in magnitude between two numerical values provides a measure of closeness—for example, the number 5 is closer to 3 than the number 10.

- *Ordinal* values are also discrete, but there is ordering associated with them. For example, {small, medium, large} may be used to characterize the size of an article. Here, there's no absolute measurement of how much smaller small is compared to medium; just that medium is larger than small, while large is larger than medium.

- *Nominal* values consist of discrete values that are in no particular order, also sometimes called categorical. For example, the color of a person's eyes could be {blue, green, black, brown}. Here, a linear distance measure isn't helpful in getting a measure of closeness between two points—for example, there's no way to state that blue is closer to green than black in the previous example.

There are a number of algorithms that work either with continuous values or with nominal values. It's possible to convert a continuous variable into a discrete variable and vice versa.

Continuous numeric values can be discretized by creating appropriate bins. For example, the number of times a user has logged in to the application in a week can be converted into discrete values, *small, medium,* and *large.* One such binning criteria might be this: if the number of logins is one, then it falls in the *small* category, two to five logins corresponds to the *medium* category, while greater than five amounts to a *large* number of logins.

Discrete variables can be converted to numerical variables in the following manner. First, let's consider the example of a person's eye color. There were four values associated with this nominal variable: {blue, green, black, brown}. This can be transformed into four attributes: *blue, green, black,* and *brown.* These attributes have a value of 1 when the color of the person's eyes matches the attribute; otherwise the value is 0.

Ordinal variables that are discrete and have an ordering associated with them can be treated differently. Let's consider an attribute that takes three values, *small, medium,* and *large.* This can be converted into three attributes, *small, medium,* and *large.* When a variable takes the *large* value, all these three attributes take the value of 1; *medium* corresponds to setting the *small* and *medium* attributes to a value of 1; while a value of *small* will correspond to simply setting the variable *small* to 1. Table 7.1 summarizes the common terms used to describe the different kinds of attributes.

Algorithms that discover relationships between different attributes in a dataset are known as *association rule* algorithms, while algorithms that analyze the importance of an attribute in relation to predicting the value of another attribute or in clustering data are known as *attribute importance* algorithms.

Table 7.1 Common terms used to describe attributes

Attribute type	Description	Discrete/ continuous	Example
Continuous	Takes real values	Continuous	The amount of time spent by a user on the site
Ordinal	There is ordering in the fixed set of values that the attribute can take	Discrete or continuous	Length of session expressed as {small, medium, large}
Nominal	There is no ordering related to the values taken from the fixed set by the attribute	Discrete	Gender of a person {male, female}

Based on how data is analyzed, algorithms can be classified into supervised and unsupervised learning, which we look at next.

7.1.2   *Supervised and unsupervised learning*

In *supervised learning*, we have a training dataset, with a set of instances or examples for which the predicted value is known. Each example consists of input attributes and a predicted attribute, as shown in figure 7.1. The aim of the algorithm is to build a mathematical model that can predict the output attribute value given a set of input attribute values. Decision trees, neural networks, regression, Bayesian belief networks, and so on are all examples of *predictive* models. The predictive models built by some algorithms such as decision trees, belief networks, and rule induction are easier to understand than those of other algorithms such as neural networks and regres-

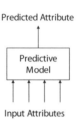

Predicted Attribute

Predictive Model

Input Attributes

Figure 7.1   A predictive model makes a prediction based on the values for the input attributes.

sion. The accuracy of a predictive model is measured by means of how well the model does on previously unseen data. When the predicted attribute—the *target*—is a categorical attribute, the prediction model is also known as a *classifier* and the problem is one of *classification*. For example, a predictive modeler might classify a blog entry into appropriate categories. When the output attribute is a continuous, it's also known as a *regressor* and the problem is one of *regression*.

In *unsupervised* learning, there's no predicted value to be learned. The algorithm analyzes the multidimensional data to form clusters—groups of similar points. For example, figure 7.2 shows two clusters formed by analyzing two-dimensional data. K-means clustering, hierarchical clustering, and density-based clustering are examples of commonly used clustering algorithms. Unsupervised learning is good at analyzing the data and discovering patterns in an automated manner.

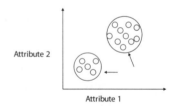

Attribute 2

Attribute 1

Figure 7.2   Two clusters in a two-dimensional attribute space found by analyzing the proximity of the data points

Now that we've classified the various learning algorithms into supervised and unsupervised learning, let's briefly look at some commonly used learning algorithms. We revisit a few of these algorithms in greater detail in chapters 9 and 10.

7.1.3   *Key learning algorithms*

In this section, we provide a high-level overview of some the commonly used learning algorithms: decision trees, clustering, regression, neural networks (MLP and RBF), SVM, and Bayesian algorithms.

A *decision tree* is one of the most commonly used classifiers and deals only with nominal attributes. Let's go through an example to understand the basic concepts. Let's assume that we want to predict whether a user will like a recently introduced new feature in our application. Assume that we've created a dataset consisting of two attributes: *user gender* and *number of logins.* The first step is to create all the attributes into nominal attributes. By the process of binning, the number of logins gets converted into three values: {small, medium, and large}. The user's gender is already nominal and can take two values: {male, female}. Let's assume that we've created a dataset where each instance is a user with these two outputs, along with whether the user liked the new feature. Figure 7.3 shows an example decision tree, which consists of *nodes* and *links.* A node in the tree corresponds to an attribute value evaluation. The root node in this example corresponds to the attribute *number of logins.* The arcs correspond to the categorical values associated with the attribute. There are three links from the parent node corresponding to the three nominal values associated with the attribute: {small, medium, large}.

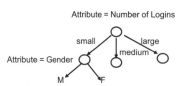

Figure 7.3   An example decision tree showing two attributes

It's easy to translate decision trees into rules to understand the logic discovered. For example, the rule for the output from the second row is

> If {number of logins = "small"} and {gender = male} then ….
> If {number of logins = "small"} and {gender = female} then ….

Among clustering algorithms, k-means is perhaps one of the most well-known. The algorithm is typically seeded with *k* randomly selected clusters, where *k* is the number of predefined clusters. Each example is then associated with the cluster whose center is closest to that point. At the end of the iteration, the means of the *k* clusters are recomputed by looking at all the points associated with the cluster. This process of learning continues until the examples don't move between clusters or a maximum number of iterations is reached.

Hierarchical clustering is another popular clustering algorithm. In this algorithm, each data point starts as its own cluster. Next, two points that are most similar are combined together into a parent node. This process is repeated until we're left with no more points to combine.

Density-based clustering algorithms try to find high-density areas that are separated by low-density areas. These algorithms automatically determine the number of clusters by omitting low-density regions, which are treated as noise. We look at clustering algorithms in greater detail in chapter 9.

Given two points in a two-dimensional space, it's fairly straightforward to compute the two constants associated to find a line that joins two points. Now extend this concept to finding the line or other higher-dimensional functions that best fit multiple points in a multi-dimensional space. Regression-based algorithms represent the data in a matrix form and transform the matrix to compute the required parameters. Regression-based techniques require numerical attributes to create the predictive models. These algorithms aim to minimize the sum of the squared error between the predicted value and the actual value for all the cases in the training dataset.

Multi-layer perceptron (MLP) and *radial basis functions (RBF)* are two of the most commonly used *neural networks.* Neural networks are useful both as predictive models and as classifiers.

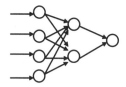

Figure 7.4   A multi-layer perceptron where the input from one layer feeds into the next layer

An MLP consists of a number of layers, beginning with the input layer as shown in figure 7.4. The number of input nodes corresponds to the number of input attributes. Depending on the nature of the transformation function used by the node, the input values may be scaled between –1 and 1. Links in the network correspond to a weight by which the output from the node is multiplied. In a three-layer network, the second set of nodes is known as *hidden nodes.* The input to a node is the sum of the outputs from the nodes, multiplied by the weight associated with the link. The third layer is the *output layer* and predicts the attribute of interest.

Building an MLP predictive model consists of estimating the weights associated with each of the links. Typically, a gradient descent algorithm is used to learn the weights associated with an MLP; the learning procedure is known as *back propagation.* With this procedure, there's no guarantee of finding a global minimum, and the learning process may be enhanced to run in conjunction with some optimization methodologies, such as simulated annealing or genetic algorithms.

In an RBF, first the data is clustered into k-clusters using the k-means clustering algorithm. Each cluster corresponds to a node in the network, the output from which is dependent on the proximity of the input to the center of the node. The output from this layer is transformed into the output using weights. Learning the weights associated with these links is a linear regression problem.

A relatively new algorithm that's becoming popular for classification problems is the *support vector machines (SVM)* algorithm. Consider a two-dimensional space with a large number of points. There are a large number of lines that can be used to divide the points into two segments; let these lines be known as *separating lines.* Now define *margin* as the distance between a separating line and a parallel line that passes through the closest point to the line. SVM selects the line that has the maximum margin associated with it. Points that this second, parallel line passes through are known as *support vector points.* SVM generalizes this concept across multiple dimensions and has been observed to work well. The output variable can be discrete, containing two values, or continuous.

Algorithms based on probability theory are commonly known as *Bayesian algorithms.* One such simple but good classifier is the Naïve Bayes' classifier. This algorithm assumes independence between the input attributes and makes a prediction based on estimating probabilities from the training data. *Bayesian belief networks (BBN),* also known as *probabilistic belief networks,* are another approach at estimating the probabilities using the Bayes' theorem. BBNs are directed acyclic graphs (DAG), where a link signifies conditional distribution function between the parent and the child node.

Table 7.2 summarizes the different kinds of algorithms used for mining data, along with the kinds of input and output attributes.

Table 7.2   Summary of different kinds of data mining algorithms

Type of algorithm	Description	Type of input	Type of output	Example
Regression	Builds a predictive model that predicts the output variable based on the values of the inputs	Continuous	Continuous	Regression, neural networks
Classification	Predicts the output value for the discrete output variable	Discrete[a]	Discrete	Decision tree, Naïve Bayes'
Clustering	Creates clusters in data to find patterns	Discrete or continuous	None	k-means, hierarchical clustering, density-based algorithms
Attribute importance	Determines the importance of attributes with respect to predicting the output attribute	Discrete or continuous	None	Minimum description length, decision tree pruning
Association rules	Finds interesting relationships in data by looking at co-occurring items	Discrete	None	Association rules, Apriori

a. Many tool sets allow the use of both continuous and discrete variables as input for regression and classification.

There's a lot more involved in understanding and implementing these algorithms. We take a more detailed look at a few of them in later chapters. Fortunately, rather than having to reimplement all these algorithms, there are a few open source data mining platforms that we can leverage, one being WEKA. You can find the list of data mining tool vendors at http://www.dmoz.org//Computers/Software/Databases/ Data_Mining/Tool_Vendors/.

With this brief overview on the different kinds of learning algorithms, we're now ready to look at the process of analyzing data to discover intelligence.

7.1.4   *The mining process*

Analyzing data to build a predictive model or discover clusters consists of the following six steps. Typically, the process is iterative, where you may repeat these steps in the quest for a better model or to refine an existing one:

1   *Modeling and selecting the attributes*—We first need to understand what we're looking for. Is our aim to build a predictive model or find patterns in the data? Based on the needs, identify the attributes that are available for use in the analysis.

2   *Creating the learning dataset*—We need a set of examples—a dataset—to be used by the algorithm. The dataset is typically broken up into two datasets: the training dataset which usually contains 90 percent of the data and is used for creating the predictive model, and the testing dataset, which is used for evaluating the quality of the predictive model. It may be computationally infeasible or too expensive to analyze all entries in a large dataset. In this case, random sampling is used to create a smaller dataset that's expected to be representative of the complete dataset.

3   *Normalizing and cleaning the data*—Instances that have missing values for any of the attributes are removed from the dataset. Further, each attribute may be normalized between the scales of [–1, 1] or [0, 1]. Typically, a distance measure is used, and normalizing the data ensures that an attribute doesn't skew the distance measurement due to a bigger range of values. For example, an attribute that takes a value between 0 and 100 will show a bigger distance measure for two points than an attribute that takes values between 0 and 1.

4   *Analyzing the data*—The training dataset is analyzed to either build a predictive model or discover clusters. A common problem to avoid in analyzing the data is overfitting the data—the model memorizes the training data, leading to poor predictive capabilities. The algorithm may be intelligent enough to prune the number of attributes being used based on their effectiveness in predicting the attribute of interest.

5   *Evaluating the quality of the predictive model*—The quality of the predictive model is evaluated using the testing dataset.

6   *Embedding the predictive model*—Once a predictive model has been built, it can be embedded in your application to make predictions.

A common approach to avoid overfitting and select the best predictive model is to use the *k-fold cross validation* strategy. This approach is typically used when the number of examples available for learning and testing is small. In this case, the dataset is broken randomly into *k* subsets. *K* sets of learning runs are executed, where one of the *k* sets is used for validating the predictive model while the other remaining (k–1) datasets are used for the learning process. Typically, the error associated with a predictive model is the average error in the test data across the *k* runs. A number of predictive models may be created using different algorithms or different settings, and the one with the least average error across the *k* runs is selected.

With this background on the data mining process and the key learning algorithms, it's helpful to work through an example to see the learning process in action. Writing learning algorithms can be complex and tedious; fortunately, a lot of work has been done in the open source community for us. We leverage one such open source data mining framework: WEKA.

7.2   *Using an open source data mining framework: WEKA*

The Waikato Environment for Knowledge Analysis, commonly known as WEKA, is one of the most popular suites of data mining algorithms that have been written in Java. WEKA is available under the GNU General Public License.[1] WEKA was developed at the University of Waikato in New Zealand. Early work on WEKA began in 1993; work on the Java version started in 1997. In September 2006, Pentaho,[2] a developer of open source business intelligence software, bought WEKA. WEKA contains tools for data preprocessing, classification, regression, clustering, association rules, and visualization. It

---

[1]   http://www.gnu.org/copyleft/gpl.html
[2]   http://www.pentaho.com/

also has a GUI application through which you can apply the various data mining algorithms to datasets. We are more interested in its Java API and will use that directly.

Over the years, the WEKA APIs have been leveraged to build additional tools and packages—you can see a list of these at http://weka.sourceforge.net/wiki/index.php/ Related_Projects. RapidMiner,[3] formerly known as Yet Another Learning Environment (YALE), is one such project that leverages WEKA to provide an environment for data mining. There's also an excellent book on data mining and WEKA written by two of the professors[4] associated with WEKA.

In this section, we familiarize ourselves with the WEKA learning platform. We begin with a brief tutorial in which we use the WEKA learning environment to orient ourselves with the WEKA Java packages and key classes. Next, we write a simple example that invokes the WEKA API. At the end of this section, you should be familiar with WEKA, its GUI application and Java API, and what's involved in embedding the platform. We leverage WEKA later in chapters 9, 10, and 12.

7.2.1 *Using the WEKA application: a step-by-step tutorial*

We begin with a brief tutorial to guide us through installing and running WEKA on Windows.

INSTALLING WEKA

First, we need to download the WEKA package from http://www.cs.waikato.ac.nz/ml/ weka/. We use the developer version 3.5.6. Note that the WEKA book uses an older version, 3.4. If you don't have Java, download the self-extracting executable that includes Java VM 5.0 (weka-3-5-6jre.exe; 31,661,572 bytes); otherwise download the WEKA version (weka-3-5-6.exe; 15,665,809 bytes) that doesn't have the JVM. Install the software using the default values. I installed mine at C:\Program Files\Weka-3-5. If you open this directory on your machine, it should look similar to figure 7.5.

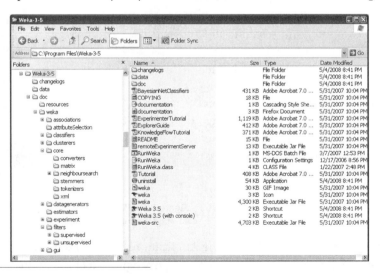

Figure 7.5 The directory structure and some of the files for WEKA

---

[3] http://rapid-i.com/content/blogcategory/10/69/

[4] Ian H. Witten and Eibe Frank *Data Mining: Practical machine learning tools and techniques*, 2nd Edition. Morgan Kaufmann, San Francisco, 2005.

Figure 7.6   **WEKA documentation that's available in the install**

A good place to start is to open the documentation.html page that's available in the Weka-3-5 directory, a screenshot of which is shown in figure 7.6.

The top three links on the page are tutorials for the three environments for which WEKA has a GUI application. These components are

- *Explorer*—An environment for exploring data
- *Experimenter*—An environment for performing experiments and comparing different learning algorithms
- *KnowledgeFlow*—An environment that's similar to Explorer but supports drag-and-drop functionality to carry out the learning process

The Package Documentation link points to the JavaDoc for the WEKA classes, which we explore later in this section. Next, it's worthwhile to spend a few minutes exploring the WEKA GUI application. Start the GUI application by going to the Start menu of your window's computer and selecting the Weka 3.5 (with console) option in the Weka 3.5.6 program menu. You should see a window similar to the one shown in figure 7.7. Before we jump into the API, you may want to spend a few minutes playing with the Explorer application. The Explorer Guide link shown in figure 7.6 is a good reference to go through.

Alternatively, here's a simple five-step exercise that you may find useful to explore the application:

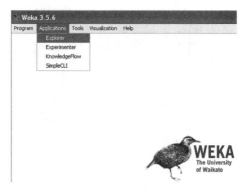

Figure 7.7   **WEKA GUI with options to start one of four applications**

1   Select the Explorer option under the Applications menu to start Explorer.
2   Click on Open File and go to the data directory data. Select the iris.arff dataset.
3   This should open up a window similar to the one in figure 7.8. Note that there are five attributes shown in the Attributes window, and you can find out the details about each attribute in the two windows on the right side.

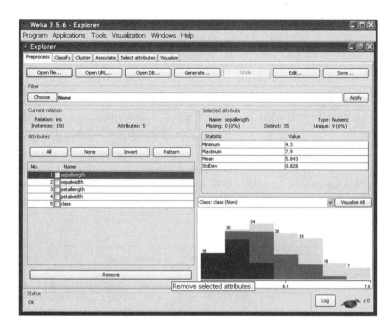

Figure 7.8　The five attributes of the iris.arff dataset, with details about the `sepallength` attribute

4　As shown in figure 7.9, we convert the `sepallength` variable into a discrete variable. Select the Choose button and then select Discretize Filter, as shown in figure 7.9. This variable is now a nominal attribute that can take three values.

5　Click the Visualize All option to see a visual representation of the five attributes.

Similarly, spend some time exploring the capabilities of the Experimenter and the KnowledgeFlow application.

With that brief overview of the WEKA application, we're now ready to explore the WEKA APIs.

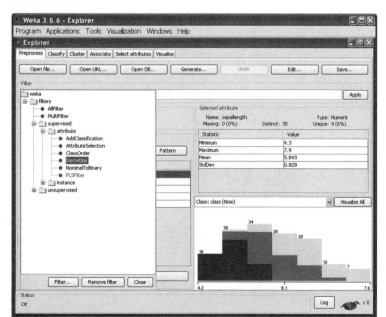

Figure 7.9　Converting a continuous variable into a discrete variable using filters in WEKA

7.2.2   *Understanding the WEKA APIs*

In this section, we explore the WEKA APIs. A good introduction to the WEKA JAVA APIs is the tutorial.pdf file, part of the WEKA installation in the C:\Program Files\Weka-3-5 directory.

If you use an IDE such as Eclipse, you may also want to add the WEKA source available in the weka-src.jar file to your Eclipse project.[5] The compiled Java classes are in weka.jar; you'll want to add the jar file to your project lib file so that Java can find it at runtime.

At this stage, it'll be useful to look at the JavaDoc for the APIs. Click on the Package Documentation link as shown in figure 7.6. Table 7.3 contains six of the most important packages that we use.

Table 7.3   The key packages in WEKA

Package	Description
weka.core	Core package containing common components used by other packages. Classes for modeling attributes, dataset, converters, matrix manipulation, text parsing, tree representation, and XML.
weka.classifiers	Contains implementation of the various classification algorithms. These include algorithms for numerical prediction.
weka.clusterers	Contains implementations of the various clustering algorithms.
weka.attributeselection	Algorithms associated with selecting attributes.
weka.associations	Algorithms related to finding associations.
weka.filters	Classes related to applying filters on the dataset; for example, to remove an attribute from analysis.

The weka.core package contains the representation for a dataset. As shown in figure 7.10, each dataset is represented by the class Instances, which contains a list of examples, represented by the class Instance. Each Instance is composed of a number of attributes. WEKA uses its own implementation for a vector, FastVector.

To load data from various sources, WEKA defines the Loader interface, as shown in figure 7.11. This has the following method to create a dataset:

```
Instances getDataSet() throws IOException;
```

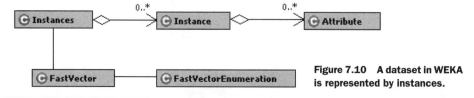

Figure 7.10   A dataset in WEKA is represented by instances.

---

[5]   Unzip this jar file in the src/java directory and include the files in your project.

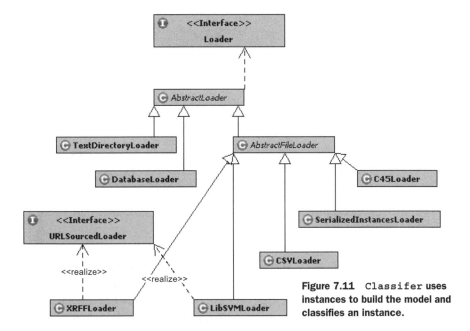

Figure 7.11 `Classifer` uses instances to build the model and classifies an instance.

There are a number of `Loader` implementations, including reading data from a csv file and from the database.

The `weka.classifier` package contains implementations for classification and prediction algorithms. As shown in figure 7.12, a `Classifier` learns its model using `Instances`. It then can classify an `Instance`. The WEKA library contains a large set of classification and prediction algorithms, some of which are shown in figure 7.12.

Similarly, the `weka.clusterer` package contains the implementation for the various clustering algorithms. Each `Clusterer` creates clusters from the `Instances` and

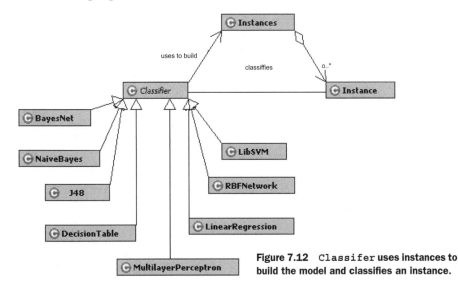

Figure 7.12 `Classifier` uses instances to build the model and classifies an instance.

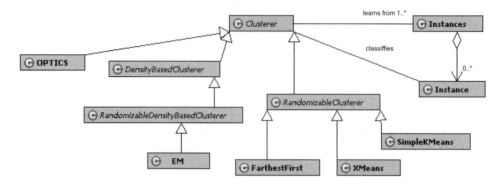

Figure 7.13 `Clusterer` **uses instances to build the model and associate an instance with the appropriate cluster.**

then associates an `Instance` with the appropriate cluster, as shown in figure 7.13. The figure also shows some of the clustering algorithms that are available.

The `weka.associations` package contains two algorithms, `Apriori` and `Predictive-Apriori`, that are available to learn association rules, as shown in figure 7.14. All association-learning algorithms extend the `Associator` interface. `CARuleMiner` is an optional interface for those schemes that can produce class association rules.

So far, you should have a good understanding about the core packages of WEKA. You're encouraged to explore other packages mentioned in table 7.3: `weka.attributeselection` and `weka.filters`. Now it's time to write some Java code to demonstrate the learning process. We create a dataset, build a model, and then evaluate it using the WEKA API.

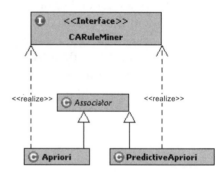

Figure 7.14 Association-learning algorithms available in WEKA

7.2.3 *Using the WEKA APIs via an example*

In this section, we use the WEKA API to create a dataset and build a predictive model to predict values. There's also a tutorial on the WEKA wiki.[6] We write the code to solve the following learning problem.

Imagine that we want to predict the number of times a user is expected to log in to our application within a week. Unfortunately, we're still a relatively new company and we have data for only four users, which is shown in table 7.4. We've captured two attributes during the registration process about the user: age and gender. Age is a

---

[6] http://weka.sourceforge.net/wiki/index.php/Programmatic_Use and http://weka.sourceforge.net/wiki/index.php/Use_Weka_in_your_Java_code

continuous attribute, while gender is a nominal attribute. We know that the learning dataset is really small, and potentially we may not even find a good predictor, but we're keen to try out the WEKA mining APIs, so we go ahead and build the predictive model in preparation for future better times.

User	Age	Gender	Number of logins
John	20	male	5
Jane	30	female	2
Ed	40	male	3
Amy	35	female	4

Table 7.4 The data associated with the WEKA API tutorial

For our example, we do the following five steps:

1 Create the attributes.
2 Create the dataset for learning.
3 Build the predictive model.
4 Evaluate the quality of the model built.
5 Predict the number of logins for a new user.

We implement a class WEKATutorial, which follows these five steps. The code for this class is shown in listing 7.1.

Listing 7.1 Implementation of the WEKATutorial

```
package com.alag.ci.weka.tutorial;

import weka.classifiers.Classifier;
import weka.classifiers.Evaluation;
import weka.classifiers.functions.RBFNetwork;
import weka.core.Attribute;
import weka.core.FastVector;
import weka.core.Instance;
import weka.core.Instances;

public class WEKATutorial {

    public static void main(String [] args) throws Exception {
        WEKATutorial wekaTut = new WEKATutorial();
        wekaTut.executeWekaTutorial();
    }

    private void executeWekaTutorial() throws Exception {
        FastVector allAttributes = createAttributes();
        Instances learningDataset =
            createLearningDataSet(allAttributes);
        Classifier predictiveModel = learnPredictiveModel( learningDataset );
        Evaluation evaluation = evaluatePredictiveModel(predictiveModel,
            learningDataset);
        System.out.println(evaluation.toSummaryString());
        predictUnknownCases(learningDataset,predictiveModel);
    }
```

Create attributes
Create dataset for learning
Build predictive model
Evaluate predictive model
Predict unknown cases

The main method for our tutorial simply invokes the method `executeWekaTutorial()`, which consists of invoking five methods that execute each of the five steps. Let's look at the first step, `createAttributes()`, the code for which is shown in listing 7.2.

Listing 7.2 Implementation of the method to create attributes

```
private FastVector createAttributes() {
    Attribute ageAttribute = new Attribute("age");          ◁──┐ Create age
    FastVector genderAttributeValues = new FastVector(2);        attribute
    genderAttributeValues.addElement("male");               ┐ Create
    genderAttributeValues.addElement("female");             │ nominal
    Attribute genderAttribute = new Attribute("gender",     │ attribute
      genderAttributeValues);                               ┘ for gender
    Attribute numLoginsAttribute = new Attribute("numLogins");
    FastVector allAttributes = new FastVector(3);       ◁─┐ Create
    allAttributes.addElement(ageAttribute);               │ FastVector
    allAttributes.addElement(genderAttribute);            │ for storing
    allAttributes.addElement(numLoginsAttribute);         ┘ attributes
    return allAttributes;
}
```

Remember, as shown in figure 7.10, WEKA uses its own implementation, `FastVector`, for creating a list of objects. There are two ways to create an `Attribute`.

For continuous attributes, such as age, we need to simply pass in the name of the attribute in the constructor:

```
Attribute ageAttribute = new Attribute("age");
```

For nominal attributes, we first need to create a `FastVector` that contains the various values that the attribute can take. In the case of attribute *gender*, we do this with the following code:

```
FastVector genderAttributeValues = new FastVector(2);
genderAttributeValues.addElement("male");
genderAttributeValues.addElement("female");
```

The constructor for nominal attributes takes in the name of the attribute and a `FastVector` containing the various values that this attribute can take. Therefore, we create the `genderAttribute` as follows:

```
Attribute genderAttribute = new Attribute("gender", genderAttributeValues);
```

Next, we need to create the dataset for the data contained in table 7.4. A dataset is represented by `Instances`, which is composed of a number of `Instance`. Each `Instance` has values associated with each of the attributes. The code for creating the `Instances` is shown in listing 7.3.

Listing 7.3 Implementation of the method `createLearningDataSet`

```
private Instances createLearningDataSet(FastVector allAttributes) {
    Instances trainingDataSet =
      new Instances("wekaTutorial", allAttributes, 4);    ◁─┐ Constructor
    trainingDataSet.setClassIndex(2);                   ◁─┘ for Instances
    addInstance(trainingDataSet, 20.,"male", 5);      Specifying attribute
    addInstance(trainingDataSet, 30.,"female", 2);    to be predicted
```

```
    addInstance(trainingDataSet, 40.,"male", 3);
    addInstance(trainingDataSet, 35.,"female", 4);
    return trainingDataSet;
}

private void addInstance(Instances trainingDataSet,
      double age, String gender, int numLogins) {
    Instance instance = createInstance(trainingDataSet,age,
       gender,numLogins);
    trainingDataSet.add(instance);
}

private Instance createInstance(Instances associatedDataSet,
      double age, String gender, int numLogins) {        ⟵⎤ Creating an
    Instance instance = new Instance(3);                     ⎦ Instance
    instance.setDataset(associatedDataSet);
    instance.setValue(0, age);
    instance.setValue(1, gender);
    instance.setValue(2, numLogins);
    return instance;
}
```

To create the dataset for our example, we need to create an instance of Instances:

```
Instances trainingDataSet = new Instances("wekaTutorial",
    allAttributes, 4);
```

The constructor takes three parameters: the name for the dataset, the FastVector of attributes, and the expected size for the dataset. The method createInstance creates an instance of Instance. Note that there needs to be a dataset associated with each Instance:

```
instance.setDataset(associatedDataSet);
```

Now that we've created the learning dataset, we're ready to create a predictive model. There are a variety of predictive models that we can use; for this example we use the radial basis function (RBF) neural network. The code for creating the predictive model is shown in listing 7.4.

Listing 7.4   Creating the predictive model

```
    private Classifier learnPredictiveModel(Instances learningDataset)
         throws Exception {
       Classifier classifier = getClassifier();      ⟵ Create Classifier to be used
       classifier.buildClassifier(learningDataset);  ⟵⎤ Build predictive
       return classifier;                               ⎥ model using
    }                                                    ⎦ learning dataset

    private Classifier getClassifier() {
       RBFNetwork rbfLearner = new RBFNetwork();
       rbfLearner.setNumClusters(2);      ⟵⎤ Set number
       return rbfLearner;                   ⎦ of clusters
    }
```

The constructor for creating the RBF is fairly simple:

```
    RBFNetwork rbfLearner = new RBFNetwork();
```

We go with the default parameters associated with RBF learning, except we set the number of clusters to be used to 2:

```
rbfLearner.setNumClusters(2);
```

Once we have an instance of a classifier, it's simple enough to build the predictive model:

```
Classifier classifier = getClassifier();
classifier.buildClassifier(learningDataset);
```

Having built the predictive model, we need to evaluate its quality. To do so we typically use another set of data, commonly known as *test dataset*; we iterate over all instances and compare the predicted value with the expected value. The code for this is shown in listing 7.5.

Listing 7.5   Evaluating the quality and predicting the number of logins

```
private Evaluation evaluatePredictiveModel(Classifier classifier,
    Instances learningDataset) throws Exception {
    Evaluation learningSetEvaluation =              Create Evaluation
        new Evaluation(learningDataset);            object
    learningSetEvaluation.evaluateModel(classifier, Evaluate the
        learningDataset);                           quality
    return learningSetEvaluation;
}
```

Evaluating the quality of the model built is fairly straightforward. We simply need to create an instance of an `Evaluation` object and pass in the classifier for evaluation:

```
Evaluation learningSetEvaluation = new Evaluation(learningDataset);
    learningSetEvaluation.evaluateModel(classifier, learningDataset);
```

Lastly, we use the predictive model for predicting the number of logins for previously unknown cases. The code is shown in listing 7.6.

Listing 7.6   Predicting the number of logins

```
private void predictUnknownCases(Instances learningDataset,
    Classifier predictiveModel)
    throws Exception {                                          Create
    Instance testMaleInstance =                                Instance
        createInstance(learningDataset,32., "male", 0) ;
    Instance testFemaleInstance =                              Pass
        createInstance(learningDataset,32., "female", 0) ;     Instance to
    double malePrediction =                                    model for
        predictiveModel.classifyInstance(testMaleInstance);    prediction
    double femalePrediction =
        predictiveModel.classifyInstance(testFemaleInstance);
    System.out.println("Predicted number of logins [age=32]: ");
    System.out.println("\tMale = " + malePrediction);
    System.out.println("\tFemale = " + femalePrediction);
}
```

We try to predict the number of logins for two users. The first user is a 32-year-old male; the second is a 32-year-old female. Listing 7.7 shows the output from running the program.

Listing 7.7   The output from the main method

```
Correlation coefficient              0.4528
Mean absolute error                  0.9968
Root mean squared error              0.9968
Relative absolute error              99.6764 %
Root relative squared error          89.16   %
Total Number of Instances            4

Predicted number of logins [age=32]:
   Male = 3.3578194529075382
   Female = 2.9503429358320865
```

Listing 7.7 shows the details of how well the predicted model performed for the training data. As shown, the correlation coefficient[7] measures the quality of the prediction; for a perfect fit, this value will be 1. The predicted model shows an error of about 1.

The model predicts that the 32-year-old male is expected to log in 3.35 times, while the 32-year-old female is expected to log in 2.95 times. Using the data presented to the model, the model predicts that male users are more likely to log in than female users.

This example has been helpful in understanding the WEKA APIs. It also brings out an important issue: the example we implemented makes our application highly dependent on WEKA. For example, the WEKA APIs use `FastVector` instead of perhaps a `List` to contain objects. What if tomorrow we wanted to switch to a different vendor or implementation? Switching to a different vendor implementation at that point would be painful and time consuming. Wouldn't it be nice if there were a standard data mining API, which different vendors implemented? This would make it easy for a developer to understand the core APIs and if needed easily switch to a different implementation of the specification with simple changes, if any, in the code. This is where the Java Data Mining (JDM) specification developed under Java Community Process JSR 73 and JSR 247 comes in.

7.3   *Standard data mining API: Java Data Mining (JDM)*

JDM aims at building a standard API for data mining, such that client applications coded to the specification aren't dependent on any specific vendor application. The JDBC specification provides a good analogy to the potential of JDM. The promise is that just like it's fairly easy to access different databases using JDBC, in the same manner, applications written to the JDM specification should make it simple to switch between different implementations of data mining functions. JDM has wide support from the industry, with representations from a number of companies including Oracle, IBM, SPSS, CA, Fair Isaac,

---

[7] See http://mathworld.wolfram.com/CorrelationCoefficient.html for more details.

SAP, SAS, BEA, and others. Oracle[8] and KXEN[9] have implementations compliant with the JDM specification as of early 2008. It's only a matter of time before other vendors and data mining toolkits adopt the specification.

Work on JSR 73[10] began in July 2000, with the final release in August 2004. JDM supports the five different types of algorithms we looked at in section 7.1: clustering, classification, regression, attribute importance, and association rules. It also supports common data mining operations such as building, evaluating, applying, and saving a model. It defines XML Schema for representing models as well as accessing data mining capabilities from a web service.

JSR 247,[11] commonly known as *JDM 2.0*, addresses features that were deferred from JDM 1.0. Some of the features JSR 247 addresses are multivariate statistics, time series analysis, anomaly detection, transformations, text mining, multi-target models, and model comparisons. Work on the project started in June 2004, and the public review draft was approved in December 2006.

If you're interested in the details of JDM, I encourage you to download and read the two specifications—they're well written and easy to follow. You should also look at a recent well-written book[12] by Mark Hornick, the specification lead for the two JSRs on data mining and JDM. He coauthored the book with two other members of the specification committee, Erik Marcadé, from KXEN, and Sunil Venkayala from Oracle.

Next, we briefly look at the JDM architecture and the core components of the API. Toward the end of the section, we write code that demonstrates how a connection can be made to a data mining engine using the JDM APIs. In later chapters, when we discuss clustering, predictive models, and other algorithms, we review relevant sections of the JDM API in more detail.

7.3.1   *JDM architecture*

The JDM architecture has the following three logical components. These components could be either collocated or distributed on different machines:

1 The API: The programming interface that's used by the client. It shields the client from knowing about any vendor-specific implementations.
2 The Data Mining Engine (DME): The engine that provides data mining functionality to the client.
3 Mining object repository (MOR): The repository to store the data mining objects.

All packages in JDM begin with `javax.datamining`. There are several key packages, which are shown in table 7.5.

---

[8] http://www.oracle.com/technology/products/bi/odm/odm_jdev_extension.html
[9] http://kxen.com/products/analytic_framework/apis.php
[10] http://www.jcp.org/en/jsr/detail?id=73
[11] http://www.jcp.org/en/jsr/detail?id=247
[12] *Java Data Mining: Strategy, Standard, and Practice*, 2007, Morgan Kaufmann.

Table 7.5 Key JDM packages

Concept	Packages	Comments
Common objects used throughout	`Javax.datamining`	Contains common objects such as `MiningObject`, `Factory` that are used throughout the JDM packages
Top-level objects used in other packages	`Javax.datamining.base`	Contains top-level interfaces such as `Task`, `Model`, `BuildSettings`, `AlgorithmSettings`. Also introduced to avoid cyclic package dependencies

Algorithms-related packages	`Javax.datamining.algorithm`
	`Javax.datamining.association`
	`Javax.datamining.attributeimportance`
	`Javax.datamining.clustering`
	`Javax.datamining.supervised`
	`Javax.datamining.rule`
		Contains interfaces associated with the different types of algorithms, namely: association, attribute importance, clustering, supervised learning—includes both classification and categorization. Also contains Java interfaces representing the predicate rules created as part of the models, such as tree model.

Connecting to the data mining engine	`Javax.datamining.resource`	Contains classes associated with connecting to a data mining engine (DME) and metadata associated with the DME.
Data-related packages	`Javax.datamining.data` `Javax.datamining.statistics`	Contains classes associated with representing both a physical and logical dataset and statistics associated with the input mining data.
Models and tasks	`Javax.datamining.task` `Javax.datamining.modeldetail`	Contains classes for the different types of tasks: build, evaluate, import and export. Provides detail on the various model representations.

Next, let's take a deeper look at some of the key JDM objects.

7.3.2   *Key JDM objects*

The `MiningObject` is a top-level interface for JDM classes. It has basic information such as a name and description, and can be saved in the MOR by the DME. JDM has the following types of `MiningObject`, as shown in figure 7.15.

- Classes associated with describing the input data, including both the physical (`PhysicalDataSet`) and logical (`LogicalDataSet`) aspects of the data.
- Classes associated with settings. There are two kinds of settings, first related to setting for the algorithm. `AlgorithmSettings` is the base class for specifying the setting associated with an algorithm. Second is the high-level specification for building a data mining model. `BuildSettings` is the base implementation for the five different kinds of models: association, clustering, regression, classification, and attribute importance.

- Model is the base class for mining models created by analyzing the data. There are five different kinds of models: association, clustering, regression, classification, and attribute importance.
- Task is the base class for the different kinds of data mining operations, such as applying, testing, importing, and exporting a model.

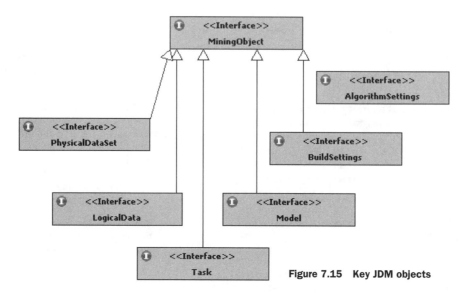

Figure 7.15   Key JDM objects

We look at each of these in more detail in the next few sections. Let's begin with representing the dataset.

7.3.3   *Representing the dataset*

JDM has different interfaces to describe the physical and logical aspects of the data, as shown in figure 7.16. PhysicalDataset is an interface to describe input data used for data mining, while LogicalData is used to represent the data used for model input. Attributes of the PhysicalDataset, represented by PhysicalAttribute, are mapped to attributes of the LogicalData, which is represented by LogicalAttribute. The separation of physical and logical data enables us to map multiple PhysicalDatasets into one LogicalData for building a model. One PhysicalDataset can also translate to multiple LogicalData objects with variations in the mappings or definitions of the attributes.

Each PhysicalDataset is composed of zero or more PhysicalAttributes. An instance of the PhysicalAttribute is created through the PhysicalAttributeFactory. Each PhysicalAttribute has an AttributeDataType, which is an enumeration and contains one of the values {double, integer, string, unknown}. The PhysicalAttribute also has a PhysicalAttributeRole; another enumeration is used to define special roles that some attributes may have. For example, taxonomyParentId represents a column of data that contains the parent identifiers for a taxonomy.

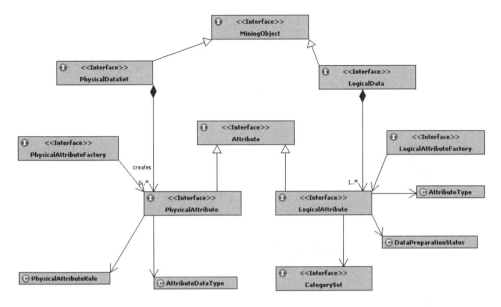

Figure 7.16   Key JDM interfaces to describe the physical and logical aspects of the data

LogicalData is composed of one or more LogicalAttributes. Each Logical-Attribute is created by the LogicalAttributeFactory and has an associated Attrib-uteType. Each AttributeType is an enumeration with values {numerical, categorical, ordinal, not specified}. Associated with a LogicalAttribute is also a DataPreparation-Status, which specifies whether the data is prepared or unprepared. For categorical attributes, there's also an associated CategorySet, which specifies the set of categorical values associated with the LogicalAttribute.

Now that we know how to represent a dataset, let's look at how models are represented in the JDM.

7.3.4   *Learning models*

The output of a data mining algorithm is represented by the Model interface. Model, which extends MiningObject, is the base class for representing the five different kinds of data mining models, as shown in figure 7.17. Each model may have an associated ModelDetail, which captures algorithm-specific implementations. For example, NeuralNetworkModelDetail in the case of a neural network model captures the detailed representation of a fully connected, MLP network model. Similarly, Tree-ModelDetail contains model details for a decision tree, and contains methods to traverse the tree and get information related to the decision tree. To keep figure 7.17 simple, the subclasses of ModelDetail are omitted.

Table 7.6 shows the six subclasses of the Model interface. Note that Supervised-Model acts as a base interface for both ClassificationModel and RegressionModel.

So far, we've looked at how to represent the data and the kinds of model representation. Next, let's look at how settings are set for the different kinds of algorithms.

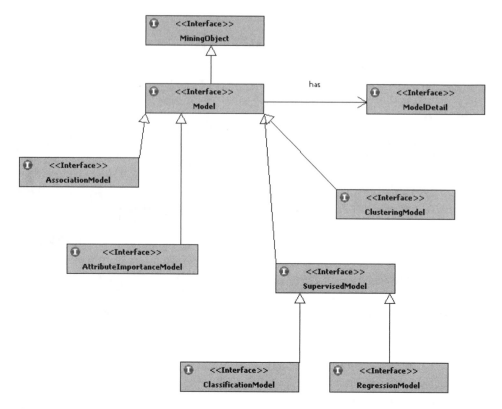

Figure 7.17   The model representation in JDM

Table 7.6   Key subclasses for Model

Model type	Description
AssociationModel	Model created by an association algorithm. It contains data associated with itemsets and rules.
AttributeImportanceModel	Ranks the attributes analyzed. Each attribute has a weight associated with it, which can be used as an input for building a model.
Clustering Model	Represents the output from a clustering algorithm. Contains information to describe the clusters and associate a point with the appropriate cluster.
SupervisedModel	Is a common interface for supervised learning–related models.
ClassificationModel	Represents the model created by a classification algorithm.
RegressionModel	Represents the model created by a regression algorithm.

7.3.5   Algorithm settings

`AlgorithmSettings`, as shown in figure 7.18, is the common base class for specifying the settings associated with the various algorithms. A DME will typically use defaults for the settings and then use the specified settings to override the defaults.

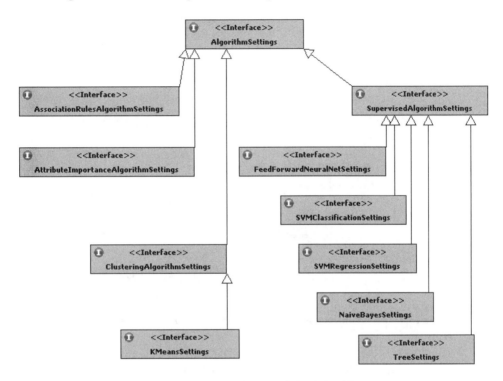

Figure 7.18   The settings associated with the different kinds of algorithms

Each specific kind of algorithm typically has its own interface to capture the settings. For example, `KMeansSettings` captures the settings associated with the k-means algorithm. This interface specifies settings such as the number of clusters, the maximum number of iterations, the distance function to be used, and the error tolerance range.

So far in this section, we've looked at the JDM objects for representing the dataset, the learning models, and the settings for the algorithms. Next, let's look at the different kinds of tasks that are supported by the JDM.

7.3.6   JDM tasks

There are five main types of tasks in JDM. These are tasks associated with building a model, evaluating a model, computing statistics, applying a model, and importing and exporting models from the MOR. Figure 7.19 shows the interfaces for some of the tasks in JDM. Tasks can be executed either synchronously or asynchronously. Some of the tasks associated with data mining, such as learning the model and evaluating a

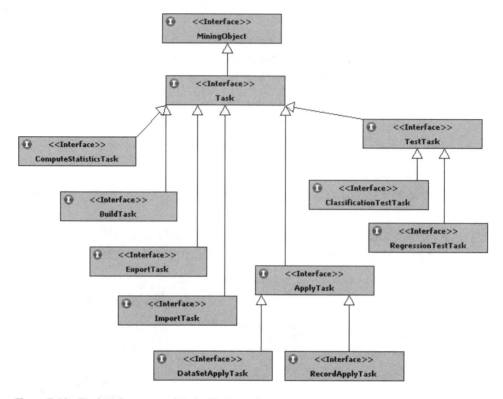

Figure 7.19 **The interfaces associated with the various tasks supported by JDM**

large dataset, take a long time to run. JDM supports specifying these as asynchronous tasks and monitoring the status associated with them.

The Task interface is an abstraction of the metadata needed to define a data-mining task. The task of applying a mining model to data is captured by ApplyTask. DataSet-ApplyTask is used to apply the model to a dataset, while RecodApplyTask is used to apply the mining model to a single record. ExportTask and ImportTask are used to export and import mining models from the MOR.

Task objects can be referenced, reexecuted, or executed at a later time. DME doesn't allow two tasks to be executed with the same name, but a task that has completed can be re-executed if required. Tasks executed asynchronously provide a reference to an ExecutionHandle. Clients can monitor and control the execution of the task using the ExecutionHandle object.

Next, we look at the details of clients connecting to the DME and the use of ExecutionHandle to monitor the status.

7.3.7 *JDM connection*

JDM allows clients to connect to the DME using vendor-neutral connection architecture. This architecture is based on the principles of Java Connection Architecture (JCX). Figure 7.20 shows the key interfaces associated with this process.

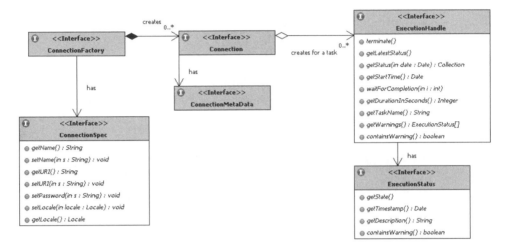

Figure 7.20 The interfaces associated with creating a `Connection` to the data-mining service

The client code looks up an instance of `ConnectionFactory`, perhaps using JNDI, and specifies a user name and password to the `ConnectionFactory`. The `Connection-Factory` creates `Connection` objects, which are expected to be single-threaded and are analogous to the `Connection` objects created while accessing the database using the JDBC protocol. The `ConnectionSpec` associated with the `ConnectionFactory` contains details about the DME name, URI, locale, and the user name and password to be used.

A `Connection` object encapsulates a connection to the DME. It authenticates users, supports the retrieval and storage of named objects, and executes tasks. Each `Connection` object is a relatively heavyweight JDM object and needs to be associated with a single thread. Clients can access the DME via either a single `Connection` object or via multiple instances. Version specification for the implementation is captured in the `ConnectionMetaData` object.

The `Connection` interface has two methods available to execute a task. The first one is used for synchronous tasks and returns an `ExecutionStatus` object:

```
public ExecutionStatus execute(Task task, java.lang.Long timeout)
    throws JDMException
```

The other one is for asynchronous execution:

```
public ExecutionHandle execute(java.lang.String taskName)
    throws JDMException
```

It returns a reference to an `ExecutionHandle`, which can be used to monitor the task's status. The `Connection` object also has methods to look for mining objects, such as the following, which looks for mining objects of the specified type that were created in a specified time period:

```
public java.util.Collection getObjectNames(java.util.Date createdAfter,
    java.util.Date createdBefore,
    NamedObject objectType) throws JDMException
```

With this overview of the connection process, let's look at some sample code that can be used to connect to the DME.

7.3.8   *Sample code for accessing DME*

It's now time to write some code to illustrate how the JDM APIs can be used to create a Connection to the DME. The first part of the code deals with the constructor and the main method, which calls the method to create a new connection. This is shown in listing 7.8.

Listing 7.8   Constructor and main method for JDMConnectionExample

```
package com.alag.ci.jdm.connect;

import java.util.Hashtable;

import javax.datamining.JDMException;
import javax.datamining.resource.Connection;
import javax.datamining.resource.ConnectionFactory;
import javax.datamining.resource.ConnectionSpec;
import javax.naming.Context;
import javax.naming.InitialContext;
import javax.naming.NamingException;

public class JDMConnectionExample {
    private String userName = null;
    private String password = null;
    private String serverURI = null;                    Constructor for
    private String providerURI = null;              JDMConnectionExample

    public JDMConnectionExample(String userName, String password,
            String serverURI, String providerURI) {  ◄─────
        this.userName = userName;
        this.password = password;
        this.serverURI = serverURI;
        this.providerURI = providerURI;                Get connection using
    }                                                  JDMConnectionExample
                                                                  instance

    public static void main(String [] args) throws Exception {
        JDMConnectionExample eg = new JDMConnectionExample("username",
        "password", "serverURI",
        "http://yourHost:yourPort/yourDMService");
        Connection connection = eg.createANewConnection();  ◄─────
    }
```

In our example, we use a JDMConnectionExample object to create a new instance of the Connection object. The constructor for JDMConnectionExample takes in four parameters: the username and password for the DME, the URI for the DME server, and the URI for the provider. Sample values are shown in the main method. The main method creates a Connection object with the following call:

```
Connection connection = eg.createANewConnection();
```

There are three steps involved in getting a new Connection, as shown in listing 7.9.

Listing 7.9 Creating a new connection in the `JDMConnectionExample`

```
public Connection createANewConnection()                        Create ConnectionFactory
  throws JDMException, NamingException {
  ConnectionFactory connectionFactory = createConnectionFactory();
  ConnectionSpec connectionSpec =
    getConnectionSpec(connectionFactory);          Get ConnectionSpec
  return connectionFactory.getConnection(connectionSpec);
}
```

First, we need to create an instance of the `ConnectionFactory`. Next, we need to obtain a `ConnectionSpec` from the `ConnectionFactory`, populate it with the credentials, and then create a new `Connection` from the `ConnectionFactory` using the `ConnectionSpec`.

Listing 7.10 contains the remaining part of the code for this example, and deals with creating the connection factory and the initial context.

Listing 7.10 Getting a `ConnectionFactory` and `ConnectionSpec`

```
private ConnectionFactory createConnectionFactory()
   throws NamingException {
   InitialContext initialJNDIContext = createInitialContext();
   return (ConnectionFactory) initialJNDIContext.lookup("java:com/env/
jdm/yourDMServer");                                 Create InitialContext
}                                                   for JNDI lookup

private InitialContext createInitialContext() throws NamingException {
   Hashtable<String,String> environment=            Environment
     new Hashtable<String,String>();                variables set
   environment.put(Context.INITIAL_CONTEXT_FACTORY, in Hashtable
"com.your-company.javax.datamining.resource.initialContextFactory-impl");
   environment.put(Context.PROVIDER_URL, this.providerURI);
   environment.put(Context.SECURITY_PRINCIPAL, this.userName);
   environment.put(Context.SECURITY_CREDENTIALS, this.password);
   return new InitialContext(environment);
}

private ConnectionSpec getConnectionSpec(
   ConnectionFactory connectionFactory) {
   ConnectionSpec connectionSpec =                  Get ConnectionSpec
     connectionFactory.getConnectionSpec();         from ConnectionFactory
   connectionSpec.setName(this.userName);
   connectionSpec.setPassword(this.password);
   connectionSpec.setURI(this.serverURI);
   return connectionSpec;
}
```

To get the `ConnectionFactory`, we first need to create the `InitialContext` for the JNDI lookup. The constructor for `InitialContext` takes a `Hashtable`, and we set the provider URL, username, and password for the lookup. Here the code

```
(ConnectionFactory) initialJNDIContext.lookup(
     "java:com/env/jdm/yourDMServer");
```

provides access to the `ConnectionFactory`. We get access to the `ConnectionSpec` with

```
ConnectionSpec connectionSpec = connectionFactory.getConnectionSpec();
```

The `ConnectionSpec` object is populated with the `serverURI`, the name, and password credentials, and a new `Connection` object is created from the `ConnectionFactory` by the following code:

```
connectionFactory.getConnection(connectionSpec);
```

Once you have a `Connection` object, you can execute the different types of `Tasks` that are available, per the JDM specification. This completes our JDM example and a brief overview of the JDM architecture and the key APIs. Before we end this chapter, it's useful to briefly discuss how JDM fits in with PMML, an XML standard for representing data mining models.

7.3.9   *JDM models and PMML*

Predictive Model Markup Language (PMML) is an XML standard developed by the Data Mining Group[13] (DMG) to represent predictive models. There's wide support among the vendors to import and/or export PMML models. But PMML doesn't specify the settings used to create the model, so there may be some loss of information when JDM models are converted to PMML format and vice versa; this is dependent on each vendor's JDM model implementation. PMML does contain adequate information to apply and test the model. PMML models map readily to JDM. JDM also influenced certain aspects of the PMML 2.0 release.

7.4   *Summary*

Data mining is the automated process of analyzing data to discover previously unknown patterns and create predictive models. Mining algorithms need test data in order to learn. A dataset is composed of a number of examples. Each example consists of values for a set of attributes. An attribute can be continuous or discrete. Discrete values that have an ordering associated with them are known as ordinal, while those that don't have any ordering are called nominal.

There are five major types of mining algorithms:

- *Attribute importance*—Ranks the available attributes in terms of importance for predicting the output variable
- *Association rules*—Finds interesting relationships in data by looking at co-occurring items
- *Clustering*—Finds clusters of similar data points
- *Regression*—Predicts the value of the output variable based on the input attributes
- *Classification*—Classifies a discrete attribute into one of enumerated value

---

[13] http://www.dmg.org/

Writing mining algorithms is complex. Fortunately, there are a few open source data mining platforms that one can use. WEKA is perhaps the most commonly used Java-based open source data mining platform. WEKA includes all the five different types of learning algorithms along with APIs to represent and manipulate the data.

You don't want to tie your application code with a specific vendor implementation of data mining algorithms. Java Data Mining (JDM) is a specification developed under Java Community Process JSR 73 and JSR 247. JDM aims at providing a set of vendor-neutral APIs for accessing and using a data-mining engine. There are couple of data-mining engines that are compliant with the JDM specification, and it's expected that more companies will implement it in the future.

With this background, you should have a basic understanding of the data mining process; the algorithms; WEKA, the open source data mining toolkit; and JDM, the Java Data Mining standard.

For the learning process, we need a dataset. In the next chapter, chapter 8, we build a text analysis toolkit, which enables us to convert unstructured text into a format that can be used by the learning algorithms. We take a more detailed look at some of the data-mining algorithms, especially those associated with clustering and predictive models in chapter 9 and chapter 10.

7.5 Resources

Burges, Christopher J. C. "A tutorial on support vector machines for pattern recognition." 1998. *Data Mining and Knowledge Discovery.* http://www.umiacs.umd.edu/~joseph/support-vector-machines4.pdf

"Familiarize yourself with data mining functions and algorithms." 2007. *JavaWorld.* http://www.javaworld.com/javaworld/jw-02-2007/jw-02-jdm.html?page=2

Hornick, Mark, Erik Marcadé, and Sunil Venkayala. *Java Data Mining: Strategy, Standard, and Practice.* 2007. Morgan Kaufmann.

Java Data Mining API 1.0. JSR 73. http://www.jcp.org/en/jsr/detail?id=73

Java Data Mining API 2.0. JSR 247. http://www.jcp.org/en/jsr/detail?id=247

Jose, Benoy. "The Java Data Mining API." Java Boutique. http://javaboutique.internet.com/articles/mining_java/

Moore, Andrew. "Statistical Data Mining Algorithms." http://www.autonlab.org/tutorials/

Sommers, Frank. "Mine Your Own Data with the JDM API." 2005. -http://www.artima.com/lejava/articles/data_mining.html

Tan, Pang-Ning, Michael Steinbach, and Vipin Kumar. *Introduction to Data Mining.* 2006.

"Use Weka in your Java Code." http://weka.sourceforge.net/wiki/index.php/Use_Weka_in_your_Java_code

Vapnik, Vladimir. *Statistical Learning Theory.* 1998. Wiley Science.

Venkayala, Sunil. "Using Java Data Mining to Develop Advanced Analytics Applications: The predictive capabilities of enterprise Java apps." Java Developer Journal, http://jdj.sys-con.com/read/49091.htm

Witten, Ian H. and Eibe Frank. *Data Mining: Practical Machine Learning Tools and Techniques, 2nd Edition.* 2005. Morgan Kaufmann, San Francisco.

Building
a text analysis toolkit

This chapter covers

- A brief introduction to Lucene
- Understanding tokenizers, TokenStream, and analyzers
- Building an analyzer to detect phrases and inject synonyms
- Use cases for leveraging the infrastructure

It's now common for most applications to leverage user-generated-content (UGC). Users may generate content through one of many ways: writing blog entries, sending messages to others, answering or posing questions on message boards, through journal entries, or by creating a list of related items. In chapter 3, we looked at the use of tagging to represent metadata associated with content. We mentioned that tags can also be detected by automated algorithm.

In this chapter, we build a toolkit to analyze content. This toolkit will enable us to extract tags and their associated weights to build a term-vector representation for the text. The term vector representation can be used to

- Build metadata about the user as described in chapter 2
- Create tag clouds as shown in chapter 3
- Mine the data to create clusters of similar documents as shown in chapter 9
- Build predictive models as shown in chapter 10
- Form a basis for understanding search as used in chapter 11
- Form a basis for developing a content-based recommendation engine as shown in chapter 12

As a precursor to this chapter, you may want to review sections 2.2.3, 3.1–3.2, and 4.3. The emphasis of this chapter is in implementation, and at the end of the chapter we'll have the tools to analyze text as described in section 4.3. We leverage Apache Lucene to use its text-parsing infrastructure. Lucene is a Java-based open source search engine developed by Doug Cutting. Nutch, which we looked at in chapter 6, is also based on Lucene. We begin with building a text-parsing infrastructure that supports the use of stop words, synonyms, and a phrase dictionary. Next, we implement the term vector with capabilities to add and compute similarities with other term vectors. We insulate our infrastructure from using any of Lucene's specific classes in its interfaces, so that in the future if you want to use a different text-parsing infrastructure, you won't have to change your core classes. This chapter is a good precursor to chapter 11, which is on intelligent search.

8.1 *Building the text analyzers*

This section deals with analyzing content—taking a piece of text and converting it into tags. Tags may contain a single term or multiple terms, known as *phrases*. In this section, we build the Java code to intelligently process text as illustrated in section 4.3. This framework is the foundation for dealing with unstructured text and converting it into a format that can be used by various algorithms, as we'll see in the remaining chapters of this book. At the end of this section, we develop the tools required to convert text into a list of tags.

In section 2.2.3, we looked at the typical steps involved in text analysis, which are shown in figure 8.1:

1 *Tokenize*—Parsing the text to generate terms. Sophisticated analyzers can also extract phrases from the text.

2 *Normalize*—Converting text to lowercase.

3 *Eliminate stop words*—Eliminating terms that appear very often.

4 *Stem*—Converting the terms into their stemmed form; removing plurals.

At this point, it's useful to look at the example in section 4.3, where we went through the various steps involved with analyzing text. We used a simple blog entry consisting of a title and a body to demonstrate analyzing text. We use the same example in this chapter.

Figure 8.1 Typical steps involved in analyzing text

Figure 8.2, which shows a typical web page with a blog entry in the center of the page, demonstrates the applicability of the framework developed in this chapter. The figure consists of five main sections:

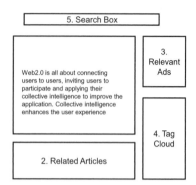

Figure 8.2   Example of how the tools developed in this chapter can be leveraged in your application

1   *Main context*—The blog entry with the title and body is at the center of the page.

2   *Related articles*—This section contains other related articles that are relevant to the user and to the blog entry in the first section. We develop this in chapter 12.

3   *Relevant ads*—This section shows advertisements that are relevant to the user and to the context in the first section. Tags extracted from the main context and the user's past behavior are used to show relevant advertisements.

4   *Tag cloud visualization*—This section shows a tag cloud representation of the tags of interest to the user. This tag cloud (see chapter 3) can be generated by analyzing the pages visited by the user in the past.

5   *Search box*—Most applications have a search box that allows users to search for content using keywords. The main content of the page—the blog entry—is indexed for retrieval via a search engine, as shown in chapter 11.

First, we need some classes that can parse text. We use Apache Lucene.

8.1.1   *Leveraging Lucene*

Apache Lucene[1] is an open source Java-based full-text search engine. In this chapter, we use the analyzers that are available with Lucene. For more on Lucene, Manning has an excellent book, *Lucene in Action*, by Gospodnetic and Hatcher. You'll find the material in chapter 4 of the book to be particularly helpful for this section.

Lucene can be freely downloaded at http://www.apache.org/dyn/closer.cgi/lucene/java/. Download the appropriate file based on your operating system. For example, I downloaded lucene-2.2.0-src.zip, which contains the Lucene 2.2.0 source, and lucene-2.2.0.zip, which contains the compiled classes. Unzip this file and make sure that lucene-core-2.2.0.jar is in your Java classpath. We use this for our analysis.

The first part of the text analysis process is tokenization—converting text into tokens. For this we need to look at Lucene classes in the package `org.apache.lucene.analysis`.

KEY LUCENE TEXT-PARSING CLASSES

In this section, we look at the key classes that are used by Lucene to parse text. Figure 8.3 shows the key classes in the analysis package of Lucene. Remember, our aim is to convert text into a series of terms. We also briefly review the five classes that are shown in figure 8.3. Later, we use these classes to write our own text analyzers.

---

[1]   http://lucene.apache.org/

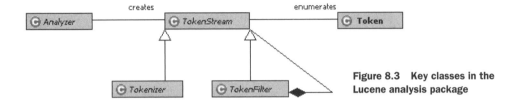

Figure 8.3 Key classes in the Lucene analysis package

An `Analyzer` is an abstract class that takes in a `java.io.Reader` and creates a Token-Stream. For doing this, an `Analyzer` has the following method:

```
public abstract TokenStream tokenStream(String fieldName, Reader reader);
```

The abstract class `TokenStream` creates an enumeration of `Token` objects. Each Tokenizer implements the method:

```
public Token next() throws IOException;
```

A `Token` represents a term occurring in the text.

There are two abstract subclasses for `TokenStream`. First is `Tokenizer`, which deals with processing text at the character level. The input to a `Tokenizer` is a `java.io.Reader`. The abstract `Tokenizer` class has two protected constructors. The first is a no-argument constructor; the second takes a `Reader` object. All subclasses of a `Tokenizer` have a public constructor that invokes the protected constructor for the parent `Tokenizer` class, passing in a `Reader` object:

```
protected abstract Tokenizer(Reader input)
```

The second subclass of `TokenStream` is `TokenFilter`. A `TokenFilter` deals with words, and its input is another `TokenStream`, which could be another `TokenFilter` or a `Tokenizer`. There's only one constructor in a `TokenFilter`, which is protected and has to be invoked by the subclasses:

```
protected TokenFilter(TokenStream input)
```

The composition link from a `TokenFilter` (see the black diamond in figure 8.3) to a `TokenStream` in figure 8.3 indicates that token filters can be chained. A `TokenFilter` follows the composite design pattern and forms a "has a" relationship with another `TokenStream`.

Table 8.1 summarizes the five classes that we have discussed so far.

Next, we need to look at some of the concrete implementations of these classes.

Table 8.1 Common terms used to describe attributes

Class	Description
Token	Represents a term occurring in the text, with positional information of where it occurs in the text.
Analyzer	Abstract class for converting text in a `java.io.Reader` into `TokenStream`.
TokenStream	An abstract class that enumerates a sequence of tokens from a text.

Table 8.1   Common terms used to describe attributes *(continued)*

Class	Description
Tokenizer	A `TokenStream` that tokenizes the input from a `Reader`. It deals with individual characters.
TokenFilter	A `TokenStream` whose input is another `TokenStream`. It deals with words.

LUCENE TOKENIZERS, FILTERS, AND ANALYZERS

In this section, we look at the available implementations for tokenizers, token filters and analyzers from Lucene. We'll leverage these when we develop our own analyzers.

First let's look at the concrete implementations of `Tokenizer` provided by Lucene. As shown in figure 8.3, we're currently interested in five of the available tokenizers. These are shown in table 8.2, which should give you a good flavor of available tokenizers. Of course, it's simple enough to extend any of these `Tokenizers`. Either a `StandardTokenizer` or a `LowercaseTokenizer` should work well for most applications.

Table 8.2   Available tokenizers from Lucene

Tokenizer	Details
StandardTokenizer	Tokenizer for most European languages. Removes punctuation and splits words at punctuation. But if a dot isn't followed by white space, it's considered part of the token. Splits words at hyphens unless there's a number, in which case the whole token isn't split. Recognizes Internet host names and email addresses.
CharTokenizer	An abstract base class for character-oriented simple `Tokenizers`.
WhitespaceTokenizer	Divides text at white spaces.
LetterTokenizer	Divides text at non-letters. Works well for European languages but not for Asian languages, where words aren't separated by spaces.
LowerCaseTokenizer	Converts text into lowercase and divides text into non-words.
RussianLetterTokenizer	Extends `LetterTokenizer` by additionally looking up letters in a given "Russian charset."

Next, let's look at the available set of `TokenFilters`, which is shown in figure 8.4. Table 8.3 contains details about a few of them.

Of particular importance to us is the `StopFilter`, which we use for adding stop words, and the `PorterStemFilter`, which we use to stem words. Note that there are language-specific filters, for example, the `RussianLowerCaseFilter` and `Russian-StemFilter` for the Russian language, and the `GermanStemFilter` for German words.

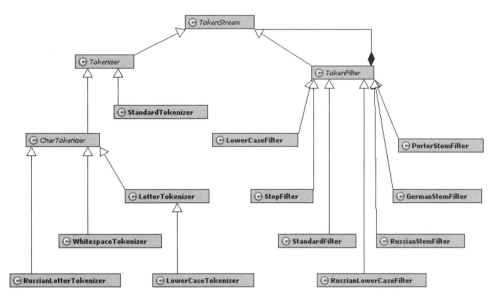

Figure 8.4 Some of the concrete implementations for Tokenizer and TokenFilter

Lastly, let's look at some of the analyzers that are available from Lucene. Figure 8.5 shows some of the Analyzer classes available to us.

Table 8.3 Available filters from Lucene

TokenFilter	Details
StandardFilter	Normalizes tokens by removing s, S, and periods. Works in conjunction with a StandardTokenizer.
LowerCaseFilter	Normalizes the token text to lowercase.
StopFilter	Removes words that appear in the provided stop word list from the token stream.
PorterStemFilter	Stems the token using the Porter stemming algorithm. Tokens are expected to be lowercase.
RussianLowerCaseFilter	Converts text into lowercase using a Russian charset.
RussianStemFilter	Stems Russian words, which are expected to be lowercase.
GermanStemFilter	A stem filter for German words.

Table 8.4 contains the details about each of the available analyzers.

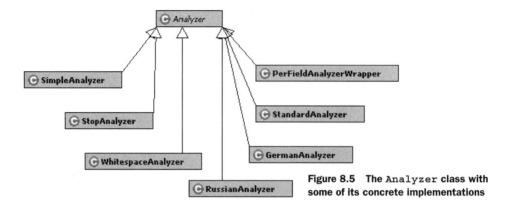

Figure 8.5   The Analyzer class with some of its concrete implementations

Table 8.4   Common Analyzer classes that are available in Lucene

Analyzer	Details
SimpleAnalyzer	Uses the LowerCaseTokenizer
StopAnalyzer	Combines a LowerCaseTokenizer with a StopFilter
WhitespaceAnalyzer	Uses the WhitespaceTokenizer
PerFieldAnalyzerWrapper	Useful for when different fields need different Analyzers
StandardAnalyzer	Uses a list of English stop words and combines StandardTokenizer, StandardFilter, LowerCaseFilter, and StopFilter
GermanAnalyzer	Analyzer for German language
RussianAnalyzer	Analyzer for Russian language

At this stage, we're done with Lucene classes. We build on what we've learned so far in this chapter by leveraging the available Lucene analyzers and token filters to write two custom Analyzers:

1 PorterStemStopWordAnalyzer: A custom analyzer that normalizes tokens; it uses stop words and Porter stemming.

2 SynonymPhraseStopWordAnalyzer: An analyzer that injects synonyms and detects phrases. It uses a custom TokenFilter that we'll build: the Synonym-PhraseStopWordFilter.

Figure 8.6 shows the class diagram for the two analyzers and token filter that we build next.

We next look at implementing the PorterStemStopWordAnalyzer.

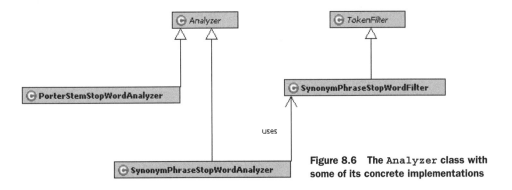

Figure 8.6 The `Analyzer` class with some of its concrete implementations

8.1.2 Writing a stemmer analyzer

It's helpful to have an analyzer that can take care of plurals by stemming words. We also want to add the capability to first normalize the tokens into lowercase and use a custom stop word list. `PorterStemStopWordAnalyzer` is such an analyzer; the code is shown in listing 8.1.

Listing 8.1 Implementation of the `PorterStemStopWordAnalyzer`

```
package com.alag.ci.textanalysis.lucene.impl;

import java.io.Reader;                                      Uses custom
                                                            stop word set
import org.apache.lucene.analysis.*;
import org.apache.lucene.analysis.standard.StandardTokenizer;

public class PorterStemStopWordAnalyzer extends Analyzer {
   private static final String [] stopWords =
      {"and","of","the","to","is";"their","can","all"};

   public TokenStream tokenStream(String fieldName, Reader reader) {
      Tokenizer tokenizer = new StandardTokenizer(reader);
      TokenFilter lowerCaseFilter =
         new LowerCaseFilter(tokenizer);
      TokenFilter stopFilter = new  StopFilter(lowerCaseFilter,
         stopWords);
      TokenFilter stemFilter =                             Takes instance of
         new PorterStemFilter(stopFilter);            StandardTokenizer as input
      return stemFilter;
   }                               Chains StopFilter  Chains LowerCaseFilter
}                                                     and uses stop word set
```

To keep things simple, we provide the analyzer with an internal stop word list. This list is customized according to the text analysis example we worked through in section 4.3. There are quite a few stop word lists that are available if you search the Web. For example, you can use Google's stop word list[2] or a more detailed list.[3] You may want to customize your stop word list based on your application and the domain to which it's applied.

---

[2] http://www.ranks.nl/tools/stopwords.html
[3] http://www.onjava.com/onjava/2003/01/15/examples/EnglishStopWords.txt

Our analyzer extends the `Analyzer` class from Lucene, and we need to implement one method:

```
public TokenStream tokenStream(String fieldName, Reader reader)
```

In this method, we first create a `Tokenizer` using the `StandardTokenizer`, which removes all punctuation and splits the text at punctuation.

```
Tokenizer tokenizer = new StandardTokenizer(reader);
```

Let's write a simple test to see the effect of `PorterStemStopWordAnalyzer` on the text "Collective Intelligence and Web2.0." Listing 8.2 shows the code for the test method.

Listing 8.2   Test method to see the effect of `PorterStemStopWordAnalyzer`

```
public void testPorterStemmingAnalyzer() throws IOException {
    Analyzer analyzer = new PorterStemStopWordAnalyzer();
    String text = "Collective Intelligence and Web2.0";
    Reader reader = new StringReader(text);
    TokenStream ts = analyzer.tokenStream(null, reader);
    Token token = ts.next();
    while (token != null) {
        System.out.println(token.termText());
        token = ts.next();
    }
}
```

The output from the test program is three tokens:

```
collect
intellig
web2.0
```

Note that *collective* is stemmed to *collect*, while *intelligence* is stemmed to *intellig*. Also, *web2.0* is a tag; the analyzer didn't split the term *web2.0*.

Next, we chain three `TokenFilter` instances, starting with the `LowerCaseFilter`, followed by the `StopFilter`, and lastly the `PorterStemFilter`. We put this analyzer into practice later in section 8.2, when we look at building our text analysis infrastructure.

8.1.3   *Writing a TokenFilter to inject synonyms and detect phrases*

In section 4.3.5, we discussed the need for detecting multiple-term tokens when analyzing text. Multiple-term tags are more specific than single-term tags and typically have a higher inverse document frequency value. If you use human-generated tags, either through professionals or users, it's necessary to detect multiple-term tags that may have been entered. These human-generated tags in essence form the universe of phrases that you'd be interested in detecting. Similarly, synonyms help in matching tags that have the same meaning. For example, *CI* is a commonly used synonym for *collective intelligence*.

In this section, we build a custom `TokenFilter` that does two things:

1 It looks at two adjoining non–stop word terms to see if they form a phrase we're interested in. If the bi-term is a valid phrase then it's injected into the token stream.

2 It looks at a synonym dictionary to see if any of the terms or phrases in the token stream have synonyms, in which case the synonyms are injected into the token stream.

To illustrate the process of how phrases can be detected, we use a fairly simple strategy—considering two adjoining non–stop word terms. You can enhance the phrase detection strategy by using more than two terms or using a longer window of terms to find phrases. A window size of two means considering the two terms adjoining to the term of interest. You'll have to balance the benefits of performing complicated logic against the additional computation time required to analyze the text. You can also use a variable size window, especially if there is a set of phrases you're trying to detect from the text.

Before we can write our custom token filter, we need to get access to phrases and synonyms. For this, we define two additional entities:

1 `PhrasesCache`: to determine whether a phrase is of interest to us

2 `SynonymsCache`: a cache of synonyms

Listing 8.3 shows the implementation for the interface `PhrasesCache`, which has only one method: `isValidPhrase`.

Listing 8.3 Interface to validate phrases

```
package com.alag.ci.textanalysis;
import java.io.IOException;

public interface PhrasesCache {
    public boolean isValidPhrase(String text) throws IOException;
}
```

Listing 8.4 shows the implementation for `SynonymsCache`. It has only one method, `getSynonym`, which returns the list of synonyms for a given text.

Listing 8.4 Interface to access synonyms

```
package com.alag.ci.textanalysis;
import java.io.IOException;
import java.util.List;

public interface SynonymsCache {
    public List<String> getSynonym(String text) throws IOException;
}
```

With this background, we're now ready to write our custom token filter. Listing 8.5 shows the first part of the implementation of the `SynonymPhraseStopWordFilter`. This part deals with the attributes, the constructor, and the implementation of the `next()` method.

Listing 8.5 The `next()` method for `SynonymPhraseStopWordFilter`

```
package com.alag.ci.textanalysis.lucene.impl;

import java.io.IOException;
import java.util.*;

import org.apache.lucene.analysis.*;                              Extends
                                                                  TokenFilter
import com.alag.ci.textanalysis.*;

public class SynonymPhraseStopWordFilter extends TokenFilter {
    private Stack<Token> injectedTokensStack = null;
    private Token previousToken = null;
    private SynonymsCache synonymsCache = null;             Takes TokenStream,
    private PhrasesCache phrasesCache = null;              SynonymsCache, and
                                                               PhraseCache
    public SynonymPhraseStopWordFilter(TokenStream input,
            SynonymsCache synonymsCache, PhrasesCache phrasesCache) {
        super(input);
        this.synonymsCache = synonymsCache;
        this.phrasesCache = phrasesCache;                 Injects additional
        this.injectedTokensStack = new Stack<Token>();     tokens in stream
    }

    public Token next() throws IOException {          Tokens on stack
        if (this.injectedTokensStack.size() > 0 ) {   passed to stream
            return this.injectedTokensStack.pop();
        }
        Token token = input.next();
        if (token != null) {                         Injects
            String phrase = injectPhrases( token);   phrases
            injectSynonyms(token.termText(), token);         Injects
            injectSynonyms(phrase, token);                   synonyms
            this.previousToken = token;
        }
        return token;
    }
}
```

The `SynonymPhraseStopWordFilter` extends the `TokenFilter` class. Its constructor takes in another `TokenStream` object, a `SynonymsCache`, and a `PhraseCache`. It internally uses a `Stack` to keep track of injected tokens. It needs to implement one method:

```
public Token next() throws IOException {
```

The attribute `previousToken` keeps track of the previous token. Phrases and synonyms are injected by the following code:

```
Token token = input.next();
if (token != null) {
    String phrase = injectPhrases( token);
    injectSynonyms(token.termText(), token);
    injectSynonyms(phrase, token);
    this.previousToken = token;
}
```

Note that the code

```
injectSynonyms(phrase, token);
```

checks for synonyms for the injected phrases also. Listing 8.6 contains the remainder of the class. It has the implementation for the methods `injectPhrases` and `injectSynonyms`.

Listing 8.6   Injecting phrases and synonyms

```
private String injectPhrases(Token currentToken) throws IOException {
    if (this.previousToken != null) {
        String phrase = this.previousToken.termText() + " " +
        currentToken.termText();
        if (this.phrasesCache.isValidPhrase(phrase)) {
            Token phraseToken = new Token(phrase,
                currentToken.startOffset(),
                 currentToken.endOffset(),"phrase");
            phraseToken.setPositionIncrement(0);
            this.injectedTokensStack.push(phraseToken);
            return phrase;
        }
    }
    return null;
}

private void injectSynonyms(String text, Token currentToken)
  throws IOException {
    if (text != null) {
        List<String> synonyms = this.synonymsCache.getSynonym(text);
        if (synonyms != null) {
            for (String synonym: synonyms) {
                Token synonymToken = new Token(synonym,
                    currentToken.startOffset(),
                     currentToken.endOffset(),"synonym");
                synonymToken.setPositionIncrement(0);
                this.injectedTokensStack.push(synonymToken);
            }
        }
    }
}
```

Concatenates previous and current tokens

Checks against dictionary

Retrieves synonyms, injects them into the stream

For injecting phrases, we first concatenate the text from the previous token, a space, and the current token text:

```
String phrase = this.previousToken.termText() + " " +
currentToken.termText();
```

We check to see if this is a phrase of interest. If it is, a new `Token` object is created with this text and injected onto the stack.

To inject synonyms, we get a list of synonyms for the text and inject each synonym into the stack. Next, we leverage this `TokenFilter` to write an analyzer that uses it. This analyzer normalizes the tokens, removes stop words, detects phrases, and injects synonyms. We build this next.

8.1.4 Writing an analyzer to inject synonyms and detect phrases

In this section we write an analyzer that uses the token filter we developed in the previous section. This analyzer normalizes tokens, removes stop words, detects phrases, and injects synonyms. We use it as part of our text analysis infrastructure.

Listing 8.7 shows the implementation for the SynonymPhraseStopWordAnalyzer.

Listing 8.7 Implementation of the SynonymPhraseStopWordAnalyzer

```
package com.alag.ci.textanalysis.lucene.impl;

import java.io.Reader;

import org.apache.lucene.analysis.*;
import org.apache.lucene.analysis.standard.StandardTokenizer;

import com.alag.ci.textanalysis.*;

public class SynonymPhraseStopWordAnalyzer extends Analyzer{
    private  SynonymsCache synonymsCache = null;
    private PhrasesCache phrasesCache = null;

    public SynonymPhraseStopWordAnalyzer(SynonymsCache synonymsCache,
            PhrasesCache phrasesCache) {            ◁────┐ Constructor
        this.synonymsCache = synonymsCache;
        this.phrasesCache = phrasesCache;
    }
                                                                 Normalizes tokens
    public TokenStream tokenStream(String fieldName, Reader reader) {
        Tokenizer tokenizer = new StandardTokenizer(reader);
        TokenFilter lowerCaseFilter = new LowerCaseFilter(tokenizer);  ◁──
        TokenFilter stopFilter = new StopFilter(lowerCaseFilter,
            PorterStemStopWordAnalyzer.stopWords);        ◁──
        return new SynonymPhraseStopWordFilter(stopFilter,          Filters for
            this.synonymsCache, this.phrasesCache);    ◁──         stop words
    }
}                      Injects synonyms and detects phrases
```

SynonymPhraseStopWordAnalyzer extends the Analyzer class. Its constructor takes an instance of the SynonymsCache and the PhrasesCache. The only method that we need to implement is

```
public TokenStream tokenStream(String fieldName, Reader reader) {
```

For this method, we first normalize the tokens, remove stop words, and then invoke our custom filter, SynonymPhraseStopWordFilter.

Next, we apply our analyzer to the sample text: "Collective Intelligence and Web2.0."

8.1.5 Putting our analyzers to work

Our custom analyzer, SynonymPhraseStopWordAnalyzer, needs access to an instance of a PhrasesCache and SynonymsCache. As shown in figure 8.7, we implement PhrasesCacheImpl and SynonymsCacheImpl. The common implementations for both classes will be in their base class, CacheImpl.

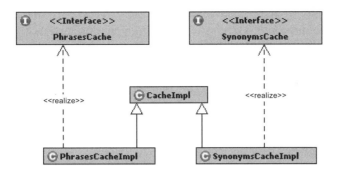

Figure 8.7   The implementations for the `PhrasesCache` and `SynonymsCache`

Listing 8.8 shows the implementation for the `CacheImpl` class. We want the lookup for phrases and synonyms to be independent of plurals; that's why we compare text using stemmed values.

Listing 8.8   Implementation of the `CacheImpl` class

```java
package com.alag.ci.textanalysis.lucene.impl;

import java.io.*;

import org.apache.lucene.analysis.*;

public class CacheImpl {
    private Analyzer stemmer = null;            // Uses PorterStemStopWordAnalyzer
                                                //               for stemming
    public CacheImpl() {
        this.stemmer = new PorterStemStopWordAnalyzer();
    }

    protected String getStemmedText(String text) throws IOException {
        StringBuilder sb = new StringBuilder();
        Reader reader = new StringReader(text);
        TokenStream tokenStream = this.stemmer.tokenStream(null, reader);
        Token token = tokenStream.next();       // Method to get
        while (token != null) {                 //   stemmed text
            sb.append(token.termText());
            token = tokenStream.next();
            if (token != null) {
                sb.append(" ");
            }
        }
        return sb.toString();
    }
}
```

There's only one method in this class:

```java
String getStemmedText(String text) throws IOException
```

We use our custom analyzer `PorterStemStopWordAnalyzer` to get the stemmed value for a text. This method iterates over all the terms in the text to get their stemmed text and converts phrases with a set of quotes (" ") between the terms.

To keep things simple, we implement a class, SynonymsCacheImpl, which has only one synonym—*collective intelligence* has the synonym *ci*. For your application, you'll probably maintain a list of synonyms either in the database or in an XML file. Listing 8.9 shows the implementation for SynonymsCacheImpl.

Listing 8.9   Implementation of SynonymsCacheImpl

```
package com.alag.ci.textanalysis.lucene.impl;

import java.io.IOException;
import java.util.*;

import com.alag.ci.textanalysis.SynonymsCache;

public class SynonymsCacheImpl extends CacheImpl implements SynonymsCache {
   private Map<String,List<String>> synonyms = null;

   public SynonymsCacheImpl() throws IOException {
      this.synonyms = new HashMap<String,List<String>>();
      List<String> ciList = new ArrayList<String>();
      ciList.add("ci");
      this.synonyms.put(getStemmedText("collective intelligence"),
         ciList);              ◁────── Has only one synonym
   }

   public List<String> getSynonym(String text) throws IOException{
      return this.synonyms.get(getStemmedText(text));   ◁── Uses stemmed values
   }                                                        for comparison
}
```

Note that to look up synonyms, the class compares stemmed values, so that plurals are automatically taken care of. Similarly, in our PhrasesCacheImpl, we have only one phrase, *collective intelligence.* Listing 8.10 shows the implementation for the Phrases-CacheImpl class.

Listing 8.10   Implementation of the PhrasesCacheImpl

```
package com.alag.ci.textanalysis.lucene.impl;

import java.io.IOException;
import java.util.*;

import com.alag.ci.textanalysis.PhrasesCache;

public class PhrasesCacheImpl extends CacheImpl implements PhrasesCache {
   private Map<String,String> validPhrases = null;

   public PhrasesCacheImpl() throws IOException {
      validPhrases = new HashMap<String,String>();
      validPhrases.put(getStemmedText("collective intelligence"), null);
   }     ◁────── Only one phrase: "collective intelligence"

   public boolean isValidPhrase(String text) throws IOException {
      return this.validPhrases.containsKey(getStemmedText(text));   ◁──
   }
}                                                        Uses stemmed values
                                                         for comparison
```

Again phrases are compared using their stemmed values. Now we're ready to write a test method to see the output for our test case, "Collective Intelligence and Web2.0." The code for analyzing this text using `SynonymPhraseStopWordAnalyzer` is shown in listing 8.11.

Listing 8.11 Test program using `SynonymPhraseStopWordAnalyzer`

```
public void testSynonymsPhrases() throws IOException {
    SynonymsCache synonymsCache = new SynonymsCacheImpl();
    PhrasesCache phrasesCache = new PhrasesCacheImpl();
    Analyzer analyzer = new SynonymPhraseStopWordAnalyzer(
        synonymsCache,phrasesCache);
    String text = "Collective Intelligence and Web2.0";
    Reader reader = new StringReader(text);
    TokenStream ts = analyzer.tokenStream(null, reader);
    Token token = ts.next();
    while (token != null) {
        System.out.println(token.termText());
        token = ts.next();
    }
}
```

The output from this program is

```
collective
intelligence
ci
collective intelligence
web2.0
```

As expected, there are five tokens. Note the token *ci*, which gets injected, as it's a synonym for the phrase *collective intelligence*, which is also detected.

So far, we've looked at the available analyzers from Lucene and built a couple of custom analyzers to process text. Text comparisons are done using stemmed values, which take care of plurals.

Next, let's look at how all this hard work we've done so far can be leveraged to build the term vector representation that we discussed in section 2.2.4 and a text analysis infrastructure that abstracts out terminology used by Lucene. That way, if tomorrow you need to use a different text-processing package, the abstractions we create will make it simple to change implementations.

8.2   *Building the text analysis infrastructure*

The core classes for our text analysis infrastructure will be independent of Lucene classes. This section is split into three parts:

1 Infrastructure related to tags
2 Infrastructure related to term vectors
3 Putting it all together to build our text analyzer class

Figure 8.8 shows the classes that will be developed for this package. We define a class, `Tag`, to represent tags in our system. Tags can contain single terms or multiple-term

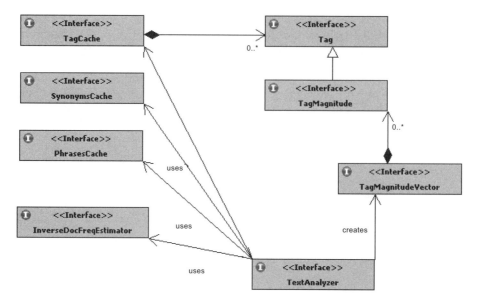

Figure 8.8   The infrastructure for text analysis

phrases. We use the flyweight design pattern, where `Tag` instances are immutable and cached by `TagCache`. The `TagMagnitude` class consists of a magnitude associated with a `Tag` instance. The term vector is represented by the `TagMagnitudeVector` class and consists of a number of `TagMagnitude` instances. In the previous section, we already looked at the `SynonymsCache` and the `PhrasesCache` classes that are used to access synonyms and phrases. The `TextAnalyzer` class is the main class for processing text. The `InverseDocFreqEstimator` is used for getting the inverse document frequency associated with a `Tag`. The `TextAnalyzer` uses the `TagCache`, `SynonymsCache`, `PhrasesCache`, and `InverseDocFreqEstimator` to create a `TagMagnitudeVector` for the text.

Next, let's look at developing the infrastructure related to tags.

8.2.1   *Building the tag infrastructure*

The four classes associated with implementing the tag infrastructure are shown in figure 8.9. These classes are `Tag` and its implementation `TagImpl`, along with `TagCache` and its implementation `TagCacheImpl`.

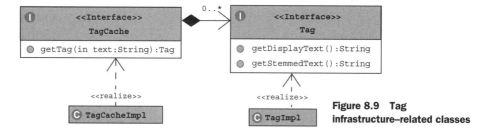

Figure 8.9   Tag infrastructure–related classes

A Tag is the smallest entity in our framework. As shown in listing 8.12, a Tag has display text and its stemmed value. Remember we want to compare tags based on their stemmed values.

Listing 8.12 The Tag interface

```
package com.alag.ci.textanalysis;

public interface Tag {
   public String getDisplayText();
   public String getStemmedText();
}
```

Listing 8.13 shows the implementation for TagImpl, which implements the Tag interface. This is implemented as an immutable object, where its display text and stemmed values are specified in the constructor.

Listing 8.13 The TagImpl implementation

```
package com.alag.ci.textanalysis.lucene.impl;

import com.alag.ci.textanalysis.Tag;

public class TagImpl implements Tag {
   private String displayText = null;
   private String stemmedText = null;
   private int hashCode ;                                    ⟵── Immutable
                                                                   object
   public TagImpl(String displayText, String stemmedText) {
      this.displayText = displayText;
      this.stemmedText = stemmedText;
      hashCode = stemmedText.hashCode();      ⟵── Hashcode
   }                                                precomputed for
                                                    faster lookup
   public String getDisplayText() {
      return displayText;
   }

   public String getStemmedText() {
      return stemmedText;
   }

   @Override
   public boolean equals(Object obj) {
      return (this.hashCode == obj.hashCode());
   }

   @Override
   public int hashCode() {
      return this.hashCode;
   }

   @Override
   public String toString() {
      return "[" + this.displayText + ", " + this.stemmedText + "]";
   }
}
```

Note that two tags with the same stemmed text are considered equivalent. Depending on your domain, you could further enhance the tag-matching logic. For example, to compare multi-term phrases, you may want to consider tags with the same terms equivalent, independent of their position. Remember, from a performance point of view, you want to keep the matching logic as efficient as possible. Tag instances are relatively heavyweight and text processing is expensive. Therefore, we use the flyweight pattern and hold on to the Tag instances. The TagCache class is used for this purpose.

We access an instance of Tag through the TagCache. The TagCache interface has only one method, getTag, as shown in listing 8.14.

Listing 8.14   The `TagCache` interface

```
package com.alag.ci.textanalysis;

import java.io.IOException;

public interface TagCache {
    public Tag getTag(String text) throws IOException ;
}
```

TagCache is implemented by TagCacheImpl, which is shown in listing 8.15. The implementation is straightforward. A Map is used to store the mapping between stemmed text and a Tag instance.

Listing 8.15   The implementation for `TagCacheImpl`

```
package com.alag.ci.textanalysis.lucene.impl;

import java.io.IOException;
import java.util.*;

import com.alag.ci.textanalysis.*;

public class TagCacheImpl extends CacheImpl implements TagCache {
    private Map<String,Tag> tagMap = null;

    public TagCacheImpl() {
        this.tagMap = new HashMap<String,Tag>();
    }

    public Tag getTag(String text) throws IOException {
        Tag tag = this.tagMap.get(text);
        if (tag == null ) {                                          ⟵ Looks up
            String stemmedText = getStemmedText(text);                 instances using
            tag = new TagImpl(text, stemmedText);                      stemmed value
            this.tagMap.put(stemmedText, tag);
        }
        return tag;
    }
}
```

Note that lookups from the cache are done using stemmed text:

```
getStemmedText(text);
```

With this background, we're now ready to develop the implementation for the term vectors.

8.2.2 Building the term vector infrastructure

Figure 8.10 shows the classes associated with extending the tag infrastructure to represent the term vector. The TagMagnitude interface associates a magnitude with the Tag, while the TagMagnitudeVector, which is a composition of TagMagnitude instances, represents the term vector.[4]

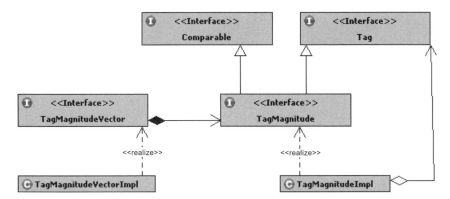

Figure 8.10   Term vector–related infrastructure

TAGMAGNITUDE-RELATED INTERFACES

Listing 8.16 shows the definition for the TagMagnitude interface. It extends the Tag and Comparable<TagMagnitude> interfaces. Implementing the Comparable interface is helpful for sorting the TagMagnitude instances by their weights.

Listing 8.16   The TagMagnitude interface

```
package com.alag.ci.textanalysis;

public interface TagMagnitude extends Tag, Comparable<TagMagnitude> {
    public double getMagnitude();
    public double getMagnitudeSqd();
    public Tag getTag();
}
```

There are only three methods associated with the TagMagnitude interface: one to get the magnitude, a utility method to get the square of the magnitudes, and one to get the associated Tag object.

The TagMagnitudeImpl class implements the TagMagnitude interface and is shown in listing 8.17.

---

[4] *Term vector* and *tag vector* are used interchangeably here, though there's a difference between terms and tags. Tags may be single terms or may contain phrases, which are multiple terms.

Listing 8.17 The implementation for `TagMagnitudeImpl`

```
package com.alag.ci.textanalysis.termvector.impl;

import com.alag.ci.textanalysis.*;

public class TagMagnitudeImpl implements TagMagnitude {
    private Tag tag = null;
    private double magnitude ;

    public TagMagnitudeImpl(Tag tag, double magnitude) {
        this.tag = tag;
        this.magnitude = magnitude;
    }

    public Tag getTag() {
        return this.tag;
    }

    public double getMagnitude() {
        return this.magnitude;
    }

    public double getMagnitudeSqd() {
        return this.magnitude*this.magnitude;
    }

    public String getDisplayText() {
        return this.tag.getDisplayText();
    }

    public String getStemmedText() {
        return this.tag.getStemmedText();
    }

    @Override
    public String toString() {
      return "[" + this.tag.getDisplayText() + ", " +
          this.tag.getStemmedText() +
          ", " + this.getMagnitude() + "]";
    }

    public int compareTo(TagMagnitude o) {
        double diff = this.magnitude - o.getMagnitude();
        if (diff > 0) {
          return -1;
        }else if (diff < 0) {
          return 1;
        }
        return 0;
    }
}
```

> Immutable object

> Useful for sorting by magnitude

Note that the `TagMagnitudeImpl` class is implemented as an immutable class. It has a magnitude attribute that's implemented as a double. The `TagMagnitudeImpl` class has access to a `Tag` instance and delegates to this object any methods related to the `Tag` interface.

TAGMAGNITUDEVECTOR-RELATED INTERFACES

Next, we're ready to define the TagMagnitudeVector interface, which represents a term vector. Listing 8.18 contains the methods associated with this interface.

Listing 8.18 The `TagMagnitudeVector` interface

```
package com.alag.ci.textanalysis;

import java.util.*;

public interface TagMagnitudeVector {
   public List<TagMagnitude> getTagMagnitudes();
   public Map<Tag,TagMagnitude> getTagMagnitudeMap() ;
   public double dotProduct(TagMagnitudeVector o) ;
   public TagMagnitudeVector add(TagMagnitudeVector o);
   public TagMagnitudeVector add(Collection<TagMagnitudeVector> tmList);
}
```

Take dot product of two term vectors

Add two term vectors

Add a collection of term vectors

The TagMagnitudeVector has four methods. The first two, getTagMagnitudes() and getTagMagnitudeMap(), are to access the TagMagnitude instance. The third method, add(), is useful for adding two term vectors, while the last method, dotProduct(), is useful for computing the similarity between two term vectors.

Lastly, let's look at the implementation for TagMagnitudeVectorImpl, which implements the TagMagnitudeVector interface. The first part of this implementation is shown in listing 8.19. We use a Map to hold the instances associated with the term vector. Typically, text contains a small subset of tags available. For example, in an application, there may be more than 100,000 different tags, but a document may contain only 25 unique tags.

Listing 8.19 The basic `TagMagnitudeVectorImpl` class

```
package com.alag.ci.textanalysis.termvector.impl;

import java.util.*;
import com.alag.ci.textanalysis.*;

public class TagMagnitudeVectorImpl implements TagMagnitudeVector {
   private Map<Tag,TagMagnitude> tagMagnitudesMap = null;

   public TagMagnitudeVectorImpl(List<TagMagnitude> tagMagnitudes) {
      normalize(tagMagnitudes);          Normalize input list
   }

   private void normalize(List<TagMagnitude> tagMagnitudes) {
      tagMagnitudesMap = new HashMap<Tag,TagMagnitude>();
      if ( (tagMagnitudes == null) || (tagMagnitudes.size() == 0)) {
         return;
      }
      double sumSqd = 0.;
      for (TagMagnitude tm: tagMagnitudes) {
         sumSqd += tm.getMagnitudeSqd();
      }
      if (sumSqd == 0. ) {
```

```
      sumSqd = 1./tagMagnitudes.size();
   }
   double normFactor = Math.sqrt(sumSqd);        ◁──  Normalization
   for (TagMagnitude tm: tagMagnitudes) {              factor set to l
      TagMagnitude otherTm = this.tagMagnitudesMap.get(tm.getTag());
      double magnitude = tm.getMagnitude();
      if (otherTm != null) {
         magnitude = mergeMagnitudes(magnitude,
               otherTm.getMagnitude()*normFactor);
      }
      TagMagnitude normalizedTm = new TagMagnitudeImpl(tm.getTag(),
            (magnitude/normFactor));
      this.tagMagnitudesMap.put(tm.getTag(), normalizedTm);
   }
}

public List<TagMagnitude> getTagMagnitudes() {
   List<TagMagnitude> sortedTagMagnitudes =
     new ArrayList<TagMagnitude>();
   sortedTagMagnitudes.addAll(tagMagnitudesMap.values());
   Collections.sort(sortedTagMagnitudes);        ◁──  Sorts results
   return sortedTagMagnitudes;                          by magnitude
}

public Map<Tag,TagMagnitude> getTagMagnitudeMap() {
   return this.tagMagnitudesMap;
}
                                                        Formula for
private double mergeMagnitudes(double a, double b) {  ◁──  merging two terms
   return Math.sqrt(a*a + b*b);
}
```

The `TagMagnitudeVectorImpl` class is implemented as an immutable object. It normalizes the input list of `TagMagnitude` objects such that the magnitude for this vector is 1.0. For the method `getTagMagnitudes`, the `TagMagnitude` instances are sorted by magnitude. Listing 8.20 contains the implementation for two methods. First is the `dotProduct`, which computes the similarity between the tag vector and another `TagMagnitudeVector`. The second method, `add()`, is useful for adding the current vector to another vector.

Listing 8.20   Computing the dot product in `TagMagnitudeVectorImpl`

```
public double dotProduct(TagMagnitudeVector o) {
   Map<Tag,TagMagnitude> otherMap = o.getTagMagnitudeMap();
   double dotProduct = 0.;
   for (Tag tag: this.tagMagnitudesMap.keySet()) {      ◁─  Computes dot product
      TagMagnitude otherTm = otherMap.get(tag);               of two vectors
      if (otherTm != null) {
         TagMagnitude tm = this.tagMagnitudesMap.get(tag);
         dotProduct += tm.getMagnitude()*otherTm.getMagnitude();
      }
   }
   return dotProduct;
}
```

```
public TagMagnitudeVector add(TagMagnitudeVector o) {
   Map<Tag,TagMagnitude> otherMap = o.getTagMagnitudeMap() ;
   Map<Tag,Tag> uniqueTags = new HashMap<Tag,Tag>();          ◁─── Creates superset
   for (Tag tag: this.tagMagnitudesMap.keySet()) {                 of all tags
      uniqueTags.put(tag,tag);
   }
   for (Tag tag:  otherMap.keySet()) {
      uniqueTags.put(tag,tag);
   }
   List<TagMagnitude> tagMagnitudesList = new
      ArrayList<TagMagnitude>(uniqueTags.size());
   for (Tag tag: uniqueTags.keySet()) {
      TagMagnitude tm = mergeTagMagnitudes(            Merges magnitudes
         this.tagMagnitudesMap.get(tag),              for same tag
            otherMap.get(tag));           ◁───┘
      tagMagnitudesList.add(tm);
   }
   return new TagMagnitudeVectorImpl(tagMagnitudesList);
}

public TagMagnitudeVector add(Collection<TagMagnitudeVector> tmList) {
   Map<Tag,Double> uniqueTags = new HashMap<Tag,Double>();
   for (TagMagnitude tagMagnitude: this.tagMagnitudesMap.values()) {
      uniqueTags.put(tagMagnitude.getTag(),
         new Double(tagMagnitude.getMagnitudeSqd()));
   }
   for (TagMagnitudeVector tmv : tmList) {                   ◁────────┐
      Map<Tag,TagMagnitude> tagMap= tmv.getTagMagnitudeMap();
      for (TagMagnitude tm: tagMap.values()) {
         Double sumSqd = uniqueTags.get(tm.getTag());
         if (sumSqd == null) {
            uniqueTags.put(tm.getTag(), tm.getMagnitudeSqd());
         } else {
            sumSqd = new Double(sumSqd.doubleValue() +    Iterates over
               tm.getMagnitudeSqd());                     all values for
            uniqueTags.put(tm.getTag(), sumSqd);                   tag
         }
      }
   }
   List<TagMagnitude> newList = new ArrayList<TagMagnitude>();
   for (Tag tag: uniqueTags.keySet()) {
      newList.add(new TagMagnitudeImpl(tag,
         Math.sqrt(uniqueTags.get(tag))));
   }
   return new TagMagnitudeVectorImpl(newList);
}

private TagMagnitude mergeTagMagnitudes(TagMagnitude a,
   TagMagnitude b) {
   if (a == null) {
      if (b == null) {
         return null;
      }
      return b;
   } else if (b == null) {
      return a;
```

```
      } else {
        double magnitude = mergeMagnitudes(a.getMagnitude(),
          b.getMagnitude());
        return new TagMagnitudeImpl(a.getTag(),magnitude);
      }
    }

    @Override
    public String toString() {
      StringBuilder sb = new StringBuilder();
      List<TagMagnitude> sortedList = getTagMagnitudes();
      double sumSqd = 0.;
      for (TagMagnitude tm: sortedList) {
        sb.append(tm);
        sumSqd += tm.getMagnitude()*tm.getMagnitude();
      }
      sb.append("\nSumSqd = " + sumSqd);
      return sb.toString();
    }
  }
}
```

To compute the dotProduct between a vector and another vector, the code finds the tags that are common between the two instances. It then sums the multiplied magnitudes between the two instances. For the add() method, we first need to find the superset for all the tags. Then the magnitude for the new vector for a tag is the sum of the magnitudes in the two vectors. At the end, the code creates a new instance

```
new TagMagnitudeVectorImpl(tagMagnitudesList);
```

which will automatically normalize the values in its constructor, such that the magnitude is one.

To compute the resulting TagMagnitudeVector by adding a number of TagMagnitudeVector instances

```
public TagMagnitudeVector add(Collection<TagMagnitudeVector> tmList)
```

we sum the squared magnitudes for a tag in all the TagMagnitudeVector instances. A new TagMagnitudeVector instance is created that has a superset of all the tags and normalized magnitudes. We use this method in clustering.

Next, let's write a simple program to show how this term vector infrastructure can be used. The output from the code sample shown in listing 8.21 is

```
[b, b, 0.6963106238227914] [c, c, 0.5222329678670935] [a, a,
0.49236596391733095]
```

Note that there are three tags, and the two instances of the *a* tag are automatically merged. The sum of the squares for all the magnitudes is also equal to one.

Listing 8.21   A simple example for TagMagnitudeImpl

```
public void testBasicOperations() throws Exception {
    TagCache tagCache = new TagCacheImpl();
    List<TagMagnitude> tmList = new ArrayList<TagMagnitude>();
```

```
        tmList.add(new TagMagnitudeImpl(tagCache.getTag("a"),1.));
        tmList.add(new TagMagnitudeImpl(tagCache.getTag("b"),2.));
        tmList.add(new TagMagnitudeImpl(tagCache.getTag("c"),1.5));
        tmList.add(new TagMagnitudeImpl(tagCache.getTag("a"),1.));
        TagMagnitudeVector tmVector1 = new TagMagnitudeVectorImpl(tmList);
        System.out.println(tmVector1);
    }
```

So far we've developed the infrastructure to represent a Tag and TagMagnitudeVector. We're down to the last couple classes. Next, we look at developing the TextAnalyzer.

8.2.3 *Building the Text Analyzer class*

In this section, we implement the remaining classes for our text analysis infrastructure. Figure 8.11 shows the four classes that we discuss. The InverseDocFreqEstimator provides an estimate for the inverse document frequency (idf) for a Tag. Remember, the idf is necessary to get an estimate of how frequently a tag is used; the less frequently a tag is used, the higher its idf value. The idf value contributes to the magnitude of the tag in the term vector. In the absence of any data on how frequently various tags appear, we implement the EqualInverseDocFreqEstimator, which simply returns 1 for all values. The TextAnalyzer class is our primary class for analyzing text. We write a concrete implementation for this class called LuceneTextAnalyzer that leverages all the infrastructure and analyzers we've developed in this chapter.

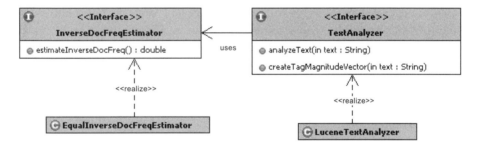

Figure 8.11 The TextAnalyzer and the InverseDocFreqEstimator

Listing 8.22 shows the InverseDocFreqEstimator interface. It has only one method, which provides the inverse document frequency for a specified Tag instance.

Listing 8.22 The interface for the InverseDocFreqEstimator

```
package com.alag.ci.textanalysis;

public interface InverseDocFreqEstimator {
    public double estimateInverseDocFreq(Tag tag);
}
```

Listing 8.23 contains a dummy implementation for InverseDocFreqEstimator. Here, EqualInverseDocFreqEstimator simply returns 1.0 for all tags.

Listing 8.23   The interface for the `EqualInverseDocFreqEstimator`

```
package com.alag.ci.textanalysis.lucene.impl;

import com.alag.ci.textanalysis.InverseDocFreqEstimator;
import com.alag.ci.textanalysis.Tag;

public class EqualInverseDocFreqEstimator implements
    InverseDocFreqEstimator {
  public double estimateInverseDocFreq(Tag tag) {
    return 1.0;
  }
}
```

Listing 8.24 contains the interface for `TextAnalyzer`, the primary class to analyze text.

Listing 8.24   The interface for the `TextAnalyzer`

```
package com.alag.ci.textanalysis;

import java.io.IOException;
import java.util.List;

public interface TextAnalyzer {
   public List<Tag> analyzeText(String text) throws IOException;
   public TagMagnitudeVector createTagMagnitudeVector(String text)
     throws IOException;
}
```

The `TextAnalyzer` interface has two methods. The first, `analyzeText`, gives back the list of `Tag` objects obtained by analyzing the text. The second, `createTagMagnitude-Vector`, returns a `TagMagnitudeVector` representation for the text. It takes into account the term frequency and the inverse document frequency for each of the tags to compute the term vector.

   Listing 8.25 shows the first part of the code for the implementation of `LuceneText-Analyzer`, which shows the constructor and the `analyzeText` method.

Listing 8.25   The core of the `LuceneTextAnalyzer` class

```
package com.alag.ci.textanalysis.lucene.impl;

import java.io.*;
import java.util.*;

import org.apache.lucene.analysis.*;

import com.alag.ci.textanalysis.*;
import com.alag.ci.textanalysis.termvector.impl.*;

public class LuceneTextAnalyzer implements TextAnalyzer {
   private TagCache tagCache = null;
   private InverseDocFreqEstimator inverseDocFreqEstimator = null;

   public LuceneTextAnalyzer(TagCache tagCache,
        InverseDocFreqEstimator inverseDocFreqEstimator) {
     this.tagCache = tagCache;
     this.inverseDocFreqEstimator = inverseDocFreqEstimator;
```

```
   }
   public List<Tag> analyzeText(String text) throws IOException {
      Reader reader = new StringReader(text);
      Analyzer analyzer = getAnalyzer();
      List<Tag> tags = new ArrayList<Tag>();
      TokenStream tokenStream = analyzer.tokenStream(null, reader) ;
      Token token = tokenStream.next();
      while ( token != null) {
         tags.add(getTag(token.termText()));
         token = tokenStream.next();
      }
      return tags;
   }
   protected Analyzer getAnalyzer() throws IOException {
      return new SynonymPhraseStopWordAnalyzer(new SynonymsCacheImpl(),
         new PhrasesCacheImpl());
   }
```

The method analyzeText gets an Analyzer. In this case, we use SynonymPhraseStop-WordAnalyzer. LuceneTextAnalyzer is really a wrapper class that wraps Lucene-specific classes into those of our infrastructure. Creating the TagMagnitudeVector from text involves computing the term frequencies for each tag and using the tag's inverse document frequency to create appropriate weights. This is shown in listing 8.26.

Listing 8.26 Creating the term vectors in LuceneTextAnalyzer

```
public TagMagnitudeVector createTagMagnitudeVector(String text)
  throws IOException {
    List<Tag> tagList = analyzeText(text);          <--- Analyze text to create tags
    Map<Tag,Integer> tagFreqMap =
       computeTermFrequency(tagList);                <--- Compute term frequencies
    return applyIDF(tagFreqMap);                     <--- Use inverse document frequency
}

private Map<Tag,Integer> computeTermFrequency(List<Tag> tagList) {
    Map<Tag,Integer> tagFreqMap = new HashMap<Tag,Integer>();
    for (Tag tag: tagList) {
       Integer count = tagFreqMap.get(tag);
       if (count == null) {
          count = new Integer(1);
       } else {
          count = new Integer(count.intValue() + 1);
       }
       tagFreqMap.put(tag, count);
    }
    return tagFreqMap;
}

private TagMagnitudeVector applyIDF(Map<Tag,Integer> tagFreqMap) {
    List<TagMagnitude> tagMagnitudes = new ArrayList<TagMagnitude>();
    for (Tag tag: tagFreqMap.keySet()) {
       double idf = this.inverseDocFreqEstimator.
         estimateInverseDocFreq(tag);
       double tf = tagFreqMap.get(tag);
```

```
        double wt = tf*idf;
        tagMagnitudes.add(new TagMagnitudeImpl(tag,wt));
    }
    return new TagMagnitudeVectorImpl(tagMagnitudes);
}

private Tag getTag(String text) throws IOException {
    return this.tagCache.getTag(text);
}
}
```

To create the `TagMagnitudeVector`, we first analyze the text to create a list of tags:

```
List<Tag> tagList = analyzeText(text);
```

Next we compute the term frequencies for each of the tags:

```
Map<Tag,Integer> tagFreqMap = computeTermFrequency(tagList);
```

And last, create the vector by combining the term frequency and the inverse document frequency:

```
return applyIDF(tagFreqMap);
```

We're done with all the classes we need to analyze text. Next, let's go through an example of how this infrastructure can be used.

8.2.4   *Applying the text analysis infrastructure*

We use the same example we introduced in section 4.3.1. Consider a blog entry with the following text (see also figure 8.2):

Title: "Collective Intelligence and Web2.0"

Body: "Web2.0 is all about connecting users to users, inviting users to participate, and applying their collective intelligence to improve the application. Collective intelligence enhances the user experience."

Let's write a simple program that shows the tags associated with analyzing the title and the body. Listing 8.27 shows the code for our simple program.

Listing 8.27   Computing the tokens for the title and body

```
private void displayTextAnalysis(String text) throws IOException {      ◁───┐
    List<Tag> tags = analyzeText(text);
    for (Tag tag: tags) {                              Method to display tags
        System.out.println(tag);
    }
}
public static void main(String [] args) throws IOException {
    String title = "Collective Intelligence and Web2.0";
    String body = "Web2.0 is all about connecting users to users, " +
        " inviting users to participate and applying their " +
        " collective  intelligence to improve the application." +
        " Collective intelligence" +
        " enhances the user experience" ;
```

```
TagCacheImpl t = new TagCacheImpl();
InverseDocFreqEstimator idfEstimator =
  new EqualInverseDocFreqEstimator();
TextAnalyzer lta = new LuceneTextAnalyzer(t, idfEstimator);    ◁──┐
System.out.print("Analyzing the title .... \n");                  │
lta.displayTextAnalysis(title);                         Creating instance
System.out.print("Analyzing the body .... \n");          of TextAnalyzer
```

First we create an instance of the TextAnalyzer class:

```
TagCacheImpl t = new TagCacheImpl();
InverseDocFreqEstimator idfEstimator =
    new EqualInverseDocFreqEstimator();
TextAnalyzer lta = new LuceneTextAnalyzer(t, idfEstimator);
```

Then we get the tags associated with the title and the body. Listing 8.28 shows the output. Note that the output for each tag consists of unstemmed text and its stemmed value.

Listing 8.28   Tag listing for our example

```
Analyzing the title ....
[collective, collect] [intelligence, intellig] [ci, ci] [collective
intelligence, collect intellig] [web2.0, web2.0]
Analyzing the body ....
[web2.0, web2.0] [about, about] [connecting, connect] [users, user] [users,
user] [inviting, invit] [users, user] [participate, particip] [applying,
appli] [collective, collect] [intelligence, intellig] [ci, ci] [collective
intelligence, collect intellig] [improve, improv] [application, applic]
[collective, collect] [intelligence, intellig] [ci, ci] [collective
intelligence, collect intellig] [enhances, enhanc] [users, user]
[experience, experi]
```

It's helpful to visualize the tag cloud using the infrastructure we developed in chapter 3. Listing 8.29 shows the code for visualizing the tag cloud.

Listing 8.29   Visualizing the term vector as a tag cloud

```
private TagCloud createTagCloud(TagMagnitudeVector tmVector) {
    List<TagCloudElement> elements = new ArrayList<TagCloudElement>();
    for (TagMagnitude tm: tmVector.getTagMagnitudes()) {
      TagCloudElement element = new TagCloudElementImpl(
        tm.getDisplayText(), tm.getMagnitude());     ◁──┐  Create
      elements.add(element);                             │  TagCloudElement
    }                                                    │  instances
    return new TagCloudImpl(elements, new
  LinearFontSizeComputationStrategy(3,"font-size: "));
  }

  private String visualizeTagCloud(TagCloud tagCloud) {
    HTMLTagCloudDecorator decorator = new HTMLTagCloudDecorator();    ◁──┐
    String html = decorator.decorateTagCloud(tagCloud);                 │
    System.out.println(html);                                           │
    return html;                                         Use decorator to
  }                                                    visualize tag cloud
```

The code for generating the HTML to visualize the tag cloud is fairly simple, since all the work was done earlier in chapter 3. We first need to create a List of TagCloud-Element instances, by iterating over the term vector. Once we create a TagCloud instance, we can generate HTML using the HTMLTagCloudDecorator class.

The title "Collective Intelligence and Web2.0" gets converted into five tags: [collective, collect] [intelligence, intellig] [ci, ci] [collective intelligence, collect intellig] [web2.0, web2.0]. This is also shown in figure 8.12.

> **TagCloud (5)**
>
> ci collective collective intelligence intelligence web2.0

Figure 8.12   The tag cloud for the title, consisting of five tags

Similarly, the body gets converted into 15 tags, as shown in figure 8.13.

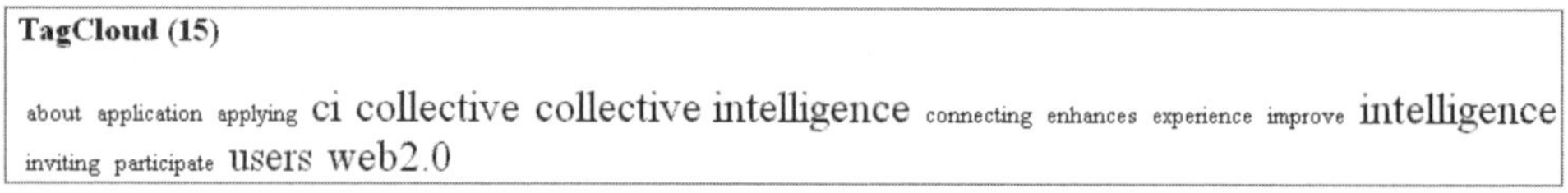

> **TagCloud (15)**
>
> about application applying ci collective collective intelligence connecting enhances experience improve intelligence inviting participate users web2.0

Figure 8.13   The tag cloud for the body, consisting of 15 tags

We can extend our example to compute the tag magnitude vectors for the title and body, and then combine the two vectors, as shown in listing 8.30.

Listing 8.30   Computing the `TagMagnitudeVector`

```
    TagMagnitudeVector tmTitle = lta.createTagMagnitudeVector(title);
    TagMagnitudeVector tmBody = lta.createTagMagnitudeVector(body);
    TagMagnitudeVector tmCombined = tmTitle.add(tmBody);
    System.out.println(tmCombined);
}
```

The output from the second part of the program is shown in listing 8.31. Note that the top tags for this blog entry are *users, collective, ci, intelligence, collective intelligence,* and *web2.0.*

Listing 8.31   Results from displaying the results for `TagMagnitudeVector`

```
[users, user, 0.4364357804719848]
[collective, collect, 0.3842122429322726]
[ci, ci, 0.3842122429322726]
[intelligence, intellig, 0.3842122429322726]
[collective intelligence, collect intellig, 0.3842122429322726]
[web2.0, web2.0, 0.3345216912320663]
[about, about, 0.1091089451179962]
[applying, appli, 0.1091089451179962]
[application, applic, 0.1091089451179962]
[enhances, enhanc, 0.1091089451179962]
[inviting, invit, 0.1091089451179962]
```

```
[improve, improv, 0.1091089451179962]
[experience, experi, 0.1091089451179962]
[participate, particip, 0.1091089451179962]
[connecting, connect, 0.1091089451179962]
```

The same data can be better visualized using the tag cloud shown in figure 8.14.

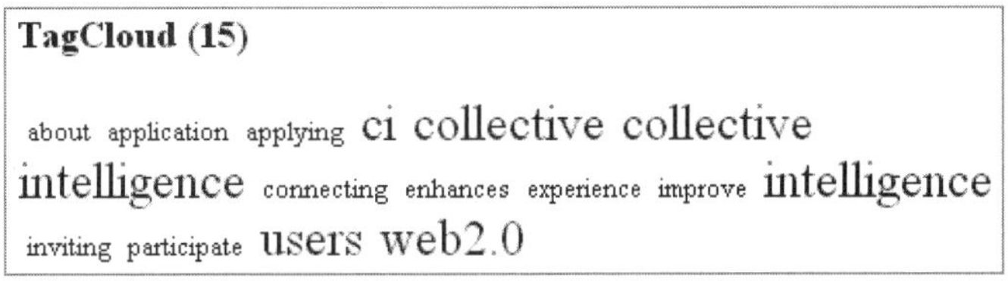

TagCloud (15)

about application applying ci collective collective intelligence connecting enhances experience improve intelligence inviting participate users web2.0

Figure 8.14   The tag cloud for the combined title and body, consisting of 15 tags

So far, we've developed an infrastructure for analyzing text. The core infrastructure interfaces are independent of Lucene-specific classes and can be implemented by other text analysis packages. The text analysis infrastructure is useful in extracting tags and creating a term vector representation for the text. This term vector representation is helpful for personalization, building predicting models, clustering to find patterns, and so on.

8.3   Use cases for applying the framework

This has been a fairly technical chapter. We've gone through a lot of effort to develop infrastructure for text analysis. It's useful to briefly review some of the use cases where this can be applied. This is shown in table 8.5.

Table 8.5   Some use cases for text analysis infrastructure

Use case	Description
Analyzing a number of text documents to extract most-relevant keywords	The term vectors associated with the documents can be combined to build a representation for the document set. You can use this approach to build an automated representation for a set of documents visited by a user, or for finding items similar to a set of documents.
Advertising	To show relevant advertisements on a page, you can take the keywords associated with the test and find the subset of keywords that have advertisements assigned.
Classification and predictive models	The term vector representation can be used as an input for building predictive models and classifiers.

We've already demonstrated the process of analyzing text to extract keywords associated with them. Figure 8.15 shows an example of how relevant terms can be detected and hyperlinked. In this case, relevant terms are hyperlinked and available for a user and web crawlers, inviting them to explore other pages of interest.

There are two main approaches for advertising that are normally used in an application. First, sites sell *search words*—certain keywords that are sold to advertisers. Let's say that the phrase *collective intelligence* has been sold to an advertiser. Whenever the

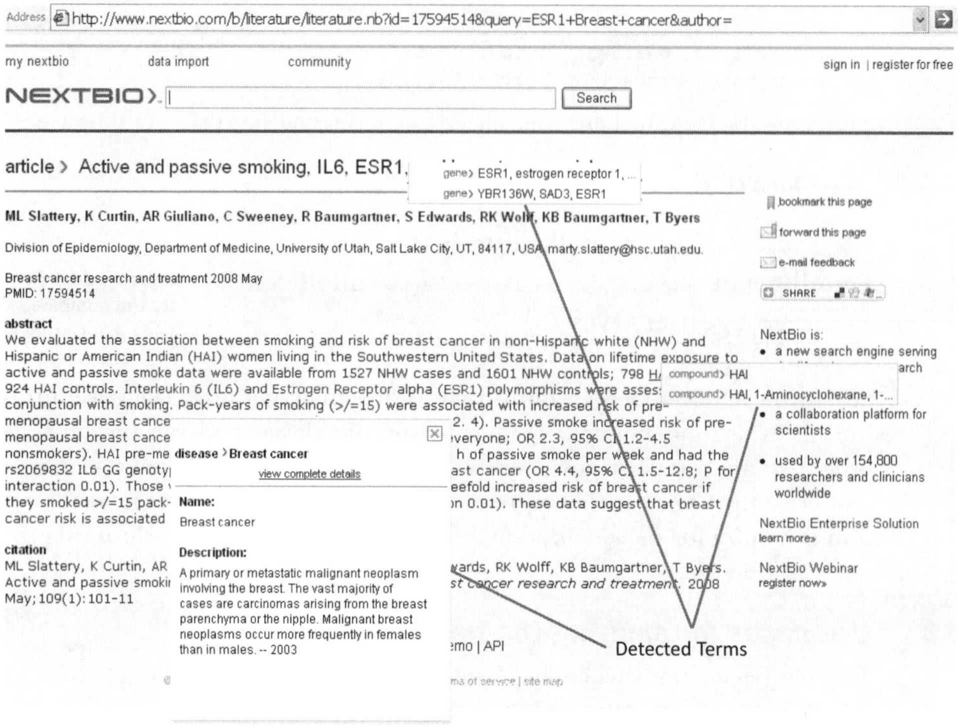

Figure 8.15 An example of automatically detecting relevant terms by analyzing text

user types *collective intelligence* in the search box or visits a page that's related to *collective intelligence*, we want to show the advertisement related to this keyword. The second approach is to associate text with an advertisement (showing relevant products works the same way), analyze the text, create a term vector representation, and then associate the relevant ad based on the main context of the page and who's viewing it dynamically. This approach is similar to building a content-based recommendation system, which we do in chapter 12.

In the next two chapters, we demonstrate how we can use the term vector representation for text to cluster documents and build predictive models and text classifiers.

8.4 Summary

Apache Lucene is a Java-based open source text analysis toolkit and search engine. The text analysis package for Lucene contains an `Analyzer`, which creates a `TokenStream`. A `TokenStream` is an enumeration of `Token` instances and is implemented by a `Tokenizer` and a `TokenFilter`. You can create custom text analyzers by subclassing available Lucene classes. In this chapter, we developed two custom text analyzers. The first one normalizes the text, applies a stop word list, and uses the Porter stemming algorithm. The second analyzer normalizes the text, applies a stop word list, detects phrases using a phrase dictionary, and injects synonyms.

Next we discussed developing a text-analysis package, whose core interfaces are independent of Lucene. A `Tag` class is the fundamental building block for this package. Tags that have the same stemmed values are considered equivalent. We introduced the following entities: `TagCache`, through which `Tag` instances are created; `PhrasesCache`, which contains the phrases of interest; `SynonymsCache`, which stores synonyms used; and `InverseDocFreqEstimator`, which provides an estimate for the inverse document frequency for a particular tag. All these entities are used by the `TextAnalyzer` to create tags and develop a term (tag) magnitude vector representation for the text.

The text analysis infrastructure developed can be used for developing the metadata associated with text. This metadata can be used to find other similar content, to build predictive models, and to find other patterns by clustering the data. Having built the infrastructure to decompose text into individual tags and magnitudes, we next take a deeper look at clustering data. We use the infrastructure developed here, along with the infrastructure to search the blogosphere developed in chapter 5, in the next chapter.

8.5 Resources

Ackerman, Rich. "Vector Model Information Retrieval." 2003. http://www.hray.com/5264/math.htm

Gospodnetic, Otis, and Erik Hatcher. *Lucene in Action.* 2004. Manning.

"Term vector theory and keywords." http://forums.searchenginewatch.com/archive/index.php/t-489.html

Discovering
patterns with clustering

9

This chapter covers

- k-means, hierarchical clustering, and probabilistic clustering
- Clustering blog entries
- Clustering using WEKA
- Clustering using the JDM APIs

It's fascinating to analyze results found by machine learning algorithms. One of the most commonly used methods for discovering groups of related users or content is the process of *clustering*, which we discussed briefly in chapter 7. Clustering algorithms run in an automated manner and can create pockets or clusters of related items. Results from clustering can be leveraged to build classifiers, to build predictors, or in collaborative filtering. These unsupervised learning algorithms can provide insight into how your data is distributed.

In the last few chapters, we built a lot of infrastructure. It's now time to have some fun and leverage this infrastructure to analyze some real-world data. In this chapter, we focus on understanding and applying some of the key clustering algorithms.

K-means, hierarchical clustering, and expectation maximization (EM) are three of the most commonly used clustering algorithms.

As discussed in section 2.2.6, there are two main representations for data. The first is the low-dimension densely populated dataset; the second is the high-dimension sparsely populated dataset, which we use with text term vectors and to represent user click-through. In this chapter, we look at clustering techniques for both kinds of datasets.

We begin the chapter by creating a dataset that contains blog entries retrieved from Technorati.[1] Next, we implement the k-means clustering algorithm to cluster the blog entries. We leverage the infrastructure developed in chapter 5 to retrieve blog entries and combine it with the text-analysis toolkit we developed in chapter 8. We also demonstrate how another clustering algorithm, hierarchical clustering, can be applied to the same problem. We look at some of the other practical data, such as user clickstream analysis that can be analyzed in a similar manner. Next, we look at how WEKA can be leveraged for clustering densely populated datasets and illustrate the process using the EM algorithm. We end the chapter by looking at the clustering-related interfaces defined by JDM and develop code to cluster instances using the JDM APIs.

9.1 Clustering blog entries

In this section, we demonstrate the process of developing and applying various clustering algorithms by discovering groups of related blog entries from the blogosphere. This example will retrieve live blog entries from the blogosphere on the topic of "collective intelligence" and convert them to tag vector format, to which we apply different clustering algorithms.

Figure 9.1 illustrates the various steps involved in this example. These steps are

1 Using the APIs developed in chapter 5 to retrieve a number of current blog entries from Technorati.

2 Using the infrastructure developed in chapter 8 to convert the blog entries into a tag vector representation.

3 Developing a clustering algorithm to cluster the blog entries. Of course, we keep our infrastructure generic so that the clustering algorithms can be applied to any tag vector representation.

We begin by creating the dataset associated with the blog entries. The clustering algorithms implemented in WEKA are for finding clusters from a dense dataset. Therefore, we develop our own implementation for different clustering algorithms. We begin with implementing k-means clustering followed by hierarchical clustering algorithms.

It's helpful to look at the set of classes that we need to build for our clustering infrastructure. We review these classes next.

---

[1] You can use any of the blog-tracking providers we discussed in chapter 5.

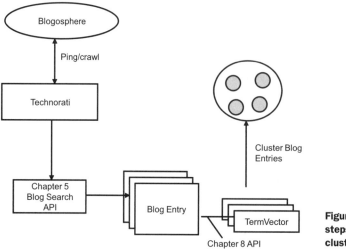

Figure 9.1   The various steps in our example of clustering blog entries

9.1.1   *Defining the text clustering infrastructure*

The key interfaces associated with clustering are shown in figure 9.2. The classes consist of

- `Clusterer`: the main interface for discovering clusters. It consists of a number of clusters represented by `TextCluster`.
- `TextCluster`: represents a cluster. Each cluster has an associated `TagMagnitudeVector` for the center of the cluster and has a number of `TextDataItem` instances.
- `TextDataItem`: represents each text instance. A dataset consists of a number of `TextDataItem` instances and is created by the `DataSetCreator`.
- `DataSetCreator`: creates the dataset used for the learning process.

Listing 9.1 contains the definition for the `Clusterer` interface.

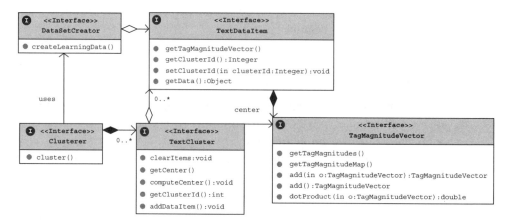

Figure 9.2   The interfaces associated with clustering text

Listing 9.1   The definition for the `Clusterer` interface

```
package com.alag.ci.cluster;

import java.util.List;

public interface Clusterer {
   public List<TextCluster> cluster();
}
```

`Clusterer` has only one method to create the `TextCluster` instances:

```
List<TextCluster> cluster()
```

Listing 9.2 shows the definition of the `TextCluster` interface.

Listing 9.2   The definition for the `TextCluster` interface

```
package com.alag.ci.cluster;

import com.alag.ci.textanalysis.TagMagnitudeVector;

public interface TextCluster {
   public void clearItems();
   public TagMagnitudeVector getCenter();
   public void computeCenter();
   public int getClusterId() ;
   public void addDataItem(TextDataItem item);
}
```

Each `TextCluster` has a unique ID associated with it. `TextCluster` has basic methods to add data items and to recompute its center based on the `TextDataItem` associated with it. The definition for the `TextDataItem` is shown in listing 9.3.

Listing 9.3   The definition for the `TextDataItem` interface

```
package com.alag.ci.cluster;

import com.alag.ci.textanalysis.TagMagnitudeVector;

public interface TextDataItem {
   public Object getData();
   public TagMagnitudeVector getTagMagnitudeVector() ;
   public Integer getClusterId();
   public void setClusterId(Integer clusterId);
}
```

Each `TextDataItem` consists of an underlying text data with its `TagMagnitudeVector`. It has basic methods to associate it with a cluster. These `TextDataItem` instances are created by the `DataSetCreator` as shown in listing 9.4.

Listing 9.4   The definition for the `DataSetCreator` interface

```
package com.alag.ci.cluster;

import java.util.List;

public interface DataSetCreator {
   public List<TextDataItem> createLearningData() throws Exception ;
}
```

Each `DataSetCreator` creates a `List` of `TextDataItem` instances that's used by the `Clusterer`. Next, we use the APIs we developed in chapter 5 to search the blogosphere. Let's build the dataset that we use in our example.

9.1.2 *Retrieving blog entries from Technorati*

In this section, we define two classes. The first class, `BlogAnalysisDataItem`, represents a blog entry and implements the `TextDataItem` interface. The second class, `BlogDataSetCreatorImpl`, implements the `DataSetCreator` and creates the data for clustering using the retrieved blog entries.

Listing 9.5 shows the definition for `BlogAnalysisDataItem`. The class is basically a wrapper for a `RetrievedBlogEntry` and has an associated `TagMagnitudeVector` representation for its text.

Listing 9.5   The definition for the `BlogAnalysisDataItem`

```
package com.alag.ci.blog.cluster.impl;

import com.alag.ci.blog.search.RetrievedBlogEntry;
import com.alag.ci.cluster.TextDataItem;
import com.alag.ci.textanalysis.TagMagnitudeVector;

public class BlogAnalysisDataItem implements TextDataItem {
    private RetrievedBlogEntry blogEntry = null;
    private TagMagnitudeVector tagMagnitudeVector = null;
    private Integer clusterId;

    public BlogAnalysisDataItem(RetrievedBlogEntry blogEntry,
            TagMagnitudeVector tagMagnitudeVector ) {
        this.blogEntry = blogEntry;
        this.tagMagnitudeVector = tagMagnitudeVector;
    }

    public Object getData() {
        return this.getBlogEntry();
    }

    public RetrievedBlogEntry getBlogEntry() {
        return blogEntry;
    }

    public TagMagnitudeVector getTagMagnitudeVector() {
        return tagMagnitudeVector;
    }

    public double distance(TagMagnitudeVector other) {
        return this.getTagMagnitudeVector().dotProduct(other);
    }

    public Integer getClusterId() {
        return clusterId;
    }

    public void setClusterId(Integer clusterId) {
        this.clusterId = clusterId;
    }
}
```

Listing 9.6 shows the first part of the implementation for `BlogDataSetCreatorImpl`, which implements the `DataSetCreator` interface for blog entries.

Listing 9.6 Retrieving blog entries from Technorati

```
package com.alag.ci.blog.cluster.impl;

import java.io.IOException;
import java.util.*;

import com.alag.ci.blog.search.*;
import com.alag.ci.blog.search.BlogQueryParameter.QueryParameter;
import com.alag.ci.blog.search.impl.technorati.*;
import com.alag.ci.cluster.*;
import com.alag.ci.textanalysis.*;
import com.alag.ci.textanalysis.lucene.impl.*;

public class BlogDataSetCreatorImpl implements DataSetCreator {

    public List<TextDataItem> createLearningData()
        throws Exception {
        BlogQueryResult bqr = getBlogsFromTechnorati(
         "collective intelligence
        return getBlogTagMagnitudeVectors(bqr);
    }

    public BlogQueryResult getBlogsFromTechnorati(String tag)
        throws BlogSearcherException{
        BlogSearcher bs = new TechnoratiBlogSearcherImpl();

        BlogQueryParameter tagQueryParam =
            new TechnoratiTagBlogQueryParameterImpl();
        tagQueryParam.setParameter(QueryParameter.KEY,
            "xxxxx");
        tagQueryParam.setParameter(QueryParameter.LIMIT, "10");
        tagQueryParam.setParameter(QueryParameter.TAG,tag);
        tagQueryParam.setParameter(QueryParameter.LANGUAGE, "en");

        return bs.getRelevantBlogs(tagQueryParam);
    }
```

Annotations:
- **Queries Technorati to get blog entries**
- **Converts to usable format**
- **Uses Technorati blog searcher**
- **Use entries tagged "collective intelligence"**

The `BlogDataSetCreatorImpl` uses the APIs developed in chapter 5 to retrieve blog entries from `Technorati`. It queries for recent blog entries that have been tagged with *collective intelligence*.

Listing 9.7 shows the how blog data retrieved from Technorati is converted into a List of `TextDataItem` objects.

Listing 9.7 Converting blog entries into a `List` of `TextDataItem` objects

```
private List<TextDataItem> getBlogTagMagnitudeVectors(
        BlogQueryResult blogQueryResult) throws IOException {
    List<RetrievedBlogEntry> blogEntries =
      blogQueryResult.getRelevantBlogs();
    List<TextDataItem> result = new ArrayList<TextDataItem>();
    InverseDocFreqEstimator freqEstimator =
        new InverseDocFreqEstimatorImpl(blogEntries.size());
    TextAnalyzer textAnalyzer = new LuceneTextAnalyzer(
```

Annotation:
- **Used for idf**

```
            new TagCacheImpl(), freqEstimator);
        for (RetrievedBlogEntry blogEntry: blogEntries) {
            String text = composeTextForAnalysis(blogEntry);
            TagMagnitudeVector tmv =
              textAnalyzer.createTagMagnitudeVector(text);
            for (TagMagnitude tm: tmv.getTagMagnitudes()) {
                freqEstimator.addCount(tm.getTag());
            }
        }

        for (RetrievedBlogEntry blogEntry: blogEntries) {
            String text = composeTextForAnalysis(blogEntry);
            TagMagnitudeVector tmv =
              textAnalyzer.createTagMagnitudeVector(text);
            result.add(new BlogAnalysisDataItem(blogEntry,tmv));
        }
        return result;
    }

    public String composeTextForAnalysis(RetrievedBlogEntry blogEntry) {
        StringBuilder sb = new StringBuilder();
        if (blogEntry.getTitle() != null) {
            sb.append(blogEntry.getTitle());
        }
        if (blogEntry.getName() != null) {
            sb.append(" " + blogEntry.getName());
        }
        if (blogEntry.getAuthor() != null) {
            sb.append(" " + blogEntry.getAuthor());
        }
        if (blogEntry.getExcerpt() != null) {
            sb.append(" " + blogEntry.getExcerpt());
        }
        return sb.toString();
    }
}
```

Annotations:
- **Combines title, name, author, and excerpt** → points to `String text = composeTextForAnalysis(blogEntry);`
- **Learns tag frequency with tags** → points to `for (TagMagnitude tm: tmv.getTagMagnitudes()) {`
- **Iterates over all blog entries** → points to second `for (RetrievedBlogEntry blogEntry: blogEntries) {`

The `BlogDataSetCreatorImpl` uses a simple implementation for estimating the frequencies associated with each of the tags:

```
InverseDocFreqEstimator freqEstimator =
    new InverseDocFreqEstimatorImpl(blogEntries.size());
```

The method `composeTextForAnalysis()` combines text from the title, name, author, and excerpt for analysis. It then uses a `TextAnalyzer`, which we developed in chapter 8, to create a `TagMagnitudeVector` representation for the text.

Listing 9.8 shows the implementation for the `InverseDocFreqEstimatorImpl`, which provides an estimate for the tag frequencies.

Listing 9.8   The implementation for `InverseDocFreqEstimatorImpl`

```
package com.alag.ci.textanalysis.lucene.impl;

import java.util.*;

import com.alag.ci.textanalysis.InverseDocFreqEstimator;
import com.alag.ci.textanalysis.Tag;
```

```
public class InverseDocFreqEstimatorImpl
      implements InverseDocFreqEstimator {

   private Map<Tag,Integer> tagFreq = null;
   private int totalNumDocs;

   public InverseDocFreqEstimatorImpl(int totalNumDocs) {
      this.totalNumDocs = totalNumDocs;
      this.tagFreq = new HashMap<Tag,Integer>();
   }
   public double estimateInverseDocFreq(Tag tag) {
      Integer freq = this.tagFreq.get(tag);
      if ((freq == null) || (freq.intValue() == 0)){
         return 1.;
      }
      return Math.log(totalNumDocs/freq.doubleValue());
   }
   public void addCount(Tag tag) {
      Integer count = this.tagFreq.get(tag);
      if (count == null) {
         count = new Integer(1);
      } else {
         count = new Integer(count.intValue() + 1);
      }
      this.tagFreq.put(tag, count);
   }
}
```

Estimates inverse document frequency

Keeps count for each tag

The inverse document frequency for a tag is estimated by computing the log of the total number of documents divided by the number of documents that the tag appears in:

```
Math.log(totalNumDocs/freq.doubleValue());
```

Note that the more rare a tag is, the higher its idf. With this background, we're now ready to implement our first text clustering algorithm. For this we use the k-means clustering algorithm.

9.1.3 *Implementing the k-means algorithms for text processing*

The k-means clustering algorithm consists of the following steps:

1. For the specified number of k clusters, initialize the clusters at random. For this, we select a point from the learning dataset and assign it to a cluster. Further, we ensure that all clusters are initialized with different data points.

2. Associate each of the data items with the cluster that's closest (most similar) to it. We use the dot product between the cluster and the data item to measure the closeness (similarity). The higher the dot product, the closer the two points.

3. Recompute the centers of the clusters using the data items associated with the cluster.

4. Continue steps 2 and 3 until there are no more changes in the association between data items and the clusters. Sometimes, some data items may oscillate between two clusters, causing the clustering algorithm to not converge. Therefore, it's a good idea to also include a maximum number of iterations.

We develop the code for k-means in more or less the same order. Let's first look at the implementation for representing a cluster. This is shown in listing 9.9.

Listing 9.9   The implementation for `ClusterImpl`

```
package com.alag.ci.blog.cluster.impl;

import java.util.*;

import com.alag.ci.blog.search.RetrievedBlogEntry;
import com.alag.ci.cluster.*;
import com.alag.ci.textanalysis.*;
import com.alag.ci.textanalysis.termvector.impl.TagMagnitudeVectorImpl;

public class ClusterImpl implements TextCluster {
   private TagMagnitudeVector center = null;          ◁──┐  Cluster center
   private List<TextDataItem> items = null;                represented by
   private int clusterId;                                  TagMagnitudeVector

   public ClusterImpl(int clusterId) {
      this.clusterId = clusterId;
      this.items = new ArrayList<TextDataItem>();
   }

   public void computeCenter() {
      if (this.items.size() == 0) {
         return;
      }
      List<TagMagnitudeVector> tmList =
         new ArrayList<TagMagnitudeVector>();               Center computed
      for (TextDataItem item: items) {                        by adding all
         tmList.add(item.getTagMagnitudeVector());             data points
      }
      List<TagMagnitude> emptyList = Collections.emptyList();
      TagMagnitudeVector empty = new TagMagnitudeVectorImpl(emptyList);  ◁──┘
      this.center = empty.add(tmList);
   }

   public int getClusterId() {
      return this.clusterId;
   }

   public void addDataItem(TextDataItem item) {
      items.add(item);
   }

   public TagMagnitudeVector getCenter() {
      return center;
   }

   public List<TextDataItem> getItems() {
      return items;
   }

   public void setCenter(TagMagnitudeVector center) {
      this.center = center;
   }

   public void clearItems() {
      this.items.clear();
   }
```

```
public String toString() {
    StringBuilder sb = new StringBuilder() ;
    sb.append("Id=" + this.clusterId);
    for (TextDataItem item: items) {
        RetrievedBlogEntry blog = (RetrievedBlogEntry) item.getData();
        sb.append("\nTitle=" + blog.getTitle());
        sb.append("\nExcerpt=" + blog.getExcerpt());
    }
    return sb.toString();
}
}
```

The center of the cluster is represented by a `TagMagnitudeVector` and is computed by adding the `TagMagnitudeVector` instances for the data items associated with the cluster.

Next, let's look at listing 9.10, which contains the implementation for the k-means algorithm.

Listing 9.10   The core of the `TextKMeansClustererImpl` implementation

```
package com.alag.ci.blog.cluster.impl;

import java.util.*;

import com.alag.ci.cluster.*;

public class TextKMeansClustererImpl implements Clusterer{
    private List<TextDataItem> textDataSet = null;
    private List<TextCluster> clusters = null;
    private int numClusters ;

    public TextKMeansClustererImpl(List<TextDataItem> textDataSet,
            int numClusters) {
        this.textDataSet = textDataSet;
        this.numClusters = numClusters;
    }
    public List<TextCluster> cluster() {
        if (this.textDataSet.size() == 0) {
            return Collections.emptyList();
        }
        this.intitializeClusters();          ◁——— Initialize clusters
        boolean change = true;
        int count = 0;
        while ((count ++ < 100) && (change)) {
            clearClusterItems();
            change = reassignClusters();      ◁——— Reassign data items to clusters
            computeClusterCenters();          ◁——— Recompute centers for clusters
        }
        return this.clusters;
    }
```

The dataset for clustering, along with the number of clusters, is specified in the constructor:

```
public TextKMeansClustererImpl(List<TextDataItem> textDataSet,
        int numClusters)
```

As explained at the beginning of the section, the algorithm is fairly simple. First, the clusters are initialized at random:

```
this.intitializeClusters();
```

This is followed by reassigning the data items to the closest clusters:

```
reassignClusters()
```

and recomputing the centers of the cluster:

```
computeClusterCenters()
```

Listing 9.11 shows the code for initializing the clusters.

Listing 9.11   Initializing the clusters

```
    private void intitializeClusters() {
        this.clusters = new ArrayList<TextCluster>();
        Map<Integer,Integer> usedIndexes = new HashMap<Integer,Integer>();
        for (int i = 0; i < this.numClusters; i++ ) {
            ClusterImpl cluster = new ClusterImpl(i);
            cluster.setCenter(getDataItemAtRandom(usedIndexes).
              getTagMagnitudeVector());
            this.clusters.add(cluster);
        }
    }

    private TextDataItem getDataItemAtRandom(
        Map<Integer,Integer> usedIndexes) {
        boolean found = false;
        while (!found) {
            int index = (int)Math.floor(
                Math.random()*this.textDataSet.size());
            if (!usedIndexes.containsKey(index)) {
                usedIndexes.put(index, index);
                return this.textDataSet.get(index);
            }
        }
        return null;
    }
```

For each of the k clusters to be initialized, a data point is selected at random. The algorithm keeps track of the points selected and ensures that the same point isn't reselected. Listing 9.12 shows the remaining code associated with the algorithm.

Listing 9.12   Recomputing the clusters

```
    private boolean reassignClusters() {
        int numChanges = 0;
        for (TextDataItem item: this.textDataSet) {
            TextCluster newCluster = getClosestCluster(item);
            if ((item.getClusterId() == null ) ||
            (item.getClusterId().intValue() !=
                newCluster.getClusterId())) {
                numChanges ++;
```

```
                    item.setClusterId(newCluster.getClusterId());
                }
                newCluster.addDataItem(item);
            }
            return (numChanges > 0);
        }
        private void computeClusterCenters() {
            for (TextCluster cluster: this.clusters) {
                cluster.computeCenter();
            }
        }
        private void clearClusterItems(){
            for (TextCluster cluster: this.clusters) {
                cluster.clearItems();
            }
        }
        private TextCluster getClosestCluster(TextDataItem item) {
            TextCluster closestCluster = null;
            Double hightSimilarity = null;
            for (TextCluster cluster: this.clusters) {
                double similarity =
                    cluster.getCenter().dotProduct(item.getTagMagnitudeVector());   ◁─┐
                if ((hightSimilarity == null) ||                                       │
                    (hightSimilarity.doubleValue() < similarity)) {                    │
                    hightSimilarity = similarity;                                      │
                    closestCluster = cluster;                        Dot product shows │
                }                                                          similarity │
            }
            return closestCluster;
        }
        public String toString() {
            StringBuilder sb = new StringBuilder();
            for (TextCluster cluster: clusters) {
                sb.append("\n\n");
                sb.append(cluster.toString());
            }
            return sb.toString();
        }
    }
}
```

The similarity between a cluster and a data item is computed by taking the dot product of the two TagMagnitudeVector instances:

```
            double similarity =
          cluster.getCenter().dotProduct(item.getTagMagnitudeVector());
```

We use the following simple main program:

```
public static final void main(String[] args) throws Exception {
    DataSetCreator bc = new BlogDataSetCreatorImpl();
    List<TextDataItem> blogData = bc.createLearningData();
    TextKMeansClustererImpl clusterer = new
            TextKMeansClustererImpl(blogData,4);
    clusterer.cluster();
}
```

The main program creates four clusters. Running this program yields different results, as the blog entries being created change dynamically, and different clustering runs with the same data can lead to different clusters depending on how the cluster nodes are initialized. Listing 9.13 shows a sample result from one of the clustering runs. Note that sometimes duplicate blog entries are returned from Technorati and that they fall in the same cluster.

Listing 9.13   Results from a clustering run

```
Id=0
Title=Viel um die Ohren
Excerpt=Leider komme ich zur Zeit nicht so viel zum Bloggen, wie ich gerne
würde, da ich mitten in 3 Projekt
Title=Viel um die Ohren
Excerpt=Leider komme ich zur Zeit nicht so viel zum Bloggen, wie ich gerne
würde, da ich mitten in 3 Projekt

Id=1
Title=Starchild Aug. 31: Choosing Simplicity & Creative Compassion..&
Releasing "Addictions" to Suffering
Excerpt=Choosing Simplicity and Creative Compassion...and Releasing
"Addictions" to SufferingAn article and
Title=Interesting read on web 2.0 and 3.0
Excerpt=I found these articles by Tim O'Reilly on web 2.0 and 3.0 today.
Quite an interesting read and nice

Id=2
Title=Corporate Social Networks
Excerpt=Corporate Social Networks Filed under: Collaboration,
Social-networking, collective intelligence, social-software — dorai @
10:28 am  Tags: applicatio

Id=3
Title=SAP Gets Business Intelligence. What Do You Get?
Excerpt=SAP Gets Business Intelligence. What Do You Get?   [IMG]
Posted by: Michael Goldberg in News
Title=SAP Gets Business Intelligence. What Do You Get?
Excerpt=SAP Gets Business Intelligence. What Do You Get?   [IMG]
Posted by: Michael Goldberg in News
Title=Che Guevara, presente!
Excerpt=Che Guevara, presente!  Posted by Arroyoribera on October 7th, 2007
Forty years ago, the Argentine
Title=Planet 2.0 meets the USA
Excerpt= This has been a quiet blogging week due to FLACSO México's visit
to the University of Minnesota. Th
Title=collective intelligence excites execs
Excerpt=collective intelligence excites execs zdnet.com's dion hinchcliffe
provides a tremendous post cov
```

In this section, we looked at the implementation of the k-means clustering algorithm. K-means is one of the simplest clustering algorithms, and it gives good results.

In k-means clustering, we provide the number of clusters. There's no theoretical solution to what is the optimal value for k. You normally try different values for k to see the effect on overall criteria, such as minimizing the overall distance between each point and its cluster mean. Let's look at an alternative algorithm called hierarchical clustering.

9.1.4 *Implementing hierarchical clustering algorithms for text processing*

Hierarchical Agglomerative Clustering (HAC) algorithms begin by assigning a cluster to each item being clustered. Then they compute the similarity between the various clusters and create a new cluster by merging the two clusters that were most similar. This process of merging clusters continues until you're left with only one cluster. This clustering algorithm is called *agglomerative*, since it continuously merges the clusters.

There are different versions of this algorithm based on how the similarity between two clusters is computed. The *single-link* method computes the distance between two clusters as the minimum distance between two points, one each of which is in each cluster. The *complete-link* method, on the other hand, computes the distance as the maximum of the similarities between a member of one cluster and any of the members in another cluster. The *average-link* method calculates the average similarity between points in the two clusters.

We demonstrate the implementation for the HAC algorithm by computing a mean for a cluster, which we do by adding the TagMagnitudeVector instances for the children. The similarity between two clusters is computed by using the dot product of the two centers.

To implement the hierarchical clustering algorithm, we need to implement four additional classes, as shown in figure 9.3. These classes are

- HierCluster: an interface for representing a hierarchical cluster
- HierClusterImpl: implements the cluster used for a hierarchical clustering algorithm
- HierDistance: an object used to represent the distance between two clusters
- HierarchialClusteringImpl: the implementation for the hierarchical clustering algorithm

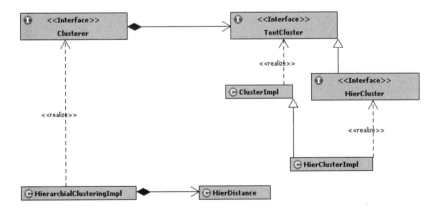

Figure 9.3   The classes for implementing the hierarchical agglomerative clustering algorithm

The interface for `HierCluster` is shown in listing 9.14. Each instance of a `HierCluster` has two children clusters and a method for computing the similarity with another cluster.

Listing 9.14   The interface for `HierCluster`

```
package com.alag.ci.cluster.hiercluster;

import com.alag.ci.cluster.TextCluster;

public interface HierCluster extends TextCluster {
   public HierCluster getChild1() ;
   public HierCluster getChild2();
   public double getSimilarity() ;
   public double computeSimilarity(HierCluster o);
}
```

You can implement multiple variants of a hierarchical clustering algorithm by having different implementations of the `computeSimilarity` method. One such implementation is shown in listing 9.15, which shows the implementation for `HierClusterImpl`.

Listing 9.15   The implementation for `HierClusterImpl`

```
package com.alag.ci.blog.cluster.impl;

import java.io.StringWriter;

import com.alag.ci.blog.search.RetrievedBlogEntry;
import com.alag.ci.cluster.TextDataItem;
import com.alag.ci.cluster.hiercluster.HierCluster;

public class HierClusterImpl extends ClusterImpl implements HierCluster {
   private HierCluster child1 = null;
   private HierCluster child2 = null;
   private double similarity;

   public HierClusterImpl(int clusterId,HierCluster child1,
       HierCluster child2, double similarity,
       TextDataItem dataItem) {                  ◁────┐  Constructor
      super(clusterId);
      this.child1 = child1;
      this.child2 = child2;
      this.similarity = similarity;
      if (dataItem != null) {
         this.addDataItem(dataItem);
      }
   }

   public HierCluster getChild1() {
      return child1;
   }

   public HierCluster getChild2() {
      return child2;
   }

   public double getSimilarity() {
      return similarity;
```

```
   }
   public double computeSimilarity (HierCluster o) {        ◁──┐  Computes similarity
      return this.getCenter().dotProduct(o.getCenter());         between clusters
   }

   public String toString() {
      StringWriter sb = new StringWriter();
      String blogDetails = getBlogDetails();
      if (blogDetails != null) {
         sb.append("Id=" + this.getClusterId() + " " + blogDetails);
      } else {
         sb.append("Id=" + this.getClusterId() + " similarity="+
            this.similarity );
      }
      if (this.getChild1() != null) {
         sb.append(" C1=" + this.getChild1().getClusterId());
      }
      if (this.getChild2() != null) {
         sb.append(" C2=" + this.getChild2().getClusterId());
      }
      return sb.toString();                    Prints out details
   }                                            of blog entry
   private String getBlogDetails() {    ◁──┘
      if ((this.getItems() != null) && (this.getItems().size() > 0)) {
         TextDataItem textDataItem = this.getItems().get(0);
         if (textDataItem != null) {
            RetrievedBlogEntry blog =
             (RetrievedBlogEntry) textDataItem.getData();
            return blog.getTitle();
         }
      }
      return null;
   }
}
```

The implementation for HierClusterImpl is straightforward. Each instance of
HierClusterImpl has two children and a similarity. The toString() and getBlog-
Details() methods are added to display the cluster.

Next, let's look at the implementation for the HierDistance class, which is shown
in listing 9.16.

Listing 9.16 The implementation for `HierDistance`

```
package com.alag.ci.blog.cluster.impl;

import com.alag.ci.cluster.hiercluster.HierCluster;

public class HierDistance implements Comparable<HierDistance> {    ◁──┐
   private HierCluster c1 = null;
   private HierCluster c2 = null;
   private double similarity ;          Implements Comparable
   private int hashCode;                interface for sorting

   public HierDistance(HierCluster c1, HierCluster c2) {
      this.c1 = c1;
      this.c2 = c2;
```

```
        hashCode = ("" + c1.getClusterId()).hashCode() +
          ("" + c2.getClusterId()).hashCode();
    }
    public boolean equals(Object obj) {                    ⟵──┐  Overrides equals and
        return (this.hashCode() == obj.hashCode());           │  hashcode methods
    }
    public int hashCode() {
        return this.hashCode;
    }

    public HierCluster getC1() {
        return c1;
    }

    public HierCluster getC2() {
        return c2;
    }

    public double getSimilarity() {
        return this.similarity;
    }

    public boolean containsCluster(HierCluster hci) {
        if ( (this.getC1() == null) || (this.getC2() == null) ) {
            return false;
        }
        if (hci.getClusterId() == this.getC1().getClusterId()) {
            return true;
        }
        if (hci.getClusterId() == this.getC2().getClusterId()) {
            return true;
        }
        return false;
    }

    public void setSimilarity(double similarity) {
        this.similarity = similarity;                      ┌─ Two distances
    }                                                      │  compared based
    public int compareTo(HierDistance o) {     ⟵──────────┘  on similarities
        double diff = o.getSimilarity() - this.similarity;
        if (diff > 0) {
            return 1;
        } else if (diff < 0) {
            return -1;
        }
        return 0;
    }
}
```

We use an instance of `HierDistance` to represent the distance between two clusters. Note that the similarity between two clusters, A and B, is the same as the distance between cluster B and A—the similarity is order-independent. The following computation for the hashCode:

```
("" + c1.getClusterId()).hashCode() +
        ("" + c2.getClusterId()).hashCode();
```

ensures that two instances of HierDistance with the same two children are equivalent. containsCluster() is a utility method that will be used by the clustering algorithm to prune out links that are no longer valid.

Finally, we look at the first part of the HierarchialClusteringImpl algorithm, which is shown in listing 9.17. This part shows the implementation of the clustering algorithm in the cluster method.

Listing 9.17 The cluster method for `HierarchialClusteringImpl`

```
package com.alag.ci.blog.cluster.impl;

import java.io.StringWriter;
import java.util.*;

import com.alag.ci.cluster.*;
import com.alag.ci.cluster.hiercluster.HierCluster;

public class HierarchialClusteringImpl implements Clusterer {
    private Map<Integer,HierCluster> availableClusters = null;      Keeps track
    private List<TextDataItem> textDataSet = null;                  of available
                                                                    clusters

    private HierCluster rootCluster ;          Root cluster at      Distances
                                               end of clustering    between
    private int idCount = 0;                                        various
    private Map<HierDistance,HierDistance> allDistance = null;      clusters

    public HierarchialClusteringImpl(List<TextDataItem> textDataSet) {
        this.textDataSet = textDataSet;
        this.availableClusters = new HashMap<Integer,HierCluster>();
        this.allDistance = new HashMap<HierDistance,HierDistance>();
    }

    public List<TextCluster> cluster() {        Clustering
        createInitialClusters();                algorithm
        while (allDistance.size() > 0) {
            addNextCluster();
        }
        List<TextCluster> clusters = new ArrayList<TextCluster>();
        clusters.add(this.rootCluster);
        return clusters;
    }
```

The clustering algorithm in HierarchialClusteringImpl is fairly simple. It first creates an initial list of clusters:

```
createInitialClusters();
```

Next it creates a new cluster from the list of available clusters. This process continues until you're left with only one cluster:

```
while (allDistance.size() > 0) {
    addNextCluster();
}
```

Let's look at the method to create the initial set of clusters, contained in listing 9.18.

Listing 9.18   Creating the initial clusters in `HierarchialClusteringImpl`

```
private void createInitialClusters() {
    createInitialSingleItemClusters();       ⟵── Create initial set of clusters
    computeInitialDistances();        ⟵──┐ Compute initial set of distances
}

private void createInitialSingleItemClusters() {
    for (TextDataItem dataItem: this.textDataSet) {
        HierClusterImpl cluster = new HierClusterImpl(this.idCount ++,
                null, null, 1.,dataItem);
        cluster.setCenter(dataItem.getTagMagnitudeVector());
        this.availableClusters.put(cluster.getClusterId(),cluster);
    }
}

private void computeInitialDistances() {
    for (HierCluster cluster: this.availableClusters.values()) {
        for (HierCluster otherCluster:
          this.availableClusters.values()) {
            if (cluster.getClusterId() !=
              otherCluster.getClusterId()) {
                HierDistance hd =
                  new HierDistance(cluster,otherCluster);
                if (!this.allDistance.containsKey(hd)) {
                    double similarity =
                      cluster.computeSimilarity(otherCluster);
                    hd.setSimilarity(similarity);
                    this.allDistance.put(hd, hd);
                }
            }
        }
    }
}
```

Creating an initial set of clusters consists of two steps. First, we create a cluster for each data item:

```
createInitialSingleItemClusters();
```

Second, we compute the distances between each of the clusters using `compute-InitialDistances()`. These distances are stored in `allDistances`.

Next, let's look at the code to add a new cluster to the initial set of clusters, shown in listing 9.19.

Listing 9.19   Merging the next cluster in `HierarchialClusteringImpl`

```
private void addNextCluster() {
    List<HierDistance> sortDist = new ArrayList<HierDistance>();
    sortDist.addAll(this.allDistance.keySet());       ┐ Get clusters with
    Collections.sort(sortDist);                       │ best similarity
    HierDistance hd = sortDist.get(0);       ⟵────────┘
    this.allDistance.remove(hd);           Create new cluster ┐
                                                              │
    HierCluster cluster = createNewCluster(hd);       ⟵───────┘   ┐ Remove invalid
    pruneDistances(hd.getC1(), hd.getC2(), sortDist);   ⟵─────────┘ distances
```

```
        addNewClusterDistances(cluster);        ⊲— Add distances from new cluster

        if (this.allDistance.size() == 0) {     ⊲— Check if we have root node
            this.rootCluster = cluster;
        }
    }

    private HierCluster createNewCluster(HierDistance hd) {
        HierClusterImpl cluster = new HierClusterImpl(this.idCount ++,
                hd.getC1(), hd.getC2(), hd.getSimilarity(),null);
        cluster.setCenter(hd.getC1().getCenter().add(
            hd.getC2().getCenter()));
        this.availableClusters.put(cluster.getClusterId(),cluster);
        this.availableClusters.remove(hd.getC1().getClusterId());
        this.availableClusters.remove(hd.getC2().getClusterId());
        return cluster;
    }

    private void pruneDistances(HierCluster c1, HierCluster c2,
        List<HierDistance> sortDist) {
        for (HierDistance hierDistance: sortDist) {
            if ((hierDistance.containsCluster(c1)) ||
                (hierDistance.containsCluster(c2))) {
                this.allDistance.remove(hierDistance);
            }
        }
    }

    private void addNewClusterDistances(HierCluster cluster) {
        for (HierCluster hc: this.availableClusters.values()) {
            if (hc.getClusterId() != cluster.getClusterId()) {
                HierDistance hierDistance = new HierDistance(cluster,hc);
                double similarity =
                    cluster.getCenter().dotProduct(hc.getCenter());
                hierDistance.setSimilarity(similarity);
                this.allDistance.put(hierDistance, hierDistance);
            }
        }
    }
```

Adding a new cluster involves finding the `HierDistance` that has the highest similarity among all the distance measures. All the distances are sorted, and the best one is used for merging clusters:

```
        Collections.sort(sortDist);
        HierDistance hd = sortDist.get(0);
```

The method `pruneDistances()` removes distances associated with the two clusters that have been merged, while the method `addNewClusterDistances()` adds the distances from the new cluster to all the other clusters that can be merged.

Listing 9.20 shows the code associated with printing the details from the hierarchical clustering algorithm.

Listing 9.20 Printing the results from `HierarchicalClusteringImpl`

```
    public String toString() {
        StringWriter sb = new StringWriter();
```

```
        sb.append("Num of clusters = " + this.idCount + "\n");
        sb.append(printClusterDetails(this.rootCluster,""));
        return sb.toString();
    }

    private String printClusterDetails(
        HierCluster cluster, String append) {
        StringWriter sb = new StringWriter();
        if (cluster != null) {
            sb.append(cluster.toString());
            String tab = "\t" + append;
            if (cluster.getChild1() != null) {
                sb.append("\n" + tab + "C1=" +
                 printClusterDetails(cluster.getChild1(),tab));
            }
            if (cluster.getChild2() != null) {
                sb.append("\n" + tab + "C2="
                 +printClusterDetails(cluster.getChild2(),tab));
            }
        }
        return sb.toString();
    }
}
```

There's nothing complicated in printing the details of the cluster that's created. The code simply formats the results; an example is shown in listing 9.21. This listing shows the results from one of the clustering runs. Note that the titles of the blog entries are shown wherever we have a leaf cluster with a blog entry. Each cluster has a unique ID associated with it and there are a total of 10 clusters.

> **Listing 9.21   Sample output from hierarchical clustering applied to blog entries**

```
Num of clusters = 19
Id=18 similarity=0.00325633040335101 C1=17 C2=9
    C1=Id=17 similarity=0.02342920655844054 C1=16 C2=14
        C1=Id=16 similarity=0.42247390457827866 C1=15 C2=13
            C1=Id=15 similarity=0.04164026486125777 C1=10 C2=6
                C1=Id=10 similarity=0.6283342717309606 C1=1 C2=0
                    C1=Id=1 Vote for Cool Software
                    C2=Id=0 Vote for Cool Software
                C2=Id=6 Collective Intelligence Applied to the Patent
Process
            C2=Id=13 similarity=0.8021265050360485 C1=12 C2=5
                C1=Id=12 similarity=0.676456586660375 C1=11 C2=7
                    C1=Id=11 similarity=0.5542920709331453 C1=4 C2=8
                        C1=Id=4 Collective Intelligence Applied to the
Patent Process
                        C2=Id=8 Collective Intelligence Applied to the
Patent Process
                    C2=Id=7 Collective Intelligence Applied to the Patent Process
                C2=Id=5 Collective Intelligence Applied to the Patent Process
        C2=Id=14 similarity=0.0604642261218513 C1=2 C2=3
            C1=Id=2 Wall Street meets social networking
            C2=Id=3 10 Ways to Build More Collaborative Teams
    C2=Id=9 Rencontres ICC'07 : on  se voit là bas ?
```

This output was generated using the following code:

```
DataSetCreator bc = new BlogDataSetCreatorImpl();
    List<TextDataItem> blogData = bc.createLearningData();
    Clusterer clusterer = new HierarchialClusteringImpl(
        blogData);
    clusterer.cluster();
    System.out.println(clusterer);
```

Hierarchical algorithms don't scale well. If n is the number of items then the order of complexity is n^2. Hierarchical algorithms, along with k-means, give good clustering results. Next, let's look at the expectation maximization clustering algorithm.

9.1.5 *Expectation maximization and other examples of clustering high-dimension sparse data*

An alternative approach to clustering is to use a model to fit the data. The clustering algorithm then tries to optimize the fit between the model and the data. Typically, for continuous attributes, the Gaussian distribution is used to model a variable. Each cluster has a mean and variance associated with it. Given another point, we can compute the probability of that point being a part of that distribution. This probability is a number between 0 and 1. The higher the probability, the higher the chance that the point belongs to the cluster.

The expectation maximization algorithm (EM) is a general-purpose framework for estimating a set of Gaussian distributions for modeling data. Unlike the k-means algorithm, the data points aren't associated with a single cluster; the association is soft in that they're associated with a cluster with a probability for each. Adapting the process to clustering, you can use the following clustering algorithms:

- *Initialize the* k *clusters at random*—Each cluster has a mean and variance.
- *Expectation step*—Compute the probability that a point belongs to the cluster.
- *Maximization step*—Maximize the parameters of the distribution to maximize the likelihood of the items.

The algorithm stops when the change in the likelihood of the objects after each iteration becomes small. In section 9.2, we apply the EM clustering algorithm using WEKA.

Analyzing the data corresponding to user click-through in a web application during a period of time leads to a high-dimension dataset, which is sparse. This is similar to the term vector representation for text. In this case, each document that a user can visit forms the terms, while the frequency count of visitation corresponds to the weight of the vector.

In chapter 3, we looked at user tagging. Analyzing the set of tags created by users leads to analysis similar to that done in this section. The tags created or visited by a user can be used to cluster similar users. Next, we look at clustering blog entries using WEKA.

9.2   *Leveraging WEKA for clustering*

Figure 7.13 in section 7.2.2 showed the classes associated with WEKA for clustering. In this section, we work through the same example of clustering blog data using the WEKA APIs.

You may recall that a dataset in WEKA is represented by the `Instances` class. `Instances` are composed of an `Instance` object, one for each data item. `Attributes` for the dataset are represented by the `Attribute` class. To apply the WEKA clustering algorithm, we do the following steps:

1 Convert the blog data from Technorati into an `Instances` representation.
2 Create an instance of the `Clusterer` and associate the learning data.
3 Evaluate the results of clustering.

It's helpful to go through figure 9.4, which maps the classes that we will be using in this section.

The class `WEKABlogDataSetClusterer`, which extends `BlogDataSetCreatorImpl`, is the main class that we develop in this section. It creates an instance of the dataset, of type `Instances`. It uses the EM class for applying the expectation maximization algorithm to the `Instances` class. The `ClusterEvaluation` class is used for evaluating the result from EM, which is an instance of the `Clusterer` class.

In this section, we first create the dataset for using the WEKA APIs. This will be followed by using the EM class to cluster the blog entries, and finally we evaluate the quality of the clustering model.

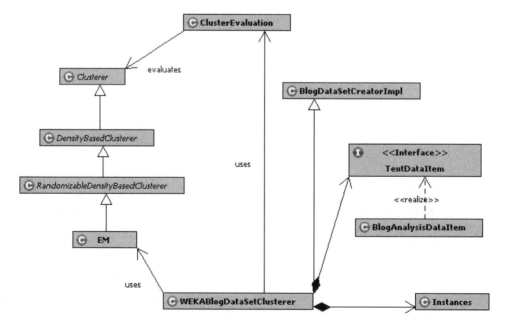

Figure 9.4   The classes for implementing the hierarchical agglomerative clustering algorithm

9.2.1 Creating the learning dataset

To create a learning dataset in WEKA, we first need to define attributes. We take a simple approach of treating each tag as an attribute. Clearly, representing text with tags leads to a high-dimensional dataset. Typically, based on your domain, you may have well over 100,000 tag instances. A common approach is to reduce the dimension space by pruning the number of tags associated with each document. In our example of classifying blog entries, for 10 blog instances, there were typically around 150 unique tags.

Listing 9.22 shows the first part of the `WEKABlogDataSetClusterer` class, which deals with creating an `Instances` dataset by retrieving live blog entries from Technorati. This class extends the `BlogDataSetCreatorImpl` class that we developed in the previous section.

Listing 9.22   The first part of `WEKABlogDataSetClusterer`

```
package com.alag.ci.blog.cluster.weka.impl;

import java.util.*;

import weka.clusterers.*;
import weka.core.*;

import com.alag.ci.blog.cluster.impl.BlogDataSetCreatorImpl;
import com.alag.ci.blog.search.RetrievedBlogEntry;
import com.alag.ci.cluster.TextDataItem;
import com.alag.ci.textanalysis.*;
import com.alag.ci.textanalysis.Tag;

public class WEKABlogDataSetClusterer extends BlogDataSetCreatorImpl {
    private List<TextDataItem> blogEntries = null;

    public Instances createLearningDataSet() throws Exception {
        this.blogEntries = createLearningData();
        FastVector allAttributes = createAttributes();
        Instances trainingDataSet = new Instances("blogClustering",
                allAttributes, blogEntries.size());
        int numAttributes = allAttributes.size();
        Collection<Tag> allTags = this.getAllTags();
        for (TextDataItem dataItem : blogEntries) {
            Instance instance = createNewInstance(numAttributes,
                    trainingDataSet,
                    allTags, dataItem );
            trainingDataSet.add(instance);
        }
        return trainingDataSet;
    }

    private FastVector createAttributes() {
        Collection<Tag> allTags = this.getAllTags();
        FastVector allAttributes = new FastVector(allTags.size());
        for (Tag tag : allTags) {
            Attribute tagAttribute = new Attribute(tag.getDisplayText());
            allAttributes.addElement(tagAttribute);
        }
        return allAttributes;
```

Keeps list of blog entries

Each tag corresponds to an attribute

Each entry corresponds to an instance

Each tag is an attribute

```
    }
    private Instance createNewInstance(int numAttributes,
        Instances trainingDataSet, Collection<Tag> allTags,
        TextDataItem dataItem) {
      Instance instance = new Instance(numAttributes);
      instance.setDataset(trainingDataSet);
      int index = 0;
      TagMagnitudeVector tmv = dataItem.getTagMagnitudeVector();
      Map<Tag, TagMagnitude> tmvMap = tmv.getTagMagnitudeMap();
      for (Tag tag : allTags) {
        TagMagnitude tm = tmvMap.get(tag);
        if (tm != null) {
          instance.setValue(index++, tm.getMagnitude());      ◁── Magnitude
        } else {                                                   corresponds
          instance.setValue(index++, 0.);                          to input value
        }                                                          for attribute
      }
      return instance;
    }
```

The method createLearningDataSet first gets the List of TextDataItem instances:

```
    this.blogEntries = createLearningData();
```

Attribute instances are created by iterating over all the tag entries:

```
        for (Tag tag : allTags) {
          Attribute tagAttribute = new Attribute(tag.getDisplayText());
          allAttributes.addElement(tagAttribute);
```

A new Instance is created by using the TagMagnitudeVector and iterating over all the tag instances. A tag attribute that isn't present in the TagMagnitudeVector instance has a magnitude of 0.

It's useful to look at listing 9.23, which shows a typical dump of the Instances class. The dump was created using the toString method for the Instances class.

Listing 9.23   An example dump of the `Instances` class

```
............ //many more attributes
@attribute zeit numeric
@attribute choosing numeric
@attribute da numeric
@attribute um numeric
@attribute sufferingan numeric
@attribute gerne numeric
@attribute articles numeric
@attribute throu numeric
@attribute years numeric
@attribute advice numeric
@attribute corporate numeric

@data
0.159381,0.228023,0,0,0,0,0,0,0,0,0,0,0.159381,0.159381,0.159381,0.159381,0
,0.159381,0,0,0,0.159381,0,0,0.159381,0,0,0,0,0,0.09074,0,0.09074,0,0.22802
3,0,0,0,0,0,0,0.159381,0,0,0,0,0,0,0.159381,0,0,0,0.159381,0,0.228023,0.228
```

023,0,0,0,0,0,0,0,0,0.228023,0.159381,0.228023,0,0,0,0,0,0.159381,0,0,0.159
381,0,0.228023,0.228023,0,0,0,0,0.09074,0,0,0,0,0,0,0.159381,0.09074,0,0,
0,0.159381,0,0,0.09074,0,0.159381,0,0,0,0.159381,0,0,0,0.159381,0,0.09074,0
,0,0,0,0,0,0,0,0.228023,0,0,0
0.21483,0,0,0,0,0,0,0,0,0,0,0,0.21483,0.21483,0.21483,0.21483,0,0.21483,0,0
,0,0.21483,0,0,0.21483,0,0,0,0,0,0.122308,0.21483,0,0,0,0,0,0,0,0,0,0,0,0,0
,0,0,0,0,0,0,0,0,0,0,0,0,0,0,0,0,0,0.21483,0,0,0,0,0.307353,0,0.21483
,0,0,0.21483,0,0,0,0.21483,0.21483,0,0,0.122308,0,0,0,0,0,0,0,0.122308,0,
0,0,0.21483,0,0,0.122308,0,0.21483,0,0,0,0.21483,0,0,0,0.21483,0,0.122308,0
,0,0,0,0,0,0,0,0,0,0
0,0,0,0,0,0,0,0,0,0,0,0,0.096607,0,0,0,0,0,0,0,0.18476,0,0,0.369519,0,0,0,0
,0,0,0,0.073523,0.554279,0,0,0,0,0,0,0.129141,0.18476,0,0,0,0,0,0.12914
1,0,0,0.18476,0.387424,0,0,0,0,0,0,0,0,0,0,0,0,0,0,0,0,0,0,0,0.18476,0,0,
0,0,0,0,0,0,0,0,0,0.18476,0,0,0,0.129141,0,0,0,0,0,0,0,0.18476,0,0,0,
0,0,0,0,0,0,0,0,0,0,0,0,0,0,0,0,0,0,0.369519
....

The first part of the dump enumerates all the attributes. Each tag instance is a numeric attribute, which takes values between 0 and 1. The data associated with three blog entries is also shown in the listing. Note that the rows are sparsely populated with most of the values being zero.

9.2.2 Creating the clusterer

Now that we've created the dataset, let's look at the second part of the implementation for WEKABlogDataSetClusterer, which corresponds to creating an instance of a Clusterer and clustering the dataset we just created. Listing 9.24 has the code.

Listing 9.24 The second part of WEKABlogDataSetClusterer

```
public void cluster() throws Exception {
    Instances instances = createLearningDataSet();    ← Creates dataset for clustering

    Clusterer clusterer = getClusterer(instances);    ← Gets Clusterer instance

    evaluateCluster(clusterer, instances);    ← Evaluates Clusterer
}

private Clusterer getClusterer(Instances instances) throws Exception {
    EM em = new EM();
    em.setNumClusters(-1);    ← Selects number of clusters by cross validation
    em.setMaxIterations(100);
    em.buildClusterer(instances);
    return em;
}
```

The clustering code is simple and consists of three steps. First, we create the learning dataset:

```
Instances instances = createLearningDataSet();
```

Next, using this Instances, we create an instance of the Clusterer. In our example, we use the expectation maximization (EM) algorithm. The class EM represents an instance of the EM algorithm. We use the no-argument constructor:

```
EM em = new EM();
```

Next, we set the parameters for the clusterer:

```
em.setNumClusters(-1);
em.setMaxIterations(100);
```

When the number of clusters is set to -1, EM uses cross validation to select the number of clusters to be used. The algorithm splits the dataset into 10 instances. It assigns the number of clusters to be 1 and then performs tenfold cross validation. The log likelihood is computed for each of the 10 runs and averaged. If the log likelihood increases, then the number of clusters is increased by one and the whole process continues. The Clusterer instance clusters the dataset using the following code:

```
em.buildClusterer(instances);
```

Next, let's look at how we can evaluate the results from clustering.

9.2.3   *Evaluating the clustering results*

To evaluate the results from clustering, we need to use a ClusterEvaluation instance. Listing 9.25 shows the third part of the code for WEKABlogDataSetClusterer, in which we evaluate the results from clustering.

Listing 9.25   The third part of WEKABlogDataSetClusterer

```
private ClusterEvaluation evaluateCluster(Clusterer clusterer,
     Instances instances) throws Exception {
   ClusterEvaluation eval = new ClusterEvaluation();
   eval.setClusterer(clusterer);
   eval.evaluateClusterer(instances);
   String evalString = eval.clusterResultsToString();    ◁── Displays
   System.out.println(evalString);                              information
                                                               about clusterer

   int numClusters = eval.getNumClusters();
   double[] assignments = eval.getClusterAssignments();
   System.out.println("NumClusters=" + numClusters);

   Map<Integer, List<RetrievedBlogEntry>> assignMap =            Associates
        associateInstancesWithClusters(assignments);     ◁──    instances with
   printClusterEntries(assignMap);                               each cluster
   return eval;                                                  created
}

private Map<Integer, List<RetrievedBlogEntry>>
associateInstancesWithClusters(double[] assignments) {
   int index = 0;
   Map<Integer, List<RetrievedBlogEntry>> assignMap =
     new HashMap<Integer, List<RetrievedBlogEntry>>();
   for (double assignment : assignments) {
      TextDataItem dataItem = this.blogEntries.get(index++);
      List<RetrievedBlogEntry> entries = assignMap.get(
       (int) assignment);
      if (entries == null) {
         entries = new ArrayList<RetrievedBlogEntry>();
         assignMap.put((int) assignment, entries);
      }
```

```
                entries.add((RetrievedBlogEntry) dataItem.getData());
        }
        return assignMap;
    }

    private void printClusterEntries(Map<Integer,
        List<RetrievedBlogEntry>> assignMap) {
        for (int clusterId = 0; clusterId < assignMap.size();
            clusterId++) {
            List<RetrievedBlogEntry> entries = assignMap.get(clusterId);
            System.out.println(clusterId);
            for (RetrievedBlogEntry blogEntry : entries) {
                System.out.println(blogEntry.getExcerpt());
            }
        }
    }
}
```

Gets retrieved blog entry

Prints blog entry details

We first create an instance of ClusterEvaluation, associate it with the Clusterer instance, and then evaluate the clusterer:

```
ClusterEvaluation eval = new ClusterEvaluation();
eval.setClusterer(clusterer);
eval.evaluateClusterer(instances);
```

Next, we get the association of each blog entry to a cluster instance:

```
double[] assignments = eval.getClusterAssignments();
```

Next, we use the assignments to create a list of retrieved blog entries with each of the clusters:

```
Map<Integer, List<RetrievedBlogEntry>>
    associateInstancesWithClusters(double[] assignments)
```

Lastly, we print out the assignments using the method printClusterEntries. Listing 9.26 shows the results from one of the clustering runs. Note that similar posts are grouped together in the same cluster. In this instance there are four clusters.

Listing 9.26 Sample output from one of the clustering runs

```
..........
Clustered Instances

0      3 ( 30%)
1      2 ( 20%)
2      2 ( 20%)
3      3 ( 30%)

Log likelihood: 222.25086

NumClusters=4
0.0
SAP Gets Business Intelligence. What Do You Get?  [IMG]     Posted by:
Michael Goldberg in News
SAP Gets Business Intelligence. What Do You Get?  [IMG]     Posted by:
Michael Goldberg in News
Che Guevara, presente! Posted by Arroyoribera on October 7th, 2007   Forty
```

```
years ago, the Argentine
1.0
[IMG ] That's what Intel wants you to do with the launch of their new
website called CoolSW. They ar
[IMG ] That's what Intel wants you to do with the launch of their new
website called CoolSW. They ar
2.0
 We Are Smarter Than Me | Podcasts  We are Smarter than Me is a great new
site on collective intelli
Corporate Social Networks Filed under: Collaboration, Social-networking,
collective intelligence, so
Choosing Simplicity and Creative Compassion...and Releasing "Addictions" to
SufferingAn article and
3.0
?[ruby] [collective intelligence] "Collective Intelligence"??????ruby???????
  [IMG Programming Collective Intelligence: Building Smart Web 2.0 Applicat
?[ruby] [collective intelligence] "Collective Intelligence"????????????????????
?  ????? del.icio.us ????
```

In this section, we've looked at applying the WEKA APIs for clustering instances. WEKA has a rich set of clustering algorithms, including `SimpleKMeans`, `OPTICS` (ordering points to identify clustering structures), `EM`, and `DBScan`.

As you must have noticed from this section, it's fairly straightforward to apply clustering using the WEKA APIs. Lastly, before we end the chapter, let's look at key interfaces related to clustering in the JDM APIs.

9.3   Clustering using the JDM APIs

The package `javax.datamining.clustering` contains interfaces for representing a clustering model, for algorithm settings associated with clustering, and for specifying the similarity matrix associated with clustering.

In this section, we briefly look at the key interfaces associated with clustering and look at code for creating a cluster using the JDM interfaces.

9.3.1   Key JDM clustering-related classes

As shown in figure 9.5, the results from a clustering run are represented by a `ClusteringModel`, which extends the `Model` interface. A `ClusteringModel` consists of a number of `Cluster` instances, which represent the metadata associated with a cluster. The `Cluster` interface has methods to return parent and children cluster instances (as with hierarchical clustering), statistics about the data associated with the cluster, rules associated with the cluster, and so on.

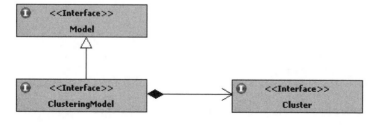

Figure 9.5   A `ClusteringModel` consists of a set of clusters obtained by analyzing the data.

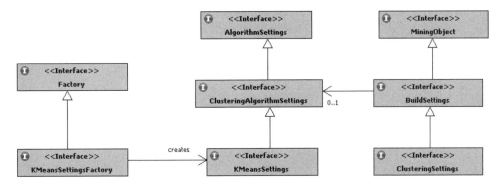

Figure 9.6 **Some of the classes associated with clustering algorithm settings and clustering settings**

For building a clustering model, there are two types of settings, as shown in figure 9.6. First are generic settings associated with the clustering process and represented by an instance of `ClusteringSettings`. Second are settings that are associated with a specific clustering algorithm. An example of such a setting is the `KMeansSettings` interface, which allows advanced users to specify the details of the k-means clustering algorithm.

The interface `BuildSettings` has a method `setAlgorithmSettings()` for setting algorithm-specific settings. Let's walk through some sample code that will make executing the clustering process through the JDM APIs clearer.

9.3.2 Clustering settings using the JDM APIs

In this section, we go through sample code to illustrate the clustering process using the JDM APIs. Our example has four steps:

1 Create the clustering settings object.
2 Create the clustering task.
3 Execute the clustering task.
4 Retrieve the clustering model.

Listing 9.27 shows the code associated with the example and the settings process.

Listing 9.27 Settings-related code for the clustering process

```
package com.alag.ci.jdm.clustering;

import java.util.Collection;

import javax.datamining.*;
import javax.datamining.algorithm.kmeans.ClusteringDistanceFunction;
import javax.datamining.algorithm.kmeans.KMeansSettings;
import javax.datamining.algorithm.kmeans.KMeansSettingsFactory;
import javax.datamining.clustering.*;
import javax.datamining.resource.Connection;
import javax.datamining.task.*;

public class JDMClusteringExample {
```

```
public void cluster(Connection connection ) throws JDMException {
   createClusteringSettings(connection);        ◄──┐ Four steps
   createClusteringTask(connection);               │ associated
   executeClusteringTask(connection);              │ with example
   retrieveClusteringModel(connection);
}

private void createClusteringSettings(Connection connection)
    throws JDMException {
   ClusteringSettingsFactory clusSettingsFactory =
     (ClusteringSettingsFactory)
   connection.getFactory(
       "javax.datamining.clustering.ClusteringSettingsFactory");
   ClusteringSettings clusteringSettings =
     clusSettingsFactory.create();
   clusteringSettings.setMaxNumberOfClusters(100);   ◄──┐ Clustering
   clusteringSettings.setMinClusterCaseCount(10);       │ process-related
   ClusteringAlgorithmSettings algorithmSettings =      │ settings
     createKMeansClusteringSettings(connection);
   clusteringSettings.setAlgorithmSettings(algorithmSettings);
   connection.saveObject("clusteringSettings",
       clusteringSettings, false);
}

private ClusteringAlgorithmSettings createKMeansClusteringSettings(
  Connection connection) throws JDMException {
   KMeansSettingsFactory kmeansSettingsFactory =
       (KMeansSettingsFactory)connection.getFactory(
         "javax.datamining.algorithm.kmeans.KMeansSettingsFactory");
   KMeansSettings kmeansSettings =
     kmeansSettingsFactory.create();               ◄──┐ Algorithm-specific
   kmeansSettings.setDistanceFunction(                │ settings
       ClusteringDistanceFunction.euclidean);
   kmeansSettings.setMaxNumberOfIterations(100);
   kmeansSettings.setMinErrorTolerance(0.001);
   return kmeansSettings;
}
```

The example first creates an instance of ClusteringSettings and sets attributes associated with the clustering process. For this, it sets the maximum and the minimum number of clusters to be created:

```
clusteringSettings.setMaxNumberOfClusters(100);
clusteringSettings.setMinClusterCaseCount(10);
```

Next, an instance of KMeansSettings is created to specify settings specific to the k-means algorithm. Here, the distance function is set to be Euclidean. The maximum number of iterations and the minimum error tolerance are also specified:

```
kmeansSettings.setDistanceFunction(ClusteringDistanceFunction.euclidean);
    kmeansSettings.setMaxNumberOfIterations(100);
    kmeansSettings.setMinErrorTolerance(0.001);
```

The algorithm settings are set in the ClusteringSettings instance:

```
clusteringSettings.setAlgorithmSettings(algorithmSettings);
```

Next, let's look at creating the clustering task.

9.3.3 Creating the clustering task using the JDM APIs

To create an instance of the BuildTask for clustering we use the BuildTaskFactory as shown in Listing 9.28.

Listing 9.28 Creating the clustering task

```
private void createClusteringTask(Connection connection) throws
JDMException {
   BuildTaskFactory buildTaskFactory = (BuildTaskFactory)
      connection.getFactory("javax.datamining.task.BuildTaskFactory");
   BuildTask buildTask =
buildTaskFactory.create("buildDataPhysicalDataSet",
      "clusteringSettings", "clusteringModel");
   connection.saveObject("clusteringBuildTask", buildTask, false);
}
```

The BuildTaskFactory creates an instance of the BuildTask. The create method to create a BuildTask needs the name of the dataset to be used, the name of the settings object, and the name of the model that is to be created. In our example, we will use the dataset "buildDataPhysicalDataSet", use the setting specified in the object "clusteringSettings", and the model that will be created from this run will be stored using the name "clusteringModel".

9.3.4 Executing the clustering task using the JDM APIs

To execute a build task, we use the execute() method on the Connection object as shown in listing 9.29.

Listing 9.29 Executing the clustering task

```
private void executeClusteringTask(Connection connection)
   throws JDMException {
   ExecutionHandle executionHandle = connection.execute(
     "clusteringBuildTask");
   int timeoutInSeconds = 100;
   ExecutionStatus executionStatus =
     executionHandle.waitForCompletion(timeoutInSeconds);
   executionStatus = executionHandle.getLatestStatus();
   if (ExecutionState.success.equals(executionStatus.getState())) {
      //successful state
   }
}
```

The following code:

```
ExecutionStatus executionStatus =
   executionHandle.waitForCompletion(timeoutInSeconds);
```

waits for the clustering task to complete and specifies a timeout of 100 seconds. Once the task completes, it looks at execution status to see whether the task was successful.

Next, let's look at how we can retrieve the clustering model that has been created.

9.3.5 *Retrieving the clustering model using the JDM APIs*

Listing 9.30 shows the code associated with retrieving a ClusteringModel using the name of the model and a Connection instance.

Listing 9.30   Retrieving the clustering model

```
private void retrieveClusteringModel(Connection connection)
    throws JDMException {
ClusteringModel clusteringModel = (ClusteringModel)
    connection.retrieveObject("clusteringModel",
      NamedObject.model);
Collection<Cluster> clusters = clusteringModel.getClusters();
for (Cluster cluster: clusters) {
  System.out.println(cluster.getClusterId() + " " +
  cluster.getName());
  }
 }
}
```

Once a ClusteringModel is retrieved, we can get the set of Cluster instances and display information related to each of the clusters.

In this section, we've looked at the key interfaces associated with clustering and the JDM APIs. As you must have noticed from this chapter, using the JDM APIs to apply clustering is fairly straightforward. We've looked at some sample code associated with creating clustering settings, creating and executing a clustering task, and retrieving the clustering model.

9.4   *Summary*

Clustering is the automated process of analyzing data to discover groups of related items. Clustering the data can provide insight into the distribution of the data, and can then be used to connect items with other similar items, build predictive models, or build a recommendation engine.

Clustering text documents involves creating a term vector representation for the text. This representation typically yields a high dimension and is sparsely populated. Analyzing the clickstream for a set of users has a similar representation. Creating a dataset using the attributes of a set of items typically leads to a dense, low-dimension representation for the data.

K-means is perhaps the simplest clustering algorithm. For this algorithm, we specify the number of clusters for the data. The algorithm iteratively assigns each item to a cluster based on a similarity or a distance measure. The centers of the clusters are recomputed based on the instances assigned to them. In hierarchical clustering, the algorithm begins with assigning a cluster to each item. Next, a new cluster is created by combining two clusters that are most similar. This process continues until you're left with only one cluster. The expectation maximization (EM) algorithm uses a probabilistic approach to cluster instances. Each item is associated with different clusters using a probabilistic distribution.

The WEKA package has a number of algorithms that can be used for clustering. The process of clustering consists of first creating an instance of `Instances` to represent the dataset, followed by an instance of a `Clusterer`, and using a `ClusterEvaluation` to evaluate the results.

The process of clustering using the JDM APIs involves creating a `ClusterSettings` instance, creating and executing a `ClusteringTask`, and retrieving the `ClusteringModel` that's created.

Now that we have a good understanding of clustering, in the next chapter we'll look at building predictive models.

9.5 Resources

Beil, Florian, Martin Ester, and Xiaowei Xu. "Frequent term-based text clustering." Proceedings of the Eighth ACM SIGKDD international Conference on Knowledge Discovery and Data Mining. (Edmonton, Alberta, Canada, 2002). KDD '02. ACM, New York, NY. 436–442. DOI= http://doi.acm.org/10.1145/775047.775110

Böhm, Christian, Christos Faloutsos, Jia-Yu Pan, and Claudia Plant. "Robust information-theoretic clustering." Proceedings of the 12th ACM SIGKDD International Conference on Knowledge Discovery and Data Mining (Philadelphia, PA, 2006). KDD '06. ACM, New York, NY. 65–75. DOI= http://doi.acm.org/10.1145/1150402.1150414

"Tutorial: Clustering Large and High-Dimensional Data." CIKM 2005. http://www.csee.umbc.edu/~nicholas/clustering/

Making predictions 10

This chapter covers

- Classification fundamentals using decision trees, Naïve Bayes, and belief networks
- Building predictors using regression and neural networks
- Leveraging the WEKA APIs for making predictions
- Classification and regression using JDM APIs

In this chapter, we build *predictive models*. A predictive model makes a prediction for the value of an output attribute using the values associated with other input attributes. Predictive models can be categorized into two types based on whether the predicted attribute is continuous or discrete. When the predicted attribute is discrete, the problem is one of *classification*, whereas when the attribute is continuous, the problem is one of *regression*. Some predictive models, as in the case of neural networks, can be built to predict multiple output attributes, while others predict a single attribute.

There are two steps involved with using predictive models: the learning phase and the application phase. In the *learning phase*, given a dataset of examples where each example has a set of input and output attributes, the learning process tries to build a mathematical model that predicts the output attribute value based on the input values. Once a mathematical model has been built, the second step is to apply the model to make predictions. The application of the mathematical model for predictions is typically fast, and can be used for real-time predictions in an application, while the amount of time taken to build the predictive model is much greater and is typically done asynchronously in the application.

In this chapter, we review some of the key supervised learning algorithms used for both classification and regression. We build on the example from the previous chapter of clustering blog entries. We use a simple example to illustrate the inner workings of the algorithms. We also demonstrate how to build classifiers and predictors by using the WEKA APIs. For this, we apply the APIs to live blog entries retrieved from Technorati. Three commonly used classification algorithms are covered in this chapter: decision trees, Naïve Bayes, and Bayesian networks (also known as belief networks or probabilistic networks). The key regression algorithms covered in this chapter include linear regression, multi-layer perceptron, and radial basis functions. We also briefly review the JDM APIs related to classification and regression. At the end of this chapter, you should have a good understanding of the key classification and regression algorithms, how they can be implemented using the WEKA APIs, and the related key JDM concepts.

10.1 Classification fundamentals

In most applications, content is typically categorized into segments or categories. For example, data mining–related content could be categorized into clustering, classification, regression, attribute importance, and association rules. It's quite useful, especially for user-generated content, to build a classifier that can classify content into the various categories. For example, you may want to automatically classify blog entries generated by users into one of the appropriate categories for the application.

One common example of a classification problem is email filtering. Here, the classifier predicts whether a given email is spam. The classifier may use a variety of information to make the prediction, such as the name of the sender, the number of individuals the email has been sent to, the content of the email, the prior history of the user interacting with similar emails, the size of the email, and so forth. The process of classifying emails is fairly involved and complex. and there are a number of commercial products that do this task. Therefore, we use a simpler example later in this section to illustrate the classification process.

In this section, we review three of the most commonly used classifiers: decision trees, Naïve Bayes, and belief networks. In Section 10.2, we use WEKA APIs to apply these classifiers to the problem of classifying blog entries.

10.1.1 Learning decision trees by example

Decision trees are one of the simplest and most intuitive classifiers used in the industry. The model generated from a decision tree can be converted to a number of if-then rules, and the relationships between the output attributes and input attributes are explicit. In section 7.1.3, we briefly described a decision tree. In this section, we work through an example to better understand the concepts related to building one.

In our example, we have a number of advertisements that we can potentially show to a user. We want to show the advertisement that the user is most likely to click (and then buy the advertised item). One such advertisement is for an expensive Rolex watch. In our example, we want to build a predictive model that will guide us as to whether we should show this Rolex advertisement to a user. Remember, we want to optimize the likelihood of the user actually buying the item as opposed to simply clicking on the ad to browse the content. In essence, we want to optimize the *look-to-book ratio* for our product—the proportion of users who've looked at an item and who then bought the item.

Based on some past analysis of the kind of people who tend to buy this watch, we've identified three attributes—in the real world, you'll probably have many more:

- *Is this a high-net-worth individual?*—Our user has provided the ZIP code of his home address during the registration process. We've correlated this ZIP code with average home values in that area and have converted this into a Boolean attribute {true, false} indicating whether this individual has a high net worth.
- *Is the user interested in watches?*—This again is a Boolean attribute. It assumes a value of {true, false}. A user is deemed to be interested in watches if recently (in the current interaction session) the user has either searched for content on the site that has a keyword *watch* or *rolex* or has visited content related to these keywords.
- *Has the user bought items before?*—This again takes a Boolean value {true, false} based on whether the user has transacted before on the site.

Some of the other attributes you can use to build such a predictive model are the user's gender, the age, the referring page, and so on.

We've collected the data of users who clicked on the ad for the watch and whether they actually bought the item. Table 10.1 contains some sample data that we use in our analysis. Note that User 3 and User 4 have the same input attributes but different outcomes. You may want to look at the data to see if you can find any patterns that you can use for predicting whether the user is likely to buy the watch.

Remember that a decision tree consists of nodes and links. Each node has an associated attribute. The number of links originating from the node equals the number of discrete values that the attribute can take. In our case, all the attributes are binary and take a value of {true, false}. Based on the given data, we need to determine the best attribute that we can use to create the decision tree.

	High net worth	Interested in watches	Has purchased before	Purchased item
User 1	F	T	T	F
User 2	T	F	T	F
User 3	T	T	F	T
User 4	T	T	F	F
User 5	T	T	T	T

Table 10.1   Raw data used in the example

Intuitively, we want to select the attribute that can best predict the output. A commonly used measurement for this is *information entropy*—this measures the amount of chaos associated with the distribution of values. The lower the entropy, the more uniform the distribution. To see how entropy is calculated, let's look at the first attribute: *high net worth*. Splitting the dataset based on the values of this attributes leads to two sets:

- False with output case {F}
- True with output cases {F, T, F, T}

Given a set of p positive cases and n negative cases, we can compute the gain[1] associated with the distribution using the code shown in listing 10.1.

Listing 10.1 Computing the gain associated with a distribution

```
public double gain(double p, double n) {
    double sum = p+n;
    double  gain = p*log2(p/sum)/sum  + n*log2(n/sum)/sum;;
    return -gain;
}

private double log2(double x) {
    if (x <= 0.) {
        return 0.;
    }
    return Math.log10(x)/Math.log10(2.);
}
```

Note that a perfect attribute will be one that splits the cases into either all positives or all negatives—in essence, Gain(1,0) = 0. On the other hand, an attribute that splits the space into two equal segments will have the following information gain: Gain(1,1) = 1.

Let's calculate the gain associated with the initial set of data, which consist of three negative cases and two positive cases:

$$\text{Gain}(2, 3) = (2/5)*\log2\,(2/5) + (3/5) * \log2\,(3/5)$$
$$= 0.97$$

Now, one can compute the entropy associated with splitting on the first attribute, which creates two sets {F} and {F, T, F, T} by the following process:

$$\text{Gain}(0,1) = 0 + (1) * \log2\,(1)$$
$$= 0$$
$$\text{Gain}(2,2) = (2/4)\,\log2\,(2/4) + (2/4)\,\log2(2/4)$$
$$= 1$$

Both these gains are added in the ratio of the number of samples that appear:

$$\text{Net Gain (attribute = high net worth)} = (1/5) * 0 + (4/5) *1$$
$$= 0.8$$

The overall *information gain* associated with splitting the data using the first attribute is

---

[1] Please refer to the references at the end of the chapter for more details on the computation of information entropy and how it came about.

$$\text{Net Info Gain (attribute = high net worth)} = \text{Gain (before split)} - \text{Gain (after split)}$$
$$= 0.97 - 0.8$$
$$= 0.17$$

Similarly, the second attribute, *interested in watches*, splits the dataset into two sets, which happen to be the same as with the first attribute:

- False with output case {F}
- True with output cases {F, T, F, T}

Therefore, Info Gain (interested in watches) = 0.17

Lastly, the third attribute, *has purchased before*, splits the dataset into the following two sets:

- False with values {T, F}
- True with values {F, F, T}

$$\text{Net Info Gain (attribute = has purchased before)} = -0.97 - \{ (2/5) \text{ Gain}(1,1) + 3/5 \text{ Gain}(1,2)\}$$
$$= 0.02$$

Selecting either the first or the second attribute leads to the highest net information gain. We arbitrarily select the first attribute to break this tie. Figure 10.1 shows the first node we've created for our decision tree, along with the set of cases that are available for the node.

Next, let's consider the case when the individual doesn't have a high net worth. Table 10.2 contains the one case that's applicable for this node.

	Interested in watches	Has purchased items	Purchased
User 1	T	T	F

Table 10.2   Data available when the user isn't a high-net-worth individual

Note that because there's just one case, all cases have the same predicted value. The information gain even without further splitting is Info Gain(0,1) = 0.

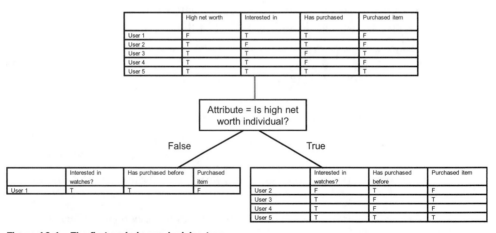

Figure 10.1   The first node in our decision tree

There's nothing to be gained by further splitting any of the other attributes when the user isn't a high-net-worth individual. We can safely predict that the user won't buy the Rolex watch.

Next, let's consider the case when the user has a high net worth. Table 10.3 shows the data associated with high-net-worth individuals.

	Interested in watches	Has purchased items	Purchased
User 2	F	T	F
User 3	T	F	T
User 4	T	F	F
User 5	T	T	T

Table 10.3   Data available when the user is a high-net-worth individual

There are two positive cases and two negative cases. The information gain associated with not splitting this node further is Info Gain(2, 2) = 1.

Next, for this dataset, let's compute the information gain associated with the two remaining attributes: is the user interested in watches, and has the user purchased items before?

Using the attribute *interested in watches*, we can split the dataset into the following two sets:

- True leads to {True, False, True}
- False leads to {False}

Net Info Gain = 1 – { (3/4) gain(2,1) + (1/4) gain(1,1)}
             = 1 – 0.69
             = 0.31

Similarly, splitting the data using the attribute *has purchased before*, leads to the following two datasets:

- True leads to {False, True}
- False leads to {True, False}

Net Info Gain = 1 – { (1/2) gain(1,1) + (1/2) gain (1,1) }
             = 0

Note that splitting on *interested in watches* has the maximum net information gain, and this is greater than zero. Therefore, we split the node using this attribute. Figure 10.2 shows the decision tree and the available data using this attribute for splitting.

Next, let's consider the case when the user has a high net worth but isn't interested in watches. Table 10.4 contains the data associated with this case.

	Has purchased items	Purchased
User 2	T	F

Table 10.4   Data when user has high-net-worth individual but is not interested in watches

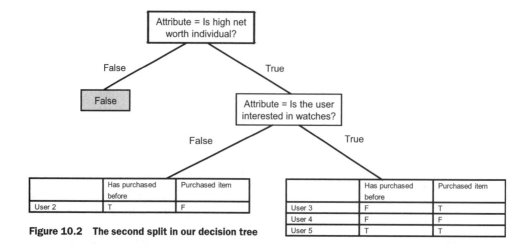

Figure 10.2   The second split in our decision tree

Again, there's only one case, so this falls into the category where all the output cases have the same prediction. Therefore, we can predict that the user won't buy the Rolex watch for this node.

Next, let's consider the case that the user has a high net worth and is interested in watches. Table 10.5 shows the set of data available for this node.

	Has purchased items	Purchased
User 3	F	T
User 4	F	F
User 5	T	T

Table 10.5   Data when user has high-net-worth individual and is interested in watches

First, the information gain by not splitting is Info Gain$(2,1) = 0.92$.

Splitting on the last attribute, *has purchased before*, leads to the following two datasets:

- False with cases {True, False}
- True with case {True}

$$\text{Net Info Gain (attribute = has purchased items before)} = 0.92 - \{(2/3) \text{ gain }(1,1) + (1/3) \text{ gain}(1,0)\}$$
$$= 0.59.$$

It's worthwhile to split on this attribute. Remember, we don't want to over-fit the data. The net information gain associated with splitting on an attribute should be greater than zero.

Figure 10.3 shows the final decision tree. Note that each leaf node can be converted into rules. We can derive the following four rules from the tree by following the paths to the leaf nodes:

1 If the user doesn't have a high net worth then she won't buy the watch.
2 If the user has a high net worth but isn't interested in watches then she won't buy the watch.

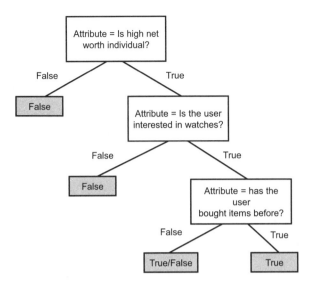

Figure 10.3 The final decision tree for our example

3 If the user has a high net worth and is interested in watches, and has bought items before, then she will buy the watch.

4 If the user has a high net worth and is interested in watches, but hasn't bought items before, then the user might or might not buy the watch, with equal probability.

With these four rules, we can decide whether it's worthwhile to show the Rolex advertisement for a user who's visiting our site. Our click-through rates for this ad should be higher than if we decide randomly whether to show the Rolex ad.

The example we've just worked through uses attributes with binary values. The same ideas are generalized for attributes with more than two discrete values. CART, ID3, C4.5, and C5.0 are some of the common implementations of decision trees. In section 10.2, we use the WEKA libraries to learn decision trees. Next, we use probability theory to build our next classifier, called Naïve Bayes' classifier.

10.1.2 Naïve Bayes' classifier

Before we look at the implementation of the Naïve Bayes' algorithm, we need to understand a few basic concepts related to *probability* theory. First, the probability of a certain event happening is a number between zero and one. The higher the number, the greater the chances of that event occurring. One of the easiest ways to compute an event's probability is to take its frequency count. For example, for the data in table 10.1, in two cases out of five, the individuals bough the watch. Therefore, the probability of a user buying the watch is $2/5 = 0.4$.

Next, let's calculate some probabilities using the data available in table 10.1. We assume that each attribute associated with the user has an underlying probability distribution. By taking the frequency count we have the probabilities shown in table 10.6.

	Value=True	Value=False
High net worth	4/5 = 0.8	1/5 =0.2
Interested in watches	4/5 = 0.8	1/5 = 0.2
Has purchased before	3/5 = 0.6	2/5 = 0.4

Table 10.6   Computing the probabilities

Now, let's find the probability that a user is both a high-net-worth individual and is interested in watches. The last three rows in table 10.1 are of interest to us. Hence, this probability is $3/5 = 0.6$.

What if we wanted to find out the probability that a user is either a high-net-worth individual or is interested in watches (or both)? Again, looking at the data in table 10.1, we're interested in all the rows that have True in either the first or second column. In this case, all five rows are of interest to us, and the associated probability is $5/5 = 1.0$.

But we could have computed the same information by adding the probability of a user being a high-net-worth individual (0.8) and the probability of the user being interested in watches (0.8) and subtracting the probability of both these attributes being present together (0.6):

$$= 0.8 + 0.8 - 0.6 = 1.0$$

More formally, the probability associated with either of the two variables occurring is the sum of their individual probabilities, subtracting the probability of both variables occurring:

$$\Pr\{A \text{ or } B\} = \Pr\{A\} + \Pr\{B\} - \Pr\{A \text{ and } B\}$$

Next, let's say that we want to compute the probability of A and B occurring. This can happen in one of two ways:

- Variable A occurs and then variable B occurs.
- Variable B occurs and then variable A occurs.

We use the notation $\Pr\{B \mid A\}$ to refer to the probability of B occurring, given that A has already occurred. Thus, the probability of A and B occurring can be computed as

$$\Pr\{A \text{ and } B\} = \Pr\{A\}\Pr\{B|A\}$$
$$= \Pr\{B\} \ \Pr\{A|B\}$$

This formula is also known as *Bayes' Rule* and is widely used in probability-based algorithms. Again, it's helpful to work through some concrete numbers to better understand the formulas.

Following this formula:

$$\Pr\{\text{high net worth and interested in watches}\}$$
$$= \Pr\{\text{high net worth}\} \ \Pr\{\text{interested in watches} \mid \text{high net worth}\}$$
$$= \Pr\{\text{interested in watches}\} \ \Pr\{\text{high net worth} \mid \text{interested in watches}\}$$

To compute the conditional probability $\Pr\{\text{interested in watches} \mid \text{high net worth}\}$, we need to look at the bottom four rows that have True in the first column. When the individual has high net worth, in three cases out of four, the user is interested in watches. Hence, the conditional probability is 3/4 = 0.75. Similarly, the conditional probability of the user having a high net worth given that the user is interested in watches is three out of four: 3/4 = 0.75.

Substituting the values, we get

Pr{high net worth and interested in watches}
= 0.8 * 0.75
= 0.8 * 0.75
= 0.6

With this basic overview of probability theory, we're now ready to apply it to the problem of classification. Our aim is to calculate the probability of a user buying a watch, given the values for the other three attributes. We need to shorten the description for the attributes. For the sake of brevity, let's call the three attributes A, B, and C, and the predicted attribute P, as shown in table 10.7.

	Description
A	Is the user a high-net-worth individual?
B	Is the user interested in watches?
C	Has the user bought items before?
P	Will the user buy the watch?

Table 10.7   Shortening the attribute descriptions

Let's assume that a user who has a high net worth, is interested in watches, and has purchased items before is visiting the site. We want to predict the probability that the user will buy the item:

Pr {P=T | A=T,B=T,C=T} = Pr {A=T,B=T, C= T | P = T} Pr{T}/ Pr {A=T,B=T, C= T }
Pr {P=F | A=T,B=T,C=T} = Pr {A=T,B=T, C= T | P = F} Pr{F}/ Pr {A=T,B=T, C= T }

Computing Pr {A=T,B=T, C= T | P = T} is typically not that easy, especially with a large number of attributes and when the learning data is sparse.[2] To simplify matters, we assume that all three attributes are *conditionally independent* of each other, given the output attribute. Therefore, to compute Pr {A=T,B=T, C= T | P = T}, let's first split the examples into two sets based on the value of the output variable, as shown in figure 10.4.

Using the cases where the output attribute is True, we can calculate the following conditional probabilities:

- Pr {A = T | P = T} = 1   - Pr {A = F | P = T} = 0
- Pr {B = T | P = T} = 1   - Pr {B = F | P = T} = 0
- Pr {C = T | P = T} = 1/2   - Pr {C = F | P = T} = 1/2

Similarly, using the cases where the output attribute if False, we can calculate the following conditional probabilities:

- Pr {A = T | P = F} = 2/3   - Pr {A = F | P = F} = 1/3
- Pr {B = T | P = F} = 2/3   - Pr {B = F | P = F} = 1/3
- Pr {C = T | P = F} = 2/3   - Pr {C = F | P = F} = 1/3

---

[2] For example, note that there is no data in our dataset to compute Pr {A=F,B=T, C= T | P = T}.

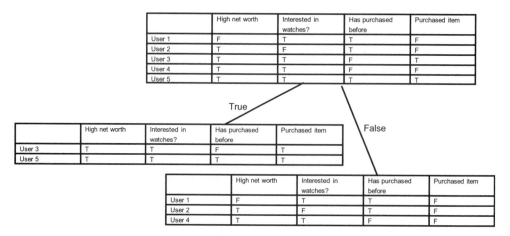

Figure 10.4   Splitting the dataset based on the value of the output attributes to compute the conditional probabilities

Also, the prior probabilities are as follows:

Pr {P = T} = 0.4 and Pr {P = F} = 0.6

Hence, we can calculate Pr {A=T, B=T, C= T | P = T}:

Pr {A=T,B=T, C= T | P = T} = Pr {A=T | P = T} Pr {B=T | P = T} Pr {C=T | P = T}
     = 1 * 1 * (1/2) = (1/2)

Here, we've simply expanded the formula and substituted the known values. Similarly:

Pr {A=T,B=T, C= T | P = F} = Pr {A=T | P = F} Pr {B=T | P=F} Pr{C=T | P=F}
     = (2/3) * (2/3) * (2/3) = 8/27

The likelihood of a user buying the watch can be computed as follows:

Pr {P=T | A=T,B=T,C=T}/ Pr {P=F | A=T,B=T,C=T}
     = Pr {A=T,B=T, C= T | P = T} Pr{T}/ Pr {A=T,B=T, C= T | P = F} Pr{F}
     =(1/2)*(2/5)/ {(8/27)* (3/5))
     = 27/24
     = 9/8

This implies that the user is more likely to buy the watch when all three conditions are met. This prediction is the same as one of the nodes that was derived by the decision tree.

When the conditional independence assumption is used, the algorithm is known as *Naïve Bayes*.

The probability-based approach can handle missing variables. For example, let's say that we don't know whether the individual has a high net worth. In this case, we can calculate the likelihood of the user buying the watch as

Pr {P=T | B=T,C=T}/ Pr {P=F | B=T,C=T}
     = Pr {B=T, C= T | P = T} Pr{T}/ Pr { B=T, C= T | P = F} Pr{F}
     = (1/2)*(2/5)/ {(1/3)*(3/5)}
     = 0.5

In this case, a user is more likely to not buy the watch—a value of 1 would imply an equal chance between buying and not buying. Given that we only have three binary inputs and there are only (23 = 8) cases, we can summarize the probabilities and make a prediction for each case. This is shown in table 10.8.

Table 10.8 The prediction table for our example

High net worth	Interested in watches	Has purchased	Will buy = True	Will buy = False	Prediction
T	T	T	1/5	8/45	Buy
T	T	F	1/5	4/45	Buy
T	F	T	0	4/45	Not Buy
T	F	F	0	2/45	Not Buy
F	T	F	0	4/45	Not Buy
F	T	F	0	2/45	Not Buy
F	F	T	0	2/45	Not Buy
F	F	F	0	1/45	Not Buy

Note that the sum of the probabilities for predicted value being true is = (1/5 + 1/5) = 0.4, and the probability for the predicted value being false is 27/45 = 0.6, which is equal to the *a priori probability*—the probability of the two events occurring in the absence of any evidence. Also, in the second row in table 10.8—when the user has a high net worth and is interested in watches but hasn't bought items before (A = T & B = T & C = F)—the Naïve Bayes' analysis predicts that the user is more likely to buy the watch, with a likelihood of 9/4. You may recall that in the previous section, using the decision tree, the prediction had an equal likelihood of the user buying the watch.

Even though the Naïve Bayes' process is simple, it's known to give results as good as, if not better than, some of the other, more complicated classifiers. The probability-based approach can be generalized and represented using a graph. The resulting network is commonly known as a *Bayesian belief network*, also called *probabilistic reasoning*, which we look at next.

10.1.3 *Belief networks*

Belief networks are a graphical representation for the Naïve Bayes' analysis that we did in the previous section. More formally, a belief network is a *directed acyclic graph (DAG)* where nodes represent random variables, and links between the nodes correspond to conditional dependence between child and parent nodes. Each variable may be discrete, in which case it assumes an arbitrary number of mutually exclusive and collectively exhaustive values, or it may be continuous. The absence of an arrow between two nodes represents conditional independence between the variables. The network is *directed*—there's a direction associated with the nodes—and *acyclic*—there are no cycles between the connections. Each node has a conditional probability table that quantifies the effects that the parents have on the node. The parents of a node are all those nodes that have arrows pointing to them. For our example, belief networks are best illustrated using a graphical representation.

Figure 10.5 shows the belief network for our example. Note the following:

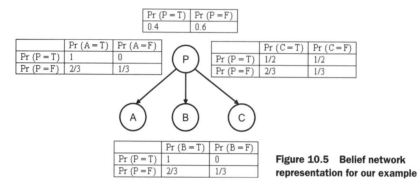

Figure 10.5   Belief network representation for our example

- The arrow from P, the predicted attribute, to the three children nodes A, B, and C implies that when P occurs, it has an effect on each of its children. There's a *causal* or *cause-effect* relationship between the parent and the child node.
- Associated with each variable is a conditional probability table. The node P has no parents and the associated probabilities with the node are known as *a priori* probabilities.
- Given the parent, P, the three children nodes A, B, and C are assumed to be conditionally independent of each other.

In the absence of any additional information about the values for A, B, and C, the network predicts the probability of Pr {P = T} = 0.4. Let's say that we know that the person has a high net worth: A = T. With this new evidence, what's the new probability associated with P? Figure 10.6 shows the belief network associated with this case. There are just two nodes in the network.

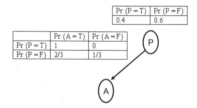

Figure 10.6   The simplified belief network when only A is known

From this, we can compute the following:

Pr {P = T | A = T} = Pr {A = T| P = T} Pr {P = T}/Pr {A = T}
   = 1 * (0.4) / 1. = 0.4

This is the same as when we didn't know whether A was True. However, if we knew that A = False, we can compute the following:

Pr {P = T | A = F} = Pr {A = F| P = T} Pr {P = T}/Pr {A = F}
   = 0 * (0.4) / 1. = 0

Doing the inference in the network to take into account new evidence amounts to applying the Bayes' Rule, and there are well-known algorithms for doing this computation.

Belief networks can be singly or multiply connected. An acyclic graph is *singly connected* if there's at most one chain (or undirected path) between a pair of variables. Networks with undirected cycles are *multiply connected.*

There are a number of inference algorithms for a simply-connected network. There are three basic algorithms for evaluating multiply connected networks: clustering methods, conditioning methods, and stochastic simulation. There are also well-known algorithms for constructing belief networks using test data. Expert-developed belief networks have been used extensively in building knowledge-based systems.

At this point, it's helpful to review the Bayesian interpretation of probability. One prevalent notion of probability is that it's a measure of the frequency with which an event occurs. A different notion of probability is the *degree of belief* held by a person that the event will occur. This interpretation of probability is called *subjective* or *Bayesian* interpretation.

We're done with our Rolex advertisement example. In the next section, we use a new example, classifying blog entries, to illustrate the use of WEKA APIs for classification.

10.2 Classifying blog entries using WEKA APIs

In this section, we build on our example of clustering blog entries from the previous chapter. We demonstrate the process of classification by retrieving blog entries from Technorati on a variety of topics. We categorize the blog entries into two sets—one of interest to us and the other not of interest to us. In this section, we apply a variety of classifiers, using the WEKA APIs to classify the items into the two categories. Later in the chapter, when we deal with regression, we use the same example to build predictors, after converting the attributes into continuous attributes. At the end of this section, you should be familiar with the classification process and the use of WEKA APIs to apply one of many classification algorithms.

Figure 10.7 outlines the four classes that we use in this chapter. You may recall that `BlogDataSetCreatorImpl`, which we developed in section 9.1.2, is used to retrieve blog entries from Technorati. `WEKAPredictiveBlogDataSetCreatorImpl` extends this class and creates the dataset that's used for classification and regression. `WEKABlogClassifier` is a wrapper class to WEKA, which invokes the WEKA APIs to classify blog entries using the dataset created by `WEKAPredictiveBlogDataSetCreatorImpl`. In section 10.5,

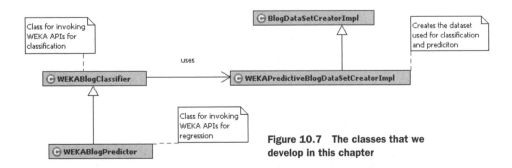

Figure 10.7 The classes that we develop in this chapter

we extend `WEKABlogClassifier` to create `WEKABlogPredictor`, which is used for invoking WEKA regression APIs.

Next, let's look at the implementation for the first of our classes, `WEKAPredictiveBlogDataSetCreatorImpl`.

10.2.1 Building the dataset for classifying blog entries

Classification algorithms typically deal with nominal or discrete attributes, while regression algorithms normally deal with continuous attributes. We build predictive models to predict whether a blog entry is of interest. To create the dataset for learning, we do the following:

1 Retrieve blog entries from Technorati for a set of tags. Blog entries associated with each tag are marked to be either an item of interest or an item in which we aren't interested.

2 Similar to our approach in chapter 9, we parse through the retrieved blog entry to create a term vector representation for each of the blog entries. Each term vector is associated with the predicted value of whether this entry is of interest.

3 Each term vector gets converted into the WEKA `Instance` object. A collection of these `Instance` objects forms the dataset and is represented by the `Instances` object.

4 For nominal attributes, we convert each of the tags into a `Boolean` attribute, which takes a value of `true` if the tag appears in the blog entry and a value of `false` if it's absent. Of course, you can use more sophisticated techniques to discretize the term vector into categorical attributes.

Listing 10.2 shows the first part of the code for `WEKAPredictiveBlogDataSetCreatorImpl`, which deals with creating the dataset with positive and negative test cases.

Listing 10.2 Retrieving blogs

```
package com.alag.ci.blog.dataset.impl;

import java.io.IOException;
import java.util.*;

import weka.core.*;

import com.alag.ci.blog.search.BlogQueryResult;
import com.alag.ci.cluster.TextDataItem;
import com.alag.ci.textanalysis.*;
import com.alag.ci.textanalysis.Tag;

public class WEKAPredictiveBlogDataSetCreatorImpl extends
        BlogDataSetCreatorImpl {
    private List<TextDataItem> blogEntries = null;

    public WEKAPredictiveBlogDataSetCreatorImpl() throws Exception {
    }

    private List<TextDataItem> createLearningDataSet(boolean isContinuous)
        throws Exception {
        String [] positiveTags = { "collective intelligence",
```

```
        "data mining", "web 2.0"};
    String [] negativeTags = { "child intelligence", "AJAX"};
    return createLearningDataSet(positiveTags, negativeTags,
        isContinuous);
}
```

```
private List<TextDataItem> createLearningDataSet(
        String [] positiveTags, String [] negativeTags,
        boolean isContinuous) throws Exception {
    List<TextDataItem> data = new ArrayList<TextDataItem>();
    for (String tag: positiveTags) {
        data.addAll(getBlogData(tag, true));
    }
    for (String tag: negativeTags) {
        data.addAll(getBlogData(tag, false));
    }
    return data;
}
```

> **Creating positive and negative test cases** ←

> **Retrieving data from Technorati**

```
private List<TextDataItem> getBlogData(String tag, boolean isRelevant)
    throws Exception {
    BlogQueryResult bqrCI = getBlogsFromTechnorati(tag);
    return getBlogTagMagnitudeVectors(bqrCI,isRelevant);
}
```
←

```
protected List<TextDataItem> getBlogTagMagnitudeVectors(
        BlogQueryResult blogQueryResult, boolean isRelevant)
         throws IOException {
    List<TextDataItem> tdiList =
        super.getBlogTagMagnitudeVectors(blogQueryResult);
    for (TextDataItem dataItem: tdiList) {
        dataItem.setCiRelated(isRelevant);
    }
    return tdiList;
}
```

To create the dataset, we specify a set of positive and negative test cases. For example, in the code

```
    String [] positiveTags = { "collective intelligence",
        "data mining", "web 2.0"};
    String [] negativeTags = { "child intelligence", "AJAX"};
```

we retrieve blog entries from Technorati using the following tags for the positive cases—*collective intelligence, data mining,* and *web 2.0*—and the following tags for the negative cases—*child intelligence* and *AJAX.*

The method `getBlogData()` uses the specified tag to retrieve relevant blog entries from Technorati, and predicts whether they'll be relevant. Of course, we're really interested in getting a WEKA dataset representation—an instance of `Instances` using the retrieved blog entries. For this, we need to look at listing 10.3.

Listing 10.3   Creating the dataset

```
protected List<TextDataItem> getBlogTagMagnitudeVectors(
        BlogQueryResult blogQueryResult, boolean isRelevant,
        boolean isContinuous) throws IOException {
```

```
        List<TextDataItem> tdiList =
           super.getBlogTagMagnitudeVectors(blogQueryResult);
        for (TextDataItem dataItem: tdiList) {
           dataItem.setCiRelated(isRelevant);
        }
        return tdiList;
    }

    public Instances createLearningDataSet(String datasetName,
        boolean isContinuous) throws Exception {
        this.blogEntries = createLearningDataSet(isContinuous);
        FastVector allAttributes = createAttributes(isContinuous);
        Instances trainingDataSet = new Instances(datasetName,
               allAttributes, blogEntries.size());
        int numAttributes = allAttributes.size();
        Collection<Tag> allTags = this.getAllTags();
        for (TextDataItem dataItem : blogEntries) {
           Instance instance = createNewInstance(numAttributes,
                  trainingDataSet,
                  allTags, dataItem, isContinuous );
           trainingDataSet.add(instance);
        }
        return trainingDataSet;
    }

    protected FastVector createAttributes(boolean isContinuous) {
        Collection<Tag> allTags = this.getAllTags();
        FastVector allAttributes = new FastVector(allTags.size());
        for (Tag tag : allTags) {
           Attribute tagAttribute =
    createAttribute(tag.getDisplayText(),isContinuous);
           allAttributes.addElement(tagAttribute);
        }
      Attribute classificationAttribute =
    createAttribute("ClassificationAttribute",isContinuous);
        allAttributes.addElement(classificationAttribute);
        return allAttributes;
    }
}
```

Creating WEKA dataset for learning

Creating Attribute representation

There's only one public method in the class WEKAPredictiveBlogDataSetCreator-Impl: createLearningDataSet(). This method takes in a name for the dataset and whether we want continuous or discrete attributes. It first retrieves all the blog entries from Technorati, creates an attribute representation, and creates the dataset by converting each blog entry into an Instance object.

The method createAttributes() creates an Attribute representation for each tag by invoking the similarly named createAttribute() method. Details of create-Attribute() are shown in listing 10.4.

Listing 10.4   Creating an Instance in WEKAPredictiveBlogDataSetCreatorImpl

```
private Attribute createAttribute(String attributeName,
    boolean isContinuous) {
    if (isContinuous) {
       return createContinuousAttribute(attributeName);
```

```
    }
    return createBinaryNominalAttribute(attributeName);
}
private Attribute createBinaryNominalAttribute(
    String attributeName) {
    FastVector attNominalValues = new FastVector(2);
    attNominalValues.addElement("true");
    attNominalValues.addElement("false");
    return new Attribute(attributeName,attNominalValues);
}
private Attribute createContinuousAttribute(
    String attributeName) {
    return new Attribute(attributeName);
}

protected Instance createNewInstance(int numAttributes,
        Instances trainingDataSet, Collection<Tag> allTags,
        TextDataItem dataItem,boolean isContinuous) {
    Instance instance = new Instance(numAttributes);
    instance.setDataset(trainingDataSet);
    int index = 0;
    TagMagnitudeVector tmv = dataItem.getTagMagnitudeVector();
    Map<Tag, TagMagnitude> tmvMap = tmv.getTagMagnitudeMap();
    for (Tag tag : allTags) {
        TagMagnitude tm = tmvMap.get(tag);
        if (tm != null) {
            setInstanceValue(instance,index++,tm.getMagnitude(),
                isContinuous);
        } else {
            setInstanceValue(instance,index++,0., isContinuous);
        }
    }
    BlogAnalysisDataItem blog = (BlogAnalysisDataItem) dataItem;
    if (blog.isCiRelated()) {
        setInstanceValue(instance,index, 1., isContinuous);
    } else {
        setInstanceValue(instance,index, 0., isContinuous);
    }
    return instance;
}

private void setInstanceValue(Instance instance, int index,
    double magnitude, boolean isContinuous) {
    if (isContinuous) {
        instance.setValue(index, magnitude);
    } else {
        if (magnitude > 0.) {
            instance.setValue(index, "true");
        } else {
            instance.setValue(index, "false");
        }
    }
}
}
```

Creates binary representation for attribute

Creates continuous representation for attribute

Creates new instance for blog entries

The method `createAttribute()` creates either discrete or continuous attributes based on the isContinuous flag. The method `createNewInstance()` creates a new instance for each blog entry. It iterates over all the tags and sets the instance value through the method `setInstanceValue()`. The value associated with an attribute in an instance is either `true` or `false` for discrete attributes, or the magnitude of the term in the term vector for continuous attributes.

Now that we have a dataset that can be used for learning, let's look at how we can leverage the WEKA APIs to apply various classification algorithms on this dataset.

10.2.2 *Building the classifier class*

In this section, we build a wrapper class for calling the WEKA APIs. `WEKABlogClassifier` is a generic class that, given an `Algorithm`, creates the dataset for learning, creates an instance of the classifier, builds the classifier using the available data, and then evaluates it. Listing 10.5 shows the implementation for the `WEKABlogClassifier` class.

> **Listing 10.5 The implementation of the `WEKABlogClassifier` class**

```
package com.alag.ci.blog.classify.weka.impl;

import java.util.Enumeration;

import weka.classifiers.Classifier;
import weka.classifiers.Evaluation;
import weka.classifiers.bayes.BayesNet;
import weka.classifiers.bayes.NaiveBayesSimple;
import weka.classifiers.functions.LibSVM;
import weka.classifiers.trees.J48;
import weka.core.Instance;
import weka.core.Instances;

import com.alag.ci.blog.dataset.impl.WEKAPredictiveBlogDataSetCreatorImpl;

public class WEKABlogClassifier {
    public enum Algorithm {DECISION_TREE, NAIVE_BAYES, BAYES_NET,
        LINEAR_REGRESSION, MLP, RBF};                                    ◁──

    public void classify(Algorithm algorithm) throws Exception {        ◁──
        Instances instances = createLearningDataset();
        Classifier classifier = getClassifier(instances,algorithm);
        evaluateModel(instances, classifier);
    }

    protected Instances createLearningDataset() throws Exception {
        WEKAPredictiveBlogDataSetCreatorImpl dataSetCreator =
            new WEKAPredictiveBlogDataSetCreatorImpl();
        return dataSetCreator.createLearningDataSet(
          "nominalBlogData",false);
    }

    protected void evaluateModel(Instances instances,
        Classifier classifier)
        throws Exception {
        Evaluation modelEval = new Evaluation(instances);
        modelEval.evaluateModel(classifier, instances);
        System.out.println(modelEval.toSummaryString("\nResults\n", true));
        for (Enumeration e = instances.enumerateInstances() ;
```

Enumeration of some algorithms

Classify using specified algorithm

```
                    e.hasMoreElements() ;) {
                print InstancePrediction((Instance)e.nextElement(),classifier);
            }
        }

    protected void print InstancePrediction(Instance instance,
            Classifier classifier) throws Exception {
        double classification = classifier.classifyInstance(instance);
        System.out.println("Classification = " + classification);
    }

    protected Classifier getClassifier(Instances instances,
        Algorithm algorithm) throws Exception {
        Classifier classifier = getClassifier(algorithm);
        instances.setClassIndex(instances.numAttributes() - 1);
        classifier.buildClassifier(instances);
        return classifier;
    }

    protected Classifier getClassifier(Algorithm algorithm)
        throws Exception {
        Classifier classifier = null;
        if (Algorithm.DECISION_TREE.equals(algorithm)) {
            classifier = new J48();
        } else if (Algorithm.NAIVE_BAYES.equals(algorithm)) {
            classifier = new NaiveBayesSimple() ;
        } else if (Algorithm.BAYES_NET.equals(algorithm)) {
            classifier = new BayesNet() ;
        }
        return classifier;
    }
}
```

(annotation: Last attribute used for prediction — pointing to `instances.setClassIndex(instances.numAttributes() - 1);`)

(annotation: Selecting right algorithm — pointing to `protected Classifier getClassifier(Algorithm algorithm)`)

We first define an enumeration, Algorithm, that contains some of the classifier and regression algorithms supported by WEKA. Note that WEKA supports many more algorithms—more than 50. The method to classify blog entries is fairly straightforward:

```
public void classify(Algorithm algorithm) throws Exception
```

It consists of three steps:

1. Creating the dataset to be used for learning
2. Getting the classifier instance based on the specified algorithm and building the model
3. Evaluating the model that's created

Note that for classification and regression algorithms, you need to specify the predicted output attribute. We do this in the method getClassifier:

```
instances.setClassIndex(instances.numAttributes() - 1);
```

It's helpful to look at the output from our classification process. Listing 10.6 shows the output from one of the runs. It shows a decision tree that correctly classified 55 of the 60 blog entries presented to it. The details of the decision tree are also shown (using System.out.println(((J48)classifier).graph());).

Listing 10.6   Sample output from a decision tree

```
Results
=======

Correctly Classified Instances       55               91.6667 %
Incorrectly Classified Instances     5                8.3333 %
Kappa statistic                      0.8052
Mean absolute error                  0.1425
Root mean squared error              0.267
Relative absolute error              31.9444 %
Root relative squared error          56.6295 %
Total Number of Instances            60

digraph J48Tree {
N0 [label="ci" ]
N0->N1 [label="= true"]
N1 [label="true (6.0)" shape=box style=filled ]
N0->N2 [label="= false"]
N2 [label="review" ]
N2->N3 [label="= true"]
N3 [label="true (3.0)" shape=box style=filled ]
N2->N4 [label="= false"]
N4 [label="machine" ]
N4->N5 [label="= true"]
N5 [label="true (3.0)" shape=box style=filled ]
N4->N6 [label="= false"]
N6 [label="technology" ]
N6->N7 [label="= true"]
N7 [label="true (3.0/1.0)" shape=box style=filled ]
N6->N8 [label="= false"]
N8 [label="web" ]
N8->N9 [label="= true"]
N9 [label="online" ]
N9->N10 [label="= true"]
N10 [label="false (2.0)" shape=box style=filled ]
N9->N11 [label="= false"]
N11 [label="true (2.0)" shape=box style=filled ]
N8->N12 [label="= false"]
N12 [label="false (41.0/4.0)" shape=box style=filled ]
}
```

In this specific example, the root node, N0, is with the term "ci". When the blog contains the term "ci", it gets classified into the node N1, which has a "true" prediction; if the blog doesn't have the term, it leads to node N2. The node N2 has two children nodes, N3 and N4. One can follow down the node hierarchy to visualize the generated decision tree.

Later in section 10.5, we discuss JDM APIs related to the classification process. So far, we've looked at building predictive models for discrete attributes. Next, let's briefly look at building predictive models for continuous attributes.

10.3   *Regression fundamentals*

Perhaps the simplest form of predictive model is to use standard statistical techniques, such as linear or quadratic regression. Unfortunately, not all real-world problems can be modeled as successfully as linear regression; therefore more complicated techniques such as neural networks and support vector machine (SVM) can be used. The process of building regression models is similar to classification algorithms, the one difference being the format of the dataset—for regression, typically all the attributes are continuous. Note that regression algorithms can also be used for classification, where the predicted numeric value is mapped to an appropriate categorical value.

In this section, we briefly review linear regression, and follow with an overview of two commonly used neural networks—the multi-layer perceptron and the radial basis function. In the next section, we use the WEKA APIs for regression.

10.3.1 *Linear regression*

In linear regression, the output value is predicted by summing all values of the input attributes multiplied by a constant. For example, consider a two-dimensional space with x and y axes. We want to build a linear model to predict the y value using x values. This in essence is the representation of a line. Therefore

$$y = a\,x + b$$
$$= [x\ 1]\,[a\ b]^T$$

where a and b are constants that need to be determined.

We can generalize this equation into a higher dimension using a matrix representation. Let Y, A, and X be matrices such that

$$Y = A\,X$$

Note that A^TA is a square matrix. The constant X can be found

$$X = (A^TA)^{-1}\,(A^TY)$$

A concrete example helps to visualize and understand the process of linear regression. To illustrate this process, we use the same example of a Rolex ad that we used earlier in the chapter. Table 10.9 shows the data that we use for our example. This is the same as table 10.1, except that we've converted the `True` values into 1.0 and `False` values into 0. Note the data for rows corresponding to User 3 and User 4—the input attribute values for both cases are the same but the output is different.

Table 10.9 The data used for regression

	High net worth	Interested in watches	Has purchased items	Bought the item
User 1	0	1	1	0
User 2	1	0	1	0
User 3	1	1	0	1
User 4	1	1	0	0
User 5	1	1	1	1

Let, Y be the predicted value, which in our case is whether the user will buy the item or not, and let $x0$, $x1$, $x2$, and $x3$ correspond to the constants that we need to find. Based on the data in table 10.9, we have

$$Y = [0\ 0\ 1\ 0\ 1]^T \qquad X = [x0\ x1\ x2\ x3]^T$$

$$A = \begin{bmatrix} 1\ 0\ 1\ 1 \\ 1\ 1\ 0\ 1 \\ 1\ 1\ 1\ 0 \\ 1\ 1\ 1\ 0 \\ 1\ 1\ 1\ 1 \end{bmatrix} \qquad A^T A = \begin{bmatrix} 1\ 0\ 1\ 1 \\ 1\ 1\ 0\ 1 \\ 1\ 1\ 1\ 0 \\ 1\ 1\ 1\ 0 \\ 1\ 1\ 1\ 1 \end{bmatrix}$$

Note that the matrix $A^T A$ is a square matrix with a number of rows and columns equal to the number of parameters being estimated, which in this case is four.

Now, we need to compute the inverse of the matrix. The inverse of a matrix is such that multiplying the matrix and its inverse gives the identity matrix. Refer to any book on linear algebra on how to compute the inverse of a matrix.[3]

And its inverse is

$$(A^T A)^{-1} = \begin{bmatrix} 6.5 & -3 & -3 & -2.5 \\ -3 & 2 & 1 & 1 \\ -3 & 1 & 2 & 1 \\ -2.5 & 1 & 1 & 1.5 \end{bmatrix}$$

Also, $A^T y = [\ 2\ 2\ 2\ 1]$

Solving for the four constants, we come to the following predictor model:

$$P = -1.5 + 1*A + 1*B + 0.5*C$$

The predicted values for the five cases are shown in table 10.10. Our linear regression–based predictive model does pretty well in predicting whether the user will purchase the item. Note that the predictions for User 3 and User 4 are the average of the two cases in the dataset.

---

[3] Or use an online matrix inverter such as http://www.bluebit.gr/matrix-calculator/ and http://www.uni-bonn.de/~manfear/matrixcalc.php for matrix multiplication. The `weka.core.matrix.Matrix` class in WEKA provides a method to compute the inverse of a matrix.

	Purchased the item	Prediction
User 1	0	0
User 2	0	0
User 3	1	0.5
User 4	0	0.5
User 5	1	1

Table 10.10 The raw and the predicted values using linear regression *(continued)*

Building a predictive model using linear regression is simple, and, based on the data, may provide good results. However, for complex nonlinear problems, linear-regression-based predictive models may have problems generalizing. This is where neural networks come in: They're particularly useful in learning complex functions. Multi-layer perceptron (MLP) and radial basis function (RBF) are the two main types of neural networks, which we look at next.

10.3.2 *Multi-layer perceptron (MLP)*

A multi-layer perceptron has been used extensively for building predictive models. As shown in figure 10.8, an MLP is a fully-connected network in which each node is connected to all the nodes in the next layer. The first layer is known as an *input layer* and the number of nodes in this layer is equal to the number of input attributes. The second layer is known as a *hidden layer* and all nodes from the input layer connect to the hidden layer. In figure 10.8 there are three nodes in the hidden layer.

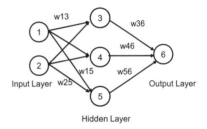

Figure 10.8 A multi-layer perceptron with one hidden layer. The weight Wxy is the weight from node x to node y. For example, W25 is the weight from node 2 to node 5.

The input feeds into each of the first-layer nodes. The output from a node is split into two computations. First, the weighted sum of the input values of a node is calculated. Next, this value is transformed into the output value of the nodes using a nonlinear activation function. Common activation functions are the sigmoid and the tan hyperbolic functions. The advantage of using these activation functions is that their derivatives can be expressed as a function of the output. Also associated with each node is a threshold that corresponds to the minimum total weighted input required for that node to fire an output. It's more convenient to replace the threshold with an extra input weight. An extra input whose activation is kept fixed at -1 is connected to each node. Linear outputs are typically used for the output layer.

For example, the output from node 3 is computed as

Activation function (W13 * value of node 1 + W23 * value of node 2 – W03)

The *back-propagation* algorithm is typically used for training the neural network. The algorithm uses a *gradient search* technique to find the network weight that minimizes the sum-of-square error between the training set and the predicted values. During the training process, the network is initialized with random weights. Example inputs are given to the network; if the network computes an output vector that matches the target, nothing is done. If there's a difference between the output and the target vector, the weights are changed in a way that reduces the error. The method tries to assess blame for the error and distributes the error among contributing weights. The algorithm uses a batch mode, where all examples are shown to the network. The corresponding error is calculated and propagated through the network. A net gradient direction is then defined that equals the sum of the gradients for each example. A step is then taken in the direction opposite to this gradient vector. The step size is chosen such that the error decreases with each step. The back-propagation algorithm normally converges to a local optimal solution; there's no guarantee of a *global solution.*

A neural network with a large number of hidden nodes is in danger of overfitting the data. Therefore, the process of *cross-validation* with a test dataset is used to avoid over-learning. Unlike linear regression, an MLP is a "black box" where it's difficult to interpret the parameters of the network, and consequently it's difficult to understand the rationale of a prediction made by a neural network. An MLP network requires a large amount of time to train the parameters associated with the network, but once the network has been trained, the computation of the output from the network is fast. An MLP works well when the problem space is large and noisy.

Next, let's look at another type of commonly used neural network: radial basis functions.

10.3.3 *Radial basis functions (RBF)*

An RBF, as shown in figure 10.9, consists of two different layers. The inputs feed into a hidden layer. The hidden layer produces a significant nonzero response only when the input vector falls within a small localized region of the input space. The output layer supplies the network's response to the activation patterns applied to the input layer. The transformation from the input space to the hidden unit space is nonlinear, whereas the transformation from the hidden unit space to the output space is

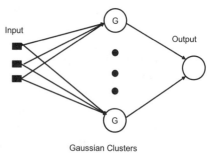

Figure 10.9   **A typical radial basis function**

linear. The most common basis for the hidden nodes is the Gaussian kernel function. The node outputs are in the range of zero to one, so that the closer the input is to the center of the Gaussian cluster, the larger the response of the node. Each node produces an identical output that lies a fixed radial distance from the center of the kernel. The output layer nodes form a weighted linear combination of the outputs from the Gaussian clusters.

Learning in the RBF network is accomplished by breaking the problem into two steps:

1 Unsupervised learning in the hidden layer
2 Supervised learning in the output layer

The k-means algorithm (see section 9.1.3) is typically used for learning the Gaussian clusters. K-means is a greedy algorithm for finding a locally optimal solution, but it generally produces good results and is efficient and simple to implement. Once learning in the hidden layer is completed, learning in the output layer is done using either the back-propagation algorithm or the matrix inversion process we identified in section 10.3.1. The output from the output node is linear. The connection weights to the output node from the Gaussian clusters can be learned using linear regression. One advantage of RBF over MLP is that learning tends to be much faster.

In theory, the RBF network, like the MLP, is capable of forming an arbitrary close approximation to any continuous nonlinear mapping. The primary difference between the two is the nature of their basis functions. The hidden layer in an MLP forms sigmoidal basis functions that are nonzero over an infinitely large region of the input space; the basis functions in the RBF network cover only small localized regions.

With this overview of some of the key regression algorithms, let's look at how to apply regression using the WEKA APIs.

10.4 *Regression using WEKA*

In this section, we use the WEKA APIs to build predictive models using regression. The section is similar to section 10.2; in fact most of the heavy lifting has already been done. As discussed in section 10.2 and in figure 10.7, we simply need to implement `WEKABlogPredictor`, which is shown in listing 10.7.

Listing 10.7   Implementing regression using the WEKA APIs

```
package com.alag.ci.blog.predict.weka.impl;

import weka.classifiers.Classifier;
import weka.classifiers.functions.LinearRegression;
import weka.classifiers.functions.MultilayerPerceptron;
import weka.classifiers.functions.RBFNetwork;
import weka.core.Instance;
import weka.core.Instances;

import com.alag.ci.blog.classify.weka.impl.WEKABlogClassifier;
import com.alag.ci.blog.dataset.impl.WEKAPredictiveBlogDataSetCreatorImpl;

public class WEKABlogPredictor extends WEKABlogClassifier {

   protected Instances createLearningDataset() throws Exception {
     WEKAPredictiveBlogDataSetCreatorImpl dataSetCreator =
       new WEKAPredictiveBlogDataSetCreatorImpl();
     return dataSetCreator.createLearningDataSet(          ⟵  Creating
       "continuousBlogData",true);                              continuous dataset
   }
   protected Classifier getClassifier(Algorithm algorithm)   ⟵  Creating correct
      throws Exception {                                          instance of
      Classifier classifier = null;                              classifier
```

```
        if (WEKABlogClassifier.Algorithm.LINEAR_REGRESSION.
          equals(algorithm)) {
            classifier = new LinearRegression();
        } else if (WEKABlogClassifier.Algorithm.MLP.equals(algorithm)) {
            classifier = new MultilayerPerceptron() ;
        } else if (WEKABlogClassifier.Algorithm.RBF.equals(algorithm)) {
            classifier = new RBFNetwork();
        }
        return classifier;
    }

    protected void printInstancePrediction(Instance instance,
            Classifier classifier) throws Exception {
        double [] prediction =
          classifier.distributionForInstance(instance);
        System.out.print("\nPrediction = " );
        for (double value: prediction) {
            System.out.print(value + ", ");
        }
    }
}
```

We simply need to overwrite two methods from the parent WEKABlogClassifier class. First, in the method createLearningDataset(), we pass in parameters indicating that we want to create continuous attributes. Second, we need to overwrite the getClassifier() method to get the appropriate classifier based on the specified algorithm. The listing shows the code for creating instances for three of the algorithms covered in this chapter: linear regression, MLP, and RBF.

So far we've looked at how we can build predictive models for both the discrete and continuous attributes. Next, let's briefly look at how the standard JDM APIs deal with classification and regression.

10.5 *Classification and regression using JDM*

In this section, we briefly review the key JDM interfaces related to classification and regression algorithms. The javax.datamining.supervised package contains the interfaces for representing the supervised learning model. It also contains subpackages for classification and regression.

This section is analogous to section 9.3, where we covered JDM-related APIs for clustering. This section covers JDM-related APIs for supervised learning—both classification and regression. We begin by looking at the key JDM supervised learning interfaces. This is followed by developing code to build and evaluate predictive models.

10.5.1 *Key JDM supervised learning–related classes*

As shown in figure 10.10, the results from supervised learning create either a ClassificationModel or a RegressionModel. Both models have a common parent, SupervisedModel, which extends Model and is a MiningObject.

For building a supervised learning model, there are two types of settings: SupervisedSettings and SupervisedAlgorithmSettings.

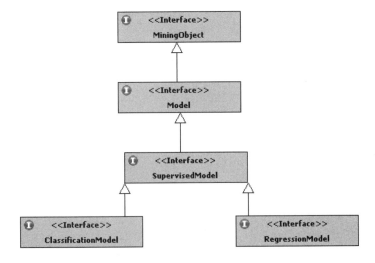

Figure 10.10   The model interfaces corresponding to supervised learning

SupervisedSettings, as shown in figure 10.11, are generic settings associated with the supervised learning process. ClassificationSettings extends this interface to contain generic classification-related settings. It supports methods for setting the cost matrix and prior probabilities that may be used by the classifier. RegressionSettings also extends SupervisedSettings and contains generic regression-related settings.

Settings that are specific to a particular algorithm extend the AlgorithmSettings interface. SupervisedAlgorithmSettings, which extends AlgorithmSettings as shown in figure 10.12, is a common interface for all algorithm-related settings. Feed-ForwardNeuralNetSettings, NaiveBayesSettings, SVMClassificationSettings, SVMRegressionSettings, and TreeSettings are five specific algorithm settings.

Next, let's walk through some sample code that will illustrate the process of creating predictive models using the JDM APIs.

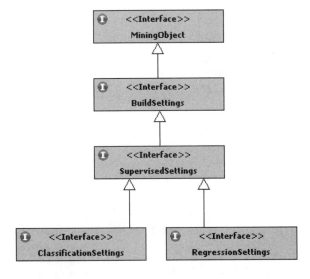

Figure 10.11   Setting interfaces related to supervised learning

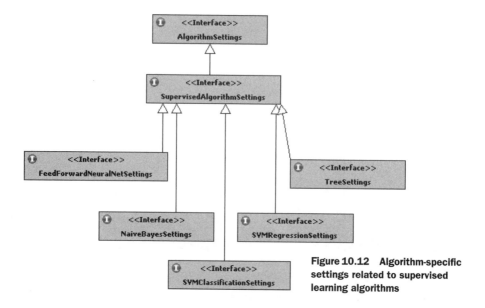

Figure 10.12   Algorithm-specific settings related to supervised learning algorithms

10.5.2 *Supervised learning settings using the JDM APIs*

In this section, we follow an approach similar to section 9.3.2, which illustrated the use of JDM APIs for clustering. The process for regression and classification is similar; we illustrate the process for classification.

We work through an example that has the following five steps:

1 Create the classification settings object.
2 Create the classification task.
3 Execute the classification task.
4 Retrieve the classification model.
5 Test the classification model.

Listing 10.8 shows the code associated with the example and the settings process.

Listing 10.8   Settings-related code for the classification process

```
package com.alag.ci.jdm.classification;

import javax.datamining.*;
import javax.datamining.algorithm.svm.KernelFunction;
import javax.datamining.algorithm.svm.classification.*;
import javax.datamining.resource.Connection;
import javax.datamining.supervised.SupervisedAlgorithmSettings;
import javax.datamining.supervised.classification.*;
import javax.datamining.task.*;

public class JDMClassificationExample {

    public void classify(Connection connection) throws JDMException {
        createClassificationSettings(connection);
        createClassificationTask(connection);
        executeClassificationTask(connection);
```

Four steps associated with example

```
        retrieveClassificationModel(connection);
        testClassificationModel(connection);
    }

    private void createClassificationSettings(Connection connection)
        throws JDMException {
        ClassificationSettingsFactory classifSettingsFactory =
            (ClassificationSettingsFactory)
        connection.getFactory(
    "javax.datamining.supervised.
                classification.ClassificationSettingsFactory");
        ClassificationSettings classificationSettings =
        classifSettingsFactory.create();
        classificationSettings.setCostMatrixName("costMatrixName");
        classificationSettings.setTargetAttributeName(
            "targetAttributeName");

        SupervisedAlgorithmSettings algorithmSettings =
        createSVMClassificationSettings(connection);
        classificationSettings.setAlgorithmSettings(algorithmSettings);
        connection.saveObject("classificationSettings",
            classificationSettings, false);
    }

    private SupervisedAlgorithmSettings
            createSVMClassificationSettings(Connection
            connection) throws JDMException {
        SVMClassificationSettingsFactory svmClassificationSettingsFactory =
            (SVMClassificationSettingsFactory)
        connection.getFactory(
            "javax.datamining.algorithm.svm.
            classification.SVMClassificationSettingsFactory");
        SVMClassificationSettings svmSettings =
            svmClassificationSettingsFactory.create();
        svmSettings.setKernelFunction(KernelFunction.kGaussian);
        return svmSettings;
    }
```

(annotation) **Classification process-related settings**

(annotation) **Algorithm-specific settings**

The example first creates an instance of `ClassificationSettings` and sets attributes associated with the classification process. For this, it sets the cost matrix and the name of the target attribute:

```
classificationSettings.setCostMatrixName("costMatrixName");
classificationSettings.setTargetAttributeName("targetAttributeName");
```

Next, an instance of `SVMClassificationSettings` is created to specify settings specific to the SVM classification algorithm. Here, the kernel function is specified to be Gaussian:

```
svmSettings.setKernelFunction(KernelFunction.kGaussian);
```

The algorithm settings are set in the `ClusteringSettings` instance:

```
classificationSettings.setAlgorithmSettings(algorithmSettings);
```

Next, let's look at creating the classification task.

10.5.3 *Creating the classification task using the JDM APIs*

To create an instance of BuildTask for clustering, we use the BuildTaskFactory as shown in listing 10.9.

Listing 10.9 Create the classification task

```
private void createClassificationTask(Connection connection)
  throws JDMException {
  BuildTaskFactory buildTaskFactory = (BuildTaskFactory)
    connection.getFactory(
    "javax.datamining.task.BuildTaskFactory");
  BuildTask buildTask = buildTaskFactory.create(
    "buildDataPhysicalDataSet",
      "classificationSettings", "classificationModel");
  connection.saveObject("classificationBuildTask", buildTask, false);
}
```

The BuildTaskFactory creates an instance of the BuildTask. The create() method to create a BuildTask needs the name of the dataset to be used, the name of the settings object, and the name of the model to be created. In our example, we use the dataset buildDataPhysicalDataSet, the setting specified in the object classificationSettings, and the model name classificationModel.

10.5.4 *Executing the classification task using the JDM APIs*

To execute a build task, we use the execute method on the Connection object, as shown in listing 10.10.

Listing 10.10 Execute the classification task

```
private void executeClassificationTask(Connection connection)
    throws JDMException {
  ExecutionHandle executionHandle =
  connection.execute("classificationBuildTask");
  int timeoutInSeconds = 100;
  ExecutionStatus executionStatus = executionHandle.
    waitForCompletion(timeoutInSeconds);
  executionStatus = executionHandle.getLatestStatus();
  if (ExecutionState.success.equals(executionStatus.getState())) {
    //successful state
  }
}
```

The code

```
ExecutionStatus executionStatus =
executionHandle.waitForCompletion(timeoutInSeconds);
```

waits for the completion of the classification task and specifies a timeout of 100 seconds. Once the task completes, it looks at execution status to see if the task was successful.

Next, let's look at how we can retrieve the classification model that has been created.

10.5.5 *Retrieving the classification model using the JDM APIs*

Listing 10.11 shows the code associated with retrieving a ClassificationModel using the name of the model and a Connection instance.

Listing 10.11   Retrieving the classification model

```
private void retrieveClassificationModel(Connection connection)
    throws JDMException {
  ClassificationModel classificationModel = (ClassificationModel)
    connection.retrieveObject("classificationModel",
    NamedObject.model);
  double classificationError = classificationModel.
    getClassificationError();
  }
}
```

Once a ClassificationModel is retrieved, we can evaluate the quality of the solution using the getClassificationError() method, which returns the percentage of incorrect predictions by the model.

10.5.6 *Retrieving the classification model using the JDM APIs*

Listing 10.12 shows the code to compute the test metrics associated with the classification model.

Listing 10.12   Testing the classification model

```
private void testClassificationModel(Connection connection)
    throws JDMException {
  ClassificationTestTaskFactory testTaskFactory =
    (ClassificationTestTaskFactory)connection.getFactory(
    "javax.datamining.supervised.classification.ClassificationTestTask");

  ClassificationTestTask classificationTestTask =
    testTaskFactory.create("testDataName", "classificationModel",
    "testResultName");
  classificationTestTask.computeMetric(
    ClassificationTestMetricOption.confusionMatrix);
  }
```

The ClassificationTestTask is used to test a classification model to measure its quality. In this example, we're testing the confusion matrix—a two-dimensional matrix that indicates the number of correct and incorrect predications a classification algorithm has made.

The JDM specification contains additional details on applying the model; for more details on this, please refer to the JDM specification.

In this section, we've looked at the key interfaces associated with supervised learning and the JDM APIs. We've looked at some sample code associated with creating classification settings, creating and executing a classification task, retrieving the classification model, and testing the classification model.

10.6   *Summary*

In your application, you'll come across a number of cases where you want to build a predictive model. The prediction may be in the form of automatically segmenting content or users, or predicting unknown attributes of a user or content.

Predictive modeling consists of creating a mathematical model to predict an output attribute using other input attributes. Predictive modeling is a kind of supervised learning where the algorithm uses training examples to build the model. There are two kinds of predictive models based on whether the output attribute is discrete or continuous. Classification models predict discrete attributes, while regression models predict continuous attributes.

A decision tree is perhaps one of the simplest and most commonly used predictive models. Decision tree learning algorithms use the concept of information gain to identify the next attribute to be used for splitting on a node. Decision trees can be easily converted into if-then rules. The Naïve Bayes' classifier uses concepts from probability theory to build a predictive model. To simplify matters, it assumes that given the output, each of the input attributes are conditionally independent of the others. Although this assumption may not be true, in practice it often produces good results. Bayes' networks or probabilistic reasoning provide a graphical representation for probability-based inference. Bayes' networks deal well with missing data.

In linear regression, the output attribute is assumed to be a linear combination of the input attributes. Typically, the process of learning the model constants involves matrix manipulation and inversion. MLP and RBF are two types of neural networks that provide good predictive capabilities in nonlinear space.

The WEKA package has a number of supervised learning algorithms, both for classification and regression. The process of classification consists of first creating an instance of `Instances` to represent the dataset, followed by creating an instance of a `Classifier` and using an `Evaluation` to evaluate the classification results.

The process of classification and regression using the JDM APIs is similar. Classification with the JDM APIs involves creating a `ClassificationSettings` instance, creating and executing a `ClassificationTask`, and retrieving the `ClassificationModel` that's created.

Now that we have a good understanding of classification and regression, in the next chapter we look at intelligent search.

10.7   *Resources*

Alag, Satnam. *A Bayesian Decision-Theoretic Framework for Real-Time Monitoring and Diagnosis.* 1996. Ph.D dissertation. University of California, Berkeley.

Jensen, Finn. *An Introduction to Bayesian Networks.* 1996. Springer-Verlag.

Quinlan, J. Ross. *C4.5: Programs for Machine Learning.* 1993. Morgan Kaufmann Series in Machine Learning.

Russel, Stuart J. and Peter Norvig. *Artificial Intelligence: A Modern Approach.* 2002. Prentice Hall.

Tan, Pang-Ning, Michael Steinbach, and Vipin Kumar. *Introduction to Data Mining.* 2005. Addison Wesley.

Witten, Ian H. and Eibe Frank. *Data Mining: Practical Machine Learning Tools and Techniques, Second Edition.* 2005. Morgan Kaufmann Series in Data Management Systems.

Part 3

Applying intelligence in your application

In this last part of the book, we focus on applying some of the concepts that we've developed throughout the book. Part 3 consists of two chapters: the first on intelligent search, and the second on building a recommendation engine.

Chapter 11 on intelligent search should give you a good overview of embedding search into your application using Lucene, along with some discussion of trends in the area of intelligent search. Chapter 12 deals with building a recommendation engine using both content-based and collaborative-based approaches. We also go through real-world case studies of personalization by Amazon, Google News, and Netflix.

Intelligent search

11

This chapter covers

- Understanding search fundamentals
- Indexing and searching using Lucene
- Useful tools and framework for intelligent search
- Six trends in the area of intelligent search

Search is ubiquitous and a multi-billion-dollar business. According to Nielsen Net Ratings, in the month of July 2008, an estimated 4.8 billion searches[1] were carried out by Google. This amounted to 60 percent of all searches performed in the US during this period. There's hardly any application now that doesn't provide a search capability within the application. In this chapter, we look at how you can add search capabilities to your application using Lucene and how you can make the search intelligent.

If you haven't done so, it's worthwhile to review chapter 6. In that chapter, we looked at intelligent web crawling using Nutch, which uses Lucene. As a precursor to this chapter, you should have also reviewed chapter 8, in which we introduced the various Lucene analyzers and the fundamentals of text parsing.

---

[1] http://www.nielsen-netratings.com/pr/pr_080819_3.pdf

We begin the chapter by looking at some of the fundamental concepts related to text search. We briefly review the process of creating an index and searching the index with Lucene. After that, we take a deeper look at indexing. Then we review the process of searching with Lucene and some of the advanced search concepts that we later use in the section about intelligent search. We look at some useful search-related tools and frameworks. Finally, we look at how search within your application can be made more intelligent and personalized for the user. At the end of this chapter, you should be able to add search to your application, make it intelligent, and personalize it for the user.

11.1   Search fundamentals

Given a query—a keyword or a phrase—search is the process of retrieving documents that are relevant to the query. The list of documents is generally returned in the order of how relevant they are to the query. You're already familiar with term vectors; in essence, search is the process of creating a term-vector representation for the query and retrieving documents whose term vector is most similar to that of the query term vector. Of course, we want the results to return quickly, and to make our search service scalable so that it can handle multiple simultaneous queries.

Recall and *precision* are two commonly used metrics to quantify the quality of search results—this is similar to evaluating the quality of documents retrieved by a crawler, as discussed in chapter 6. Recall is the percentage of relevant documents that were returned, while precision is the percentage of documents that you found relevant. For example, if there are 10 relevant documents and a search result returned 8 results, 5 of which were relevant, then recall is $5/10 = 50\%$, while precision is $5/8 = 62.5\%$. Furthermore, we want to make our search intelligent by using additional contextual information, such as the user's interests.

Manning has an excellent book on Lucene, *Lucene in Action*, by Gospodnetic and Hatcher. This book is a must read if you're going to be doing any serious work with Lucene in your application.

In this section, we briefly introduce some of the key search concepts. We review the key Lucene classes that will be used and end the section by implementing an example that demonstrates the search process. We begin with a brief introduction reviewing the process involved in adding search to your application. This is followed by looking at some of the core Lucene classes and working through an example.

11.1.1   Search architecture

As shown in figure 11.1, there are four entities involved in adding search to your application: documents to be indexed, an asynchronous indexing service, the search index, and a synchronous query service.

There are two main services that you need to build to add search to your application. First is an asynchronous indexing service, which is responsible for creating a search index—a reverse index of terms with related documents. Depending on the

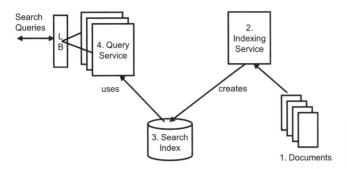

Figure 11.1 The entities involved with adding search to your application

size of your documents, it may take a long time to create a full index, and this process is typically done offline or asynchronously. Once a search index has been created, this service may update the index, either through periodic polling for document changes or by being notified of changes through an event notification. The indexing service is responsible for keeping the search index created up-to-date.

The second service is the query or search service. This service is responsible for taking a user query and converting it into an appropriate term-vector representation and retrieving relevant documents from the search index. This search service is stateless—it receives a query and returns a response back, without holding on to any state information—which makes it possible to have multiple instances of this service servicing client requests. The service can be collocated in the same JVM as your web application, or it may be distributed on remote machines. Having multiple instances of the stateless search services, front-ended with a load balancer and servicing requests over HTTP, is a common architecture used to deploy search services. In this architecture, as load increases, more instances of the service are added to the load balancer.

With that brief overview, let's look at some of the core classes that are used for indexing and searching using Lucene.

11.1.2 *Core Lucene classes*

As shown in figure 11.2, `IndexWriter` is the main class for creating and maintaining a Lucene index. An `IndexWriter` uses a `Directory` object to create an index. It also uses an `Analyzer` (refer to section 8.1) to analyze documents. A `Document` is a set of fields with a name and a textual value. Each field should correspond to information that you'll search against or display in the search results. Documents are atomic entities that are added to an index and retrieved from the index through search. Not all documents in an index need have the same set of fields. Also, the weight associated with each document or field for searching can be different, using a process known as *boosting*.

The `IndexReader` class contains methods for deleting `Document` instances from the index. At any given time, only one thread, either `IndexReader` or `IndexWriter`, should modify an index. If you look at the source of the `IndexWriter` and `IndexReader`, you'll find a number of synchronized checks that ensure that the same instance can be shared across multiple threads. An `IndexReader` is unaware of any changes to the index once it's been opened; you may need to periodically reopen it to see any changes made after it was opened.

A QueryParser uses an Analyzer—this should be the same as the one used for indexing—to convert a user query into a Query object. An instance of a Searcher then uses this Query to search through the search index to return a Hits object. It's safe to have multiple search queries—read-only operations—executed on an index in parallel, even while an index is being created or modified by a different thread.

The search index is accessed using the Directory object. The Hits object contains by composition a number of Hit objects. Each Hit object provides access to the underlying document. Figure 11.2 shows two types of the Searcher—the IndexSearcher for searching a single index and the MultiSearcher for searching through multiple indexes sequentially. ParallelMultiSearcher searches multiple indexes in parallel. Figure 11.2 also shows two kinds of Directory classes—the first, FSDirectory, is used for storing the index on the file system, while the second one, RAMDirectory, is used for creating an in-memory index. The in-memory index is useful for writing tests, whereas the index is created as a part of the test and then destroyed at the end of the test. Since RAMDirectory does everything in memory, it's much faster than FSDirectory and can also be used for services that require fast performance, such as an auto-complete service.

Next, let's put these core classes into action. We illustrate the basic process of indexing and searching by applying it to an example.

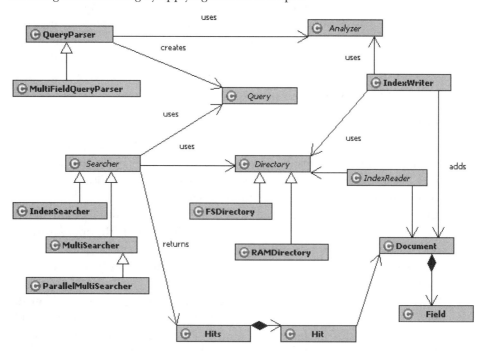

Figure 11.2   The key Lucene classes for creating and searching an index

11.1.3 *Basic indexing and searching via example*

We build on our example from the previous chapters of retrieving blog entries from the blogosphere using Technorati. We first create an index of all the blog entries we've retrieved and then search through them using the Lucene APIs. If you haven't done so, it'll be worthwhile to review chapter 5 and section 9.1.2, which contains the implementation for `BlogDataSetCreatorImpl`. `BlogDataSetCreatorImpl` is used in this example to retrieve data from the blogosphere.

This example is split into three main parts and relates to the steps shown in figure 11.1:

1 Retrieving blog data from the blogosphere
2 Creating a Lucene index using the blog entries
3 Searching the Lucene index for certain phrases

We implement a class called `BlogSearchExample` for this section. The code for this class is split into three parts, one for each of the three parts. At this stage it's helpful to look at listing 11.1, which shows the main method for the `BlogSearchExample`.

Listing 11.1 The main method for the `BlogSearchExample`

```
public static void main(String [] args) throws Exception {
    BlogSearchExample bs = new BlogSearchExample();
    String tag = "collective intelligence";
    String luceneIndexPath = "blogSearchIndex";

    BlogQueryResult blogQueryResult =
        bs.getBlogsFromTechnorati(tag);          ◁──┤ Retrieve blog entries
    Directory indexDirectory = bs.createSearchIndex(luceneIndexPath,
        blogQueryResult);                        ◁── Create search index
    bs.searchForBlogs(indexDirectory, tag);      ◁──┐
}                                                   │ Search for blog entries
```

The main method consists of three main lines of code, corresponding to the three parts enumerated previously.

RETRIEVING BLOG ENTRIES FROM TECHNORATI

Listing 11.2 shows the first part of the code for `BlogSearchExample`, which deals with retrieving blog entries from Technorati.

Listing 11.2 Retrieving blog entries from Technorati

```
package com.alag.ci.search.lucene;

import java.io.IOException;
import java.util.*;

import org.apache.lucene.analysis.Analyzer;
import org.apache.lucene.document.*;
import org.apache.lucene.index.IndexWriter;
import org.apache.lucene.queryParser.QueryParser;
import org.apache.lucene.search.*;
import org.apache.lucene.store.Directory;
```

```
import com.alag.ci.blog.dataset.impl.BlogDataSetCreatorImpl;
import com.alag.ci.blog.search.*;
import com.alag.ci.textanalysis.lucene.impl.*;

public class BlogSearchExample {

    public BlogQueryResult getBlogsFromTechnorati(String tag)
        throws BlogSearcherException {
        return (new BlogDataSetCreatorImpl()).getBlogsFromTechnorati(tag);
    }
```

To retrieve data from Technorati, we use `BlogDataSetCreatorImpl`, which we developed in section 9.1.2 and listing 9.6. The method `getBlogsFromTechnorati` returns a `BlogQueryResult` object using the passed-in tag. Next, let's look at how this data is converted into a search index.

CREATING A SEARCH INDEX

Listing 11.3 shows the next part of the code for `BlogSearchExample`, which deals with creating a search index.

Listing 11.3 Creating a search index

```
public Directory createSearchIndex(String path,          Create
    BlogQueryResult blogQueryResult) throws  Exception{    IndexWriter
    IndexWriter indexWriter = new IndexWriter(path,        using
        getAnalyzer(), true);                              specified path

    indexWriter.setUseCompoundFile(false);    ←— Don't use compound file
    Directory indexDirectory = indexWriter.getDirectory();
    indexBlogEntries(indexWriter,                          Add blog
        blogQueryResult.getRelevantBlogs());               entries to index
    System.out.println("Number of docs indexed = " +
        indexWriter.docCount());
    indexWriter.optimize();
    indexWriter.close();    ←—┐ Optimize and
    return indexDirectory;     │ close index
}

private void indexBlogEntries(IndexWriter indexWriter,
    List<RetrievedBlogEntry> blogEntries) throws Exception {
    int count = 1;
    for (RetrievedBlogEntry blogEntry: blogEntries) {
        indexWriter.addDocument(getDocument(blogEntry));
        System.out.println("" + count ++ + blogEntry + "\n");
    }
}

private Document getDocument(RetrievedBlogEntry blogEntry) {
    Document document = new Document();
    BlogDataSetCreatorImpl dataSetCreator =               Create field with
        new BlogDataSetCreatorImpl();                     complete text
    String completeText = dataSetCreator.composeTextForAnalysis(
        blogEntry);
    addField(document,"completeText",completeText, Field.Store.YES,
        Field.Index.TOKENIZED , Field.TermVector.YES);   ←—
    addField(document,"name",blogEntry.getName(), Field.Store.YES,
```

```
            Field.Index.TOKENIZED , Field.TermVector.YES);
        addField(document,"title",blogEntry.getTitle(), Field.Store.YES,
            Field.Index.TOKENIZED , Field.TermVector.YES);
        addField(document,"excerpt",blogEntry.getExcerpt(),
            Field.Store.YES,
            Field.Index.TOKENIZED , Field.TermVector.YES);
        addField(document,"url",blogEntry.getUrl(), Field.Store.YES,
            Field.Index.UN_TOKENIZED , Field.TermVector.YES);
        addField(document,"author",blogEntry.getAuthor(), Field.Store.NO,
            Field.Index.UN_TOKENIZED , Field.TermVector.YES);
        return document;
    }

  private void addField(Document document, String fieldName,String value,
        Field.Store fieldStore, Field.Index fieldIndex,
        Field.TermVector fieldTermVector) {
     Field field = new Field(fieldName, getNotNullValue(value),
         fieldStore, fieldIndex, fieldTermVector);
     document.add(field);
   }

   private String getNotNullValue(String s) {
      if (s != null) {
        return s;
      }
      return "";
   }                                              Custom Analyzer
                                                  from section 8.1.4
   private Analyzer getAnalyzer() throws IOException {    ◄─────
      return new SynonymPhraseStopWordAnalyzer(
          new SynonymsCacheImpl(),new PhrasesCacheImpl());
   }
```

We first create an instance of the `IndexWriter` using the specified directory path name and the `Analyzer`. The last parameter, `true`, specifies that it's okay to create the index or overwrite the existing one. Passing in `false` would've appended to an existing index:

```
IndexWriter indexWriter = new IndexWriter(path, getAnalyzer(), true);
```

Note that we use the `SynonymPhraseStopWordAnalyzer`, which we developed in section 8.1.4. The following code

```
indexWriter.setUseCompoundFile(false);
```

implies that we don't want to use compound files. If it had been turned on, it would signify that multiple files for each segment would be merged into a single file when a new segment is flushed. Refer to http://lucene.apache.org/java/docs/fileformats.html if you're interested in learning more about the Lucene index format.

The following line of code

```
indexBlogEntries(indexWriter, blogQueryResult.getRelevantBlogs());
```

iterates over each blog entry, creates a document, and adds it to the index. The method `getDocument()` creates a `Document` object from a blog entry. For each blog entry, we first create a `Field` using the complete text representation for the blog entry:

```
String completeText = dataSetCreator.composeTextForAnalysis(
        blogEntry);
```

To create the `Field`:

```
Field field = new Field(fieldName, getNotNullValue(value),
        Field.Store.YES, fieldIndex, fieldTermVector);
```

We specify the field name, set a non-null value and specify whether the field is to be stored in the index and whether it's to be tokenized, and whether we want to store the term vector for that field in the index. Storing a field implies that the content of the field will be literally stored in the index and can be retrieved later from search results. A field that isn't stored is still indexed by Lucene. Note that we don't tokenize the URL. `Fields` that are tokenized (`Field.Index.TOKENIZED`) can't be used for sorting the results obtained by querying the index. So if you plan to use Lucene for sorting the results using a sort order other than relevance, you need to add a field that's `Field.Index.UN_TOKENIZED`. Setting the option to `Field.Index.NO` implies that the value of the field won't be indexed by Lucene. When the `document.add()` method is called multiple times with the same field name but different value objects, Lucene internally will concatenate all the values together for that particular field. As a rule of thumb, in most applications, you want to store all the parameters that you'll show in your search results. This typically includes title, URL, and abstract; avoid having to make a database call to show each of the results in your search results page. Try to retrieve all the information that's displayed from Lucene.

Once all the blog entries have been added to the index, we print out the number of entries added to the index using `indexWriter.docCount()`. Lastly, we optimize and close the index using

```
indexWriter.optimize();
    indexWriter.close();
```

Listing 11.4 shows sample output from the code for one of the runs.

Listing 11.4 Sample output from indexing the blogs

```
1 Name: Wikinomics
Url: http://204.15.36.163:8080/blog
Title: Is Digg Making Us Dumber?
Excerpt: If you started reading this post based on the title, you've
already half proven the point I'm about to argue. Sensationalism
combined with social med
LastUpdateTime: Mon Feb 25 20:03:23 PST 2008

2 Name: Wikinomics
Url: http://www.wikinomics.com/blog
Title: Is Digg Making Us Dumber?
Excerpt: If you started reading this post based on the title, you've
already half proven the point I'm about
```

```
LastUpdateTime: Tue Feb 26 06:19:03 PST 2008

3 Name: BSG Alliance - Next Generation Enterprises. On Demand.
Url: http://www.bsgalliance.com
Title: Is Digg Making Us Dumber?
Excerpt: Citation - content was aggregated by Kalivo Listener from 3rd
party: Credited Author: Naumi Haque So
LastUpdateTime: Mon Feb 25 22:40:00 PST 2008

4 Name: Social Media Explorer
Url: http://www.socialmediaexplorer.com
Title: Exploring Social Media Measurement: Collective Intellect
Excerpt:  This entry in our ongoing exploration of social media
measurement firms focuses on Collective Intel
LastUpdateTime: Mon Feb 25 11:00:53 PST 2008
Author: Jason Falls

..........

10 Name: Et si l'on parlait Marketing
Url: http://henrikaufman.typepad.com/et_si_lon_parlait_marketi
Title: Imagination 3.0
Excerpt:  En Octobre 2007, j'avais analysé l'excellent livre de mon ami
Brice Auckenthaler : L'Imagination C
LastUpdateTime: Mon Feb 25 23:22:20 PST 2008
```

That's it! We've added all the blog entries to our index and we can now search the index.

SEARCHING THE INDEX

Searching the index using a query is fairly straightforward. Listing 11.5 shows the third part of the code for this example, which deals with searching the index.

Listing 11.5 Searching the index

```
public void searchForBlogs(Directory directory, String queryString)
  throws Exception {
    IndexSearcher indexSearcher =
      new IndexSearcher(directory);      ◁── Create instance of IndexSearcher
    QueryParser queryParser = new QueryParser(
      "completeText",getAnalyzer());     ◁── Create instance of QueryParser
    Query query =
      queryParser.parse(queryString);    ◁── Create Query from QueryParser
    Hits hits =
      indexSearcher.search(query);       ◁── Retrieve Hits from IndexSearcher
    System.out.println("Number of results = " + hits.length() +
        " for " + queryString);
    Iterator iterator = hits.iterator();
    while (iterator.hasNext()) {                        Retrieve
        Hit hit = (Hit) iterator.next();                Document from
        Document document = hit.getDocument();    ◁──┘  Hit object
        System.out.println(document.get("completeText"));

        Explanation explanation = indexSearcher.explain(weight,
            hit.getId());                                     Explain
        System.out.println(explanation.toString());          query
                                                             result
```

```
        }
    }
    indexSearcher.close();
}
```

We first create an instance of the `IndexSearcher` using the `Directory` that was passed in to the index. Alternatively, you can use the path to the index to create an instance of a `Directory` using the static method in `FSDirectory`:

```
Directory directory = FSDirectory.getDirectory(luceneIndexPath);
```

Next, we create an instance of the `QueryParser` using the same analyzer that we used for indexing. The first parameter in the `QueryParser` specifies the name of the default field to be used for searching. For this we specify the completeText field that we created during indexing. Alternatively, one could use `MultiFieldQueryParser` to search across multiple fields. Next, we create a `Query` object using the query string and the `QueryParser`. To search the index, we simply invoke the search method in the `Index-Searcher`:

```
Hits hits = indexSearcher.search(query);
```

The `Hits` object holds the ranked list of resulting documents. It has a method to return an `Iterator` over all the instances, along with retrieving a document based on the resulting index. You can also get the number of results returned using `hits.length()`. For each of the returned documents, we print out the title and excerpt fields using the `get()` method on the document. Note that in this example, we know that the number of returned blog entries is small. In general, you should iterate over only the hits that you need. Iterating over all hits may cause performance issues. If you need to iterate over many or all hits, you should use a `HitCollector`, as shown later in section 11.3.7.

The following code demonstrates how Lucene scored the document for the query:

```
Explanation explanation = indexSearcher.explain(weight, hit.getId());
```

We discuss this in more detail in section 11.3.1.

It is useful to look at listing 11.6, which shows sample output from running the example. Note that your output will be different based on when you run the example—it's a function of whichever blog entries on collective intelligence have been created in the blogosphere around the time you run the program.

Listing 11.6   Sample output from our example

```
Number of docs indexed = 10
Number of results = 3 for collective intelligence
Collective Knowing  Gates of the Future       From the Middle    I
recently wrote an article on collective intelligence that I will share h
0.8109757 = (MATCH) sum of:
  0.35089532 = (MATCH) weight(completeText:collective in 7), product of:
    0.5919065 = queryWeight(completeText:collective), product of:
      1.9162908 = idf(docFreq=3)
```

```
        0.30888134 = queryNorm
      0.5928222 = (MATCH) fieldWeight(completeText:collective in 7),
  product of:
        1.4142135 = tf(termFreq(completeText:collective)=2)
        1.9162908 = idf(docFreq=3)
        0.21875 = fieldNorm(field=completeText, doc=7)
     0.46008033 = (MATCH) weight(completeText:intelligence in 7), product of:
      0.80600667 = queryWeight(completeText:intelligence), product of:
        2.609438 = idf(docFreq=1)
        0.30888134 = queryNorm
      0.57081455 = (MATCH) fieldWeight(completeText:intelligence in 7),
  product of:
        1.0 = tf(termFreq(completeText:intelligence)=1)
        2.609438 = idf(docFreq=1)
        0.21875 = fieldNorm(field=completeText, doc=7)

Exploring Social Media Measurement: Collective Intellect Social Media
Explorer Jason Falls  This entry in our ongoing exploration of
social media measurement firms focuses on Collective Intel
0.1503837 = (MATCH) product of:
  0.3007674 = (MATCH) sum of:
    0.3007674 = (MATCH) weight(completeText:collective in 3), product of:
      0.5919065 = queryWeight(completeText:collective), product of:
        1.9162908 = idf(docFreq=3)
        0.30888134 = queryNorm
      0.5081333 = (MATCH) fieldWeight(completeText:collective in 3),
         product of:
        1.4142135 = tf(termFreq(completeText:collective)=2)
        1.9162908 = idf(docFreq=3)
        0.1875 = fieldNorm(field=completeText, doc=3)
  0.5 = coord(1/2)

Boites a idées et ingeniosité collective Le perfologue, le blog pro de
la performance et du techno management en entreprise. Alain Fernandez
Alain Fernandez Les boîte à idées de new génération  Pour capter
l'ingéniosité collective, passez donc de la boîte à
0.1002558 = (MATCH) product of:
  0.2005116 = (MATCH) sum of:
    0.2005116 = (MATCH) weight(completeText:collective in 4), product of:
      0.5919065 = queryWeight(completeText:collective), product of:
        1.9162908 = idf(docFreq=3)
        0.30888134 = queryNorm
      0.33875555 = (MATCH) fieldWeight(completeText:collective in 4),
    product of:
        1.4142135 = tf(termFreq(completeText:collective)=2)
        1.9162908 = idf(docFreq=3)
        0.125 = fieldNorm(field=completeText, doc=4)
  0.5 = coord(1/2)
```

As expected, 10 documents were retrieved from Technorati and indexed. One of them had *collective intelligence* appear in the retrieved text and was ranked the highest, while the other two contained the term *collective*.

This completes our overview and example of the basic Lucene classes. You should have a good understanding of what's required to create a Lucene index and for searching the index. Next, let's take a more detailed look at the process of indexing in Lucene.

11.2   Indexing with Lucene

During the indexing process, Lucene takes in `Document` objects composed of `Fields`. It analyzes the text associated with the `Fields` to extract terms. Lucene deals only with text. If you have documents in nontext format such as PDF or Microsoft Word, you need to convert it into plain text that Lucene can understand. A number of open source tool kits are available for this conversion; for example PDFBox is an open source library available for handling PDF documents.

In this section, we'take a deeper look at the indexing process. We begin with a brief introduction of the two Lucene index formats. This is followed by a review of the APIs related to maintaining the Lucene index, some coverage of adding incremental indexing to your application, ways to access the term vectors, and finally a note on optimizing the indexing process.

11.2.1   Understanding the index format

A Lucene index is an *inverted text index*, where each term is associated with documents in which the term appears. A Lucene index is composed of multiple segments. Each segment is a fully independent, searchable index. Indexes evolve when new documents are added to the index and when existing segments are merged together. Each document within a segment has a unique ID within that segment. The ID associated with a document in a segment may change as new segments are merged and deleted documents are removed. All files belonging to a segment have the same filename with different file extensions. When the compound file format is used, all the files are merged into a single file with a .CFS extension. Figure 11.3 shows the files created for our example in section 11.1.3 using a non-compound file structure and a compound file structure.

Once an index has been created, chances are that you may need to modify the index. Let's next look at how this is done.

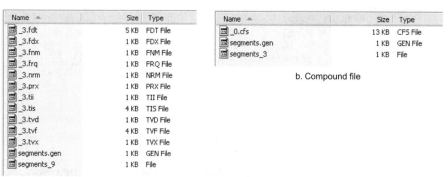

a. Non-compound file

Figure 11.3   Non-compound and compound index files

11.2.2 *Modifying the index*

`Document` instances in an index can be deleted using the `IndexReader` class. If a document has been modified, you first need to delete the document and then add the new version of the document to the index. An `IndexReader` can be opened on a directory that has an `IndexWriter` opened already, but it can't be used to delete documents from the index at that point.

There are two ways to delete documents from an index, as shown in listing 11.7.

Listing 11.7 Deleting documents using the `IndexReader`

```
public void deleteByIndexId(Directory indexDirectory, int docIndexNum)
  throws Exception {
    IndexReader indexReader = IndexReader.open(indexDirectory);
    indexReader.deleteDocument(docIndexNum);
    indexReader.close();
}
```
Delete document based on index number

```
public void deleteByTerm(Directory indexDirectory, String externalId)
  throws Exception {
    Term deletionTerm = new Term("externalId", externalId);
    IndexReader indexReader = IndexReader.open(indexDirectory);
    indexReader.deleteDocuments(deletionTerm);
    indexReader.close();
}
```
Delete documents based on term

Each document in the index has a unique ID associated with it. Unfortunately, these IDs can change as documents are added and deleted from the index and as segments are merged. For fast lookup, the `IndexReader` provides access to documents via their document number. There are four static methods that provide access to an `IndexReader` using the `open` command. In our example, we get an instance of the `IndexReader` using the `Directory` object. Alternatively, we could have used a `File` or `String` representation to the index directory.

```
IndexReader indexReader = IndexReader.open(indexDirectory);
```

To delete a document with a specific document number, we simply call the `delete-Document` method:

```
indexReader.deleteDocument(docIndexNum);
```

Note that at this stage, the document hasn't been actually deleted from the index—it's simply been marked for deletion. It'll be deleted from the index when we close the index:

```
indexReader.close();
```

A more useful way of deleting entries from the index is to create a `Field` object within the document that contains a unique ID string for the document. As things change in your application, simply create a `Term` object with the appropriate ID and field name and use it to delete the appropriate document from the index. This is illustrated in the method `deleteByTerm()`. The `IndexReader` provides a convenient method, `undeleteAll()`, to undelete all documents that have been marked for deletion.

Opening and closing indexes for writing tends to be expensive, especially for large indexes. It's more efficient to do all the modifications in a batch. Further, it's more efficient to first delete all the required documents and then add new documents, as shown in listing 11.8.

Listing 11.8   Batch deletion and addition of documents

```
public void illustrateBatchModifications(Directory indexDirectory,
      List<Term> deletionTerms,
      List<Document> addDocuments) throws Exception {
   IndexReader indexReader = IndexReader.open(indexDirectory);      ◁─┐
   for (Term deletionTerm: deletionTerms) {                           │
      indexReader.deleteDocuments(deletionTerm);        Batch deletion │
   }
   indexReader.close();
   IndexWriter indexWriter = new IndexWriter(indexDirectory,
      getAnalyzer(),false);                 ◁───┐
   for (Document document: addDocuments) {       Batch addition
      indexWriter.addDocument(document);
   }
   indexWriter.optimize();
   indexWriter.close();
}
```

Note that an instance of `IndexReader` is used for deleting the documents, while an instance of `IndexWriter` is used for adding new `Document` instances.

Next, let's look at how you can leverage this to keep your index up to date by incrementally updating your index.

11.2.3   *Incremental indexing*

Once an index has been created, it needs to be updated to reflect changes in the application. For example, if your application is leveraging user-generated content, the index needs to be updated with new content being added, modified, or deleted by the users. A simple approach some sites follow is to periodically—perhaps every few hours—re-create the complete index and update the search service with the new index. In this mode, the index, once created, is never modified. However, such an approach may be impractical if the requirement is that once a user generates new content, the user should be able to find the content shortly after addition. Furthermore, the amount of time taken to create a complete index may be too long to make this approach feasible. This is where *incremental indexing* comes into play. You may still want to re-create the complete index periodically, perhaps over a longer period of time.

As shown in figure 11.4, one of the simplest deployment architectures for search is to have multiple instances of the search service, each having its own index instance. These search services never update the index themselves—they access the index in read-only mode. An external indexing service creates the index and then propagates the changes to the search service instances. Periodically, the external indexing service batches all the changes that need to be propagated to the index and incrementally updates the index. On completion, it then propagates the updated index to the

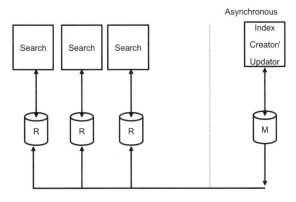

Figure 11.4 A simple deployment architecture where each search instance has its own copy of a read-only index. An external service creates and updates the index, pushing the changes periodically to the servers.

search instances, which periodically create a new version of the `IndexSearcher`. One downside of such an approach is the amount of data that needs to be propagated between the machines, especially for very large indexes.

Note that in the absence of an external index updater, each of the search service instances would have to do work to update their indexes, in essence duplicating the work.

Figure 11.5 shows an alternate architecture in which multiple search instances are accessing and modifying the same index. Let's assume that we're building a service, `IndexUpdaterService`, that's responsible for updating the search index. For incremental indexing, the first thing we need to ensure is that at any given time, there's only one instance of an `IndexReader` modifying the index.

First, we need to ensure that there's only one instance of `IndexUpdaterService` in a JVM—perhaps by using the Singleton pattern or using a Spring bean instance. Next, if multiple JVMs are accessing the same index, you'll need to

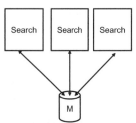

Figure 11.5 Multiple search instances sharing the same index

implement a global-lock system to ensure that only one instance is active at any given time. We discuss two solutions for this, first using an implementation that involves the database, and second using the `Lock` class available in Lucene. The second approach involves less code, but doesn't guard against JVM crashes. When a JVM crashes, the lock is left in an acquired state and you have to manually release or delete the lock file.

The first approach uses a timer-based mechanism that periodically invokes the `IndexUpdaterService` and uses a row in a database table to create a lock. The `Index-UpdaterService` first checks to see whether any other service is currently updating the index. If no services are updating the index—if there's no active row in the database table—it inserts a row and sets its state to be active. This service now has a lease on updating the index for a period of time. This service would then process all the changes—up to a maximum number that can be processed in the time frame of the lease—that have to be made to the index since the last update. Once it's done, it sets the state to inactive in the database, allowing other service instances to then do an update. To avoid JVM crashes, there's also a timeout associated with the active state for a service.

The second approach is similar, but uses the file-based locking provided by Lucene. When using `FSDirectory`, lock files are created in the directory specified by the system property `org.apache.lucene.lockdir` if it's set; otherwise the files are created in the computer's temporary directory (the directory specified by the `java.io.tmpdir` system directory). When multiple JVM instances are accessing the same index directory, you need to explicitly set the lock directory so that the same lock file is seen by all instances.

There are two kinds of locks: *write locks* and *commit locks*. Write locks are used whenever the index needs to be modified, and tend to be held for longer periods of time than commit locks. The `IndexWriter` holds on to the write lock when it's instantiated and releases it only when it's closed. The `IndexReader` obtains a write lock for three operations: deleting documents, undeleting documents, and changing the normalization factor for a field. Commit locks are used whenever segments are to be merged or committed. A file called *segments* names all of the other files in an index. An `IndexReader` obtains a commit lock before it reads the segments file. `IndexReader` keeps the lock until all the other files in the index have been read. The `IndexWriter` also obtains the commit lock when it has to write the segments file. It keeps the lock until it deletes obsolete index files. Commit locks are accessed more often than write locks, but for smaller durations, as they're obtained only when files are opened or deleted and the small segments file is read or written.

Listing 11.9 illustrates the use of the `isLocked()` method in the `IndexReader` to check whether the index is currently locked.

Listing 11.9   Adding code to check whether the index is locked

```
public void illustrateLockingCode(Directory indexDirectory,
    List<Term> deletionTerms,
    List<Document> addDocuments) throws Exception {
  if (!IndexReader.isLocked(indexDirectory)) {
    IndexReader indexReader = IndexReader.open(indexDirectory);
    //do work
  } else {
    //wait
  }
}
```

Another alternative is to use an application package such as Solr (see section 11.4.2), which takes care of a lot of these issues. Having looked at how to incrementally update the index, next let's look at how we can access the term frequency vector using Lucene.

11.2.4   *Accessing the term frequency vector*

You can access the term vectors associated with each of the fields using the `IndexReader`. Note that when creating the `Field` object as shown in listing 11.3, you need to set the third argument in the static method for creating a field to `Field.TermVector.YES`. Listing 11.10 shows some sample code for accessing the term frequency vector.

Listing 11.10 Sample code to access the term frequency vector for a field

```
public void illustrateTermFreqVector(Directory indexDirectory)
    throws Exception {
  IndexReader indexReader = IndexReader.open(indexDirectory);
  for (int i = 0; i < indexReader.numDocs(); i ++) {
    System.out.println("Blog " + i);
    TermFreqVector termFreqVector =
        indexReader.getTermFreqVector(i, "completeText");
    String [] terms = termFreqVector.getTerms();
    int [] freq = termFreqVector.getTermFrequencies();
    for (int j =0 ; j < terms.length; j ++) {
        System.out.println(terms[j] + " " + freq[j]);
    }
  }
}
```

The following code

```
TermFreqVector termFreqVector =
indexReader.getTermFreqVector(i, "completeText");
```

passes in the index number for a document along with the name of the field for which the term frequency vector is required. The `IndexReader` supports another method for returning all the term frequencies for a document:

```
TermFreqVector[] getTermFreqVectors(int docNumber)
```

Finally, let's look at some ways to manage performance during the indexing process.

11.2.5 *Optimizing indexing performance*

Methods to improve[2] the time required by Lucene to create its index can be broken down into the following three categories:

- Memory settings
- Architecture for indexing
- Other ways to improve performance

OPTIMIZING MEMORY SETTINGS

When a document is added to an index (`addDocument` in `IndexWriter`), Lucene first stores the document in its memory and then periodically flushes the documents to disk and merges the segment. `setMaxBufferedDocs` controls how often the documents in the memory are flushed to the disk, while `setMergeFactor` sets how often index segments are merged together. Both these parameters are by default set to 10. You can control this number by invoking `setMergeFactor()` and `setMaxBufferedDocs()` in the `IndexWriter`. More RAM is used for larger values of `mergeFactor`. Making this number

---

[2] http://wiki.apache.org/lucene-java/ImproveIndexingSpeed

large helps improve the indexing time, but slows down searching, since searching over an unoptimized index is slower than searching an optimized index. Making this value too large may also slow down the indexing process, since merging more indexes at once may require more frequent access to the disk. As a rule of thumb, large values for this parameter (greater than 10) are recommended for batch indexing and smaller values (less than 10) are recommended during incremental indexing.

Another alternative to flushing the memory based on the number of documents added to the index is to flush based on the amount of memory being used by Lucene. For indexing, you want to use as much RAM as you can afford—with the caveat that it doesn't help beyond a certain point.[3] Listing 11.11 illustrates the process of flushing the Lucene index based pm the amount of RAM used.

Listing 11.11   Illustrate flushing by RAM

```
public void illustrateFlushByRAM(IndexWriter indexWriter,
    List<Document> documents) throws Exception {
  indexWriter.setMaxBufferedDocs(MAX_BUFFER_VERY_LARGE_NUMBER);      ⟵  Set max to large value
  for (Document document: documents) {
    indexWriter.addDocument(document);
    long currentSize = indexWriter.ramSizeInBytes();   ⟵  Check RAM used after every addition
    if (currentSize > LUCENE_MAX_RAM) {
      indexWriter.flush();    ⟵  Flush RAM when it exceeds maximum
    }
  }
}
```

It's important to first set the number of maximum documents that will be used before merging to a large number, to prevent the writer from flushing based on the document count.[4] Next, the RAM size is checked after each document addition. When the amount of memory used exceeds the maximum RAM for Lucene, invoking the flush() method flushes the changes to disk.

To avoid the problem of very large files causing the indexing to run out of memory, Lucene by default indexes only the first 10,000 terms for a document. You can change this by setting setMaxFieldLength in the IndexWriter. Documents with large values for this parameter will require more memory.

INDEXING ARCHITECTURE

Here are some tips for optimizing indexing performance:

- In memory indexing, using RAMDirectory is much faster than disk indexing using FSDirectory. To take advantage of this, create a RAMDirectory-based index and periodically flush the index to disk using the FSDirectory index's addIndexes() method.

- To speed up the process of adding documents to the index, it may be helpful to use multiple threads to add documents. This approach is especially helpful

---

[3] See discussion http://www.gossamer-threads.com/lists/lucene/java-dev/51041.

[4] See discussion http://issues.apache.org/jira/browse/LUCENE-845.

when it may take time to create a `Document` instance and when using hardware that can effectively parallelize multiple threads. Note that a part of the `addDoc-ument()` method is synchronized in the `IndexWriter`.

- For indexes with large number of documents, you can split the index into n instances created on separate machines and then merge the indexes into one index using the `addIndexesNoOptimize` method.
- Use a local file system rather than a remote file system.

OTHER WAYS TO OPTIMIZE

Here are some way to optimize indexing time:

- Version 2.3 of Lucene exposes methods that allow you to set the value of a `Field`, enabling it to be reused across documents. It's efficient to reuse `Docu-ment` and `Field` instances. To do this, create a single `Document` instance. Add to it multiple `Field` instances, but reuse the `Field` instances across multiple document additions. You obviously can't reuse the same `Field` instance within a doc-ument until the document has been added to the index, but you can reuse `Field` instances across documents.
- Make the analyzer reuse `Token` instances, thus avoiding unnecessary object creation.
- In Lucene 2.3, a `Token` can represent its text as a character array, avoiding the creation of `String` instances. By using the `char []` API along with reusing `Token` instances, the creation of new objects can be avoided, which helps improve performance.
- Select the right analyzer for the kind of text being indexed. For example, index-ing time increases if you use a stemmer, such as `PorterStemmer`, or if the ana-lyzer is sophisticated enough to detect phrases or applies additional heuristics.

So far, we've looked in detail at how to create an index using Lucene. Next, we take a more detailed look at searching through this index.

11.3 Searching with Lucene

In section 11.3, we worked through a simple example that demonstrated how the Lucene index can be searched using a `QueryParser`. In this section, we take a more detailed look at searching.

In this section, we look at how Lucene does its scoring, the various query parsers avail-able, how to incorporate sorting, querying on multiple fields, filtering results, searching across multiple indexes, using a `HitCollector`, and optimizing search performance.

11.3.1 Understanding Lucene scoring

At the heart of Lucene scoring is the vector-space model representation of text (see section 2.2.4). There is a term-vector representation associated with each field of a document. You may recall from our discussions in sections 2.2.4 and 8.2 that the weight associated with each term in the term vector is the product of two terms—the term frequency in the document and the inverse document frequency associated with the term across all documents. For comparison purposes, we also normalize the term vector so that shorter documents aren't penalized. Lucene uses a similar approach, where in addition to the two terms, there's a third term based on how the document and field have been boosted—we call this the boost value. Within Lucene, it's possible to boost the value associated with a field and a document; see the setBoost() method in Field and Document. By default, the boost value associated with the field and document is 1.0. The final field boost value used by Lucene is the product of the boost values for the field and the document. Boosting fields and documents is a useful method for emphasizing certain documents or fields, depending on the business logic for your domain. For example, you may want to emphasis documents that are newer than historical ones, or documents written by users who have a higher authority (more well-known) within your application.

Given a query, which itself is converted into a normalized term vector, documents that are found to be most similar using the dot product of the vectors are returned. Lucene further multiplies the dot product for a document with a term that's proportional to the number of matching terms in the document. For example, for a three-term query, this factor will be larger for a document that has two of the queried terms than a document that has one of the query terms.

More formally, using the nomenclature used by Lucene, the Similarity[5] class outlines the score that's computed between a document d for a given query q:

$$Score(q, d) = coord(q, d) \cdot (norm(q)) \sum_{t \, in \, q} tf(t \cdot in \cdot d) \cdot (idf(t)) \cdot boost(t \cdot field \cdot in \cdot d) \cdot (norm(t, d))$$

Note that the summation is in essence taking a dot product. Table 11.1 contains an explanation of the various terms used in scoring.

Table 11.1 Explanation of terms used for computing the relevance of a query to a document

Term	Description
Score(q,d)	Relevance of query q to a document d
tf(t in d)	Term frequency of term t in the document
Idf(t)	Inverse document frequency of term t across all documents
Boost(t field in d)	Boost for the field—product of field and document boost factors
Norm(t,d)	Normalization factor for term t in the document
Coord(q,d)	Score factor based on the number of query terms found in document d
Norm(q)	Normalization factor for the query

The DefaultSimilarity class provides a default implementation for Lucene's similarity computation, as shown in Figure 11.6. You can extend this class if you want to override the computation of any of the terms.

---

[5] http://lucene.zones.apache.org:8080/hudson/job/Lucene-Nightly/javadoc/org/apache/lucene/search/Similarity.html

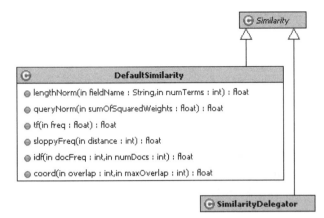

Figure 11.6 The default implementation for the `Similarity` **class**

The `IndexSearcher` class has a method that returns an `Explanation` object for a `Weight` and a particular document. The `Weight` object is created from a `Query` (`query.weight(Searcher)`). The `Explanation` object contains details about the scoring; listing 11.12 shows a sample explanation provided for the query term *collective intelligence,* using the code as in listing 11.4 for searching through blog entries.

Listing 11.12 Sample explanation of Lucene scoring

```
Link permanente a Collective Intelligence  SocialKnowledge
Collective Intelligence  Pubblicato da Rosario Sica su
Novembre 18, 2007   [IMG David Thorburn]Segna
0.64706594 = (MATCH) sum of:
  0.24803483 = (MATCH) weight(completeText:collective in 9), product of:
    0.6191303 = queryWeight(completeText:collective), product of:
      1.5108256 = idf(docFreq=5)
      0.409796 = queryNorm
    0.40061814 = (MATCH) fieldWeight(completeText:collective in 9),
product of:
      1.4142135 = tf(termFreq(completeText:collective)=2)
      1.5108256 = idf(docFreq=5)
      0.1875 = fieldNorm(field=completeText, doc=9)
  0.3990311 = (MATCH) weight(completeText:intelligence in 9), product of:
    0.7852883 = queryWeight(completeText:intelligence), product of:
      1.9162908 = idf(docFreq=3)
      0.409796 = queryNorm
    0.5081333 = (MATCH) fieldWeight(completeText:intelligence in 9),
product of:
      1.4142135 = tf(termFreq(completeText:intelligence)=2)
      1.9162908 = idf(docFreq=3)
      0.1875 = fieldNorm(field=completeText, doc=9)
```

Using the code in listing 11.4, first a `Weight` instance is created:

```
Weight weight = query.weight(indexSearcher);
```

Next, while iterating over all result sets, an `Explanation` object is created:

```
Iterator iterator = hits.iterator();
while (iterator.hasNext()) {
   Hit hit = (Hit) iterator.next();
```

```
        Document document = hit.getDocument();
        System.out.println(document.get("completeText"));
        Explanation explanation = indexSearcher.explain(weight,
          hit.getId());
        System.out.println(explanation.toString());
    }
```

Next, let's look at how the query object is composed in Lucene.

11.3.2 Querying Lucene

In listing 11.4, we illustrated the use of a `QueryParser` to create a `Query` instance by parsing the query string. Lucene provides a family of `Query` classes, as shown in figure 11.7, which allow you to construct a `Query` instance based on the requirements.

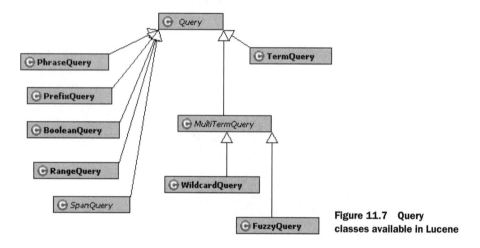

Figure 11.7   Query classes available in Lucene

Table 11.2 contains a brief description for queries shown in figure 11.7. Next, let's work through an example that combines a few of these queries, to illustrate how they can be used.

Table 11.2   Description of the query classes

Query class name	Description
Query	Abstract base class for all queries
TermQuery	A query that matches a document containing a term
PhraseQuery	A query that matches documents containing a particular sequence of terms
PrefixQuery	Prefix search query
BooleanQuery	A query that matches documents matching Boolean combinations of other queries
RangeQuery	A query that matches documents within an exclusive range
SpanQuery	Base class for span-based queries
MultiTermQuery	A generalized version of `PhraseQuery`, with an added method `add(Term[])`

Table 11.2   Description of the query classes *(continued)*

Query class name	Description
WildCardQuery	Wildcard search query
FuzzyQuery	Fuzzy search query

Let's extend our example in section 11.1.3, where we wanted to search for blog entries that have the phrase *collective intelligence* as well as a term that begins with *web**. Listing 11.13 shows the code for this query.

Listing 11.13   Example code showing the use of various `Query` classes

```
public void illustrateQueryCombination(Directory indexDirectory)
  throws Exception {
    IndexSearcher indexSearcher = new IndexSearcher(indexDirectory);
    PhraseQuery phraseQuery = new PhraseQuery();
    phraseQuery.add(new Term("completeText","collective"));          Adding
    phraseQuery.add(new Term("completeText","intelligence"));        phrase
    phraseQuery.setSlop(1);                        Setting slop      terms
                                                   for terms
    PrefixQuery prefixQuery = new PrefixQuery(
      new Term("completeText","web"));             Creating prefix query

    BooleanQuery booleanQuery = new BooleanQuery();       Combining queries
    booleanQuery.add(phraseQuery, BooleanClause.Occur.MUST);
    booleanQuery.add(prefixQuery, BooleanClause.Occur.MUST);
    System.out.println(booleanQuery.toString());

    Hits hits = indexSearcher.search(booleanQuery);
}
```

We first create an instance of the `PhraseQuery` and add the terms *collective* and *intelligence*. Each phrase query has a parameter called `slop`. Slop by default is set to 0, which enables only exact phrase matches. When the slop value is greater than 0, the phrase query works like a `within` or `near` operator. The `slop` is the number of moves required to convert the terms of interest into the query term. For example, if we're interested in the query *collective intelligence* and we come across a phrase *collective xxxx intelligence*, the slop associated with this phrase match is 1, since one term —*xxx*—needs to be moved. The slop associated with the phrase *intelligence collective* is 2, since the term *intelligence* needs to be moved two positions to the right. Lucene matches exact matches higher than sloppy matches.

For the preceding Boolean query, invoking the `toString()` method prints out the following Lucene query:

+completeText:"collective intelligence"~1 +completeText:web*

Next, let's look at how search results can be sorted using Lucene.

11.3.3   *Sorting search results*

In a typical search application, the user types in a query and the application returns a list of items sorted in order of relevance to the query. There may be a requirement in the application to return the result set sorted in a different order. For example, the requirement may be to show the top 100 results sorted by the name of the author, or the date it was created. One naïve way of implementing this feature would be to query Lucene, retrieve all the results, and then sort the results in memory. There are a couple of problems with this approach, both related to performance and scalability. First, we need to retrieve all the results into memory and sort them. Retrieving all items consumes valuable time and computing resources. The second problem is that all the items are retrieved even though only a subset of the results will eventually be shown in the application. For example, the second page of results may just need to show items 11 to 20 in the result list. Fortunately, Lucene has built-in support for sorting the results sets, which we briefly review in this section.

The `Sort` class in Lucene encapsulates the sort criteria. `Searcher` has a number of overloaded search methods that, in addition to the query, also accept `Sort` as an input, and as we see in section 11.3.5, a `Filter` for filtering results. The `Sort` class has two static constants: `Sort.INDEXORDER`, which sorts the results based on the index order, and `Sort.RELEVANCE`, which sorts the results based on relevance to the query. Fields used for sorting must contain a single term. The term value indicates the document's relative position in the sort order. The field needs to be indexed, but not tokenized, and there's no need to store the field. Lucene supports three data types for sorting fields: `String`, `Integer`, and `Float`. `Integers` and `Floats` are sorted from low to high. The sort order can be reversed by creating the `Sort` instance using either the constructor:

```
public Sort(String field, boolean reverse)
```

or the `setSort()` method:

```
setSort(String field, boolean reverse)
```

The `Sort` object is thread safe and can be reused by using the `setSort()` method.

In listing 11.3, we created a field called "`author`". Let's use this field for sorting the results:

```
addField(document,"author",blogEntry.getAuthor(), Field.Store.NO,
    Field.Index.UN_TOKENIZED , Field.TermVector.YES);
```

Listing 11.14 shows the implementation for the sorting example using the "`author`" field.

Listing 11.14   Sorting example

```
public void illustrateSorting(Directory indexDirectory)
    throws Exception {
    IndexSearcher indexSearcher = new IndexSearcher(indexDirectory);
    Sort sort = new Sort("author");   ⟵── Create Sort object specifying field for sorting
    Query query = new TermQuery(
        new Term("completeText","intelligence"));   ⟵─── Create query
                                                         specifying
    Hits hits =                                          field for
        indexSearcher.search(query, sort);   ⟵─┐ Search using    searching
    Iterator iterator = hits.iterator();         query and
    while (iterator.hasNext()) {                 sort objects
```

```
            Hit hit = (Hit) iterator.next();
            Document document = hit.getDocument();
            System.out.println("Author = " + document.get("author"));
        }
    }
```

In the case of two documents that have the same values in the Sort field, the document number is used for displaying the items. You can also create a multiple field Sort by using the SortField class. For example, the following code first sorts by the author field, in reverse alphabetical order, followed by document relevance to the query, and lastly by using the document index number:

```
    SortField [] sortFields = {new SortField("author", false),
        SortField.FIELD_SCORE, SortField.FIELD_DOC};
        Sort multiFieldSort = new Sort(sortFields);
```

So far we've been dealing with searching across a single field. Let's look next at how we can query across multiple fields.

11.3.4 *Querying on multiple fields*

In listing 11.3, we created a "completeText" field that concatenated text from the title and excerpt fields of the blog entries. In this section, we illustrate how you can search across multiple fields using the MultiFieldQueryParser, which extends FieldQueryParser as shown in figure 11.2.

Let's continue with our example from section 11.1.3. We're interested in searching across three fields—"name", "title", and "excerpt". For this, we first create a String array:

```
    String [] fields = {"name", "title", "excerpt"};
```

Next, a new instance of the MultiFieldQueryParser is created using the constructor:

```
    new MultiFieldQueryParser(fields, getAnalyzer());
```

Lucene will search for terms using the OR operator—the query needs to match any one of the three fields. Next, let's look at how we can query multiple fields using different matching conditions. Listing 11.15 illustrates how a multifield query can be composed, specifying that the match should occur in the "name" field, and the "title" field, and shouldn't occur in the "excerpt" field.

Listing 11.15 MultiFieldQueryParser **example**

```
    public Query getMultiFieldAndQuery(String query) throws Exception {
        String [] fields =
            {"name", "title", "excerpt"};           ◁── Create
        BooleanClause.Occur[] flags = {                  array with
            BooleanClause.Occur.SHOULD,                  field names
            BooleanClause.Occur.MUST,
            BooleanClause.Occur.MUST_NOT};
        return MultiFieldQueryParser.parse(query, fields,
            flags, getAnalyzer());
    }
```

Create array with conditions for combining

Invoke parse method

This example constructs the following query for Lucene:

```
(name:query) +(title:query) -(excerpt:query)
```

Next, let's look at how we can use `Filters` for filtering out results using Lucene.

11.3.5 *Filtering*

Lots of times, you may need to constrain your search to a subset of available documents. For example, in an SaaS application, where there are multiple domains or companies supported by the same software and hardware instance, you need to search through documents only within the domain of the user. As shown in figure 11.8, there are five `Filter` classes available in Lucene.

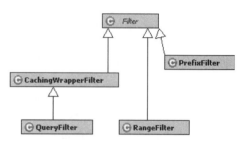

Figure 11.8   Filters available in Lucene

Table 11.3 contains a brief description of the various filters that are available in Lucene.

Table 11.3   Description of the filter classes

Class	Description
Filter	Abstract base class for all filters. Provides a mechanism to restrict the search to a subset of the index.
CachingWrapperFilter	Wraps another filter's results and caches it. The intent is to allow filters to simply filter and then add caching using this filter.
QueryFilter	Constrains search results to only those that match the required query. It also caches the result so that searches on the same index using this filter are much faster.
RangeFilter	Restricts the search results to a range of values. This is similar to a `RangeQuery`.
PrefixFilter	Restricts the search results to those that match the prefix. This is similar to a `PrefixQuery`.

Next, let's look at some code that illustrates how to create a filter and invoke the search method using the filter. Listing 11.16 shows the code for creating a `RangeFilter` using the `"modifiedDate"` field. Note that the date the document was modified is converted into a `String` representation using yyyymmdd format.

Listing 11.16   Filtering the results

```
public void illustrateFilterSearch(IndexSearcher indexSearcher,
        Query query, Sort sort) throws Exception {
    Filter rangeFilter = new RangeFilter(
        "modifiedDate", "20080101",          Create instance
        "20080131", true, true);        ◁──  of RangeFilter
```

```
        CachingWrapperFilter cachedFilter =                    | Wrap RangeFilter in
          new CachingWrapperFilter(rangeFilter);     ◁──────┘  CachingWrapperFilter
        Hits hits = indexSearcher.search(query, cachedFilter, sort);
    }
```

The constructor for a `RangeFilter` takes five parameters. First is the name of the field to which the filter has to be applied. Next are the lower and the upper term for the range, followed by two `Boolean` flags indicating whether to include the lower and upper values. One of the advantages of using `Filters` is the caching of the results. It's easy enough to wrap the `RangeFilter` instance using the `CachingWrapperFilter`. As long as the same `IndexReader` or `IndexSearcher` instance is used, Lucene will use the cached results after the first query is made, which populates the cache.

11.3.6 *Searching multiple indexes*

In figure 11.2, you may have noticed two `Searcher` classes, `MultiSearcher` and `ParallelMultiSearcher`. These classes are useful if you need to search across multiple indexes. It's common practice to partition your Lucene indexes, once they become large. Both `MultiSearcher` and `ParallelMultiSearcher`, which extends `MultiSearcher`, can search across multiple index instances and present search results combined together as if the results were obtained from searching a single index. Listing 11.17 shows the code for creating and searching using the `MultiSearcher` and `ParallelMultiSearcher` classes.

Listing 11.17 Searching across multiple instances

```
    public void illustrateMultipleIndexSearchers(Directory index1,
            Directory index2, Query query, Filter filter) throws Exception {
        IndexSearcher indexSearcher1 = new IndexSearcher(index1);
        IndexSearcher indexSearcher2 = new IndexSearcher(index2);
        Searchable [] searchables = {indexSearcher1, indexSearcher2};   ◁─┐

        Searcher searcher = new MultiSearcher(searchables);           ◁─┐ │
        Searcher parallelSearcher = new ParallelMultiSearcher(searchables); │

        Hits hits = searcher.search(query, filter);        Create array of │
    //use the hits                                    Searchable instances │
        indexSearcher1.close();
        indexSearcher2.close();                      Constructor takes array of
    }                                                   Searchable instances
```

`ParallelMultiSearcher` parallelizes the search and filter operations across each index by using a separate thread for each `Searchable`.

Next, let's look at how we can efficiently iterate through a large number of documents.

11.3.7 *Using a HitCollector*

So far in this chapter, we've been using `Hits` to iterate over the search results. `Hits` has been optimized for a specific use case. You should never use `Hits` for anything other than retrieving a page of results, or around 10–30 instances. `Hits` caches documents, normalizes the scores (between 0 and 1), and stores IDs associated with the document using the Hit class. If you retrieve a Document from Hit past the first 100 results, a new search will be issued by Lucene to grab double the required Hit instances. This process is repeated every time the Hit instance goes beyond the existing cache. If you need to iterate over all the results, a HitCollector is a better choice. Note that the scores passed to the HitCollector aren't normalized.

In this section, we briefly review some of the HitCollector classes available in Lucene and shown in figure 11.9. This will be followed by writing our own HitCollector for the blog searching example we introduced in section 11.1.

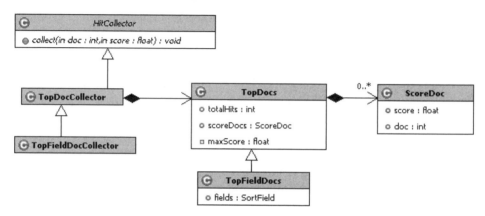

Figure 11.9   HitCollector-related classes

Table 11.4 contains a brief description for the list of classes related to a HitCollector. HitCollector is an abstract base class that has one abstract method that each HitCollector object needs to implement:

```
public abstract void collect(int doc, float score)
```

In a search, this method is called once for every matching document, with the following arguments: its document number and raw score. Note that this method is called in an inner search loop. For optimal performance, a HitCollector shouldn't call Searcher.doc(int) or IndexReader.document(int) on every document number encountered. The TopDocCollector contains TopDocs, which has methods to return the total number of hits along with an array of ScoreDoc instances. Each ScoreDoc has the document number, along with the unnormalized score for the document. TopFieldDocs extends TopDocs and contains the list of fields that were used for sorting.

Table 11.4   Description of the HitCollector-related classes

Class	Description
HitCollector	Base abstract class for all HitCollector classes. It has one primary abstract method: collect().
TopDocCollector	HitCollector implementation that collects the specified number of top documents. It has a method that returns the TopDocs.

Table 11.4 Description of the `HitCollector`-related classes *(continued)*

Class	Description
TopDocs	Contains the number of results returned and an array of ScoreDoc, one for each returned document.
ScoreDoc	Bean class containing the document number and its score.
TopFieldDocCollector	HitCollector that returns the top sorted documents, returning them as TopFieldDocs.
TopFieldDocs	Extends TopDocs. Also contains the list of fields that were used for the sort.

Next, let's look at a simple example to demonstrate how the `HitCollector`-related APIs can be used. This is shown in listing 11.18.

Listing 11.18 Example using `TopDocCollector`

```
public void illustrateTopDocs(Directory indexDirectory, Query query,
        int maxNumHits) throws Exception {
    IndexSearcher indexSearcher =
        new IndexSearcher(indexDirectory);
    TopDocCollector hitCollector =
        new TopDocCollector(maxNumHits);
    indexSearcher.search(query, hitCollector);
    TopDocs topDocs = hitCollector.topDocs();
    System.out.println("Total number results=" + topDocs.totalHits);
    for (ScoreDoc scoreDoc: topDocs.scoreDocs) {
        Document document = indexSearcher.doc(scoreDoc.doc);
        System.out.println(document.get("completeText"));
    }
    indexSearcher.close();
}
```

Create instance of **TopDocCollector**

Query searcher using **HitCollector**

Retrieve document from **ScoreDoc**

In this example, we first create an instance of the `TopDocCollector`, specifying the maximum number of documents that need to be collected. We invoke a different variant of the search method for the `Searcher`, which takes in a `HitCollector`. We then iterate over the results, retrieving the `Document` instance using the `ScoreDoc`.

Next, it's helpful to write a custom `HitCollector` for our example. Listing 11.19 contains the code for `RetrievedBlogHitCollector`, which is useful for collecting `RetrievedBlogEntry` instances obtained from searching.

Listing 11.19 Implementing a custom `HitCollector`

```
package com.alag.ci.search.lucene;

import java.io.IOException;
import java.util.*;

import org.apache.lucene.document.Document;
import org.apache.lucene.search.*;

import com.alag.ci.blog.search.RetrievedBlogEntry;
import com.alag.ci.blog.search.impl.RetrievedBlogEntryImpl;
```

```
public class RetrievedBlogHitCollector extends HitCollector{
    private List<RetrievedBlogEntry> blogs = null;
    private Searcher searcher = null;

    public RetrievedBlogHitCollector(Searcher searcher) {
        this.searcher = searcher;
        this.blogs = new ArrayList<RetrievedBlogEntry>();
    }

    public void collect(int docNum, float score) {
        try {
            Document document = this.searcher.doc(docNum);
            RetrievedBlogEntryImpl blogEntry =
                new RetrievedBlogEntryImpl();
            blogEntry.setAuthor(document.get("author"));
            blogEntry.setTitle(document.get("title"));
            blogEntry.setUrl(document.get("url"));
            this.blogs.add(blogEntry);
        } catch (IOException e) {
            //ignored
        }
    }

    public List<RetrievedBlogEntry> getBlogEntries() {
        return this.blogs;
    }
}
```

> **Collect method needs to be implemented**

In our example, we create an instance of RetrievedBlogEntryImpl and populate it with the attributes that will be displayed in the UI. The list of resulting RetrievedBlog-Entry instances can be obtained by invoking the getBlogEntries() method.

Before we end this section, it's useful to look at some tips for improving search performance.

11.3.8 *Optimizing search performance*

In section 11.2.5, we briefly reviewed some ways to make Lucene indexing faster. In this section, we briefly review some ways to make searching using Lucene faster[6]:

- If the amount of available memory exceeds the amount of memory required to hold the Lucene index in memory, the complete index can be read into memory using the RAMDirectory. This will allow the SearchIndexer to search through an in-memory index, which is much faster than the index being stored on the disk. This may be particularly useful for creating auto-complete services—services that provide a list of options based on a few characters typed by a user.

- Use adequate RAM and avoid remote file systems.

- Share a single instance of the IndexSearcher. Avoid reopening the Index-Searcher, which can be slow for large indexes.

---

[6] Refer to http://wiki.apache.org/lucene-java/ImproveSearchingSpeed.

- Optimized indexes have only one segment to search and can be much faster than a multi-segment index. If the index doesn't change much once it's created, it's worthwhile to optimize the index once it's built. However, if the index is being constantly updated, optimizing will likely be too costly, and you should decrease mergeFactor instead. Optimizing indexes is expensive.

- Don't iterate over more hits than necessary. Don't retrieve term vectors and fields for documents that won't be shown on the results page.

At this stage, you should have a good understanding of using Lucene, the process of creating an index, searching using Lucene, sorting and filtering in Lucene, and using a HitCollector. With this background, we're ready to look at some ways to make searching using Lucene intelligent. Before that, let's briefly review some tools and frameworks that may be helpful.

11.4   Useful tools and frameworks

Given the wide popularity and use of Lucene, a number of tools and frameworks have been built. In chapter 6, we used Nutch, which is an open source crawler built using Lucene. In section 6.3.4, we also discussed Apache Hadoop, a framework to run applications that need to process large datasets using commodity hardware in a distributed platform. In this section, we briefly look at Luke, a useful tool for looking at the Lucene index, and three other frameworks related to Lucene that you should be aware of: Solr, Compass, and Hibernate search. Based on your application and need, you may find it useful to use one of these frameworks.

11.4.1   Luke

Luke is an open source toolkit for browsing and modifying the Lucene index. It was created by Andrzej Bialecki and is extensible using plug-ins and scripting. Using Luke, you can get an overview of the documents in the index; you can browse through documents and see details about their fields and term vectors. There's also an interface where you can search and see the results of the search query. You can start Luke using the Java Web Start link from the Luke home page at http://www.getopt.org/luke/. Figure 11.10 shows a screenshot of Luke in the document browse mode. You can browse through the various documents and look at their fields and associated terms and term vector. If you're experimenting with different analyzers or building your own analyzer, it's helpful to look at the contents of the created index using Luke.

11.4.2   Solr

Solr is an open source enterprise search server built using Lucene that provides simple XML/HTTP and JSON APIs for access. Solr needs a Java servlet container, such as Tomcat. It provides features such as hit highlighting, caching, replication, and a web administration interface.

Solr began as an in-house project at CNET Networks and was contributed to the Apache Foundation as a subproject of Lucene in early 2006. In January 2007, Solr graduated from an incubation period to an official Apache project. Even though it's a

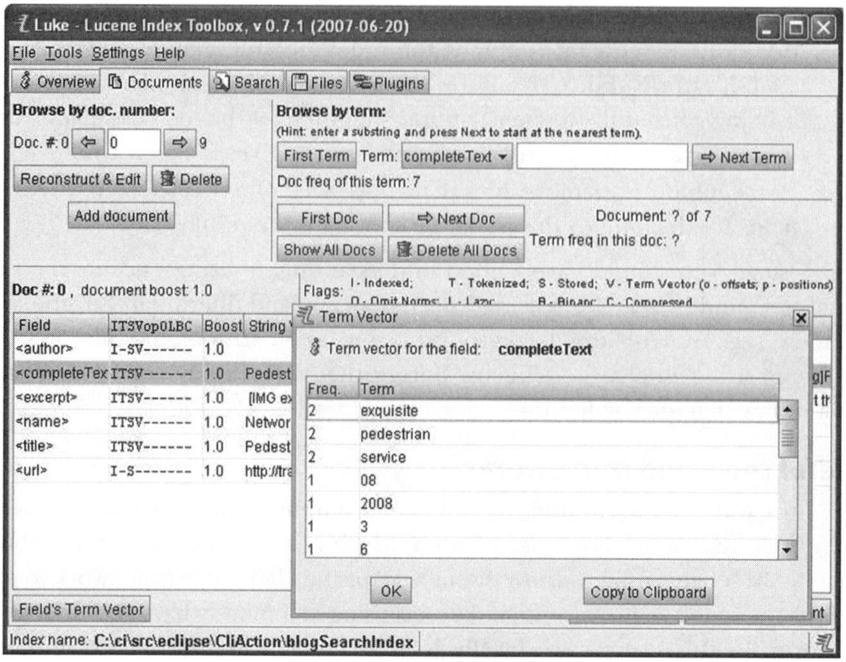

Figure 11.10   Screenshot of Luke in the Documents tab

relatively new project, it's being used extensively by a number of high-traffic sites.[7] Figure 11.11 shows a screenshot of the Solr admin page.

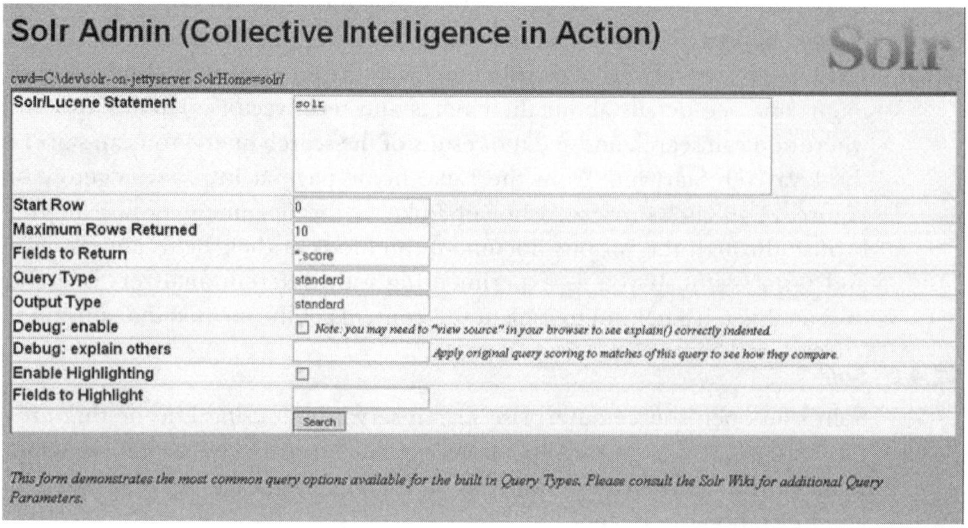

Figure 11.11   Screenshot of the Solr admin page

[7] http://wiki.apache.org/solr/PublicServers

11.4.3 *Compass*

Compass is a Java search engine framework that was built on top of Lucene. It provides a high level of abstraction. It integrates with both Hibernate and Spring, and allows you to declaratively map your object domain model to the underlying search engine and synchronize changes with the data source. Compass also provides a Lucene JDBC, allowing Lucene to store the search index in the database. Compass is available using the Apache 2.0 license. Read more about Compass at http://www.opensymphony.com/compass/.

11.4.4 *Hibernate search*

Hibernate search solves the problem of mapping a complex object-oriented domain model to a full-text search-based index. Hibernate search aims to synchronize changes between the domain objects and the index transparently, and returns objects in response to a search query. Hibernate is an open source project distributed under the GNU Lesser General Public License. Read more about Hibernate at http://www.hibernate.org/410.html.

In this section, we've looked at tools built on top of Lucene. For most applications, using a framework such as Solr should be adequate, and should expedite adding search capabilities. Now that we have a good understanding of the basics of search, let's look at how we can make our search intelligent.

11.5 *Approaches to intelligent search*

One of the aims of this chapter is to make search more intelligent. In this section, we focus on techniques that leverage some of the clustering, classification, and predictive models that we developed in part 2 of the book. We also look at some of the current approaches being used by search companies. There are a lot of companies innovating within the search space.[8] While it's impossible to cover them all, we discuss a few of the well-known ones.

In this section, we cover six main approaches to making search more intelligent:

- Augmenting the document by creating new fields using one or more of the following: clustering, classification, and regression models
- Clustering the results from a search query to determine clusters of higher-level concepts
- Using contextual and user information to boost the search results toward a particular term vector
- Creating personal search engines, which search through a subset of sites, where the list of sites is provided by a community of users; and using social networking, where users can tag sites, and the search engine blocks out irrelevant sites and selects sites selected by other users
- Linguistic-based search, where the level of words and their meanings is used
- Searching through data and looking for relevant correlations

---

[8] http://www.allthingsweb2.com/mtree/SEARCH_2.0/

For most of them, we also briefly look at how you could apply the same concept in your application.

11.5.1 *Augmenting search with classifiers and predictors*

Consider a typical application that uses user-generated comment (UGC). The UGC could be in many forms; for example, it could be questions and answers asked by users, images, articles or videos uploaded and shared by the user, or tagged bookmarks created by the user. In most applications, content can be classified into one or more categories. For example, one possible classification for this book's content could be tagging, data collection, web crawling, machine learning, algorithms, search, and so on. Note that these classifications need not be mutually exclusive—content can belong to multiple categories. For most applications, it's either too expensive or just not possible to manually classify all the content. Most applications like to provide a "narrow by" feature to the search results. For example, you may want to provide a general search feature and then allow the user to subfilter the results based on a subset of classification topics that she's interested in.

One way to build such functionality is to build a classifier that predicts whether a given piece of content belongs to a particular category. Here is the recipe for adding this functionality:

- Create a classifier for each of the categories. Given a document, each classifier predicts whether the document belongs to that category.
- During indexing, add a field, `classificationField`, to the Lucene `Document`, which contains the list of applicable classifiers for that document.
- During search, create a `Filter` that narrows the search to appropriate terms in the `classificationField`.

Predictive models can be used in a manner similar to classifiers.

An example of using a classification model to categorize content and use it in search is Kosmix[9]: Kosmix, which aims at building a home page for every topic, uses a categorization engine that automatically categorizes web sites. Figure 11.12 shows a screenshot of the home page for *collective intelligence* generated by Kosmix.

11.5.2 *Clustering search results*

The typical search user rarely goes beyond the second or third page of results and prefers to rephrase the search query based on the initial results. Clustering results, so as to provide categories of concepts gathered from analyzing the search results, is an alternative approach to displaying search results. Figure 11.13 shows the results of clustering using Carrot2[10] clustering for the query *collective intelligence*. You can see the higher-level concepts discovered by clustering the results. The user can then navigate

---

[9] http://www.kosmix.com/.
[10] http://project.carrot2.org/index.html

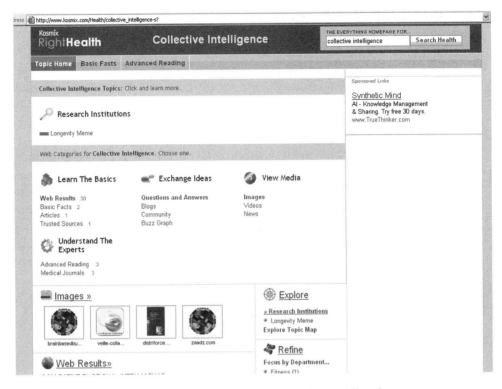

Figure 11.12   Screenshot of the home page for *collective intelligence* at Kosmix

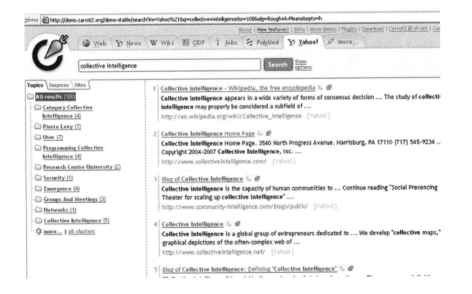

Figure 11.13   Clustering search results using Carrot2 clustering

to dig deeper into concepts of interest. Clusty[11] is a well-known search engine that applies this principle. Clusty carries out a meta-search across multiple search engines and then clusters the results.

Carrot2 is an open source engine that automatically clusters search results. Integration with Lucene results is fairly straightforward.[12] Carrot2 has been successfully used in a number of commercial applications.

11.5.3 *Personalizing results for the user*

The main motivation behind this approach is to use any available contextual information to modify the search query to make the search more relevant. The contextual information could be in the form of a term-vector representation for the user's interests or profile. Or a click on a tag might modify the search query to add additional contextual information. An example should help you understand the concept better. Let's say that a user makes a general query *computers* on a site that sells computers. Now, if there is a profile associated with the user that has information on the kind of products that the user tends to buy or look at—perhaps whether the user enjoys expensive products or a particular brand—this additional information can be used to modify and sort the information that's retrieved.

11.5.4 *Community-based search*

Community-based search engines allow users to create custom search engines by specifying a set of web sites. These sites are either emphasized or are the only web sites searched. This approach is useful for creating vertically focused search engines. Google custom search (http://www.google.com/coop/), Eurekster (http://www.eurekster.com/), and Rollyo (http://rollyo.com/) are a few of the companies that follow this approach and allow users to create custom search engines. Figure 11.14 shows a screenshot of a personalized search engine that I created on Google using the URLs that I obtained running the focused crawler we developed in chapter 6.

One way of applying this concept within your application is to allow your users to tag content within the application. In essence, each tag categorizes the content. You can allow users to create custom search engines within your application by allowing them to combine sets of tags. Hence, when a search is carried out within a custom search engine, only content that has one or more of the required tags is considered for search results.

---

[11] http://clusty.com

[12] http://carrot2.svn.sourceforge.net/viewvc/carrot2/trunk/carrot2/applications/carrot2-demo-api-example/src/org/carrot2/apiexample/LuceneExample.java?view=markup

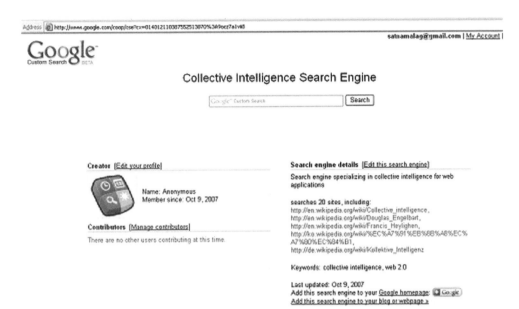

Figure 11.14   **Screenshot of a personalized search engine on collective intelligence developed using Google Custom Search**

11.5.5 *Linguistic-based search*

Natural language–based search engines, such as Hakia (http://www.hakia.com/), Powerset (http://www.powerset.com/), and Lexee (http://www.lexxe.com/), aim to go beyond simple text matching by trying to get the content of the query. They look at the syntactic relationships and try to retrieve pages that are similar based on analyzing their content.

11.5.6 *Data search*

On February 29, 2008, Bloomberg.com reported that George Church, a professor of genetics at Harvard Medical School, plans to spend $1 billion to create a database for finding new drugs by correlating each person's personal health history to DNA-related information. Church, whose research led to the first direct genomic sequencing method and also helped initiate the Human Genome Project, is backed by Google and OrbiMed Advisors, LLC. Church plans to decode the DNA of 100,000 people in the world's biggest gene sequencing project.

The entire human genome has more than 3 billion DNA base pairs. Humans have 24 unique chromosomes and an estimated 20,000–25,000 unique genes. A *gene* is a portion of the genomic sequence that encodes proteins—building blocks of cells and tissues. Variations in genes and other parts of the DNA have been linked to various types of diseases. DNA chips or microarrays enable researchers to generate large amounts of DNA-related data. *Computational biology* or *bioinformatics* is an active area of research that deals with deriving intelligence from biological data. Companies such as 23andme.com, navigenics.com, and decodeme.com provide a service by which consumers' DNA is converted into single nucleotide polymorphisms (SNP) data, with the promise that it can be used to calculate the levels of risks associated with various diseases.

These are just some examples of the growing trends in the life sciences area. Data is being generated at a fast pace within this field. So far in this chapter, we've mainly concentrated on text-based search. However, searching through large amounts of experimental data, where you normalize the data and use actual experimental values from the data along with any meta-text or associated annotations to discover new relationships, is a form of *data-based search*. Such search engines typically also leverage an ontology and complex biological relationships to guide their searches. One such company that I'm associated with is NextBio.[13] At NextBio, we leverage all publicly available life sciences–related data, along with user-contributed data, to provide a platform for life scientists to discover new relationships, perhaps between genes, diseases, and treatments. Going back to the original example of Church's plan to decode the DNA of 100,000 people, I hope that all that data will be publicly available in the future for search engines to use and help discover new drugs for diseases.

Figure 11.15 shows a screenshot from NextBio for the gene TP53. Note that the search engine has returned lists of diseases, tissues, and treatments that may be related to this gene.

Figure 11.15 Screenshot from NextBio showing the Gene TP53, along with inferences from analyzing the data

---

[13] www.nextbio.com. Disclaimer: I'm currently the VP of engineering at NextBio.

In this section, we've looked at six current trends in the area of making search more intelligent. It is impossible to discuss all the innovation happening in the large number of new search engines being built. You may want to look at a couple of additional upcoming search engines: Cuil,[14] which claims to have a larger index than Google, and Searchme,[15] which has an innovative way of displaying search results. Search is a multi-billion-dollar business, so expect more innovation in this area in the years to come.

11.6 Summary

Search is the process of retrieving relevant results in response to a query. The process of searching consists of first creating an inverted index of terms and then searching through the inverted index. The vector-space model and the term-vector representation of content are the basis for retrieving relevant documents in response to a search query.

Lucene provides two main classes, `FSDirectory` and `RAMDirectory`, for creating an index. Content is added to the index using a `Document` instance. Each `Document` instance consists of `Field` instances, each of which has a name and a `String` value. `Field` objects can be stored in the index for future retrieval, tokenized for search, or untokenized for sorting, and can have an associated term vector stored with them. The same analyzer needs to be used for both indexing and searching.

Searches within Lucene are carried out using an instance of a `Searcher` and a `Query` object. `Query` instances are created using either a `QueryParser` or by instantiating appropriate `Query` instances. `Hits`, which is a container for results from a query, contains access to the resulting documents. It's more appropriate to use a `HitCollector` when you need to traverse through a large number of result documents. Lucene provides extensive support for sorting and filtering the results.

Approaches to make search more intelligent include using classification and prediction algorithms to classify content, clustering results to present concepts, creating personal search engines, leveraging user tagging information to filter results, and using natural language processing to determine concepts to aid search.

Now that we have a good understanding of search, in the next chapter, we look at how we can build a recommendation engine using both collaborative and content-based analysis.

11.7 Resources

Apache Lucene Index File Format. http://lucene.apache.org/java/docs/fileformats.html

Apache Lucene Scoring. http://lucene.apache.org/java/docs/scoring.html

"The Best of Web 2.0 Searching and Search Engine." http://www.allthingsweb2.com/mtree/SEARCH_2.0/

Carrot and Lucene. http://project.carrot2.org/faq.html#lucene-integration

Carrot Clustering. http://project.carrot2.org/

Compass. http://www.opensymphony.com/compass/content/about.html

Delecretaz, Bertrand. "Solr: Indexing XML with Lucene and REST." xml.com, August 2006. http://www.xml.com/pub/a/2006/08/09/solr-indexing-xml-with-lucene-andrest.html

---

[14] http://www.cuil.com/
[15] http://www.searchme.com/

Ezzy, Ebharim. Search 2.0 Vs Traditional Search. 2006. http://www.readwriteweb.com/archives/search_20_vs_tr.php

Fleisher, Peter. "Google's search policy puts the user in charge." *Financial Times*, May 2007. http://www.ft.com/cms/s/2/560c6a06-0a63-11dc-93ae-000b5df10621.html

Google Custom Search. http://www.google.com/coop/

Hatcher, Otis Gospodnetic and Erik. *Lucene in Action*. 2004. Manning Publications.

Hibernate Search Apache Lucene Integration. http://www.hibernate.org/hib_docs/search/reference/en/html/index.html

Hibernate Search. http://www.hibernate.org/410.html

Hotchkiss, Gord. "The Pros & Cons Of Personalized Search." Search Engine Land, March 2007. http://searchengineland.com/070309-081324.php

Hunter, David J., Muin J. Khoury, and Jeffrey M. Drazen. "Letting the genome out of the bottle—will we get our wish?" *New England Journal of Medicine*. 2008 Jan 10;358(2):105-7 http://content.nejm.org/cgi/content/full/358/2/105

Improve Indexing Speed. Lucene Wiki. http://wiki.apache.org/lucene-java/ImproveIndexingSpeed

Lauerman, John. "Google Backs Harvard Scientist's 100,000-Genome Quest." February 29, 2008. http://www.bloomberg.com/apps/news?pid=newsarchive&sid=abC4lpqJ0TZs

Lucene FAQ. http://wiki.apache.org/lucene-java/LuceneFAQ

Lucene Resources. http://wiki.apache.org/lucene-java/Resources

Luke. http://www.getopt.org/luke/

Newcomb, Kevin. "A Look at the Next Generation of Search?" February, 2007. http://searchenginewatch.com/showPage.html?page=3624837

Nielsen online. "Nielsen Announces February US Search Share Rankings." March 2–8. http://www.nielsen-netratings.com/pr/pr_080326.pdf

Owens, Steven J. Lucene Tutorial. http://www.darksleep.com/lucene/

Rich Il's Conference Trip. http://ils501.blogspot.com/

Smart, John Ferguson. Integrate advanced search functionalities into your apps. JavaWorld.com. 2006. http://www.javaworld.com/javaworld/jw-09-2006/jw-0925-lucene.html

Solr. http://lucene.apache.org/solr/

"Updating an index." http://wiki.apache.org/lucene-java/UpdatingAnIndex

12

Building a recommendation engine

This chapter covers

- Fundamentals for building a recommendation engine
- A content-based approach for building a recommendation engine
- A collaborative-based approach for building a recommendation engine
- Real-world case studies of Amazon, Google News, and Netflix

In recent years, increasing amount of user interaction has provided applications with a large amount of information that can be converted into intelligence. This interaction may be in the form of rating an item, writing a blog entry, tagging an item, connecting with other users, or sharing items of interest with others. This increased interaction has led to the problem of information overload. What we need is a system that can recommend or present items to the user based on the user's interests and interactions. This is where personalization and recommendation engines come in.

Recommendation engines aim to show items of interest to a user. Recommendation engines in essence are matching engines that take into account the context of where the items are being shown and to whom they're being shown.

Recommendation engines are one of the best ways of utilizing collective intelligence in your application.

Netflix, the world's largest online movie rental service, provides a good proof-point of how important recommendation engines are to commerce. Netflix offers personalized recommendations to over 8.4 million subscribers with a catalog of more than 100,000 movie titles.[1] Netflix's recommendation engine is very effective, with about 60 percent of Netflix members selecting their movies based on movie recommendations that have been tailored to their individual tastes. Later in this chapter (see section 12.4.3), we briefly review the approach Netflix took to build their recommendation system.

In this chapter, we look at how to develop a recommendation engine. To do this, we use most of the concepts that we've developed in previous chapters. We begin with a brief introduction to various concepts related to building a recommendation engine. Next, continuing with our running example of using blog entries from Technorati, we build a recommendation engine using a content-analysis approach. For this, we first leverage Lucene and then use the text analytics framework developed in chapter 8. Next, we look at the various collaborative approaches to building recommendation engines. This will be followed by reviewing a few approaches—Amazon, Google News, and Netflix—to building recommendation engines in the industry. At the end of this chapter, you should be comfortable building a recommendation engine using both content-based and collaborative approaches.

12.1 *Recommendation engine fundamentals*

One of the best-known examples of a recommendation engine is Amazon.com. Amazon provides personalized recommendations in a number of ways, one of which is shown in figure 12.1. Figure 12.1 shows the recommendations provided by Amazon when you look at the book *Lucene in Action* by Gospodnetic and Hatcher. Note that they recommend a number of books under the heading "Customers Who Bought

Figure 12.1 An example of the output of a recommendation engine at Amazon.com

---

[1] As of September 2008; see http://www.netflix.com/MediaCenter?id=5379#about

This Item Also Bought." This is an example of an *item-based* recommendation, where items related to a particular item are being recommended.

In this section, we introduce basic concepts related to building a recommendation engine. Let's begin by taking a deeper look at the many forms of recommendation engines.

12.1.1 Introducing the recommendation engine

As shown in figure 12.2, a recommendation engine takes the following four inputs to make a recommendation to a user:

- *The user's profile*—age, gender, geographical location, net worth, and so on
- *Information about the various items available*—content associated with the item
- *The interactions of the users*—ratings, tagging, bookmarking, saving, emailing, browsing content
- *The context of where the items will be shown*—the subcategory of items that are to be considered

As we mentioned in section 2.2.1, a user is also an item. In social networking, other users are recommended based on the context of the application.

One of the easiest forms of a recommendation list is the "Top Item List," where items that have been viewed, tagged, bought, or saved the most in a period of time are presented to the user. While promoting top products is useful, what we really want is to create a personalized list of recommendations for users.

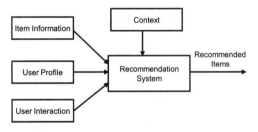

Figure 12.2   The inputs and outputs of a recommendation engine

Recommendation engines can help build the following types of features in your application:

- Users who *acted on* this item also took *action on* these other items, where the *acted on* could be watched, purchased, viewed, saved, emailed, bookmarked, added to favorites, shared, created, and so on
- Other users you may be interested in
- Items related to this item
- Recommended items

Here are some concrete examples of these use cases:

- Users who watched this video and also watched these other videos
- New items related to this particular article
- Users who are similar to you
- Products that you may be interested in

In recommendation systems, there's always a conflict between *exploitation* and *exploration*. Exploitation is the process of recommending items that fall into the user's sweet spot, based on things you already know about the user. Exploration is being presented with items that don't fall into the user's sweet spot, with the aim that you may find a new sweet spot that can be exploited later. Greedy recommenders, with little exploration, will recommend items that are similar to the ones that the user has rated in the past. In essence, the user will never be presented with items that are outside their current spot. A common approach to facilitating exploration is to not necessarily recommend just the top n items, but to add a few items selected at random from candidate items. It's desirable to build in some diversity in the recommendation set provided to the user.

Next, let's look at the two basic approaches to building recommendation engines.

12.1.2 *Item-based and user-based analysis*

There are two main approaches to building recommendation systems, based on whether the system searches for related items or related users.

In item-based analysis, items related to a particular item are determined. When a user likes a particular item, items related to that item are recommended. As shown in figure 12.3, if items A and C are highly similar and a user likes item A, then item C is

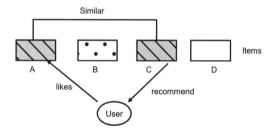

Figure 12.3   Item-based analysis: similar items are recommended

recommended to the user. You may recall our discussion in section 2.2.3, where we looked at two approaches to finding similar items. First was content-based analysis, where the term vector associated with the content was used. The second was collaborative filtering, where user actions such as rating, bookmarking, and so forth are used to find similar items.

In user-based analysis, users similar to the user are first determined. As shown in figure 12.4, if a user likes item A, then the same item can be recommended to other users who are similar to user A. Similar users can be obtained by using profile-based information about the user—for example cluster the users based on their attributes, such as age, gender, geographic location, net worth, and so on. Alternatively, you can find similar users using a collaborative-based approach by analyzing the users' actions.

Later on in section 12.4, we look at examples of both: item-based analysis as used in Amazon and user-based analysis as used by Google News. Here are some tips that may help you decide which approach is most suitable for your application:

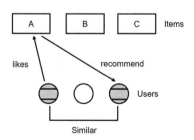

Figure 12.4   User-based analysis: items liked by similar users are recommended

- If your item list doesn't change much, it's useful to create an item-to-item correlation table using item-based analysis. This table can then be used in the recommendation engine.

- If your item list changes frequently, for example for news-related items, it may be useful to find related users for recommendations.

- If the recommended item is a user, there's no option but to find related users.

- The dimensionality of the item and user space can be helpful in deciding which approach may be easier to implement. For example, if you have millions of users and an order of magnitude fewer items, it may be easier to do item-based analysis. Whenever users are considered, you'll deal with sparse matrices. For example, a typical user may have bought only a handful of items from the thousands or millions of items that are available in an application.

- If there are only a small number of users, it may be worthwhile to bootstrap your application using item-based analysis. Furthermore, there's no reason (other than perhaps time to implement and performance) why these two approaches can't be combined.

- It's been shown empirically that item-based algorithms are computationally faster to implement than user-based algorithms and provide comparable or better results.

Both user- and item-based analysis require the computation of a *similarity* metric. Next, let's look at how this is done.

12.1.3 Computing similarity using content-based and collaborative techniques

Regardless of whether you use item-based or user-based analysis, there are two main approaches for computing similarity, depending on whether you're analyzing text or user actions. If you can represent the content associated with an item or a user in terms of a term vector, then taking the dot product of two normalized vectors provides a measure of how close two term vectors are. This corresponds to invoking the method for the TagMagnitudeVector class we introduced in section 8.2.2.

```
public double dotProduct(TagMagnitudeVector o)
```

In content-based analysis, recommending items simply amounts to finding items that have similar term vectors.

As described in section 2.4 and illustrated in table 12.1, a typical collaborative filtering algorithm represents each customer as an N-dimensional vector of items, where N is the number of distinct items in the system. Each cell value in the vector corresponds to either a positive number quantifying how well the user liked the item or a negative number if the user disliked the item. Similar to the inverse-document frequency, where commonly used words have less weight, a factor may be used to compensate for best-selling or highly rated items—the weight for this factor is inversely proportional to the number of entries that this item has in its column.

	Item 1	Item 2	...	...	Item N
User 1	2				
User 2	5	1			
......					1
User m				2	

Table 12.1   Representing the user as an N-dimensional vector

Note that this vector will be sparse for almost all users—a typical user would have acted on only a handful of the *N* items. In section 12.3.3, we look at one of the ways to deal with sparse matrices: reducing dimensionality using singular value decomposition (SVD).

We look at collaborative filtering algorithms in more detail in section 12.3. For now, you may recall from section 2.4 that there are three main approaches to computing the similarities while using collaborative filtering:

1 Cosine-based similarity computation
2 Correlation-based similarity computation (Pearson-r correlation)
3 Adjusted cosine-based similarity computation

In section 12.3, we develop the infrastructure to compute these similarities. Next, let's look at the advantages and disadvantages of content-based and collaborative techniques.

12.1.4 *Comparison of content-based and collaborative techniques*

The following are some advantages and disadvantages of collaborative and content-based techniques.

- Collaborative-based techniques have the advantage that they treat an item as a black-box—they don't use any information about the content itself. Unlike content-based techniques, the same infrastructure is applicable across domains and languages. So if you build a recommendation engine that works well in the English language, you can use the same infrastructure for your site in Chinese. For content such as images, music, and videos that might not have text associated with them, content-based analysis may not be an option, unless of course you allow users to tag the items (see chapter 3 for more on tagging).

- In content-based analysis, the algorithm has no notion of the item's quality—it's all based on the term vector. There's no notion of how good or bad a particular item is—the algorithm doesn't know whether an article is well-written or poorly written. On the other hand, in collaborative-based approaches, you have usable quantitative information about the quality of the item. Web search engines provide a good analogy to this. Prior to Google, most search engines used content-based approaches for showing search results. Google, with its page rank, uses a collaborative approach—it uses how various sites have been linked together to compute a rank for each site.

- Over a period of time, the results from content-based analysis don't change much; text associated with the item may not change much. As time progresses, there may be some changes in the term vector due to changes in the inverse document frequency for the terms in the document, but on the whole things don't change much for an item. Collaborative-based approaches rely on user interaction, and over a period of time user interaction on the item may change. For example, a video on a current topic may be rated highly. Over a period of time, as new content comes in and the video is no longer relevant to current issues, it may get lower ratings.

- Collaborative-based systems rely on using the information provided by a user to find other related users and recommend items based on the ratings from similar users. In the absence of an adequate amount of data, these systems can perform poorly in their prediction capabilities. For a new user with little interaction history, there may not be enough information to find similar users using the user's interaction history for a collaborative approach. Typically, to overcome this, user-profile information—age, gender, demographics, and so forth—is also used to find similar users.

- Collaborative-based systems won't recommend new items added to the system unless they've been rated by a substantial number of users.

Some recommendation systems use a hybrid approach, combining content-based and collaborative analysis. The combination could be in the form of implementing the two methods separately and then combining the results. Another way is to use the user's profile to find similar users when a user hasn't rated enough items. Recommendation systems may also leverage additional information that may affect the prediction, for example, the time of the year, or month, or week.

Now that we have a basic understanding of content-based and collaborative-based approaches, we take a more detailed look at how to implement these two approaches. In the next two sections, we first cover content-based analysis, followed by collaborative-based analysis.

12.2 Content-based analysis

Fortunately, most of the work that needs to be done to build a recommendation engine based on content analysis has already been done in prior chapters, more specifically in chapters 8, 9, and 11. In this section, we demonstrate finding related items using Lucene; using the text analytics framework developed in chapter 8; finding related items for a set of documents; and lastly how content-based results can be further personalized for a user.

12.2.1 Finding similar items using a search engine (Lucene)

In this section, we demonstrate how you can find similar items using a search engine such as Lucene. The basic approach is to compose a query, based on the content of the document you want to find related items for, and query the index for items that best match this query.

At this stage, it's helpful to look at the output from some of the code that we write in this section. Listing 12.1 shows the output from one of the runs from the sample code we implement next (listing 12.2). In this example, 10 blog entries for the tag *collective intelligence* were retrieved from Technorati and indexed using Lucene. Then related blog entries for each blog entry were computed—these are shown as tabbed entries below the blog entry.

Listing 12.1 Sample output from related blogs

```
Social Media is Just the Next Logical Step in Technology
http://mindblogging.typepad.com/whataconcept
    our learning wiki http://www.estuyajuan.com/blog
    The Dilemma of Personalized Library Services
http://sowebup.wordpress.com
Companies using the Power of WE - The Consumers! http://www.we-magazine.net
    our learning wiki http://www.estuyajuan.com/blog
    The Dilemma of Personalized Library Services
http://sowebup.wordpress.com
Pagerank isn' for humans http://fmeyer.org
    our learning wiki http://www.estuyajuan.com/blog
    A Tool to Attract More People to Your Cause
http://www.movingfrommetowe.com
    Le web 2.0 affiche ses vraies valeurs : financières, s'ntend. A
l'xemple de Google et son
    The Dilemma of Personalized Library Services
http://sowebup.wordpress.com
    Programming Collective Intelligence: Building Smart Web 2.0
Applications http://2.smilesquare.com
    Supporting occupation - Gordon Brown in Israel
http://heathlander.wordpress.com
Programming Collective Intelligence: Building Smart Web 2.0 Applications
http://2.smilesquare.com
    our learning wiki http://www.estuyajuan.com/blog
    Le web 2.0 affiche ses vraies valeurs : financières, s'ntend. A
l'xemple de Google et son
    Pagerank isn' for humans http://fmeyer.org
    The Dilemma of Personalized Library Services
http://sowebup.wordpress.com
```

First, let's take a simple approach of hand-crafting this query. Listing 12.2 shows a simple method that uses the `TermFreqVector` associated with a document field to create a `BooleanQuery`.

Listing 12.2 Creating a `BooleanQuery` using the term vector in Lucene

```
private Query composeTermVectorBooleanQuery(IndexReader indexReader,
    int docNum,String fieldName, float boost ) throws Exception {
    TermFreqVector termFreqVector =
        indexReader.getTermFreqVector(docNum, fieldName);      ◁─── Retrieves
                                                                    term
    BooleanQuery booleanQuery = new BooleanQuery();                 frequency
    String [] terms = termFreqVector.getTerms();                    vector
    for (String term: terms) {
```

```
        Query termQuery = new TermQuery(new Term(fieldName,term));
        booleanQuery.add(termQuery, BooleanClause.Occur.SHOULD);      ◁──┐
    }                                                            ┌──────────┐
    booleanQuery.setBoost(boost);    ◁──┐  ┌──────────┐          │ Creates  │
    return booleanQuery;                 │  │ Applies  │          │BooleanQuery,│
}                                           │ boost factor │      │adding in terms│
                                            │ for query │         └──────────┘
                                            └──────────┘
```

We first obtain the `TermFreqVector` associated with the specified document and the field. Next, we create an instance of `BooleanQuery`, to which we add all the terms (or a subset of terms) from the term vector. Note that we specify the condition `Boolean-Clause.Occur.SHOULD`, which means that not all the terms are required. Lastly, since we combine the query with other `Boolean` queries, we set a boost factor for this query.

Let's apply this approach to our running example of blog entries. We build on our example from chapter 11, where we indexed blog entries. Let's find related blog entries for each blog entry in our Lucene index. Listing 12.3 shows the code for obtaining related blog entries for a given blog in our index.

Listing 12.3 Creating a composite `BooleanQuery` and retrieving blog entries

```
private List<RetrievedBlogEntry> getRelatedBlogEntries(    ┌──────────┐
    IndexSearcher indexSearcher, int docNum)               │ Creates  │
    throws Exception {                                      │BooleanQuery for│
  IndexReader indexReader = indexSearcher.getIndexReader(); │title and boosts it│
                                                            └──────────┘
  Query booleanTitleQuery = composeTermVectorBooleanQuery(
     indexReader,       docNum,"title", 3.0f);      ◁───────────────────┘

  Query booleanCompleteTextQuery =composeTermVectorBooleanQuery(
     indexReader, docNum,
     "completeText", 1.0f);                  ◁──┐  ┌──────────────┐
                                                 │  │ Creates BooleanQuery │
  BooleanQuery likeThisQuery = new BooleanQuery();│ for complete text │
  likeThisQuery.add(booleanTitleQuery, BooleanClause.Occur.SHOULD);
  likeThisQuery.add(booleanCompleteTextQuery,
     BooleanClause.Occur.SHOULD);     ◁── Combines two queries

  return getRelatedBlogEntries(indexSearcher, likeThisQuery);
}

private List<RetrievedBlogEntry> getRelatedBlogEntries(
  IndexSearcher indexSearcher,
     Query query) throws Exception {        ┌──────────┐
  RetrievedBlogHitCollector blogHitCollector =│ Retrieves │
     new RetrievedBlogHitCollector(indexSearcher);│ related entries │
  indexSearcher.search(query, blogHitCollector);   ◁────┘ using query │
  return blogHitCollector.getBlogEntries();                └──────────┘
}
```

Since we want to weigh the title more than other text, we first create an instance of `BooleanQuery` using the title and apply a boost factor of 3. This is combined with a `BooleanQuery` representation for the complete text. Lastly, related blog entries are obtained from the index using the `RetrievedBlogHitCollector` class we implemented in section 11.3.7.

Finally, listing 12.4 shows the code for retrieving all the blog instances from the index and getting the related items for each blog entry.

Listing 12.4   Iterating over all documents in the index

```java
public void illustrateMoreLikeThisByQuery(Directory indexDirectory)
    throws Exception {
    IndexSearcher indexSearcher = new IndexSearcher(indexDirectory);
    for (int i = 0; i < indexSearcher.maxDoc(); i ++) {
        Document document = indexSearcher.doc(i);
        System.out.println(document.get("title") + " " +
        document.get("url"));
        if (document != null) {
            List<RetrievedBlogEntry> relatedBlogs =
            getRelatedBlogEntries( indexSearcher, i) ;
            for (RetrievedBlogEntry relatedBlog : relatedBlogs ) {
                System.out.println("\t" + relatedBlog.getTitle() + +
                " " + relatedBlog.getUrl());
            }
        }
    }
}
```

Our rather simplistic approach doesn't take into account the term frequency and inverse document frequencies associated with each term in the query. Fortunately, Lucene's `contrib/query` package provides a fairly good version of this functionality. Download and compile the following Lucene similarity package:

http://svn.apache.org/repos/asf/lucene/java/trunk/contrib/queries/src/java/ org/apache/lucene/search/similar/MoreLikeThis.java

Listing 12.5 shows the same functionality developed using the `MoreLikeThis` class.

Listing 12.5   Iterating over all documents in the index

```java
public List<RetrievedBlogEntry>
  getRelatedBlogsUsingLuceneMoreLikeThis(            Specifies fields to
      IndexSearcher indexSearcher,                      create query
        int docNum) throws Exception {
    IndexReader indexReader = indexSearcher.getIndexReader();
    MoreLikeThis moreLikeThis = new MoreLikeThis(indexReader);   Min
    moreLikeThis.setAnalyzer(getAnalyzer());                     number of
    String [] fieldNames = {"title", "completeText"};            documents
    moreLikeThis.setFieldNames(fieldNames);                      containing
    moreLikeThis.setMinDocFreq(0);                               each term
    Query query = moreLikeThis.like(docNum);
    System.out.println(query.toString());                Creates query
    return getRelatedBlogEntries( indexSearcher, query); for document
}
```

`MoreLikeThis` is a fairly sophisticated class that creates a query to find items similar to a particular document. It has a number of settings, such as the minimum number of documents in which a term should appear, the minimum term frequency, the minimum and maximum length of words, stop words, and the maximum number of query terms. Using this class is fairly straightforward. We create an instance of More-LikeThis, set the analyzer, specify the fields to be used, and set the minimum document frequency to be 0, because we have few blog entries in our Lucene index.

Next, let's look at building a content-based recommendation engine using the text analytics infrastructure we developed in chapter 8.

12.2.2 Building a content-based recommendation engine

You may recall the TagMagnitudeVector class from section 8.2.2 and listing 8.18. The TagMagnitudeVector class contains a list of tags with magnitudes, where the magnitude terms are normalized such that the sum of the squares of the magnitudes for all the terms is 1. Each term magnitude is obtained by computing the term frequency and the inverse document frequency for the terms. The similarity between two documents can be computed by taking their dot products. For example, for a Tag-MagnitudeVector, use the following method:

```
public double dotProduct(TagMagnitudeVector o) ;
```

Finding similar items for an item amounts to finding items that have the highest dot products with the given item's term vector. Let's illustrate how to build such a recommendation engine. First, we need to define a simple Java bean class RelevanceText-DataItem, which is a container for a TextDataItem along with a double relevance value. Listing 12.6 contains the implementation for RelevanceTextDataItem.

Listing 12.6 Implementation for `RelevanceTextDataItem`

```
package com.alag.ci.recoengine;

import com.alag.ci.cluster.TextDataItem;

public class RelevanceTextDataItem implements
    Comparable<RelevanceTextDataItem>{
  private double relevance = 0;
  private TextDataItem dataItem = null;

  public RelevanceTextDataItem(TextDataItem dataItem, double relevance) {
    this.relevance = relevance;
    this.dataItem = dataItem;
  }

  public int compareTo(RelevanceTextDataItem other) {      ⟵  Implementation
    if( this.relevance > other.getRelevance()) {                for interface
      return -1;
    }
    if( this.relevance < other.getRelevance()) {
      return 1;
    }
    return 0;
  }

  public TextDataItem getDataItem() {
    return dataItem;
  }
```

```
    public double getRelevance() {
       return relevance;
    }
}
```

Next, let's define a class, `ContentBasedBlogRecoEngine`, which will retrieve blog entries from Technorati and then find relevant blog entries for each blog entry. Listing 12.7 shows the first part of the code for `ContentBasedBlogRecoEngine`. This listing shows the main steps in building a content-based recommendation engine—creating the dataset, finding relevant items, and printing it out.

Listing 12.7   The main steps for building a content-based recommendation engine

```
package com.alag.ci.recoengine;

import java.util.ArrayList;
import java.util.Collections;
import java.util.List;

import com.alag.ci.blog.dataset.impl.BlogDataSetCreatorImpl;
import com.alag.ci.blog.search.RetrievedBlogEntry;
import com.alag.ci.cluster.DataSetCreator;
import com.alag.ci.cluster.TextDataItem;
import com.alag.ci.textanalysis.TagMagnitudeVector;

public class ContentBasedBlogRecoEngine {

   public static void main(String [] args) throws Exception{
      ContentBasedBlogRecoEngine recoEngine =
        new ContentBasedBlogRecoEngine();
      List<TextDataItem> dataItems = recoEngine.createLearningData();
      recoEngine.illustrateContentRecoEngine(dataItems);
   }

   public List<TextDataItem> createLearningData() throws Exception {
      DataSetCreator creator = new BlogDataSetCreatorImpl();
      return creator.createLearningData();
   }

   public void illustrateContentRecoEngine(List<TextDataItem> dataItems) {
      for (TextDataItem dataItem: dataItems) {
         RetrievedBlogEntry blogEntry =                    Retrieves blog entries
           (RetrievedBlogEntry)dataItem.getData();        from Technorati
         System.out.println(blogEntry.getTitle());
         List<RelevanceTextDataItem> relevantItems =
              getRelevantDataItems(
              dataItem,dataItems ) ;
         for (RelevanceTextDataItem relevantItem: relevantItems) {
           blogEntry =
            (RetrievedBlogEntry)(
            relevantItem.getDataItem().getData());
           System.out.println("\t" + blogEntry.getTitle() +
            " " + relevantItem.getRelevance());
         }
      }
   }
```

The method `createLearningData()` uses an instance of `BlogDataSetCreatorImpl` (see chapter 8) to create a `List` of `TextDataItems`. `illustrateContentRecoEngine` simply iterates over all blog entry instances to print out related items for each entry. Listing 12.8 shows the implementation for the method to find the related items for the blogs.

Listing 12.8 Getting relevant items in `ContentBasedBlogRecoEngine`

```
private List<RelevanceTextDataItem> getRelevantDataItems(
    TextDataItem parentDataItem,
    List<TextDataItem> candidateDataItems ) {
  TagMagnitudeVector tmv = parentDataItem.getTagMagnitudeVector();
  List<RelevanceTextDataItem> relevantItems = new
ArrayList<RelevanceTextDataItem>();
    for (TextDataItem candidateDataItem: candidateDataItems) {
      if (!parentDataItem.equals(candidateDataItem)) {
        double relevance =
tmv.dotProduct(candidateDataItem.getTagMagnitudeVector());        ⟵ Dot
        if (relevance > 0.) {                                          product
          relevantItems.add(new RelevanceTextDataItem(                 of term
          candidateDataItem, relevance));                              vectors
        }
      }
    }
    Collections.sort(relevantItems);        ⟵┐ Sort results based
    return relevantItems;                      on relevance
  }
}
```

To find related blogs, we simply iterate over all blog instances, compute the similarity with the blog of interest, and then sort all relevant blog items based on the similarity. Listing 12.9 shows sample output from the code developed in this section. Here, you can see the related blog entries for a blog along with the level of relevance between the parent and the children blogs.

Listing 12.9 Related entries for a blog

```
Social Media is Just the Next Logical Step in Technology http://
   mindblogging.typepad.com/whataconcept
   our learning wiki http://www.estuyajuan.com/blog 0.01720982414882634
   The Dilemma of Personalized Library Services
http://sowebup.wordpress.com 0.01403890610073534
Companies using the Power of WE - The Consumers! http://www.we-magazine.net
   our learning wiki http://www.estuyajuan.com/blog 0.0396024241655864
   The Dilemma of Personalized Library Services
http://sowebup.wordpress.com 0.016152829610989242
Pagerank isn' for humans http://fmeyer.org
   our learning wiki http://www.estuyajuan.com/blog 0.04675732078317664
   A Tool to Attract More People to Your Cause
...http://www.movingfrommetowe.com 0.038080852316322855
   Le web 2.0 affiche ses vraies valeurs : financières, s'ntend. A
l'xemple de Google et son 0.029162920196574908
   The Dilemma of Personalized Library Services
http://sowebup.wordpress.com 0.0153460076524816
```

```
Programming Collective Intelligence: Building Smart Web 2.0
Applications http://2.smilesquare.com 0.01044583466318214
   Supporting occupation - Gordon Brown in Israel
http://heathlander.wordpress.com 0.006828125603489045
Programming Collective Intelligence: Building Smart Web 2.0
Applications http://2.smilesquare.com
   our learning wiki http://www.estuyajuan.com/blog 0.031064220852246284
   Le web 2.0 affiche ses vraies valeurs : financières, s'ntend. A
l'xemple de Google et son 0.027501197695123845
   Pagerank isn' for humans http://fmeyer.org 0.01044583466318214
   The Dilemma of Personalized Library Services
http://sowebup.wordpress.com 0.0036025401391830475
```

So far we've looked at how to build a content-based recommendation engine using a search engine and using the text processing toolkit we built in chapter 8. A common use case is when we have a collection of items, such as a topic or subtopic, and we want to find items that are similar to this collection. We look at this next.

12.2.3 *Related items for document clusters*

In an application, it's common to define topics or subtopics that have underlying documents associated with them. For example, if you're building a site about data mining, you may have five subtopics: association rules, attribute importance, clustering, classification, and regression. For each of these subtopics, you may have filed a number of documents. You want to build a representation for each of these subtopics by using the content that's been associated with each subtopic.

Fortunately, each document has an associated normalized term vector, and finding a composite representation from the document set simply amounts to adding all the term vectors for the documents. Listing 12.10 illustrates the code for combining the different term vectors.

> **Listing 12.10   Code to illustrate merging of documents**

```
public void illustrateMergingOfDocuments(
    List<TagMagnitudeVector> tagMagnitudeVectors) {
    List<TagMagnitude> tagMagnitudes = Collections.emptyList();
    TagMagnitudeVector emptyTMV =
      new TagMagnitudeVectorImpl(tagMagnitudes);
    TagMagnitudeVector mergedTMV = emptyTMV.add(tagMagnitudeVectors);
    System.out.println(mergedTMV);
}
```

Once we have a combined term vector representation for the subtopic, finding similar items is the same as in section 12.2.2. In section 11.6.3, we looked at trends in intelligent search where you can further personalize search results using metadata associated with the user. We briefly look at this next.

12.2.4 *Personalizing content for a user*

When there's a tag vector representation for the user, it's also possible to sort the candidate list of items using the term vector representation for the user. Typically, a candidate list of items is stored for each item of interest (around 20–30 items). Then, based on which user is visiting the content, the user's term vector is used to bubble up the content that may be of most interest to the user. Make sure that the recommendation list isn't completely homogenous and there's enough diversity in the recommendation list to allow the user to explore new areas of interest.

With this overview of content-based recommendation systems, we're now ready to take a more detailed look at collaborative filtering.

12.3 *Collaborative filtering*

In collaborative filtering, an item is considered as a black box—we don't look at its content—and user interactions (such as rating, saving, purchasing) with the item are used to recommend an item of interest to the user. More formally, given a dataset of user actions (also called the *user-item dataset*), we want to recommend items to a user. As discussed in section 12.1.2, we either find similar users and recommend items liked by these users, or we find items similar to an item of interest. There are two main classes of collaborative filtering algorithms—*memory*-based and *model*-based.

In memory-based algorithms, the entire user-item database is used. The algorithm first finds a set of similar users and then makes a recommendation or set of recommendations (top *n* recommendations) by combining the preferences of the similar users. This approach is also known as *nearest neighbor.* Typically, the expected rating for an item is estimated by combining the ratings of similar users, using the degree of similarity as a measure to combine the ratings. One problem with using the weighted sum to predict the rating is the bias that different users may have in rating items. For example, one user may provide ratings that average 3 while another may provide ratings that are similar but which average 3.5. Therefore, it's also common to predict the ratings for a user using the weighted sum of the deviations in ratings of similar users. In section 12.1.3, we looked at the three approaches to computing the similarities between users: cosine-based similarity computation, Pearson-r correlation, and the adjusted cosine-based similarity computation. In an application with a large number of users, it isn't practical to compute similar users for a user in real-time. Therefore, it's common to pre-compute this association either in a lookup table or by creating user clusters.

Model-based collaborative filtering algorithms create a model (see chapters 9 and 10) using the user-item data to predict ratings that a user is likely to give. Model-based algorithms try to model the user based on past ratings and then use the models to predict the ratings on items the user hasn't visited or rated. Commonly used model-based approaches include latent semantic indexing (LSI), Bayesian clustering, probabilistic latent semantic indexing (PLSI), multiple multiplication factor model, Markov Decision process, and latent Dirichlet allocation.

12.3.1 *k-nearest neighbor*

In section 2.4, we worked through the process of collaborative filtering for generating both an item-to-item correlation matrix and a user-to-user similarity matrix.

Collaborative filtering algorithms use the user-item matrix shown in table 12.1 as input. The matrix is transposed—each item becomes a row and users become columns—when related items are to be found.

There are really two steps in applying collaborative filtering. First, we need to determine similar items or users, and then make a prediction using the similar items. This approach is also commonly known as *k-nearest neighbor (k-NN)*. The predicted value is typically a weighted sum of the ratings for the *k* neighboring items. To take care of different biases in ratings among the *k* neighbors, the weighted sum of the deviations in ratings from the user's average rating value is also used. Let's look at this computation via an example.

We illustrate the process of predicting ratings using the ratings of similar users by working through the example we introduced in section 2.4.1. Table 12.2 shows the user-item matrix associated with this example.

	Photo1	**Photo2**	**Photo3**	**Average**
John	3	4	2	3
Jane	2	2	4	8/3
Doe	1	3	5	3
Average	2	3	11/3	26/3

Table 12.2   Ratings data used in the example

In section 2.4.1, we worked through three methods for computing the similarities. Using the Pearson-r correlation computation, we arrived at the user-to-user similarity matrix shown in table 12.3.

	John	**Jane**	**Doe**
John	1	-0.866	-0.5
Jane	-0.866	1	0.87
Doe	-0.5	0.87	1

Table 12.3   Correlation matrix for the users

John is correlated with Jane by -0.866, while he's correlated to Doe by -0.5. Next, let's look at how we can predict John's expected rating for Photo1 using the ratings of similar users Jane and Doe.

John's expected rating for Photo1 = John's average rating + w1 * (Jane's rating – Jane's average rating) + w2 * (Doe's rating – Doe's average rating)

$$= 3 + (-0.866/1.366) * (2 - 8/3) + (-0.5/1.366) * (1 - 3)$$
$$= 4.2$$

Similarly, the predicted rating for Photo2 from John is

$$= 3 + (-0.866/1.366) * (2 - 8/3) + (-0.5/1.366) * (3 - 3)$$
$$= 3.4$$

If you remember from our discussions in earlier chapters, the inverse document frequency (idf) is used in the term vector to emphasize terms that aren't common across documents. A similar concept, *inverse user frequency*, is used to pre-process the user-item data. Items that are popular aren't very good at capturing similarities between users and items. Therefore, if n is the total number of users and ni of them have rated a particular item, then the inverse user frequency is defined as log (n/ni). Entries in the user-item table are multiplied by their inverse user frequencies before the computation of the similarities.

For large-scale systems, it can be expensive to find k neighbors in real-time. Users are typically clustered offline so as to retrieve the k nearest neighbors in real time. K-NN algorithms need to deal with sparse data, which can affect the quality of the solution. Furthermore, these algorithms can run into scalability issues, as their computation grows with both the number of users and the number of items being processed.

For this reason, large sites, such as Amazon, use item-based collaborative filtering. The example in section 2.4 illustrated the process of item-to-item collaborative filtering. In this process, the user-item table (table 12.1) is transposed to have items as rows and users as columns. In essence, every item has a vector associated with it, each user being a dimension. For every item, the k (a number typically between 10 and 30) closest items are obtained using a similarity function (vector dot product or correlation computation). Related items for an item are stored in the database. Once the related item table has been computed for each item, displaying related items to a user is a simple lookup. This approach scales independently of the number of users on the system.

Next, let's look at how we can implement these algorithms.

12.3.2 *Packages for implementing collaborative filtering*

There are a number of different options in implementing k-nearest neighbor, which we go through in this section.

The collaborative filtering problem is similar to the text analysis problem—both of them deal with large-dimensional sparse matrices. In chapter 8, we developed the `TagMagnitudeVector` infrastructure for representing a term vector and computing the cosine similarity between two term vectors. The first option is to leverage this infrastructure. For data represented in the user-item table (see table 12.1), each row corresponding to a user is equivalent to a term vector for a document. This can be represented by a `TagMagnitudeVector`, and cosine-similarity can be computed by taking the dot product of two `TagMagnitudeVector` instances. Furthermore, if we wanted to compute the similarity by computing the Pearson-r correlation, we can extend the `TagMagnitudeVector` class so that all the terms would be normalized to have a zero mean and unit magnitude. Again, the correlation between two such normalized vectors would be their dot product.

The second option is to leverage WEKA (see section 7.2). The `weka.core.neighboursearch` package contains a number of classes that implement the nearest-neighbor search algorithms. Some of these classes are described in table 12.4 and shown in figure 12.5. All these search classes extend the abstract base class `NearestNeigbourSearch`.

Table 12.4 `NearestNeighborSearch` **classes in WEKA**

Class	Description
`NearestNeighbourSearch`	Abstract class for nearest-neighbor search
`BallTree`	Implements the BallTree/Metric Tree algorithm for nearest-neighbor search
`CoverTree`	Implements the CoverTree data structure for nearest-neighbor search
`KDTree`	Implements the KDTree search algorithm for nearest-neighbor search
`LinearNNSearch`	Implements the brute force search algorithm for nearest-neighbor search

In section 10.4, we looked at classifiers available in WEKA. The `weka.classifiers.lazy` class contains classification algorithms that are based on nearest-neighbor search algorithms. Some of these algorithms are shown in figure 12.5 and described in table 12.5.

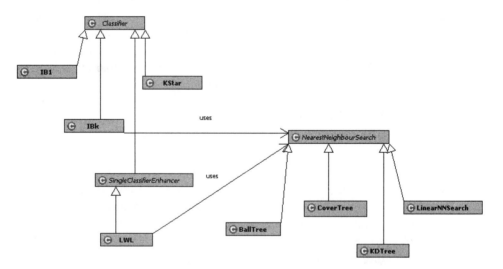

Figure 12.5   WEKA classes related to instance-based learning and nearest-neighbor search

Table 12.5   Classifiers in WEKA based on nearest-neighbor search

Class	Description
`IB1`	Nearest-neighbor classifier.
`IBk`	K-nearest neighbors classifier.
`KStar`	K* is an instance-based classifier that uses an entropy-based distance function.

Next, let's walk through a simple example that illustrates what's involved in implementing the k-nearest neighbor algorithm using WEKA. We split the implementation into two sections and use the dataset in table 12.2 as our example. The first part deals with creating the Instances to represent the data, while the second part deals with building a classifier and evaluating it. Listing 12.11 shows the implementation for creating the Instances dataset along with the main method that enumerates the three things this example will do: create the attributes, create the learning dataset, and illustrate the k-NN algorithm.

Listing 12.11 Creating the dataset for implementing k-NN

```java
package com.alag.ci.cf;

import weka.classifiers.lazy.IBk;
import weka.core.Attribute;
import weka.core.FastVector;
import weka.core.Instance;
import weka.core.Instances;

public class KNNWEKAExample {

    public static final void main(String [] args) throws Exception {
        KNNWEKAExample eg = new KNNWEKAExample();
        FastVector attributes = eg.createAttributes();
        Instances instances = eg.createLearningDataSet(attributes);
        eg.illustrateClassification(instances);
    }

    private FastVector createAttributes() {
        FastVector allAttributes = new FastVector(3);
        allAttributes.addElement(new Attribute("item1"));
        allAttributes.addElement(new Attribute("item2"));
        allAttributes.addElement(new Attribute("item3"));
        return allAttributes;
    }

    private Instances createLearningDataSet(FastVector allAttributes) {
        Instances trainingDataSet =
            new Instances("wekaCF", allAttributes, 3);
        trainingDataSet.setClassIndex(2);
        addInstance(trainingDataSet, 3,4,2);
        addInstance(trainingDataSet, 2,2,4);
        addInstance(trainingDataSet, 1,3,5);
        System.out.println(trainingDataSet);
        return trainingDataSet;
    }

    private void addInstance(Instances trainingDataSet,
            double item1, double item2, double item3) {
        Instance instance = new Instance(3);
        instance.setDataset(trainingDataSet);
        instance.setValue(0, item1);
        instance.setValue(1, item2);
        instance.setValue(2, item3);
        trainingDataSet.add(instance);
    }
```

Annotations:
- Create three numerical attributes (pointing to `eg.createAttributes();`)
- Create learning dataset (pointing to `eg.createLearningDataSet(attributes);`)
- Set third attribute to be predicted (pointing to `trainingDataSet.setClassIndex(2);`)

The implementation is fairly straightforward. We first create the attributes and then the set of instances:

```
FastVector attributes = eg.createAttributes();
Instances instances = eg.createLearningDataSet(attributes);
```

Note that we set the third attribute, `item3`, to be the predicted attribute:

```
trainingDataSet.setClassIndex(2);
```

Listing 12.12 shows the output generated by printing out the `Instances`:

```
System.out.println(trainingDataSet);
```

Note that all the three attributes are mapped as numerical attributes.

Listing 12.12   The dataset created from the first part of code

```
@relation wekaCF

@attribute item1 numeric
@attribute item2 numeric
@attribute item3 numeric

@data
3,4,2
2,2,4
1,3,5
```

Next, let's look at the second part of the code, which deals with creating a classifier and querying the classifier for the expected values. This is shown in listing 12.13.

Listing 12.13   Making predictions using k-nearest neighbor

```
public void illustrateClassification(Instances instances)
  throws Exception {
    IBk ibk = new IBk(1);                                    ◁  Create instance of IBk classifier
    ibk.buildClassifier(instances);                          ◁  Build classifier
    System.out.println("\nPrediction:");
    for (int i = 0; i < instances.numInstances(); i++) {
       Instance instance = instances.instance(i);
       double  result = ibk.classifyInstance(instance);      ◁
       System.out.println("Expected=" + instance.value(2) +
       " Predicted=" + result);
    }                                                        Classify single instance
  }
}
```

First, we create an instance of the k-nearest neighbor classifier. Since we have only three data points in our example, we set *k* to be 1:

```
IBk ibk = new IBk(1);
```

Next, we build the classifier (`ibk.buildClassifier(instances);`) and then evaluate each instance for the predicted value for `item3`. We only have three examples and each query instance is a perfect match for one of the three cases. Listing 12.14 shows the output for item3 for each of the three cases—as expected, the expected and predicted values matched perfectly.

> **Listing 12.14 The output predicted and expected values for our example**

```
Prediction:
Expected=2.0 Predicted=2.0
Expected=4.0 Predicted=4.0
Expected=5.0 Predicted=5.0
```

The third alternative is to use one of a number of free packages that implement collaborative filtering in Java. We briefly go through three of the popular Java-based open source packages. Cofi (http://www.nongnu.org/cofi/) is a project available under GPL and is led by Daniel Lemire. The music recommendation site Racofi (http://racofi.elg.ca/index.html) uses the Cofi package. The Cofi package is fairly lightweight and easy to use. A number of memory-based collaborative filtering algorithms are implemented in this package.

Taste (http://taste.sourceforge.net/) is another collaborative filtering package that's fast and lightweight. It supports both item-based and user-based memory-based collaborative filtering algorithms. It's fairly well-documented and easy to use.

Cofe (http://eecs.oregonstate.edu/iis/CoFE//?q=taxonomy/term/6) is yet another collaborative filtering package that's freely available. It's well-documented and fairly easy to use.

Next, let's look at a commonly used model-based collaborative filtering method known as *latent semantic indexing (LSI)*, which reduces the dimensionality of the user-item matrix using a technique known as *singular value decomposition (SVD)*.

12.3.3 *Dimensionality reduction with latent semantic indexing*

As noted in section 3.5.2, LSI has been used in content-based analysis to solve the problems of synonymy and polysemy. Consider a term-document matrix as shown in table 12.6, where each row corresponds to terms across documents, while a column represents a document. The ith column in this matrix corresponds to the term-vector representation for the ith document. In essence, to create this matrix, we first need to create the term vector for each document and then join all the term vectors vertically to create this matrix. Note that a cell value corresponds to the product of the term frequency and inverse document frequency for that term and document.

	Document 1	Document 2	....	Document n
Term 1				
Term 2				
....				
Term m				

Table 12.6
Term-document matrix

This matrix is similar to the user-item matrix in table 12.1. In LSI,[2] the dimensionality of the term-document matrix is reduced using the process of singular value decomposition (SVD). The following are a few motivations for doing such a transformation on the term-document matrix:

- *Necessary evil*—If the term-document matrix is too large from a computational standpoint, an approximation may be more computationally friendly.
- *Filtering noise*—If the term-document matrix is noisy, the transformed matrix may be a better approximation of the concepts.
- *Sparse matrix*—If the term-document matrix is sparse, transforming the matrix may increase its density.

This is analogous to applying SVD to the term-document matrix. To understand this further, we need to first understand SVD and how it transforms the matrix.

An arbitrary matrix A of size m x n can be decomposed into three matrices using SVD. Let r be the rank of A. As shown in figure 12.6, the matrices are

- U, an orthogonal[3] square matrix of size m x r.
- S, a diagonal matrix of size r x r, with each diagonal value being the eigen value for the matrix. All values of S are positive and stored top to bottom in decreasing order of magnitude.
- V is an orthogonal square matrix of size n x r.

We can reduce the r x r dimensionality of the matrix S to use only the top k singular values. As shown in figure 12.6, the matrices U and Vt are reduced in dimensionality for this approximation of A. The lower dimensionality allows us to approximate using k singular values.

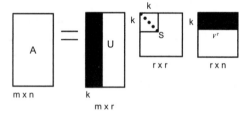

Next, let's work through the same example as in the previous section, but this time we apply dimensionality reduction to illustrate the SVD process.

Figure 12.6   Illustration of the dimensionality reduction

12.3.4 *Implementing dimensionality reduction*

JAMA[4] is a widely used linear algebra package developed by MathWorks[5] and is intended to be the standard matrix class for Java. WEKA uses JAMA; the `weka.core.matrix.Matrix` class represents a matrix and has a number of methods, including one to compute the SVD of a matrix. In this section, we develop the Java code to implement dimensionality reduction using the example from section 12.3.1.

---

[2] http://lsirwww.epfl.ch/courses/dis/2003ws/papers/ut-cs-94-270.pdf

[3] The product of the matrix and its transpose gives the identity matrix. See http://en.wikipedia.org/wiki/Orthogonal_matrix.

[4] http://math.nist.gov/javanumerics/jama/

[5] http://www.mathworks.com/

We develop SVDExample, a simple class that first creates a matrix representation for the data in table 12.2 and computes the SVD for the matrix. Then we approximate the matrix using reduced dimensionality. Listing 12.15 shows the first part of the code that deals with representing the data in a Matrix instance and computing its SVD.

Listing 12.15 Representing the data to illustrate dimensionality reduction

```
package com.alag.ci.cf;

import weka.core.matrix.Matrix;
import weka.core.matrix.SingularValueDecomposition;

public class SVDExample {

    public static final void main(String [] args) {            Develop Matrix
        SVDExample eg = new SVDExample();                        representation
        Matrix userItem = eg.createUserItemMatrix();    ⟵─┘    for data
        SingularValueDecomposition svd =
          eg.computeSVD(userItem);         ⟵── Compute SVD for matrix
        eg.reduceDimension(userItem, svd, 1);    ⟵
        eg.reduceDimension(userItem, svd, 2);         Illustrate
        eg.reduceDimension(userItem, svd, 3);         dimensionality
    }                                                 reduction

    public Matrix createUserItemMatrix() {
        double [] [] values = { {3,4,2}, {2,2,4}, {1,3,5} };
        Matrix userItem = new Matrix(values);
        System.out.println("UserItem: Rank=" + userItem.rank());    ⟵─┐
        System.out.println(userItem);
        return userItem;                        Print rank of original matrix
    }

    public SingularValueDecomposition computeSVD(Matrix matrix) {
        SingularValueDecomposition svd = matrix.svd();
        System.out.println("U:\n" + svd.getU());
        System.out.println("UtU is orthogonal:\n" +
        svd.getU().transpose().times(svd.getU()));    ⟵
        System.out.println("S:\n" + svd.getS());              U and V are
        System.out.println("Vt:\n" + svd.getV().transpose());  orthogonal
        System.out.println("VtV is orhogonal:\n" +            matrices
        svd.getV().transpose().times(svd.getV()));    ⟵
        return svd;
    }
}
```

The example first creates a Matrix representation for the data. Note that the rank of the matrix is also printed in the method createUserItemMatrix(). The output from the first part of the program is shown in listing 12.16. Note that the rank for our matrix is 3.

Listing 12.16 Output from running the first part of the code

```
UserItem: Rank=3
 3 4 2
 2 2 4
 1 3 5
```

```
U:
 0.55 -0.83 0.12
 0.54 0.23 -0.81
 0.64 0.51 0.57

UtU is orthogonal:
 1 0 0
 0 1 0
 0 0 1

S:
 8.93 0    0
 0    2.71 0
 0    0    0.91

Vt:
 0.38 0.58 0.72
 -0.55 -0.48 0.68
 -0.74 0.66 -0.14

VtV is orthogonal:
 1 0 0
 0 1 0
 0 0 1
```

As shown in listing 12.16, *S* contains three eigen values: 8.93, 2.71, and 0.91. Note that they appear in descending order in the diagonal of the matrix. Also, both *U* and *V* are orthogonal matrices. Next, let's approximate the matrices by reducing the dimensionality of the matrix, the code for which is shown in listing 12.17.

Listing 12.17   Code illustrating dimensionality reduction

```
public Matrix reduceDimension(Matrix userItem,
   SingularValueDecomposition svd, int k) {
      int m = userItem.getRowDimension();
      int n = userItem.getColumnDimension();          Compute appropriate
      Matrix Uk = matrixSubset(svd.getU(),m,k);       subsets of matrices
      Matrix Sk = matrixSubset(svd.getS(),k,k);
      Matrix Vtk = matrixSubset(svd.getV().transpose(),k,n);
      Matrix approx = Uk.times(Sk).times(Vtk);
      System.out.println(k + " dimensional approx matrix:\n " + approx);
      return approx;
}

private Matrix matrixSubset(Matrix orig, int m, int k ) {
   Matrix newMatrix = new Matrix(m,k);
   for (int i = 0; i < m; i++) {                   Approximate original matrix
      for (int j = 0; j < k; j ++) {               using reduced matrices
         newMatrix.set(i, j, orig.get(i,j));
      }
   }
   return newMatrix;
}
}
```

For a given value of *k*—in our example, this is shown for the values 1, 2, and 3—we compute the subset of the three matrices *U*, *S*, and *V*. Next, we approximate the original matrix using these reduced matrices, the output of which is shown in listing 12.18 for the three different *k* values.

Listing 12.18   Output from running the second part of the code

```
1 dimensional approx matrix:
  1.84 2.84 3.53
  1.81 2.79 3.47
  2.15 3.33 4.14

2 dimensional approx matrix:
  3.08 3.93 2.02
  1.45 2.48 3.9
  1.39 2.66 5.07

3 dimensional approx matrix:
  3 4 2
  2 2 4
  1 3 5
```

Note that the approximation using k=2 is fairly close to the original values of the initial matrix, and we get back the original matrix for k=3. Lastly, let's look at a probabilistic model–based approach in collaborative filtering.

12.3.5 *Probabilistic model–based approach*

In chapter 10, we briefly introduced the Bayesian belief network—a directed acyclic graph where nodes correspond to random variables and directed arcs between nodes signify conditional probability between the parent and child nodes. In probabilistic collaborative filtering, each item corresponds to a node in the belief network. The states of a node correspond to the different rating values, with an additional state corresponding to the missing or "no vote" state. The learning algorithm searches for different network topologies corresponding to dependencies for each item. Once the network has been learned, each item will have parent nodes corresponding to items that are best predictors for the expected ratings.

In this section, we've covered various approaches to implementing collaborative filtering. Next, let's look at some real-world examples of how this technology has been applied.

12.4 *Real-world solutions*

In this section, we cover three case studies of how large-scale recommendation systems have been developed at Amazon.com, Google News, and at Netflix. These three case studies should give you an insight into how large-scale (millions of users and millions of items) recommendation systems have been developed in the real world. We learn something new with each use case. First, we learn about Amazon's item-to-item recommendation engine that scales to millions of users and millions of items. Next, we look at Google News personalization to learn about how to deal with noisy user input high item churn. Lastly, we look at Netflix and learn the approach taken by various researchers to improve the results of a recommendation engine, along with Netflix's approach.

12.4.1 *Amazon item-to-item recommendation*

Perhaps one of the best-known examples of a recommendation system is at Amazon.com. Amazon reports high click-through and email advertising conversion rates using their recommendation engine, compared to untargeted content such as banner advertisements and top-seller lists. The content of this section is drawn from two sources: first from a paper[6] published on item-to-item collaborative filtering, and second from Greg Linden's blog[7] entries. (Linden developed Amazon's recommendation system.)

Figure 12.1 showed an example of the recommendations Amazon provides to a user browsing a book. For a given item (book), Amazon shows related items by analyzing customer purchasing patterns. Figure 12.7 shows another example of personalized recommendations based on items that the user has purchased in the past.

Users can browse through the list of recommended items, and as shown in Figure 12.8, can rate an item and/or remove items from consideration from the recommendation engine.

Figure 12.7   Screenshot of recommendations to a user at Amazon.com

---

[6] Linden, G., Smith, B., and York, J. 2003. "Amazon.com Recommendations: Item-to-Item Collaborative Filtering." *IEEE Internet Computing* 7, 1 (Jan. 2003), 76-80. DOI= http://dx.doi.org/10.1109/MIC.2003.1167344.

[7] http://glinden.blogspot.com/

Figure 12.8   To help the recommendation engine at Amazon, a user can rate an item and/or remove items from consideration.

Amazon makes recommendations based on information from multiple contexts, including

- *Short term information*—Recommendations based on recent search terms and item browsing history, as shown in figure 12.9.
- *Items available in the shopping basket.*
- *Purchasing history*—Recommendations based on past purchasing history, as shown in figure 12.7. The system also uses available information about the user to send out targeted emails suggesting recommended items.

Figure 12.9   Recommendations based on browsing history

The recommendation system at Amazon has a number of challenges:

- *Large number of items and users*—The system contains huge amounts of data with tens of millions of customers and millions of distinct catalog items.
- *Performance and scalability*—Results need to be returned within half a second. There are a very large number of transactions—for example, on December 10, 2007,[8] which was one of Amazon's strongest days, customers ordered more than 5.4 million items, or 62.5 items per second.

---

[8]   http://phx.corporate-ir.net/phoenix.zhtml?c=97664&p=irol-newsArticle&ID=1089861&highlight=

- *Limited information for new customers*—New customers may have purchased or rated only a few items. Older customers may have purchased or rated a large number (thousands) of items.
- *Responsiveness to new information*—The algorithm must respond immediately to new information from the customer.

As described in section 12.1.2, Amazon uses an item-based approach, where related items for an item are used for recommendations. This also means that all users get the same list of items as recommended items when they look at a particular item. Given the large number of users[9] and items, it was found that implementing a typical k-nearest neighbor search ran into severe performance and scalability issues. It was deemed that reducing the dimensionality of the search space—by clustering and partitioning items, or by discarding most popular and unpopular items—would degrade the recommendation quality. Again, from a performance and scalability point of view, a content-based approach for recommendations was not used—for users with thousands of purchases, you would need to combine the term vectors across all instances and query the catalog for related items.

The item-to-item collaborative filtering algorithm implemented by Amazon scales independent of the number of users, and develops the expensive item-to-item table offline. During runtime computing, the list of recommended items is simply a table lookup. You can compute the item-to-item similarity table by iterating over the user-item purchase matrix (similar to table 12.1), but the following iterative algorithm provides a better utilization of memory and computing resources:

- Assume that there are *n* items and a *n* x *n* matrix with items corresponding to rows and columns. Iterate the following steps across all items.
- For a given item (parent item), iterate over all customers who have bought the particular item. For each item purchased (child item) by the customer, increment the count for that item—this is stored in the child item row and parent item column.

At the end of the iteration, to find related items for a the parent item, simply go to the parent item column and retrieve the items in the order of their counts.

A simple example helps illustrate the process. Table 12.7 contains the purchasing pattern for four customers in a catalog with four items. To keep things simple, we ignore modifications to the matrix to reflect the frequency of purchase for the four items (idf).

	Item 1	Item 2	Item 3	Item 4
User 1	1		1	
User 2		1		1

Table 12.7 Sample data for iterative item-to-item algorithm

---

[9] Even at 10 million users and 1 million items

	Item 1	Item 2	Item 3	Item 4
User 3	1	1	1	
User 4			1	1

Table 12.7 Sample data for iterative item-to-item algorithm *(continued)*

Applying our algorithm should result in the item-to-tem matrix shown in Table 12.8. As shown in the table, the items most related to Item 1 are Item 3, followed by Item 2.

	Item 1	Item 2	Item 3	Item 4
Item 1	-	1	2	
Item 2	1	-	1	1
Item 3	2	1	-	1
Item 4		1		-

Table 12.8 Item-to-item matrix

Once the item-to-item matrix has been computed offline, the recommended items are determined using the related items for each item and combining the scores across all instances.

The item-to-item recommendation algorithm used by Amazon is one of the simplest collaborative filtering algorithms, which works well and scales to huge amounts of data.

12.4.2 Google News personalization

Google News (news.google.com) is a computer-generated news site that aggregates headlines from more than 4,500 news sites, clusters them into related stories, and displays it all in a personalized manner for a user. Figure 12.10 shows a typical news page for a logged-in user.

Google provides personalized recommendations to users who opt in to the search history feature provided by various Google web sites. As a part of the search history, Google records search queries made by the user along with a list of news articles visited. When a user has adequate history of news items clicked, the site recommends news stories of interest to the user in two sections. The first is the Recommended for *youremailaddress* section in the center of the page, just below the Top Stories section. The second place is the Recommended link on the left side, just below the Top Stories link, where the user can get a larger list of recommended items. An example of this page is shown in figure 12.11.

Google News is a good example of building a scalable recommendation system for a large number of users (several million unique visitors in a month) and a large number of items (several million new stories in a two-month period) with constant item churn. This is different from Amazon, where the rate of item churn is much smaller.

Figure 12.10   Google News with recommended stories using the user's web history

The content of this section is drawn from a paper[10] published on this topic and a talk[11] given by Mayur Datar from Google.

Figure 12.11   Personalized news stories for a logged-in user

---

[10] Das, A. S., Datar, M., Garg, A., and Rajaram, S. 2007. Google news personalization: scalable online collaborative filtering. In *Proceedings of the 16th international Conference on World Wide Web* (Banff, Alberta, Canada, May 08 - 12, 2007). WWW '07. ACM, New York, NY, 271-280. DOI= http://doi.acm.org/10.1145/1242572.1242610.

[11] Slides and video can be obtained from http://sfbayacm.org/events/2007-10-10.php.

Google decided to use collaborative filtering to build the recommendation system, mainly due to the availability of data from Google's large user base, and the advantage that the same collaborative filtering approach could be applied to other application domains, countries, and languages. A content-based recommendation system perhaps may have worked just as well, but may have required language/section-specific tweaking. Google also wanted to leverage the same collaborative filtering technology for recommending images, videos, and music, where it's more difficult to analyze the underlying content.

There are a number of things that are of interest to us in this case study:

- *High churn in items*—One of the unique challenges for the news site has been the high rate of churn associated with the news stories—news stories change every 10–15 minutes. This is unlike our case study of Amazon, where the rate of churn isn't as high. The rapid change in the item set makes it difficult to compute a model representation for item-to-item, since computing that would probably take a few hours, and the news would be obsolete by that time.
- *Noisy ratings*—A user clicking on a story is used as a noisy positive vote for that story. A click is noisier than an explicit 1–5 star rating (see section 2.3) or treating a purchase as a positive vote. As discussed in sections 2.3.4 and 2.4.2, a click on a story corresponds to a rating of 1, while a non-click corresponds to a 0 rating.
- *Instant gratification*—The system incorporates user clicks instantly in its recommendations, thus providing instant gratification to the user.
- *High performance requirements*—Google has a high performance requirement for the recommendation system—typically the recommendation engine needs to provide a recommendation within a few hundred milliseconds.

The problem of recommending news stories to a user can be modeled into a standard collaborative filtering user-item table, as shown in table 12.1. Here, an item is a news story, while rows are users. The dimensionality of *m* and *n* is a few million. The matrix is sparse, where a typical user may have clicked on a few stories, while some users may have clicked on hundreds of stories. Google's approach focuses on algorithms that are scalable and combines three different algorithms—one is a memory-based algorithm while the other two are model-based algorithms. The recommendation engine weighs the scores for each recommended item across the three approaches. The memory-based algorithm uses the related-item approach. Here we use the covisitation algorithm (similar to Amazon's algorithm), where users are clustered together based on which pages they've visited. The other two algorithms, MinHash and PLSI, group users into clusters, and recommend stories clicked by one user to others in the same cluster.

User clustering is a batch process that should be done offline and run periodically to not affect the performance of the regular application. While the cluster story-counts are maintained in real-time, new users that haven't been clustered in the previous clustering run are recommended stories based on a covisitation algorithm. Google leverages BigTable[12] and MapReduce to scale the algorithms to the large volume of data. Next, we briefly describe the three algorithms used.

---

[12] http://labs.google.com/papers/bigtable.html

MEMORY-BASED ALGORITHM: COVISITATION

The first algorithm, known as *covisitation*, uses an item-based approach to compute recommended news items. Similar to Amazon and covered in the previous section, the algorithm displays items that have been viewed by other users who have viewed a given item.

Conceptually, the algorithm is simple, and works as follows. Consider a window of time, typically a few hours. Two stories that have been visited by the same user during this period of time are said to have been *covisited*. Associated with each user is a list of items that have been visited by the user in the given window of time; we call this the user's *click history*. For each item, the system keeps a running count of how many times this story has been covisited with each other story. If two stories have never been covisited then this count is 0. When a user clicks on a new item, the system uses the user's click history and updates the covisitation count for this new item and each item in the user's click history. Given an item, related items are thus other items that have the largest covisitation numbers associated with them. The algorithm also takes into account the temporal nature of the clicks, and discounts the count based on the age of the click and story. These counts are also normalized to a 0 and 1 scale. To generate a list of candidate items for a user, the system uses the user's click history. For each of the items in the user's click history, the list of covisited items along with their scores is retrieved. The scores for the items are added over all items in the user's click history set, and the items with the highest summed weight are recommended to the user.

MODEL-BASED ALGORITHMS

Minwise Independent Permutation Hashing (MinHash) is a probabilistic clustering algorithm that assigns two users to the same cluster, with a probability proportional to the overlap in items they've clicked. A simple similarity function, also known as *Jaccard coefficient*, is used to compute the similarity between two users. The Jaccard coefficient, a number between 0 and 1, is the ratio of number of items that have been covisited by the two users divided by the total number of unique items that have been visited by either of the two users. A simple approach is to compute the similarities of the users with all the other users and recommend stories using these similarities to weigh the recommendations. However, given the large number of users, this approach isn't scalable. Google therefore uses a sublinear time near-neighbor search technique called *Locality Sensitive Hashing (LSH)*. The algorithm works as follows. The complete set of items are randomly arranged. A user is assigned a hash value equal to the index of the first item that the user has visited in this permutation. This process is repeated a number of times (10–20) in parallel. The hash value for a user is equal to the sum of the hash values assigned to the user in each of the runs. Users having the same hash values are assigned to the same cluster. For scalability and performance, the MinHash clustering algorithm is implemented as a MapReduce problem.

PLSI is a collaborative filtering algorithm developed by Hoffmann and is based on probabilistic latent semantic models. It models users and items as random variables, where the relationship between users and items is modeled as a mixture distribution.

Hidden variables are used to capture the relationships between the users and the items. The expectation-maximization algorithm is used to learn the parameters of the algorithm. For scalability, the algorithm was reformulated to fit into the Map-Reduce paradigm.

Experiments on the live Google site have shown better click-through rates for recommended stories than those for the top stories for the day. The large dimensionality for items and users along with a high degree of item churn makes this case study interesting.

Lastly, let's look at Netflix.

12.4.3 *Netflix and the BellKor Solution for the Netflix Prize*

In November 2007, a little over a year after announcing a million-dollar prize for the winning entry in a contest to improve the prediction accuracy of movie ratings by 10 percent, Netflix awarded the first progress prize of $50,000 to BellKor,[13] a group of researchers at AT&T Labs. The BellKor (a.k.a. KorBell) team consisting of Yehuda Koren, Robert Bell, and Chris Volinsky, improved on the Netflix recommendation system by 8.43 percent, a little short of the 10 percent required to achieve the million dollar prize. Of course, this improvement is on a test dataset that Netflix provided as a part of the contest, and not integrated into Netflix's recommendation engine yet. The contest in its first year attracted more than 27,000 contestants on more than 2,550 teams from 161 countries.

Netflix believes that any improvements in their recommendation engine will provide them with a competitive advantage. Opening up the process of finding a better recommendation engine with a public contest is yet another example of collective intelligence, where the collective efforts of other users is being used to improve the recommendation engine.

Before we go on to the BellKor solution, it's useful to look at Netflix's recommendation engine. This part of the section draws from a talk given by Jim Bennett, VP of recommendation systems, at the Recommender06.com conference[14] in September 2006.

When a user signs up at Netflix, the user is urged to rate movies in an attempt to learn the user's tastes. Netflix's recommendation engine, Cinematch, uses an item-to-item algorithm (similar to Amazon) with a number of heuristics that aren't disclosed to the public. The offline computation of the item-to-item matrix takes two days to train. To solve the problem of "cold startup" for new titles, items are set up manually; this manual setup is retired over a period of time. Figure 12.12 shows a typical recommendation screen that's shown to a user. Here, movies similar to the movie "Babel" are being recommended to the user.

Figure 12.13 shows the home page for a user, which shows the user's recommended movies.

---

[13] http://www.research.att.com/~volinsky/netflix/
[14] http://blog.recommenders06.com/wp-content/uploads/2006/09/bennett.pdf

Figure 12.12   Movies related to a movie being recommended at Netflix

Figure 12.13   Home page for a user at Netflix showing the user's recommended movies

The current Netflix recommendation system uses about 2 billion movie ratings that have been collected from more than 10 million customers. However, Netflix estimates that by sometime around 2010 to 2012, it will

- Have more than 10 billion ratings
- Generate 10 million ratings a day
- Make 5 billion recommendations a day
- Have more than 20 million customers

NETFLIX COMPETITION

The learning dataset for the competition consists of more than 100 million anonymous movie ratings, on a scale of one to five stars, made by 480,000 users on 17,770 movies. Note that the user-item dataset for this problem is sparsely populated, with nearly 99 percent of user-item entries being zero. The distribution of movies per user is skewed. The median number of ratings per user is 93. About 10 percent of the users rated 16 or fewer movies, while 25 percent of the users rated 36 or fewer. Two users rated as many as 17,000movies. Similarly, the ratings per movie are also skewed, with almost half the user base rating one of the popular movies (Miss Congeniality). About 25 percent of the movies had 190 or fewer ratings associated with them. A handful of movies were rated fewer than 10 times. The dataset doesn't contain any personal identifiable information. It contains user ID, movie titles, star ratings, and dates—there are no text reviews in the dataset. In the absence of any content associated with the movies, there's no option but to apply a collaborative-based approach to analyze the data.

The Netflix competition doesn't take into account speed of implementation or scalability of the approach used. It simply focuses on the quality of the recommendation system in terms of minimizing the error between the user rating and the predicted rating. The Netflix data doesn't contain much information to allow the use of a content-based approach; it's for this reason that teams focused on collaborative-based techniques.

The winning team, BellKor, spent more than 2,000 combined hours poring through data to find the winning solution. The winning solution was a linear combination of 107 sets of predictions. Many of the algorithms involved either nearest neighbor method (k-nearest neighbor) or latent factor models such as SVD/factorization and Restricted Boltzmann Machines (RBMs).[15]

The winning solution uses k-NN to predict the rating for a user using both the Pearson-r correlation and cosine methods to compute the similarities. Similar to our discussion in section 12.3.1, they found that it was useful to remove item-specific and user-specific biases in the computation. Latent semantic models (see sections 12.3.4 and 12.3.5) were also used widely in the winning solution. RBMs are stochastic neural networks that contains two layers. The first layer corresponds to the observed ratings, while the second layer is hidden and is connected to the first layer.

---

[15] See http://www.scholarpedia.org/article/Boltzmann_machine and Google Tech Talk "Next Generation of Neural Networks" by Geoffrey Hinton of University of Toronto, http://www.youtube.com/watch?v=AyzOUbkUf3M.

The BellKor team found that it was important to utilize a variety of models that complemented each others' shortcomings. None of the models by itself could get the BellKor team to the top of the competition. The combined set of models achieved an improvement of 8.43 percent over Cinematch, while the best model—a hybrid of applying k-NN to output from RBMs—improved on the result by 6.43 percent. The biggest improvement by LSI methods was 5.1 percent, with the best pure k-NN model scoring below that. (*K* for the k-NN methods was in the range of 20 to 50.) The BellKor team also applied a number of heuristics to further improve the results.

The BellKor team provides a number of recommendations on what's needed to build a winning solution for a competition:

- Combining complementary models helps improve the overall solution. Note that a linear combination of three models, one each for k-NN, LSI, and RBM, would have resulted in fairly good results—an improvement of 7.58 percent.
- You need a principled approach to optimizing the solution.
- The key to winning is to build models that can predict accurately where there's sufficient data, without over-fitting in the absence of adequate data.

The Netflix competition—the data, the prize money, and the fame factor—have generated a large amount of interest in the field of collaborative filtering. Teams have collaborated with each other and have published their solutions, allowing others to build on their work. Figure 12.14 shows the leaderboard for the competition as of early

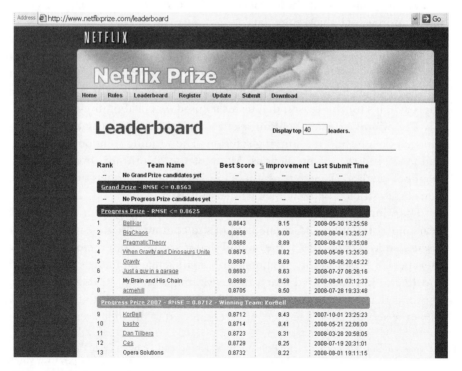

Figure 12.14   A screenshot of the Netflix leaderboard as of early 2008 (http://www.netflixprize.com/leaderboard)

August 2008. Note that the best score is an improvement of 9.15 percent over the benchmark result. The million-dollar question is, Will someone come up with the solution that's good enough to surpass the 10 percent improvement mark? Only time will tell, but given the interest and efforts being made, it's perhaps only a question of time.

In this section, we've covered the solutions for three large-scale recommendation systems—Amazon, Google News, and Netflix. By now, you should understand what a recommendation engine is, and how it can be used and built. In your application, you should be able to start with building perhaps a simple content-based item-to-item recommendation engine and then augment it with a collaborative-based approach. This should help you to personalize your application for every user. The challenge with personalization and building recommendation systems is to find the right balance between the delta improvement in quality and the additional time the user needs to wait for the response. I've found the strategy of starting with something simple and gradually building on top of it over time, along with lots of asynchronous pre-computation, to work well in most cases.

12.5 Summary

One of the best ways to personalize a site for a user is to use a recommendation engine. There are two main approaches to building a recommendation engine: content-based and collaborative-based. In content-based analysis, similar content is recommended by computing the similarity in term vectors between various items. But content-based algorithms can't determine the quality of an item being recommended. For this, we need to use a collaborative approach. In collaborative filtering, each item is treated as black box, and user interactions with the item are used to compute similarities. Collaborative approaches are language-agnostic and are particularly suited for analyzing images, video, and music that might not have any content associated with them.

Approaches to building recommendation systems can be further divided into item-based and user-based analysis. In item-based analysis, items that are similar to items of interest are recommended to the user, while in user-based analysis, first similar users to a user are found, and them items liked by those users are recommended.

The recommendation problem uses a user-item matrix containing rating information (purchasing/voting/click-through) for cell values. In this matrix, a row corresponds to a user, while each column corresponds to an item. This matrix is typically of large dimension and sparse. This large dimensional matrix may be approximated to lower dimensions using singular value decomposition. The k-nearest neighbor algorithm determines the k closest users to predict the ratings for a user.

We also looked at three well-known, large-scale recommendation systems: Amazon.com, Google News personalization, and Netflix.

Using the concepts developed in this book, you should now be able to apply collective intelligence to your application. Good luck at providing a personalized experience to your users.

12.6   *Resources*

ACM Transactions on Computer-Human Interaction (TOCHI) Special Section on Recommender Systems. Volume 12, Issue 3 (September 2005).

Adomavicius, Gediminas and Alexander Tuzhilin. "Toward the Next Generation of Recommender Systems: A Survey of the State-of-the-Art and Possible Extensions," IEEE Transactions on Knowledge and Data Engineering, Vol. 17, no. 6, pp. 734–749. June, 2005.

Bell, Robert and Yehuda Koren. "Improved Neighborhood-based Collaborative Filtering." http://public.research.att.com/~yehuda/pubs/cf-workshop.pdf

————"Scalable Collaborative Filtering with Jointly Derived Neighborhood Interpolation Weights." IEEE Conference on Data Mining (ICDM'07). 2007, IEEE.

————"Improved Neighborhood Based Collaborative Filtering." KDD 2007 Netflix Competition Workshop. http://public.research.att.com/~yehuda/pubs/cf-workshop.pdf

Bell, Robertl, Yehuda Koren, and Chris Volinsky. "The BellKor Solution to Netflix Prize." 2007. http://www.research.att.com/~volinsky/netflix/ProgressPrize2007BellKorSolution.pdf and http://www.netflixprize.com/assets/ProgressPrize2007_KorBell.pdf

————"Modeling relationships at multiple scales to improve accuracy of large recommender systems." http://portal.acm.org/citation.cfm?id=1281192.1281206

————"Chasing $1,000,000: How We Won The Netflix Progress Prize." ASA Statistical and Computing Graphics Newsletter. Volume 18, Number 2, December 2007. http://stat-computing.org/newsletter/v182.pdf

BellKor home page. http://www.research.att.com/~volinsky/netflix/

Berry, M. W., S. T. Dumais, and G. W. O'Brien. "Using linear algebra for intelligent information retrieval." SIAM Review 37(4):573–595. 1995. http://citeseer.ist.psu.edu/berry95using.html

Breese, John, David Heckerman, and Carl Kadie. "Empirical Analysis of Predictive Algorithms for Collaborative Filtering." Proceedings of the 14th Annual Conference on Uncertainty in Artificial Intelligence (UAI-98), pgs 43-52. 2002. Morgan Kaufmann.

Chang, Fay, Jeffrey Dean, Sanjay Ghemawat, Wilson C. Hsieh, Deborah A. Wallach, Mike Burrows, Tushar Chandra, Andrew Fikes, and Robert E. Gruber. "Bigtable: A Distributed Storage System for Structured Data." OSDI '06: Seventh Symposium on Operating System Design and Implementation, Seattle, WA. November, 2006. http://209.85.163.132/papers/bigtable-osdi06.pdf

COFE: Collaborative Filtering Engine. http://eecs.oregonstate.edu/iis/CoFE/

Cofi: A Java-based collaborative filtering library. http://www.nongnu.org/cofi/

Das, Abhinandan S., Mayur Datar, Ashutosh Garg, and Shyam Rajaram. "Google news personalization: scalable online collaborative filtering." In Proceedings of the 16th international Conference on World Wide Web (Banff, Alberta, Canada, May 08–12, 2007). WWW '07. ACM, New York, NY, 271-280. DOI= http://doi.acm.org/10.1145/1242572.1242610

Deshpande, Mukund and George Karypis. "Item-based top-n recommendation algorithms." ACM Transactions on Information Systems, 22(1):1–34, 2004. http://citeseer.ist.psu.edu/article/deshpande04item.html

Fleder, Daniel M. and Kartik Hosangar. "Recommender systems and their impact on sales diversity." Proceedings of the 8th ACM conference on Electronic commerce. 2007. http://portal.acm.org/citation.cfm?id=1250910.1250939

Hoffman, Thomas. "Latent semantic models for collaborative filtering." ACM Transactions on Information Systems (TOIS) , Volume 22, Issue 1 (January 2004).

The Homepage of Nearest Neighbors and Similarity Search. Maintained by Yury Lifshits. http://simsearch.yury.name/tutorial.html

IEEE Intelligent Systems Special Issue on Recommender Systems. vol. 22(3), 2007International Journal of Electronic Commerce Special Issue on Recommender Systems. Volume 11, Number 2 (Winter 2006-07).

Johnson, Aaron. "Using Lucene and MoreLikeThis to Show Related Content." Nov. 2006. http://cephas.net/blog/2006/11/14/using-lucene-and-morelikethis-to-show-related-content/

KDD Cup and Workshop (KDD'07). ACM Press (2007).

Kim, Juntae. "Effect of Dimensionality Reduction in Recommendation Systems." AI Workshop, 2002. http://ai.dgu.ac.kr/seminar/pds/AIWorkshop2002.ppt

Lemire, Daniel and Anna Maclachlan. "Slope One Predictors for Online Rating-Based Collaborative Filtering." Proceedings of SIAM Data Mining (SDM '05), 2005. http://www.daniel-lemire.com/fr/abstracts/SDM2005.html

Linden, Greg. Geeking with Greg. Blog. http://glinden.blogspot.com/

Linden, Greg, Brent Smith, and Jeremy York. "Amazon.com Recommendations: Item-to-Item Collaborative Filtering." *IEEE Internet Computing*. 7, 1 (Jan, 2003), 76-80. DOI= http://dx.doi.org/10.1109/MIC.2003.1167344

Porter, Joshua. "Watch and Learn: How Recommendation Systems are Redefining the Web." 2006. http://www.uie.com/articles/recommendation_systems/

"The Present and Future of Recommender Systems." September 12-13, 2006. Bilbao, Spain. http://www.mystrands.com/corp/summerschool06.vm

Proceedings of the 13th ACM SIGKDD international conference on Knowledge discovery and data mining (KDD'07). ACM Press (2007).

"Reinforcing the Blockbuster Nature of Media: The Impact of Online Recommenders." http://knowledge.wharton.upenn.edu/article.cfm?articleid=1818

Salakhutdinov, Ruslan, Andriy Mnih, and Geoffrey Hinton. "Restricted Boltzmann machines for collaborative filtering." In Proceedings of the 24th International Conference on Machine Learning (Corvalis, Oregon, June 20 - 24, 2007). Z. Ghahramani, Ed. ICML '07, vol. 227. ACM, New York, NY, 791-798. DOI= http://doi.acm.org/10.1145/1273496.1273596

Sarwra, Badrul, George Karypis, Joseph Konstan, and John Riedl. "Item-based collaborative filtering recommendation algorithms." Proceedings of the 10th International World Wide Web Conference (WWW10), Hong Kong, May 2001. http://citeseer.ist.psu.edu/sarwar01itembased.html

————"Application of dimensionality reduction in recommender systems—a case study." In ACM WebKDD Workshop, 2000. http://citeseer.ist.psu.edu/sarwar00application.html

SVD Recommendation System in Ruby. 2007. http://www.igvita.com/blog/2007/01/15/svd-recommendation-system-in-ruby/

Taste: Collaborative filtering for Java. http://taste.sourceforge.net/

Taste. http://code.google.com/soc/2007/taste/about.html

Yahoo Launchcast. http://new.music.yahoo.com/

index

MORE TITLES FROM MANNING

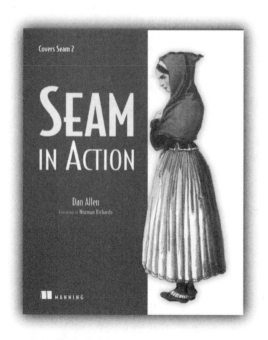

Seam in Action
by Dan Allen

   ISBN: 1-933988-40-1
   624 pages
   $44.99
   September 2008

jQuery in Action
by Bear Bibeault
  and Yehuda Katz

   ISBN: 1-933988-35-5
   376 pages
   $39.99
   February 2008

For ordering information go to www.manning.com